In Fondest Memory of
Jacques Derrida

Stanford University Press
Stanford, California

Printed in the United States of America
on acid-free, archival-quality paper

Library of Congress Cataloging-in-Publication Data

Kamuf, Peggy, 1947–
Book of addresses / Peggy Kamuf.
p.   cm. — (Meridian)
Includes bibliographical references and index.
ISBN 0-8047-5058-0 (hardcover : alk. paper)
ISBN 0-8047-5059-9 (pbk. : alk. paper)
1. Deconstruction.   I. Title.
II. Series: Meridian (Stanford, Calif.)

B809.6.K36 2005
149—DC22

2004023136

Original Printing 2005

Last figure below indicates year of this printing:
14   13   12   11   10   09   08   07   06   05

Contents

Acknowledgments

All of the chapters in this book were originally written in response to invitations: to participate in a conference or contribute to a publication. I am grateful to the many friends and colleagues who worked to provide these occasions: Geoff Bennington, Jean Bessière, Elizabeth Beaumont Bissell, John Brannigan, Monique Chefdor, Tom Cohen, Hafid Gafaiti, Nancy Holland, Lynne Huffer, Michel Lisse, Ian Maclachlan, Martin Mc-Quillan, Richard Rand, Alison Rice, Ruth Robbins, Nicholas Royle, Michael Syrotinski, Christine Thuau, and Julian Wolfreys. Several chapters benefited greatly from responses by Derek Attridge, Michel Lisse, Nick Royle, and Sam Weber, all incomparable readers. My thanks to David Agruss for his careful help checking the final manuscript and to Christopher Peterson for his splendid assistance preparing the index. Having had the good fortune to spend fall semester 2002 at the Society for the Humanities at Cornell University, I want to thank all my colleagues there for their hospitality and fellowship. For their generous support, I thank the deans of the College of Letters, Arts, and Sciences at the University of Southern California, as well as my department chairs and friends, Karen Pinkus and Peter Starr.

I'm especially indebted to Branka Arsić, who from the beginning helped me to see the shape of this book and who bestowed on it the gift of her Afterword. And we are both very grateful to Kristina Pribićević Zorić for her remarkable translation of this text.

To acknowledge debts is also to practice ingratitude. For awareness of that paradox, along with so many other things, I have two great writers to thank (or not), Hélène Cixous and Jacques Derrida.

I acknowledge and thank all the publishers that granted permission to reprint material that appeared in earlier versions in the following publications: chapter 1, in Nicholas Royle, ed., *Deconstructions: A User's Guide*, 2000, Palgrave, reproduced with permission of Palgrave Macmillan; chapter 2, in Nancy Holland, ed., *Feminist Interpretations of Jacques Derrida*, University Park, The Pennsylvania State University Press, 1996, pp. 103-26, © The Pennsylvania State University, reproduced by permission of the publisher; chapter 4, in Tom Cohen, ed., *Jacques Derrida and the Humanities: A Critical Reader*, Cambridge University Press, 2001, © Cambridge University Press, reprinted with permission; chapter 6, in *Yale French Studies* 85, ed. Lynne Huffer; chapter 7, in *The Question of Literature and the Place of the Literary in Contemporary Theory*, ed. Elizabeth Beaumont Bissell, Manchester University Press, 2002; chapter 8, in *Angelaki: A Journal of the Theoretical Humanities* 4, 3 (December 1999), http://www.tandf.co.uk; chapter 12, in *Tympanum* 1, 2 (1999); chapter 13, in *Paroles Gelées*, 19, 2 (2001), © Regents of the University of California; chapter 14, in John Branigan, et al., eds., *Applying to Derrida*, 1996, Macmillan, reproduced with permission of Palgrave Macmillan; chapter 15, in Michael Syrotinski and Ian Maclachlan, eds., *Sensual Reading: New Approaches to Reading in Its Relation to the Senses*, 2001, Bucknell University Press.

Los Angeles
August 2004

Introduction: Disavowals
(A Foreword)

—Aren't you going to write an introduction?

—An editor once put it to me that whereas a preface presents the book, an introduction presents the book's argument. But *Book of Addresses* doesn't have an argument, or else it has too many.

—Well, how about a preface then?

—I know you're right to insist on the conventions, but here's the thing: a preface would have to refer to *Book of Addresses* as, well, a book, which despite appearances may be a misnomer.

—You're saying that you've given this book a title that may be a misnomer? Is that even possible?

—I don't know, but admit that a book that puts "book" in its title also puts irony in play, whether or not that was the intent.[1] As a result, it may always be impossible to say whether a book that calls itself such in fact deserves the title.

—Still, how could it ever deny that it is a book? But wait a minute, let's back up. We were just having an ordinary conversation about how you needed to finish your book, and I asked—mostly just to keep the conversation going—whether you were going to write an introduction. And now suddenly we're beginning to talk ontological nonsense about books that *are* and yet maybe *are not* books. Can we at least slow down even if we can't change the subject?

—Yes, well, thanks for keeping the conversation going. And you're right, I don't want to change the subject now. But that was your doing. You reminded me of the expectation that certain books will have introductions or prefaces. Which led me to the "nonsense" that this book's name may be ironic.

—Ok, I understand the dilemma. I can even see how it accelerates into what I just called ontological nonsense (sorry about that). But you also said a moment ago that I was right to expect that, whether introduction or preface, there would be some presentation of your book, I mean, of *Book of Addresses*—written, of course, after the fact. So maybe I don't understand after all . . .

—Yes, yes you do, of course you do, you're right that you do. Except maybe this is not so much a dilemma, which is to say, "a situation requiring a choice between equally undesirable alternatives" (Webster's Unabridged, 2001), as something else, a chance to invent a liminal text that is both and yet neither, neither introduction nor preface, but . . .

— . . . foreword? There's another kind of preliminary writing, at or before the threshold of the book proper. A foreword is also part of the apparatus of paratext (to use Genette's term),[2] a part of that paratextual part that precedes the rest, rather than running below it (like footnotes) or following it (like appendices or index). So what about a foreword?

—Wouldn't that be inappropriate? Here's Webster's again: "foreword: a short introductory statement in a published work, as a book, esp. when written by someone other than the author." That "esp." says it's inappropriate, unusual, unconventional for the author to write a book's foreword.

—But I thought you were prepared to set aside such conventional expectations?

—True enough. Perhaps I should write a foreword presenting these essays as though they were the work of someone else. That would not be difficult and, above all, it would not be false.

—Hold it. What do you mean? Is that another riddle? Are you saying not only is this not a book, but you are not its author?

—A riddle if you like, but it goes to what is in question throughout *Book of Addresses*, which is to say, addresses, the condition of addressing, of address, of being addressed. It is not just *about* address, it doesn't just present arguments or theses on that subject, even though there is a good deal of that. But the chapters are all also in the condition of address; in other words, *they are addressed.* You who are so fond of commonsensical grammar will recognize that this altogether ordinary phrase in English becomes irreducibly ambiguous when isolated and left undetermined or unconditioned by anything else. To be precise, the phrase suspends the certainty of "voice": active or passive. So, to say "these pieces are addressed" can mean, grammatically, both that they are spoken, delivered, or written to another's address *and* they are addressed *by* another, they exist in the condition of being addressed by another. Not all other languages—maybe none?—tolerate such an ambiguous grammar as to the *direction* of "address." In French, for example, I cannot say "elles sont adressées" unless I'm talking about something like the envelopes of letters and then there is no ambiguity of grammatical voice. French is quite fussy about the way it uses *adresser* and *adresse*. One addresses oneself to another (*on s'adresse à quelqu'un*), but no one can ever be simply or *directly* (?) *adressée* by another, in the passive voice (at least not grammatically). Nor can I say that I delivered an *adresse*, meaning a talk, a lecture, a plenary address, and so forth.[3] All these strictures keep tighter reins over the direction of addressing ("address" and "direction" both derive from *rectus, directus*: right, a straight line, etc.), especially as regards personal address, which is buffered with a reflexive construction, as if to make things less direct, thus more polite, if you see what I mean. So, at least in grammatical French, the ambiguity I just called the condition of address (as in "they are addressed") has generally to signal itself elsewhere and otherwise than directly in this lexicon of address. But the English idiom signals the indirection in the very saying of direction, that is, of address. It can say the indirection more directly. Or more indirectly, as you like.

—Let me see if I still follow where you're going with this, in which direction. You were evoking the riddle of authorship, when the phrase "they are addressed" got cast up on our shores, in all its wonderful ambiguity.

—Wonderful? Did I say it was wonderful?

—No, but isn't that where this is going? You were about to show me that the condition of address in *Book of Addresses* suspends the direction of origination, in other words, of authorship. And that there is something wonderful about that. Did I get it wrong again?

—No you're right (*rectus*, again), but as for "wonderful," well, that is such a worn word, a cliché, I don't know. . . . But, yes, ok, it is "wonderful" if between us we can agree to hear still the surprise, the wonder, long lost in the cliché. There is cause to wonder when one's "own" address is suspended from the address *by* the other, *coming* from the other, and that this *coming* is always a surprise, registered or cognized, therefore, only *après coup*. Otherwise it wouldn't be a surprise. So, yes, it is "wonderful," I say grasping at an almost-dead designator, to realize, *après coup*, the condition of *après coup* address. I realize, *après coup*, that everything was addressed *to me* by another. "Authorship," as a consequence, is but the appropriation (disavowed and therefore guilty) of the other's address, and it is not at all "wonderful," but just what everyone expects to happen anyway, according to all the conventions of authorship. By convention, am I not the author of these pieces? The sole and rightful author and owner? Nothing wonderful about that, on the contrary. If "authorship," as construed by conventions and contracts, is a disavowal of the "wonder" before the suspension of the address's direction, well, then, can one disavow the disavowal? If so, wouldn't *that* really be wonderful? In a foreword, perhaps, as "written by someone other than the author."

—You would avow that, because these pieces are addressed, you are not the author, not the only author, or not only the author? Something like that? But who else then? And in that case aren't we talking about plagiarism?

—Plagiarism is a matter of intention; as always, the law recognizes fault or guilt only when an intentional, self-directed, and self-present subject is concerned (I'm talking obviously about modern law). That's why, when a charge of plagiarism is upheld, the plagiarist's only excuse is to say it was unintentional. Doris Kearns Goodwin, for example, blamed careless note-taking for her failure to distinguish here and there between her words and those of other biographers she cited without specific acknowledgment.[4] To plead an absence of intention to appropriate the other's words, however, she had to confess an absence to herself, therefore a discontinuous self, which the law naturally disallows from its purview, since it recognizes only self-present subjects. Well, not exactly, because it also recognizes the condition it terms "temporary insanity." Goodwin, in sum, pleaded a species of temporary insanity, the kind of absence from oneself or "madness" that is in force when one reads and writes, when one reads *and then* writes, maybe years later, only to discover, *après coup*, that one has perhaps confused reading and writing, what one read and what one, or rather, the other wrote.

—Isn't that an apology for plagiarism? I mean, does it not offer an excuse or even an alibi, a defense that is a justification? Because you mean, I suppose, to refer this self-absence to what you're calling the condition of address? If that is where this is going, then I'm not sure I want to follow anymore, at least not without some firm distinctions and clear differentiations. It would be irresponsible, would it not, to undermine the distinction made in law between guilty and guiltless acts? And therefore the concept of the legal subject . . .

—Yes, well, as usual, you are not following me, but already in front, pointing out the direction things must take. But I did warn you that a "disavowal of the disavowal" is a most improbable, even impossible undertaking. Now perhaps you see a little what I mean. The distinction you fear to see undermined, as you put it, the one between guilty and guiltless acts, will never disappear from the law, for that simply is what the law is, or rather what it *does* and what it exists to do: make the distinction, i.e., judge, decide, between guilty and not guilty. It determines the responsibility of those subject to it. Your fear, therefore, cannot be for the law itself, as such, which will always be powerless to cease making the distinction (which does not mean, of course, that such decisions are always or even ever just). So what, then, may be put at risk, beyond the law that decides responsibility in those terms? What other responsibility might there be?

—Are you asking me? I don't know, do you mean like a higher responsibility? The responsibility to justice and not just to or before the law?

—Certainly, if one understands by justice, and with Levinas, the other: "the relation to others—that is to say, justice."[5] And if, in "responsibility," one begins to hear the reawakened "metaphor" of response, that is, of answering another, but also answering to, before, and even for another. That there is response in responsibility, in other words, that there is always some other for whom, before whom, or to whom one is responding when one does what is called *taking* responsibility, this is perhaps what is too daunting to think about, and therefore one doesn't let oneself think about it too much, but takes refuge in rational law and the law of reason, where there is responsibility only for a subject or a self. It is reason itself, one feigns to believe, that would be at risk if I were to begin to take responsibility beyond the subject.

—Well, wouldn't it?

—That depends on whether you would call what we are having right now a reasonable conversation. Your word "nonsense" a moment ago suggests you have your doubts, but we are still here talking, which means I'm not just talking nonsense to myself, despite some appearances to the contrary. Only you can decide to go on assuming it is reasonable to say what we are saying to each other and in response. Whatever you decide, by the way, will certainly be right, that is, reasonable.

—That's it, I've got it. I can finally put a name to the vague echo I've been hearing for some time now in our talk, or rather in yours. It's Derrida's post card–writer, in *Envois*, isn't it? That's who you are echoing, repeating, citing without acknowledgment. I'm right, aren't I, that the very first words of that text are "Yes, you were right," that is, "tu avais raison"?[6] In French, one says "you are right" by giving or rendering *reason* to you, saying, literally: "you have reason." The text thus begins with this response that gives or gives *back* reason to the other. It renders reason to the other and in that it responds—to him or to her. Derrida's text begins there, which is to say, with the other. It begins by giving (back) reason, and in that it accepts the other's decision. Whatever the decision, the response of love (for the premise of *Envois* is that this is part of a correspondence between lovers) is "You are right, you have reason." That's what finally gave you away, when you said the same thing to me, or almost. You said, whatever I decide will be right and reasonable. And, of course, Derrida's text is a demonstration of undecidable address as the very condition of the relation to the other, in speech, writing, or whatever. Whereas Plato, in the *Phaedrus*, has Socrates appear to say (and the post cards in *Envois* picture Plato dictating to Socrates from behind his back) that this condition afflicts *logos* only when it is written and begins to roll and unroll a scroll or script in any old direction: "Every word [*logos*], when once it is written, is bandied about, alike among those who understand it and those who have no interest in it, *and it knows not to whom to speak or not to speak*."[7] In other words, writing afflicts *logos* with a loss of address. This is where *Book of Addresses* is coming from, isn't it?

—Yes, but if your next step is to charge that I've appropriated texts of Derrida's without acknowledgment, well, I'd be truly at a loss to defend myself—except to say, once again, you're right, no doubt, it must be true! You see how much I love discoursing with you! Yes, yes, it's true! Truth to tell, you tell me the truth. And yet, haven't I already confessed, acknowledged this appropriation, and in every chapter of *Book of Addresses*? There's not one of the texts assembled here that does not, to a greater or lesser extent, move to comprehend some piece of writing by Derrida, that is, to take it in, appropriate it in a way. However, one could also describe this relation in the language of responsibility and response I was using a moment ago: by citing and referring to texts of Derrida, I would be taking responsibility for them, not in the legal sense of claiming they return to me as to their author or cause or that they belong to me as does some property, but rather in the sense of responding to what I understand them to be saying, because I hold them to be saying something reasonable, that is, within the call of reason. So, there is *giving* reason and *taking* responsibility, give and take. Here giving and taking signal neither a simple reciprocity, nor a conceptual opposition. The relation between them is other, precisely because it is a matter of response/responsibility to, before, and for another than the one who or which is said to be doing this giving and taking. Like what you and I are doing now.

—So you haven't altogether forgotten I'm here? It had begun to sound like you were giving a lecture. But where is all this taking us? And must we follow it?

—Yes, because it follows that the thinking of responsibility has to be allowed to shift out of its traditional circles around the epistemological, phenomenological, or legal subject (take your pick), where it has always been assailed by contradictions at every attempt to determine its own responsibilities for itself.[8] These circles, the ideal form of reason, do not adequately describe the movement of appropriation, which is *movement* precisely because the circle cannot properly close on itself, at least not without taking another in. The point would be *not to disavow* the links between giving (back) the response of reason (or of love or of love of reason), taking another in, and taking responsibility, in whatever discourse that expression is commonly understood (legal, ethical, political, economic).

—Why is that the point? And the point of what? Moreover, who gave you the compass? Don't try appeasing me again with another "You're right"!

—So you need appeasing now? Suddenly we're at war? . . . Well, listen, I suppose it is the point of linkage, precisely, our being linked, bound together, and we hope more in peace than at war. That cannot be just an empty sentiment, for whoever professes still to love reason, once reason is acknowledged to be on the side of the other. But I must say something more about my appropriating from Derrida (from others as well, but less voluminously) so many sentences, paragraphs, pages, whole texts, but often just single words, phrases without quotation marks that could distinguish them from the rest, from "my own" words. I just indicated how one might understand responsibility here in terms of response, and I marked that off in distinction to the legal concept. But consider this: if responsibility stopped there, if it didn't have to take things further, would one have taken responsibility for anything *oneself*? Responsibility does not act by itself, without someone taking it for or to himself/herself. In other words, in order to take a responsibility, one has to engage the movement of appropriation. Which means, in principle, that the act enters, irreversibly, into communication with acts of misappropriation as these can be determined, for example, by laws regarding plagiarism, and so forth. It is this principle of communication (or contamination) that prompted you a moment ago to raise an alarm about irresponsibility. You demanded "firm distinctions and clear differentiations" (I'm quoting you). Perhaps now you will see that you wanted to make distinctions and differentiations *within* the movement of appropriation, rather than between it and something else, all that would be outside it as, precisely, inappropriable. Well, this is also what interests me, although I believe that the distinctions and differentiations you call for can never come to stand, stand still, become established, not even by a strictly legal establishment, because they are always of the order of decisions, acts, performatives, or even just what are loosely called "value judgments," and thus imply a context that is both particular and not closed. The contexts of decision are infinite, and each time, the act of (taking) responsibility has to do with a singularity, and therefore with a factor of unknowability.[9] If it were simply a matter of following general axioms, rules, conventions, or a program, the act (or actor) could not take anything upon or into itself as *its* responsibility. We're led back to the link between responsibility and the movement of appropriation, between a response that *begins* by giving reason (back) to another and a taking-of-responsibility that *begins* to take (itself) away from the response.

—Don't take this the wrong way, but what you just said sounds like so many things Derrida has written about responsibility, decision, giving/taking and gift, speech acts, context, all boiled down into a few sentences.[10]

—"Don't take this the wrong way"? Which way do you mean? That's usually something one says to try to avoid giving offense. (But isn't the expression almost always, well, a little offensive? Shall I ignore that?) I don't imagine you're worried I'll hear another insinuation of plagiarism, or some other misappropriation. I know, and you know that I know, that I wrote those sentences, just now, "off the top of my head," as we say. You might as well have been there, here, inside the head from off the top of which they came—that's how much you know about them, where they come from, and that they are not pilfered as such, *tel quel*, from any specific place, not even from, as you put it, "so many things Derrida has written." So by "wrong way" you don't mean anything like plagiarism. But apparently there's another wrong way to take the observation, which I might fall into even though I entirely agree with what you say, at least on the surface, and thus once again I take it the "right way" by saying, once again, you're right. The other "wrong" way would be (I'm guessing) to hear you charging: "There is too much Derrida in that head of yours, which is therefore not finally yours at all, and everything you say . . . "

—Wait, I didn't say that at all! You're not quoting anyone but yourself!

—True enough. I'm just remarking on the uncertain pragmatics of the words spoken, the way they can be doing things at a level of the unspoken. This structure can be compared to the symptom Freud called *Verneinung*, whereby a negation stands for its contrary, an assent, confirmation, or affirmation. Freud analyzes *Verneinung* as produced by repression acting against or in resistance to recognition of an unconscious desire or drive. A classic example illustrates the symptom well enough: when the analysand says something like "the woman I desired in my dream is not like my mother, not at all" then the analyst is ready to retort, on Freud's authority, that "'no' is the hall-mark of repression."[11] "Don't take this the wrong way" might be another illustration of *Verneinung* inhabiting our most polite discourse or even constituting it. (In fact, the first sentence Freud invents to illustrate the symptom is pragmatically very similar: "Now you'll think I mean to say something insulting, but really I've no such intention" [235]). It says, in effect, don't take this, what I'm about to say, the wrong way, and at the same time it also says that there is a wrong way, and thus "you are right to hear that I am also saying (without saying it) the 'wrong way,' which is therefore not simply the wrong way, but also the right way to hear what I say."

—That's twisted! And there you go again adding quotation marks as if I myself had said all that, instead of you. I didn't. Now I suppose you're going to tell me that "I didn't" is another, whaddayacallit? *Verneinung*? Go ahead . . .

—You just said it, I didn't . . . You see the difficulty we face extricating ourselves from this structure? It's the reason I said that a disavowal of disavowal would indeed be "wonderful."

—Why "disavowal of disavowal"? Doesn't that just raise the level of difficulty to a new power, thus guaranteeing failure? Why can't the disavowal simply be undone, that is, confessed? But what am I saying? Which disavowal? Whose? Of what? Of whom? I think you're losing me again . . .

—No, no, you're still ahead of me. For those are precisely the questions one would have to ask on the way to distinguishing and differentiating *within* the movement of appropriation, that task neither of us thinks to

avoid, although we have very different ways of imagining this non-avoid-
ance (parenthetically, and so as not to insist too much on our imaginary
difference, you call for such decisions, distinctions, and differentiations to
be made once and for all, more or less, whereas I insist on the infinite it-
erations of the task at hand, never finished once and for all, and never just
a task for the moral philosopher, but for all those who have to get on with
life and thus with death, with others, in every context imaginable); leaving our differences aside, what is it we are both asking *about*? A structure
of disavowed appropriation: if that sounds almost sinister, remember that
the same structure is also *involved in* what we both still call and want to
call by the noble names of reason and responsibility. I know, "involved in"
sounds pretty imprecise, but that's just it. If we could measure, plot, describe precisely, once and for all, this "involvement," if we could lay out
an *involuted* (from *involvere*, to roll in or up) relation in the flat dimension
of logical definition, if, in other words, taking responsibility were a matter of just reading off from this definition, well, then, would we even be
raising questions about it? No, because there would be no question about
what one should, ought to, must do (but also should not, ought not to,
must not do) to take his/her/its responsibility. And that's clearly not the
case, the question is always on everyone's lips, including ours . . .

   — . . . and Derrida's, who I still hear echoing in all you say. All right. Responsibility "involves," is folded into a movement of appropriation, i.e., a
"self" who or which alone takes responsibility. This means that this "self"
also acts for, before, in place of, in response to, or simply *as* the involuted
other(s) "within," all the others involved or with whom one "is involved,"
to use that common expression, but to include all manner of involvements,
not just intimate ones, even the most abstract, for example, what one sees
on television or learns of through the news or is able to understand at some
remove. All the others who are within without being only within so long as
they are also without, without and therefore also within (to graft on here
some of your convoluted syntax!). I know Derrida has affirmed many times
something like "it is the other in me who—or which—decides."[12] Well,
isn't this exactly the sort of statement of truth, the confession or avowal that
is routinely disavowed by, well, by someone like "me" who relies on an idea
of responsibility fully grounded in the subject? And who wonders, upon
hearing the assertion "it is the other in me who decides, who has decided,"
whether it describes a responsible act, a responsible decision when it puts responsibility on the shoulders of a phantom other, an other "in me"?

—You wonder, you say. That's wonderful. For indeed who is wondering, who is asking the question? Who has just said these things? Is it you or rather "someone like you"? Or is it someone else, someone other for whom you speak up or on whose shoulders you stand? Are you speaking for yourself or for another when you worry these matters? And what about the quotation of Derrida? Isn't he another who is speaking here as well, through a textual proxy? These are not easily decidable questions once one suspends the axiomatics of subjectivity that are usually invoked to decide them. No subject's knowledge has ever been sufficient in itself to make decisions, what are called "decisions," which do not merely unfold the consequences of knowledge and calculation, because they have to step off at some point into an unknown, beyond the subject's knowledge or ability to calculate outcomes.

—Yes, yes, this is the necessary distinction between calculated program and decision. But admit it's not easy to do without the axiomatics of subjectivity. Didn't Nietzsche say something to the effect that we won't get rid belief in the subject so long as we haven't given up grammar?[13]

—Or the law, for which the responsibilizable subject is a conditioning belief, construction, or simply what Joyce called (he was speaking of paternity) a legal fiction. The subject is a legal fiction, which means that, before the law, no one is given the choice to "do without" it. But in the whole lived complexity of involvements and responsibilities, decisions, acts, and sufferings, the legal fiction can be and does get suspended, all the time, even if, by law, it will always be enforced. Before or beyond the law, however, there is always good reason to "do without" the fiction, effectively or practically and through all kinds of "practices," which include experiences of suffering (one's "own" and that of others, the suffering of others as one's own, the suffering of compassion). Practically or pragmatically, we might say that, through these "practices" or experiences, the legal fiction is disavowed, even as it remains in force in every manner of recognized discourse of knowledge (for the fiction concerns above all the epistemological subject, the subject of knowledge, about whom one can ask: what did he know and when did he know it?). Such practical "disavowals," however, would not necessarily be speech acts, in the narrow sense, even though the term disavowal itself calls up speech, or at least voice. *Advocare*, the root of our words avow, avowal, figures the action of calling to or calling up a voice, more specifically, calling to one's aid the voice or speech of another. The advocate is called to speak in place of the other, to lend his/her voice to the other's cause, thereby to act as an aid or supplement to the one who stands accused. Likewise, the word vow implies something spoken, a speech act, a voice swearing a vow. Vow, avow, avowal all call up not only voice and speech, but the scene of the law, once again, and the very particular speech acts performed there under the law's command.

—Yes, I see that, but what's your point?

—Merely to point or call to this call to language and even to underscore it, redouble it as when I spoke of "disavowal of disavowal." Perhaps all such a phrase can do is repeat, redouble the call to another's "voice," that is, to language and therefore to thought. And it calls on the other disavowal to disavow the first. The structure of disavowal, we saw, is inextricable for the subject, or for the ego, if you prefer Freud's terminology. By itself, the subject can only disavow that it is not itself. Which is why its disavowal has to call for another to repeat it but with the difference of a spacing that marks the site of another's speech, another speaking. This other site is what no discourse of subject-based knowledge can know, cognize, and therefore recognize, avow. In the strict court of law, the legal subject cannot confess, give testimony, or respond as anyone other than itself. That is why these very discourses themselves need to be supplemented by others, many others, many other sites of the difference they disavow. They thus call up or call for a repetition that does not just repeat the same thing, but changes or displaces something, *does* something, which is what I'm here calling: disavowal of disavowal.

—But where are these sites? In what space?

—I'm speaking now of the necessity to put into language, to bring thought before itself in some form (language as power of formalization) so that it may continue to try to grasp its own contradictions, false ideas, and inadequate understandings. This is not to suggest that language is the only site that matters or the one that comprises all others or any similar such thing. Just a moment ago I pointed to "the whole lived complexity of involvements and responsibilities, decisions, acts, and sufferings," in other words, to the innumerable sites where effectively, pragmatically, something like the disavowal of disavowal goes on, unceasingly in fact, and without any necessary recourse to the formalization of language or even to elementary linguistic expression. It may, it certainly does take place in utter silence, before or beyond any articulated speech: e.g., a caress that is answered by another caress, or an exchange of glances. But if I'm also insisting on the properly linguistic site, that's because this site will and does get called up all the time to supplement and speak for the silent witness to experience as experience of the other.[14] It is true that, still most often, what steps up in answer to this call is a discursive advocate for the subject (for example, as the subject of knowledge of its own experience); what takes over, in other words, is a disavowing discourse.

—Can there be any other?

—Perhaps that is what is in question here and throughout *Book of Addresses*. If so, would that explain the constant reference to writings of Derrida, Nancy, Cixous, Blanchot, and others, all of whom consign the truth of thought to something other than the subject? Their texts would thus be what I called sites for the disavowal of the disavowal of this "something other."

—That phrase is becoming so awkward! Can't you find a better one?

—How about "deconstruction"?

—Less awkward, but not very original. Besides, how does it mean "disavowal of disavowal"?

—If you want a serious answer to that question, we'd have to take the time to recall what "deconstruction" sought to name when it was initially proposed, when it began to be, as Plato put it, "bandied about, alike among those who understand it and those who have no interest in it." If we were being serious here, if we were, say, sitting around a seminar table, I'd suggest we reread (for discussion next week) the 1966 essay by Derrida titled "Freud and the Scene of Writing." And then, next week having arrived, the discussion could begin by situating the essay. So, we'd remark that it begins with a kind of preface or presentation of its provenance in a long lecture for a seminar that met at the Institut de Psychanalyse. In telescopic prose, this prologue sketches the background of the lecture-essay, and indicates which question was "in the air" at the seminar, namely: what is the relation, if any, between deconstruction and psychoanalysis? This question leads to a very concise description of what deconstruction does, and thus of what that term was meant to name, to put into language. Well, although the word disavowal never occurs, I would say that "deconstruction" is here made to designate as well and from the outset a kind of disavowal of disavowal, not first of all as an event within the psychoanalytic transference, but rather as a historical force.

To see this, we'd have to pay attention to what is being said about repression (and you recall that *Verneinung* is an effect of repression). Psychoanalysis and deconstruction share an interest in repression *inasmuch as it fails.*[15] Derrida cites Freud declaring, quite reasonably: "Repressions that have failed have more claim on our interest than those that may have been successful; for the latter will for the most part escape our examination." And Derrida comments that it is a comparable failure that "interests us," in other words, those who speak (for example, in a seminar) for the *historical* interest of deconstruction. "An unsuccessful repression, on the road to historical dismantling. It is this dismantling that interests us, this un-successfulness [*non-réussite*, that is, non-success] which confers upon its becoming a certain legibility and limits its historical opaqueness" (197).

This is very near the crux of the question we're asking in our own little seminar; one glimpses here, in outline, the idea of disavowal of disavowal, as well as the necessity of its structure: a repetition that does not merely repeat the same, but also dismantles or assists at the dismantling of what remains nevertheless legible. This crux comes fully into view when it is aligned with a certain practice of, precisely, crossing out or erasing. For-malized in writing, deconstruction disavows, puts a cross through the his-tory to which it does not simply belong since it also *thinks* the condition of belonging, i.e., the condition of a self proper to itself, belonging to it-self. When deconstruction begins to write this history of belonging, it does so with the double gesture of inscribing and erasing, inscribing, on the one hand, the historical epoch of metaphysics, while with the other hand erasing its archive, but in a manner that does not render it illegible, on the contrary "This erasure, *which maintains the legibility of the archia* [*archie*, emphases added], signifies a relationship of *conceived* [that is, *pen-sée*, emphasis in the original] belonging to the history of metaphysics."[16]

So, what is interesting to reflect upon now is how, from the beginning, deconstruction has advocated itself (so to speak!) as a different practice of *disavowal,* which is both related to and distinguishable from the psycho-analytic structure of *Verneinung.* This practice is that of an inscribing era-sure (or erasing inscription) that does not prevent legibility. Whereas *Verneinung* belongs essentially to the structure of repression as constitutive of the individual psyche, erasure is a practice of *thinking* ("erasure . . . sig-nifies a relationship of conceived [*pensée*] belonging . . . ") that reads the failure of repression as historical dismantling (i.e., the historical decon-struction of metaphysics). It is thus a matter of conceiving differently the relation between these two, *Verneinung* and erasure: "Logocentric repres-sion is not comprehensible on the basis of the Freudian concept of repression; on the contrary, logocentric repression permits an understanding of how an original and individual repression became possible within the horizon of a culture and a historical structure of belonging" (197).

Did you just sigh? Or was that a groan?

—Maybe I was just testing to see if you were still listening. Anyway, isn't it time for the seminar to end? But seriously, I'm wondering why you took us back to this most classic *mise en place* of deconstruction, as double gesture, reinscription and erasure, writing *sous rature*, the closure of metaphysics, and all the rest . . .

—Were *you* listening? It's because I proposed deconstruction as another name for "disavowal of disavowal," and since to justify that rash translation would take the time of a seminar, I employed a fiction . . .

—A fiction? Yes, go on.

—Fiction: there's perhaps another name for "disavowal of disavowal."[17] I could point to the places in *Book of Addresses* where this idea is worked out with help from Blanchot, Cixous, Derrida again. But also with the help of a literary fiction, a novella by Henry James, *The Aspern Papers*, a partial reading of which opens the collection (and gives some of the most sustained argument here about the condition of address).[18] Now, if we could prolong our seminar, I would choose to add a different text by James to our reading list for next week, his preface for the New York edition of *The Golden Bowl*.[19]

—Surely you're kidding? Look at the clock . . .

—All right, I see, but stay and help me read just three words of the text, in fact just one word, because it is essentially the same word repeated three times. Each time, however, it seems to have a different force of meaning, or it goes in a different direction. If I've counted right, James writes "disavowing," "disavowing," "disavowal" at three different junctures in this preface, the first and last falling very close to the beginning and the end of the text. The first time it occurs in the midst or at the turning point of a reflection on what it means for an author of a novel to be responsible, or rather what it has meant, what it must have meant for this author, writing now, *après coup*, a preface for his own book, to have been responsible. As he so often does in these prefaces, James is remarking on his preference for narrating another's impression of an affair or event (the "subject-matter," as he calls it), rather than narrating it directly as the author. "I have already betrayed, as an accepted habit, and even to extravagance commented on, my preference for dealing with my subject-matter, for 'seeing my story,' through the opportunity and the sensibility of some more or less detached, some not strictly involved, though thoroughly interested and intelligent, witness or reporter. . . . The somebody is often . . . but an unnamed, unintroduced and . . . unwarranted participant, the impersonal author's concrete deputy or delegate, a convenient substitute or apologist for the creative power otherwise so veiled and disembodied."[20] The prefacer is then going to be led to analyze this preference in terms of the responsibility that is assumed by letting another stand in as the painter or the poet in his place. Let me cite the whole passage.

—You promised we were going to read just three words, three occurrences of "disavowal"?

—The word comes later, but we need the context to be able to read it. And besides, James's text performs a disavowal before it ever confesses the word. The disavowed thing is mockingly called "the mere muffled majesty of irresponsible 'authorship.'" But that gesture is immediately followed by another whereby the other, that is, "the painter of the picture or chanter of the ballad," is declared never "responsible *enough* and for every inch of his surface and note of his song." Those are James's italics, by the way. And after several more turns and changes of direction, it turns out that the preference declared here is to give oneself "most instead of least to answer for." You won't mind, will you, if I continue inserting some bracketed remarks into the full quotation?

—!!!

—

Anything, in short, I now reflect, must always have seemed to me better [this "to me" signals that James is speaking still for himself and for his own preference in the matter]—better for the process and the effect of representation, my irrepressible ideal—than the mere muffled majesty of irresponsible "authorship." [Do you think that "irrepressible" might have called up the look-alike "irresponsible," which follows it so closely? How does one take responsibility for one's own irrepressible preference? Especially if the preference one is declaring is to let another take one's place as "deputy," "delegate," "substitute," or "apologist," to recall all of James's terms?] Beset constantly by the sense that the painter of the picture or the chanter of the ballad (whatever we may call him) can never be responsible *enough*, and for every inch of his surface and note of his song, I track my uncontrollable footsteps, right and left [i.e., through changes of direction], after the fact [*après coup*], while they take their quick turn, even on stealthiest tiptoe, toward the point of view that, within the compass, will give me most instead of least to answer for. (347)

This image of James going back over his own stealthy tracks, watching himself read directions off a compass that points always toward *more* responsibility, is compelling for the note struck of the uncontrollability of it all, I mean the way the footsteps are being drawn once again, right here in the preface, into another's wake, the other that he pretended to be in writing his fictions, but also now, the other that he was when he so pretended.

—I'm still waiting for James finally to call this "disavowing" by name.

—Here it is, in the next paragraph: "It's not that the muffled majesty of authorship doesn't here [i.e., in *The Golden Bowl*] ostensibly reign; but I catch myself again shaking it off and *disavowing* [my emphases] the pretence of it while I get down into the arena and do my best to live and breathe and rub shoulders and converse with the persons engaged in the struggle . . . " So, the disavowal of authorship is the condition of doing one's best at what authors do best, which according to James, and he just confessed it again, means representing "the persons engaged in the struggle."

—Why didn't you quote the end of the sentence: " . . . engaged in the struggle that provides for the others in the circling tiers the entertainment of the great game"? This representation, which James has just called his "irrepressible ideal," is itself represented as theatrical. James always insists that a novel must interest, entertain, give its audience pleasure. Here that audience is figured as "the others in the circling tiers" of a theater, even though the "great game" entertaining them is a novel. I seem to recall that Henry James dreamed of triumph as a playwright, but that his plays were far less successful than his novels and tales. But, don't you see that the theatrical figure can also work to disavow the disavowal of "the muffled majesty of authorship"! For what has had to be muffled in novel-writing is the applause from the circling tiers; a novel's readers are always absent and thus silent, there's no call for "Author! Author!" at the end of a play. So James here manages to procure for himself some substitute for that moment by way of the theatrical image.[21] That's really rather clever.

—Or it may be just another demonstration of the impossible disavowal that James nevertheless meant to declare. For he would say, if only he could, that ostensibly reigning authorship is a pretense, to be shaken off, and yet what he says shows how it still sticks to one, comes back on stage no sooner the disavowal is published.

—But look how late it's getting! I must be off.

—Wait, wait! We can just glance at the second occurrence. At this point, James is going on about the photographs accompanying this edition as frontispieces to each volume. Even though he collaborated extensively with the photographer, Alvin Langdon Coburn, choosing the sites to be photographed for each volume and even dictating the angles of the shots, James betrays some ambivalence about their inclusion here. In particular, he is determined to forestall any notion that the frontispieces serve as "illustrations" of the novels they accompany.[22] But at least, notes James, the photographer found a way, "not to keep, or to pretend to keep, anything like dramatic step with [the] suggestive matter [of the volumes]" (331). That is, the photographer did not pretend that he could emulate with his pictures James's own dramas (we're in the theater again). "This," James comments, "would quite have disqualified them, to my rigour; but they were 'all right,' in the so analytic modern critical phrase, through their discreetly *disavowing* emulation" (my emphasis). Saying "all right" (but in quotation marks and with marked irony), James consents to receive the "discreetly disavowing emulation" of the photographs. Does it strike you that this three-word phrase is quite unstable? "Disavowing" can be either a verbal or adjectival participle, and depending on how you read it makes quite a difference for the sense. Do the photographs actively disavow any emulation, that is, not even attempt it, or on the contrary, do they present the novel with their "disavowing emulation" of its grand, dramatic achievement? And what about "discreetly"? Right now that looks to me like the revealing mark of its opposite, the witting or unwitting immodesty of all this disavowed emulation. What do you think?

—I think you've nearly persuaded me that one should not write a preface to one's own writings. But suppose someone had convinced Henry James of that? For all their disavowals, the prefaces are quite wonderful texts in their own right. Still, and again don't take this the wrong way, you're no Henry James . . .

—But who could ever deny it? And these are great texts not *in spite of* the disavowals displayed, but *because* they display them so well, so inextricably, so seemingly inexorably. As if disavowal were even the law of their composition. Or rather, since the novels are written in and as the movement that would disavow "the muffled majesty of authorship," the prefaces are composed according to the principle of a disavowal of that disavowal, in other words, a reappropriation of what only *seemed* to be painted or chanted by another. But before we can close the book, there is the last occurrence of our theme word, which falls a few lines before the end, in the last paragraph of this, the last of the prefaces. James here is giving a final assessment of what has been done, of the "done things" that are not just the novels and tales, the fictions, but also now these prefaces. It's rather long, but I beg your indulgence to cite *in extenso*.

All of which amounts but to saying . . .

—Wait, wait!

—

. . . that as the whole conduct of life consists of things done, which do other things in their turn, just so our behaviour and its fruits are essentially one and continuous and persistent and unquenchable, so the act has its way of abiding and showing and testifying, and so, among our innumerable acts, are no arbitrary, no senseless separations. The more we are capable of acting the less gropingly we plead such differences; whereby, with any capability, we recognise betimes that to "put" things is very exactly and responsibly and interminably to do them. Our expression of them, and the terms on which we understand that, belong as nearly to our conduct and our life as every other feature of our freedom; these things yield in fact some of its most exquisite material to the religion of doing. More than that, our literary deeds enjoy this marked advantage over many of our acts, that, though they go forth into the world and stray even in the desert, they don't to the same extent lose themselves; their attachment and reference to us, however, strained, needn't necessarily lapse—while of the tie that binds us to *them* we may make almost anything we like. We are condemned, in other words, whether we will or no, to abandon and outlive, to forget and disown and hand over to desolation, many vital or social performances—if only because the traces, records, connexions, the very memorials we would fain preserve, are practically impossible to rescue for that purpose from the general mixture. We give them up even when we wouldn't—it is not a question of choice. Not so on the other hand our really "done" things of this superior and more appreciable order—which leave us indeed all licence of disconnexion and *disavowal* [my emphasis], but positively impose on us no such necessity. (347–48)

It's getting dark. Are you still there? Did you follow the last turn toward a disavowal that may be freely undertaken, because no necessity imposes it? Unlike those acts that are abandoned, outlived, forgotten, disowned, or handed over to desolation, not always by choice or even against our wish to hold them fast, the act of literature, the act of "putting" things in such a way as "very exactly and responsibly and interminably to do them," leaves one free to disavow them—or not. There is then a structure (if we can call it that) of disconnection that "is not a question of choice" but of the "general mixture," where connection is lost "whether we will or no," over against which James is adumbrating the "marked advantage" of the literary deed, of our "really 'done' things" whose "attachment and refer- ence to us, however strained, needn't necessarily lapse." Despite certain appearances, however, there is not an opposition being made here be- tween irresponsible life and responsible art. For one thing, James says clearly that the act of "putting" things is very much part of the deeds and doings that make up the "whole conduct of life."[23] "Our expression of [things], and the terms on which we understand that, belong as nearly to our conduct and our life as every other feature of our freedom." Not an opposition, then, but a relation within life between modes of disavowal, the disavowals that "just happen" and are even imposed by necessity, and a kind of disavowal that one would always be free not to make, not to have to make. But can a disavowal "just happen"? Haven't I been saying that a disavowal is always some kind of act or deed or speech act? Perhaps in the idea of disavowal or disconnection that "just happens," there is, precisely, a disavowal of connection? James appears to suggest this at one point, before he puts in place the distinction of literary deeds from any other kind of deed: "our behaviour and its fruits are essentially one and continuous and persistent and unquenchable, so the act has its way of abiding and showing and testifying [notice the language of testimony], and so, among our innumerable acts, there are no arbitrary, no senseless separations."[24] That is, just as with our literary deeds, the connection abides and is attested to between acts and behaviours: "there are no arbi- trary, senseless separations." To declare otherwise would be to engage in a disavowal, and it is this speech act that James figures in the following sen- tence: "The more we are capable of acting the less gropingly we *plead* such differences." Even if the superior actor (the one who is capable of acting the most, of giving himself "the most instead of the least to answer for") will be identified, for James, with the doer of literary deeds (or in general with the artist), the "we" of "we plead" is all-inclusive. It includes, that is, whoever *pleads* disconnection (before some court or before one's con- science), and therefore poses a limit to his or her own responsibility for some attested act. The legal subject must always plead the differences ever more gropingly, for that is its law: so that it may know itself as and at the limit of its responsibility. The speech act figured in this pleading is thus the disavowal *constitutive* of the subject.

But the same general, unspecified "we" is also subject to the experience of finitude whereby "we are condemned . . . whether we will or no, to abandon and outlive, to forget and disown and hand over to desolation, many vital or social performances." What I earlier, and gropingly, called disavowals that "just happen" was a reference to this description of finite experience. What's still unclear is whether James noticed or meant us to notice the connection between his two characterizations of "disconnection": the first, an act of disavowal that pleads disconnection, while the second is a disconnection that "just happens" by virtue of the finitude, alas, of experience. Is there a connection being made here between these two disconnects, or is the connection being disavowed, precisely, in the figure of what "just happens"? What do you think?

—That, as James said, one can never be responsible *enough*. You're right. Leave *Book of Addresses* alone, without preface or introduction. But if you like, I'll write a foreword and confess everything in your place.

—Oh, if only you could, that would indeed be wonderful.

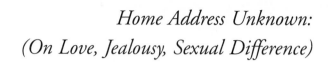

Home Address Unknown:
(On Love, Jealousy, Sexual Difference)

§ 1 Deconstruction and Love

> Can one speak of loving without declaring love, without declaring war,
> beyond all possible neutrality? Without confessing, be it the
> unspeakable?
>
> —Jacques Derrida

The conjunction of deconstruction and love will seem an unexpected one to some. It is an association excluded by the widely circulated image of deconstruction as an essentially negative operation, as if the term were really a synonym of "destruction" and the additional syllable simply superfluous. This persistent reduction has come about only after many repetitions, performed most often so as to give someone a pretext for denunciation. Deconstruction has had bad press almost since it first appeared in Derrida's writings. Things got quickly worse when others began to pick up the term, perhaps because this could be taken as a signal that something larger was afoot and would have to be dealt with more severely. Thus it is that, after several decades of such severity, one cannot approach an essay on deconstruction and love without anticipating a resistance fed by the rumor that deconstruction is essentially destructive and even that it destroys everything we, as members of civilized societies, ought to work to preserve from destruction, which is to say, everything we love or at least everything we are told we ought to love. Beginning with love itself. At its core, this resistance would be working to protect love itself from destruction, and thus to protect everything and everyone we love. And what could be more natural than that? The nature of this resistance would thus be that of the tautology assumed between acts of loving and acts of preserving or protecting from destruction. As such, the resistance is likely to be activated by very powerful forces indeed.

The task of this chapter cannot be to overcome this powerful resistance, assuming that such a thing were even possible. It cannot aim, in other words, simply to dismantle the resistant idea that love essentially seeks to preserve from destruction and is therefore what must, above all, be preserved. Rather, I will try to make apparent how a loving movement is the indispensable key to understanding what deconstruction does. In the process—and this would be the ultimate stakes of the undertaking—the idea will have to be approached that even if it is essentially preservative, love (but also deconstruction) is nevertheless no stranger to destruction, to loss, and to ruin. To put it less litotically, in other words, to avoid that figure of speech whereby an affirmation is expressed by the negative of the contrary, we will be approaching the figure of love as affirmation that deconstructs the opposition between preservation and destruction, of love, therefore, as that which, like deconstruction, takes place along the divided, ruined border of this alternative.

Let's begin by citing just one of the many occasions on which Derrida has sought to arrest the assimilation of deconstruction to a negative operation, to a destruction. It is from the transcription of a discussion he had with some colleagues in Montreal in 1979 (Derrida is thus not the only signatory of this text). He is explaining how he initially never intended to attach any privilege to the term "deconstruction," which he began using in a chain with many others. This privilege got assigned when others began to repeat the term as the principal designation for what he and soon many others were interested in doing. But insofar as the word carried connotations, as he puts it, "of a technical operation used to dismantle systems," he has never much liked it.[1] The technical reference, he explains, tends to screen out the more important association for him: that the deconstructive gesture be "accompanied, or can be accompanied (in any case, I would hope to accompany it), by an affirmation. It is not negative, it is not destructive." He goes on to recount that, once it became clear how this word was being singled out by others, he tried "to determine this concept," as he writes, "in my own manner, that is, according to what I thought was the right manner, which I did by insisting on the fact that it was not a question of a negative operation" (87). And then, so as to make his insistence on the non-negative, affirmative concept of deconstruction clearer still, Derrida speaks of love:

> I don't feel that I'm in a position to *choose* between an operation that we'll call negative or nihilist, an operation that would set about furiously dismantling systems, and the other operation. I love very much everything that I decon-

struct in my own manner; the texts I want to read from the deconstructive point of view are texts I love, with that impulse of identification which is indispensable for reading. They are texts whose future, I think, will not be exhausted for a long time. . . . [M]y relation to these texts is characterized by loving jealousy and not at all by nihilistic fury (one can't read anything in the latter condition) . . . (ibid.)

Before underscoring a few points about these remarks, one might ask: Is it certain that this is the most auspicious place to begin a discussion of deconstruction and love? When one says that one loves a *text*,[2] when the object of the transitive verb "love" is not an animate thing, then is there not a very large distance taken at the outset from the heart of the love relation, which has to be (does it not?) either interpersonal or at least a relation formed between animate, living beings? In other words, by setting out from a remark about love for something like texts, are we not going off in a wrong direction, which has to lead wide of the animate heart or soul of love? Worse still, beginning in this fashion might risk confirming yet another facet of deconstruction's negative association in many people's minds, all those for whom, for example, Derrida's famous assertion "there is no outside-the-text" is heard only as an intellectual's negation of all activity other than writing and reading. To even seem to imply that the love in question in deconstruction is *first of all* the love of texts appears designed to discourage at the outset anyone who might harbor this misguided notion from giving it up.[3]

That is always possible. Yet, if these risks seem worth taking, it could well be for a reason not unlike the one that leads Derrida, in the above passage, to insist to the extent he does that, contrary to a common perception, his own practice of deconstruction proceeds out of love rather than under the sway of a destructive impulse: that reason is to add the force of *affirmation* to what otherwise appears destined to have only the negative force of its technical, dismantling operation. Likewise, if we begin here by speaking of the love of texts with some faith that we will thereby be led to the heart of the matter, then it must be because we have already begun to affirm something about love's heart: it is that which would be able to hold together in an essential relation the movement toward the animate as well as toward the inanimate, toward life as well as non-life, or death, and therefore toward that which can be preserved in life as well as that which has never had or no longer has any life as such to be preserved. At the heart of love, all of these apparent oppositions would be suspended, no longer or not yet in force, or already ruined, in ruins.[4]

But this is indeed to anticipate where the opening quotation, on loving the texts one deconstructs, may lead. To consider these remarks less precipitously, one should recall that they were improvised for a specific occasion and in response to another's question; as such, they are perhaps less guarded, less policed than they might otherwise be for publication under an author's sole signature. Derrida here is sharing with others the responsibility for signing this text. Which is not to say, of course, that they are unsigned or unattributable, but merely that they bear a particular relation to the movement whereby one signs something. Indeed, Derrida had been invited on the occasion in question to air thoughts about that movement itself, to characterize his own gesture when he signed other texts elsewhere, to offer reflections from a certain remove about what put them and his signature in motion.[5] As remarks about the relation one may have to the writing and reading one does (or to which one submits), they would attempt to configure those activities (or those passions) from somewhere exterior to them, at some distance before or beyond what is being described. And since what is being described or characterized is the relation, passion, and impulse called love, then the external vantage point aimed for here would itself have to stand outside that love relation, in a position of "objective neutrality," as it is called, which would be the position of the would-be scientist or scholar. But is this attempt in fact a success? Is there, in other words, an objectively neutral, scholarly position that can be identified there?

That is very doubtful, for reasons one may quickly see. As already pointed out, the remarks summarize how Derrida had to work to counter a prevalent understanding of the deconstructive gesture as negative or destructive. They give a condensed account of his efforts to resituate this concept "according to what [he] thought was the right manner," which was the manner of an affirmation. Notice, however, that at a certain point, the point at which the quoted extract begins, the speaker is no longer giving simply an account of what he has done, of other texts he has signed; the mode or manner of his remarks also shifts to that of affirmation. And it is at this point that he invokes love: "I love very much everything that I deconstruct in my own manner; the texts I want to read from a deconstructive point of view are texts I love . . . " Such phrases, and those that surround them, can no longer be heard as merely descriptive—or constative, as speech act theorists would say; in other words, they do not only describe a state of affairs, which led someone to do something, and then the something that he did ("to determine this concept in my own manner") or that he continues to do ("I love very much everything that I deconstruct in my own manner"). Without drama, but with indisputable emphasis, these phrases also do something: they *declare love*, and as such they perform the affirmation by which, as Derrida had earlier observed, the deconstructive gesture "is accompanied, or can be accompanied (in any case, I would hope to accompany it)." In doing so, in declaring love, they affirm the accompanying affirmation in the present of their performance, at the scene of discussion with some colleagues in Montreal in 1979, but also, of course, at every other scene at which these remarks can be and have been repeated, including this one. Each repetition differs in force, but with each quotation or repetition, the affirmative declaration remains, as it were, in excess over the descriptive value of these sentences. In excess, or rather let us say that the affirmative force of the declaration is that which conditions the description as more, less, or simply other than the description that it also is, but that it is only by virtue of having been declared. In other words, when Derrida (or anyone else) says or writes: "I love X very much," he is describing a certain relation, but he can describe it only by affirming again that he loves X very much. Because an affirmative accompaniment puts in place the description, which it thereby precedes and conditions, no objective neutrality is to be found outside this structure, for one is already within it, which is to say, within a structure conditioned by the non-objective, non-neutral, affirmative declaration: "I love . . . ."[6]

This suggests that, without much apparent calculation (for that is the character of improvisation), the remarks I've quoted and then partially analyzed would have performed once again the accompanying affirmation that Derrida finds to be missing whenever deconstruction is construed as a merely technical operation of dismantling, whenever its gesture is taken up and repeated as technique or mere method, whenever an external, objectively neutral position is assumed as the place from which to deconstruct whatever by whomever, and by anyone at all like everyone else. The affirmation by which Derrida would wish to accompany the deconstructive gesture cannot be neutral;[7] it is, rather, of the nature of love, that is, of that whose non-neutrality must be thought of in at least two different ways.

On the one hand, when one loves something or someone, one is partial to it, to him, or to her; one even has a passion, as we say, for that thing or that person or that creature. That is why, for example, in allegories of love (e.g., Cupid), love's passion will be represented somehow as a blindness. But this impaired visibility or vision is precisely not the blindness we believe to be required of justice, which is conceived of or allegorized as a blindness in the interest of dispensing a neutral, or just, justice. The blindness of love, in its partiality, is assumed to prevent, overturn, or at least make improbable the blind, impartial neutrality of justice.[8] *On the other hand,* love is not neutral in the sense that he or she who loves is not just anyone, no matter who; it is *he* who loves, *she* who loves. Each has his or her idiom of love, but this idiom is less something one *has* or *knows* than something one *does*. (We will return to this notion of idiom below).

Now, these two faces or figures of love's non-neutrality might be called objective and subjective if it were not that such a distinction is suspended by or from the *passion* of love, in other words, by or from that which one experiences in a certain passivity under the influence or the pull of another whom one loves, that is, the other to whom one's feeling of love becomes addressed and by whom it is therefore determined as address. Determined by the other, the address of love is never issued by a pre-existent subject in the direction of an object, its object, or destination. As Jean-Luc Nancy has put it:

> Love re-presents the "I" to itself as broken . . . To the "I" it presents this: that it, this subject, has been touched, breached, in its subjectivity, and from now on, it *is*; for the time of love, broken or cracked, however slightly. It *is* so, which means that the break or the wound is neither an accident nor a property that the subject could make its own. Since it is a break of its property as subject, it is, essentially, an interruption in the process of relating to oneself outside oneself. . . . For as long as it lasts, love does not cease to come from without and to remain, not outside but this outside itself, each time singular, a blade plunged into me and that I cannot rejoin because it disjoins me.[9]

One could say, in somewhat simple terms, that the position of subject, the subject position, the positionality of subject/object are, as such, incapable of the experience of love's passion or even that they are *opposed* to that experience insofar as it knows no subject, no "I" who loves "X," outside or before the passion of the subject's address of love. In other words, love is not a matter of position, whether of subject or object, and therefore of opposition, but of an address that does not originate from any home, as it were. An address without home, without the property of a subject from which it is sent and to which it returns, love always brushes up against the uncanny, the *unheimlich*, which might also be translated for the occasion as "un-homelike." Love brings with it the un-homelike because it is the experience of the sudden or not-so-sudden arrival of the other who *expropriates* address, which is to say *appropriates* it, *exappropriates* it: when I say "I love . . . ," it is always the declaration of the other at my address.

There is at least one more thing to notice about the improvised character of the remarks that led Derrida to make his declaration of love. The repetition of a phrase, "à ma manière" ("in my own manner"), scans the declaration in a manner that, had this been a more calculated, written text, would probably have either provoked the style censor or else prompted a reflection about that idiomatic phrase. As it is, however, the phrase repeats of itself and insists—idiomatically, mechanically, or manneristically—on doing what one does in one's own manner. "I tried to determine this concept in my own manner, that is, according to what I thought was the right manner . . . "; "I love very much everything I deconstruct in my own manner . . . " This modest adverbial modifier can in fact be read as a key to the affirmative tenor of the passage, which culminates in the declaration of love's conjunction with deconstruction. The affirmation that would accompany the deconstructive gesture, at least when that gesture is performed by the one who signs here in his own manner, would always proceed in some manner or another, according to someone's idiom. It is thus, as well, an affirmation of the idiom in the idiom. This is to underscore once again that deconstruction in the "right manner," deconstruction accompanied by affirmation rather than confined to a negative or technical operation, has never been performed by just anyone at all and no one in particular, for example, by *the* philosopher of pure reason, an ideal subject, or from some position of objective neutrality. The accompanying affirmation, which makes for all the difference from the idea of philosophy or from the notion of a pure technique, is carried, as it were, in an idiom, by which is not meant only a particular language, but everything that can inform and deform anyone's use of a common, so-called natural language: the domain of personal and family history, of conscious experience and unconscious desire, of civil, public identity and private identifications, and so forth. In other words, all that, all that is in play whenever anyone says "I love . . . " The affirmation, carried by the idiom, will be an affirmation of all that, all that is in play whenever anyone says, declares, affirms: "I love . . . ," "j'aime . . . ," "yo quiero . . . ," "ich liebe . . . " in whatever idiom.[10]

I have, it seems, let myself be tempted to read these few phrases of an impromptu exchange as if they supplied all the coordinates needed to plot the conjunction of deconstruction with love. As yet, however, little has been said about what is most striking, perhaps, about these lines, the fact that they declare a love of texts. Recall the initial question about the risks this kind of declaration might present for the task here, the risk of being led astray from the heart of the matter of love. Nevertheless, it was wagered at the beginning that, by keeping to this course, we would be able to affirm something about love's heart, as that which can accommodate, in a relation of love, the animate and the inanimate, the living and the dead, persons and texts. It is time now to renew the wager.

~

—Before you take that step, remember the questions placed in epigraph: "Can one speak of loving without declaring love, without declaring war, beyond all possible neutrality? Without confessing, be it the unspeakable?"[11]

—Are those rhetorical questions? If so, they are themselves a declaration, a non-neutral act.

—Indeed. So, do you think an essay titled "Deconstruction and Love" escapes the necessity to risk confessing the unspeakable? Somewhere have you not begun to answer the question: whom or what do you love?

—If that is not another rhetorical question, then it is the police who are asking it.

—How could it be a rhetorical question?

—Perhaps not in the usual sense, as a question that *forces* a response and only one response. But if rhetorical or poetic force can indeed be other than police force, then it must somewhere be allied with whatever permits the response of *more than one, other than one, other than just one.* Rhetoric allows also for allegory, and an allegory is always some kind of text.

—So you would declare you love a text?

—Yes, if that is possible.

~

How is it possible to love a text? That is, how is it possible to say one loves a text, of any and every sort, without that declaration being simply an abuse of the language, a stretching of the proper sense of love to the point of breaking? Or even an abasement of the highest sense, which should be reserved for the love of one's fellow human beings, if not, indeed, for the love of God, for God's love?[12] To be sure, the idea of a loving God is preserved in texts, which are themselves revered as sacred by the "religions of the book." But this consecration is precisely whatever, for those religions or those cultures, sets sacred texts apart from texts of any and every sort, from the non-sacred texts that one cannot say one loves without improperly invoking the very notion of sacrality. In other words, as soon as one declares love for a text classified as, for example, fiction or poetry or philosophy,[13] then a whole theologically buttressed doctrine of love is at stake. It is, therefore, no small matter when someone says such a thing, provided he or she means to declare more than just a passing appreciation. It is especially no small matter if it can be shown not only that such a declaration does not abuse or abase love in the proper or highest sense, but also and more affirmatively, that from its possibility is suspended whatever anyone can mean as the most proper or most sacred sense of love, the most sacred address of "I love you" for him or her—love, therefore, in all its mysteriously infinite singularity. This means, in a terrifyingly simple sense, that if we ceased, for some barely imaginable reason, to be able to *declare* a love of texts, to renew and preserve the force of that declaration, then we would also have ceased being able to love anything or anyone at all. So, yes, indeed, much is at stake; perhaps everything.

Which is why one should not take lightly the fact that for such a declaration to be possible, we cannot know ultimately either to whom it will have been declared or who is the *object*, as we say, of such a declaration. Suppose I want to declare I love something of this sort, a novel, a work of poetry, or even a critical essay. To whom can I say such a thing so that it may have the performative force of a declaration? If I announce it just to anyone within earshot, it may indeed provoke various interpretations about my state of mind or my taste in literature, or perhaps even my "raceclassgender" coefficient, but all such interpretations would take my statement as having solely constative value, that is, as a statement concerning some fact. True, it is a strange kind of fact because no neutral observer can verify it or falsify it, but fact it remains for this "neutral observer" nonetheless, that is, for whoever can hear such a statement without taking it as a *declaration* of love made to him or to her and to which he or she can and even *must* respond (walking away or pretending one has not heard the declaration would also be responses to such a declaration). It is, then, this address with the possibility and even the necessity of response that makes the difference between the constative statement and the performative declaration. So the question we were asking becomes the following: to whom, to which addressee, does one address a love of texts? For whom can such an address have the force of declaration, or the force of love, without which all such statements circulate as merely unverifiable, neutral, and finally indifferent facts?

Suppose the novel, poem, or essay I love was written by a still-living author. I might therefore declare my love to him or to her, as if there were finally no difference between author and text, signature and that which it signs. This happens everywhere, every day, which for many is no doubt a sufficient reason to write or to make any kind of work that another can love. If one dares to be lucid about this situation, however, then one knows that such tributes carry with them the recognition that one's name, one's signature is, as Juliet analyzes it, "no part of thee."[14] Because the name, the signature is not the bearer of the name, it is also always the mark of the definitive detachment that others must experience upon the death of the name's bearer, when the name will cease to be a possible form of address to someone else living and commence to function, as it were, independently of any individual bearer. But this functioning *simply is* the general possibility of naming, of language, or more generally still, of *iterability*, to use the term Derrida has made available.[15] Which means, of course, that it does not await anyone's individual, punctual death to begin to accompany every use we make of his or her proper name, including that most proper use: to call one to respond to a declaration of love. Here, then, is something no one likes to think about too much, even as it always accompanies every thought we ever have of love for another; here is an unbearable thing that must be born, which is also to say carried and renewed beyond any single one's ability to bear it: the names we give to love when we declare it are the names of mortals. Whenever we declare love to another by addressing him or her by name, we address it also to his or her mortality.[16]

We call "text," however, that which bears its name not as the mark of mortality but rather as the very possibility of its living on and continuing to be called by its name. I can thus say "I love Emily Dickinson" without much risk that my meaning will be mistaken: I love a text, the text that is now, seemingly, *inseparable* from the name it bears but the name it also just *is*, its name *as* text. But if I *can* say such a thing, and if I can say it not just as some kind of fact but affirm or declare the love I say I bear, if, in other words, I can *address* love to another with these words, then the name "Emily Dickinson" will also have to be able to name, *still*, this other who would be addressed and the other to whom I am already responding. The other, who? Emily Dickinson herself? No, of course not, but rather "someone" to whom I give that name, all the same, within myself, a site of and for another within me.[17] When one declares love to a text, one declares it *necessarily* to another within oneself. Is there, then, a distinction that has to be made between this act and the act of addressing love to another who is *also* other than oneself, a presently living person, that is, one who is not only an other within me?

Yes and no. Yes, because the independent exteriority of the other is the condition of my being able to address love or anything else to him or her, as well as the condition for any such declaration to receive from another a response that is not already determined by the address. That the other exists independently from the subject of the declaration is simply, we could say, the condition of love as other than self-love, other than a love whose object is oneself or any part of oneself. However, the distinction cannot be made in these terms, because a declaration of love is also a declaration that some internalization of the other has at least begun; the subject of the declaration is already not just itself, and that is what it declares. It declares that between itself alone and the self that shelters another within, there is no line that can be drawn separating the two as simply exterior to each other. There is at once a division, an other within the self who is not the self, and no division, the other internalized by the self as the self. But if both these conditions are necessary, if both the other's exteriority and internalization are the conditions of love, this means, doesn't it, that no strict difference can ever be laid down with certainty between, on the one hand, what is called, most often reprovingly, self-love and, on the other hand, its other, the other love that is love for the other, addressed to another.

If this is so—and it is so—then who could ever affirm love for another, to another, without at the same time addressing love to himself or to herself? And therefore without also appropriating back to the self what is meant for the other? Perhaps indeed this is always what happens, one way or the other; perhaps there has never been a declaration of love that did not keep for itself what it wanted the other to have or to feel.[18] The very least we can say is that we cannot know that there has ever been *in fact* a declaration of love that did not appropriate the address to itself, because every such address will have been conditioned by the possibility of its cancellation as address to another outside the self. I have already remarked this condition when I said, a moment ago, that love is declared to mortals, by mortals, that is, beings who internalize and are internalized in the face of the impossibility, inevitable one day, of addressing those whom they love in any other way. Yet, is that also a reason to question that there has ever been a declaration of love for another, a truly other other? Doubtless no, because we do *not* question this possibility so long as we can still think a love that does not address only itself, that does not appropriate the address of love for itself. So long as we do have this thought, it is even what we think love *must be*: the love of another. It is what we think must be given or received in the name of love, without, nevertheless, being able to affirm in absolute certainty that we have ever given or received such a thing. We can and do think this; moreover, we can cite examples, which is to say, texts.

For example, Henry James's *The Aspern Papers,* a love story in which the only love declared is finally for a text, and even for *this* text here, the one we are reading. Because the title designates both this text and the text in this text, it embeds, at the outset, a figure for itself, a set of "papers" that will be the object of blinding love. (In a moment, we'll consider what this figure of the self-loving text may be doing here.) These papers are presumed to be letters from the great American poet Jeffrey Aspern, dead for many years when the novel opens, and, if they exist, they may still be in the possession of the woman to whom they were originally addressed, the now-ancient Miss Juliana Bordereau. Miss Bordereau lives, a virtual recluse, in a Venetian villa, which is why, the narrator reasons, she has been able to keep the papers secret for so long. That secrecy is about to end, if the narrator succeeds in doing what he has come to Venice to do: he wants the papers more than anything in the world and will try to get them away somehow from their owner. The first-person narrator, who never mentions his name, is one of the two foremost editors of Aspern's works; he shares with his co-editor the responsibility for preserving the poet's name, which had been somewhat forgotten in the world of letters before their edition. In other words, Aspern's now-celebrated greatness (if, at least, we can believe the narrator) is at least partially owed to the narrator-editor's own labors. I note this circumstance because it alone would be sufficient to cast doubt on the claim that, as the narrator confides, he is doing what he does for "Jeffrey Aspern's sake," for the sake, then, of this other whom he loves.[19] This is doubtful not just because the name of the dead poet can only be the name of some other in himself, but because, as a name, it is *bound up* with the narrator's own, in the edition that both will have signed. For "Jeffrey Aspern's sake" is also always for his own sake or the sake of his own name.

The novel, then, is narrated from the position of one who can never know whether he acts for his own sake or for the sake of the other. As such, the text of *The Aspern Papers* evinces a considerable lucidity about love. In its lucidity, this text would declare: Love just *is* that impossible knowledge, the impossibility of discerning for whose sake, in whose name, one acts. Now, if this sounds like a contradiction, or worse yet, an obfuscation, that is probably because we too readily locate lucidity in a subject, and in just one subject. It is clearly not, however, the narrator himself who is lucid about what he is doing; he declares—or wants to de-clare—that he is acting out of love for another, rather than in view of an appropriation for himself of the papers and all they represent for him. We believe we can see through the narrator's conscious self-justifications ("it is all for Jeffrey Aspern's sake"), which can only have the force of *self*-justi-fications because they invoke justice done to the other. Because this dis-course holds up the other's name in self-defense, it creates the window through which to see through it—to the other other, the other who is ex-propriated when a subject would claim *to know* that whatever he does, no matter how deceitful, duplicitous, or even murderous, he does for another and not for himself. So, the "lucidity" I alluded to above is not to be found in the narrator's conscious discourse, and this is true despite the fact that every single word of the text (with the exception of the title) belongs to that discourse, is re-cited and narrated by the narrator. Despite that, there is an excess to be accounted for because, as I said, beyond the blinded *discourse*, there is a *text* that can evince a lucidity about love that the narrator seems unable to see for himself. If such a text can be "lucid," it is because it figures somehow *in itself* this border between everything it contains, all the words constituting the text, and what is *at the same time* an excess of text over all the words it contains. A border is thereby traced or re-marked setting off an outside within.

Notice, however, that to call this re-marking of textuality "lucid" and lucid about love (but is there anything else to be lucid about?) is already to begin to *configure* it once again as a subject, a *seeing* subject, that is, as what I have just said it is not. This configuration is inevitable because it is part of the very movement by which one reads a text, by which one reads as figures and as faces what has in itself nothing of a face.[20] If, then, a text re-marks itself in excess of any subject, any one subject, it also does so by figuring within itself the viewpoint of subjects. (And there is necessarily always more than one of these if a text evinces lucidity about love.) In *The Aspern Papers*, the figure of lucidity, as opposed to the narrating figure of blindness, is Juliana Bordereau, the other other who stands to be expropriated by the narrator if ever he succeeds in justifying to himself the theft he has come to perpetrate. Hers, then, is perhaps the lucidity about love that, as I said, the narrator cannot see for himself.

There is much in the novel to suggest that this is so. In particular, there is a device that holds in place the structure of a blindness that is not just opposed to lucidity, face to face, as it were, but *pierced* by it: This device is the strange, disfiguring apparatus, "a horrible green shade,"[21] that Juliana Bordereau wears over her eyes. It is the focus of all the narrator's thoughts when he sees her for the first time, without, however, being able to come face to face with her:

> it almost exceeded my courage (much as I longed for the event) to be left alone with such a terrible relic as [Juliana Bordereau]. She was too strange, too literally resurgent. Then came a check, with the perception that we were not really face to face, inasmuch as she had over her eyes a horrible green shade which for her, served almost as a mask. I believed for the instant that she had put it on expressly, so that from underneath it she might scrutinise me without being scrutinised herself. At the same time it increased the presumption that there was a ghastly death's-head lurking behind it. The divine Juliana as a grinning skull—the vision hung there until it passed. Then it came to me that she *was* tremendously old—so old that death might take her at any moment, before I had time to get what I wanted from her. The next thought was a correction to that; it lighted up the situation. She would die next week, she would die to-morrow—then I could seize her papers. (229–30)

That he sees himself or believes himself to be seen without seeing, scrutinized without scrutinizing in return, has the curious effect here of bringing the narrator as close as he can come to confessing the event he most longs to see: the death of the other who sits before him. It suggests that he does not need to say as much to her; she sees all. Hers is the point of view of that most powerful spectator, the one who can pierce the plane of deceptive appearance because her own faculty of vision is not implicated in the scene she sees. She is a purely seeing subject who cannot become an object in the other's sight or purview. Hence it can seem that she sees what he vainly attempts to hide from her and even that she foresees, from the first, the terrible scene that is going to unfold close to the end of the novel, after months of proximity to her deadly enemy, the narrator.

One evening as Miss Bordereau lies close to death (or so he believes) in an adjacent room, the narrator slips into the salon and approaches the secretary where he is convinced the letters lie concealed. As he is about to test the lock by touching its button, protesting as he does that it was not his intention to steal the papers ("I did not propose to do anything, not even—not in the least—to let down the lid; I only wanted to test my theory, to see if the cover *would* move"),[22] he happens to look over his shoulder and sees there Miss Bordereau herself, as if risen from the dead; she no longer wears the shade over her eyes, with the result that he beheld "for the first, the last, and the only time . . . her extraordinary eyes. They glared at me, they made me horribly ashamed." As he turns to look into those eyes, for the first and last time, "she hissed out passionately, furiously: 'Ah you publishing scoundrel!'" before she falls back "with a quick spasm, as if death had descended on her . . . " (286). The next day, the shamed narrator quits Venice for a week of distracted tourism, leaving others to bury the consequences of his failed theft and successful murder.

To be sure, the novel does not telescope (as I have just done) these two scenes, the first and last meetings between the adversaries who are locked in a death struggle over the possession of the letters. By juxtaposing them, I have sought only to bring out the pattern that opposes the narrator's love, which makes him blind, to Juliana's love, which makes her lucid. Can she, however, be lucid about what opposes her to the "publishing scoundrel"? That is, about the love whose object is the papers? In other words, can the love she bears for them be simply opposed to the thieving narrator's? One assumes that it can only by virtue of the letters' address: her own name on the letters is what makes them precious to her. She loves above all their *singular, unique* address, and that is what she want to preserve from the destruction of publication, which would send the letters to innumerable addresses. What she hates is the idea of repetition or reproduction of her name when she is not there to respond to it as addressed to her alone. This would also be what she shows through the act of veiling or shrouding her eyes; no other may ever gaze into them, that is, no other may read there Jeffrey Aspern's address to her. One might even go so far as to say that Juliana Bordereau has to *hate* the letter of the address, which will always make the papers she holds readable and repeatable for another. In all of this, she is apparently opposed to the narrator, who loves not the singular address on the letters (and especially not their addressee, whom he would rather see dead) but precisely their reproducibility. He indeed wants to publish them, and under his own name. As we have already noticed, the narrator can never be certain that he is not acting out of love for his own name; his efforts to appropriate the letters could be driven above all by the wish to appropriate their address to himself. But if Juliana Bordereau is indeed able to see through to this wish expressed in each of his acts (or so we may imagine), it is because she has the same wish: to appropriate the address of the letters. But, you will ask, aren't the letters already addressed to her? Yes, but only because they *can* be addressed to anyone at all, only because they are repeatable. Since they are repeatable, which is the condition of their arriving at an address, they also do not arrive once and for all, if ever.[23] Doubtless, Juliana Bordereau, for all her lucidity, cannot see this, but more important, it is what she, unlike the narrator perhaps, cannot love.

In the charged space between the narrator and Miss Bordereau, there is, then, love for a text as that which can be *both* repeated because addressed, *and* addressed because repeated/repeatable. This struggle thereby spaces out and opposes what the iterability of the name does not and cannot dissociate. Neither of them can love the letters without wanting to destroy them, either by publishing them, and therefore destroying their unique address, or by assuring that they can never be published, and therefore destroying any chance of repetition. That Miss Bordereau may think to destroy the letters is the narrator's greatest fear:

> "But why should she not destroy her papers?"
> "Oh, she loves them too much."
> "Even now, when she may be near her end?"
> "Perhaps when she's sure of that she will."

When it is said, "she loves them too much," one understands first: she loves them too much to destroy them. And we understand this simply enough because, like the characters in dialogue here, one wants to believe love is simply that which could never destroy what it loves. However, one may also overhear this exchange as reflecting someone's judgment that Juliana loves the letters *too much*, she is wrong to love them as much as she does, to the exclusion perhaps of anyone or anything else. But who can make such a judgment?

This is not the narrator speaking but the third principal character in the narrative, or rather, I should say the fourth since the great Jeffrey Aspern is already the third party to a triangle. The speaker is another Miss Bordereau, the middle-aged (perhaps even elderly) relation of Juliana's, and her constant companion for an untold number of years.[24] Miss Tita, as she is called,[25] plies the middle ground between the other two. She ministers to the love each of them bears toward the letters, apparently promising *both of them* that she will prevent the destruction of what they love. Her compliance, her pliability with one and the other (the narrator repeatedly qualifies her by this pliability) makes her the site or the shuttling vehicle between the poles placed in deadly opposition to one another: *both* her aunt and the narrator want *both* to preserve and destroy the letters, either to destroy them *by* preserving them or to preserve them *by* destroying them. Between the poles of this reversal, Tita Bordereau *complies without contradiction* to one and the other, to the other and to the other of the other. The mortal combat in which these two are locked is at the same time unlocked by her capacity to fold somehow the opposition of the other two into a non-opposition. It is as if, with her name, she were the *border* across which they stand opposed. She would thus figure that oddly bordered space in which each of them is interiorized by the other but within her. As such a figure, she is the heart or at the heart of this text because she is the *possibility of love* between these two mortal enemies.

Toward the end of his narrative, when he has returned to the villa after Juliana Bordereau's death and funeral, the narrator has two further interviews with the niece of his nemesis. In the first, she lets him know that, if he wishes it, the letters could be his. "I would give you everything—and she would understand, where she is—she would forgive me." This offer is made in the conditional but the condition is never stated, never declared by either of the interlocutors.[26] The narrator has no doubt, however, that she is inviting him to propose marriage to her. In reply to this non-declaration, he can only stammer and make "a wild, vague movement, in consequence of which I found myself at the door. . . . The next thing I remember I was downstairs and out of the house" (296). He continues to run in the other direction until he wakes the next morning with a start and only one question in his calculating heart: "Was I still in time to save my goods? That question was in my heart . . . " He goes to the final interview and there, through some strange "optical trick," he has a startling vision:

> Now I perceived it; I can scarcely tell how it startled me. She stood in the middle of the room with a face of mildness bent upon me, and her look of forgiveness, of absolution made her angelic. It beautified her; she was younger; she was not a ridiculous old woman. This optical trick gave her a sort of phantasmagoric brightness . . . (300)

It is a vision that might have lasted if Tita Bordereau had not had the "force of soul," as he calls it (and the idea of the compliant "Miss Tita with force of soul was a new conception"), to tell him the "great thing" she has done.

> "I have done the great thing. I have destroyed the papers."
> "Destroyed them?" I faltered.
> "Yes; what was I to keep them for? I burnt them last night, one by one, in the kitchen."
> "One by one?" I repeated, mechanically.
> "It took a long time—there were so many." The room seemed to go round me as she said this and a real darkness for a moment descended upon my eyes. When it passed Miss Tita was there still, but the transfiguration was over and she had changed back to a plain, dingy, elderly person. (301)[27]

When Miss Tita declares that she has burnt the papers and in that she has done "the great thing," she affirms something in two apparently different senses: on the one hand, she declares something to be the case, a fact, an event, a truth. "I burnt them last night, one by one, in the kitchen." This affirmation of fact is preceded, on the other hand, by a different and seemingly tautological affirmation. With "I have done the great thing," she says in effect: I myself affirm that I have done this affirmatively, with a greatness of love for the great thing I was doing, performing, bringing in to the world, and here I repeat all this to you, in my truthful declaration or confession to you of what I have done. Unlike the confession of a fact, this other affirmation does not merely confirm a state of affairs, an event, or a fact that pre-exists the statement. It affirms also that it affirms its own act. It says, yes, yes, I sign this event. I *love* it. I myself love what I have done.

But still, can we know what the "great thing" is that she has done? Is it an act of destruction? An act of preservation? Of revenge? Of memory? Of forgetting? Of forgiveness? Or, if indeed it is great, then wouldn't that have to be the *possibility* of any one and all of those meanings, a possibility that can only be *declared* or *opened* by some kind of affirmation? Here, then, with this double affirmation or double declaration, *The Aspern Pa-*

pers addresses the possibility of love beyond what any subject can want to mean by it. "I have done the great thing" it says. The text constitutes itself as text, in excess of any subject's discourse, with this affirmation that can never be mistaken for a statement of fact or mere opinion. This is because the distinguishing border between the two kinds of affirmation depends *in fact* on a fiction, on the fiction according to which Tita Bordereau can be believed when she says she has burned the papers, or even when she says they ever existed. If we *can* believe her, if that possibility exists, it exists only in fiction, that is, *as and in a fictional text.* As such a text, then, it would suspend the difference between the affirmative declaration of "greatness" and the affirmation of the truth of fact, of "what really happened." In "reality," what has "burned" is but a *figure* in the text for itself, which it must figure *allegorically.* The self-affirmation of the self-loving greatness of the text for what it has done, for the text it is and for the text it signed. This is the seal burned into the text, turned into a text. The allegorizing figure of self-love has to let itself burn up and to love the growing pile of ashes. Only then has it done a great thing, affirmed nothing but the affirmation itself, so that it may repeat: yes, yes.

Yes, yes, they burned, one by one, each one, each singular one. And already, yes, one by one, they begin to repeat mechanically: "'One by one,' I repeated mechanically." If this is the heart of the text, it is also an artificial or mechanical heart.

But this cannot surprise us altogether because "the great thing" is done *in* a text and *by* a text, the artifice, fiction, or allegory we have been reading, one by one. Or rather, *not* one by one but all shoved together into a bundle behind the scrutinizing mask of critical commentary, as if there were only one pair of eyes able to take in the whole complex scene. Can such coldly analytic, selective, reductive, non-singularizing commentary ever declare love to the text it takes as its object? That seems unlikely, which is why I will not risk any more of it here. I have already said that I love this text, *too much.*

—To whom or to what do you think you have you said it?

—Look there: on the shelf, its pages yellow around the borders, their acid beginning to consume them, a cheap (i.e., non-scholarly) volume titled *Great Short Works of Henry James.* Who ever came up with such a great title? Who could have written such a thing?

—If you really want to know, ask the publisher.

—Oh, you scoundrel you!

§ 2   Deconstruction and Feminism: A Repetition

I

Othello, act 3, scene 4: Emilia is putting Desdemona on guard against her husband's jealousy while the latter seeks to explain Othello's "strange unquietness" to herself as surely "something of state" that has "puddled his clear spirit." "Pray heaven it be state matters, as you think, / And no conception nor no jealous toy / Concerning you," says Emilia. Desdemona protests: "Alas the day, I never gave him cause," to which Emilia then rejoins with this observation about "jealous souls": "But jealous souls will not be answered so. / They are not jealous for the cause, / But jealous for they're jealous. It is a monster / Begot upon itself, born on itself." Here, then, the older, married woman speaks of a monstrousness that the new bride, in her virginal innocence, has never conceived: a self-begetting that turns on itself and returns to itself in a tautological repetition without cause and therefore, it is implied, without end: "they're jealous for they're jealous." This is no natural birth, but a production, if we can call it that, without any other parent than itself, a parent that is also its own monstrous child.

Women speaking together, in private, apparently of a man's jealousy. Yet Emilia speaks of "jealous souls" without distinguishing men from women, even if everything else about the scene seems to override this equivocation. She then shifts the referent altogether when she says, "It is a monster," speaking now of neither men, nor women, nor perhaps even anything human. It is, we understand, jealousy itself that she is evoking in the traits of a certain monstrousness. But "jealousy itself," begotten upon and from itself as "it"—neither man nor woman—is that not precisely what is mon-

44

strous? Therefore, do we not seek to contain the self-begotten monster with a sex, and only one sex? And to define such a monstrosity as we define one sex over against the other? For if jealousy is monstrous because it suspends or effaces the difference called sexual, if only in its desire or its phantasm, then to contain it thus is to suspend that suspension and give it a human face, perhaps all too human.

These questions about Shakespeare's monster may serve to introduce a reflection on jealousy, which is taken here as the angle of entry into the all-too-bewildering and perhaps monstrous topic of "deconstruction and feminism." This choice is prompted by what seems to be an avoidance or a silence somewhere close to the heart or the soul of feminist theory regarding the subject—presuming that theory to be unified, and unified around something like a heart or a soul. The silence has followed on the critique of the Freudian theory of *Penisneid,* penis envy, a critique which one may justifiably take to be indispensable to feminist thought of the last seventy-five years. The critique accompanied from the first Freud's elaboration of the theory; indeed, his most succinct formulations of penis envy—in the "lecture" on Femininity in *New Introductory Lectures on Psychoanalysis* (1933) and the essay "Female Sexuality" (1931)—are responses to objections already raised by members of the first generation of psychoanalysts: Karen Horney, Helene Deutsch, Ernest Jones among the most prominent of them.[1] That critique has been reelaborated by, among others, Luce Irigaray and Sarah Kofman. Their similar but competing studies of the lecture "Femininity" have had a significant influence on a certain thinking about women's sexuality and subjectivity that we cannot document here. Rather, we take merely as a point of departure the sense that this thinking has assumed or assimilated the deconstruction of *Penisneid* to the benefit of a notion of the feminine subject that would be, in theory or in principle, free of any *constitutive* envy or jealousy, and most particularly of that constitutive formation Freud called penis envy. In other words, envy or jealousy (and we will say something further below about this apparent semantic distinction) would be thought of as accidental or contingent states that can characterize this subject at any given moment or in certain circumstances; its manifestations, however, would remain essentially external to the subject's own constitution before and beyond jealousy. This idea of a feminine subject would grant no essential place to jealousy or envy, would recognize or allow for no effects of jealousy in the constitution of a subject by sexual difference as feminine. To the extent, therefore, that jealousy operates as a constitutive, irreducible determinant in sexual differentiation, it is a masculine determinant and a determining factor of masculinity. Unlike contingent feminine jealousy, unlike the historically conditioned feminine resentment of masculine privilege that Freud, for example, would have all but ignored and neglected to take into account, there would be an essential masculine jealousy that is the effect of the thwarted drive to possess or appropriate feminine difference. Such a theory of the nonjealous feminine subject would therefore have to answer our earlier question—does the self-begotten monster have a sex and only one sex?—in the affirmative: Yes, and it is masculine.

This assertion and the preceding ones are attributed less to some feminist discourse than, as already mentioned, to a silence observed or imposed there around the topic or topos of jealousy. *On the one hand,* this silence closes out the Freudian account of penis envy, that unconscious formation to which women would owe virtually all affective, social, and intellectual development, including, as Sarah Kofman recalls, feminism itself. From the essay "The Psychogenesis of a Case of Homosexuality in a Woman," she cites this description of Freud's patient:

> The analysis showed, further, that the girl had suffered from childhood from a strongly marked "masculinity complex." A spirited girl, always ready for romping and fighting, she was not at all prepared to be second to her slightly older brother; after inspecting his genital organs she had developed a pronounced envy of the penis, and the thoughts derived from this envy continued to fill her mind. She was in fact a feminist; she felt it to be unjust that girls should not enjoy the same freedom as boys, and rebelled against the lot of woman in general.[2]

Elsewhere, in the "Taboo of Virginity," Freud writes: "Behind this envy for the penis, there comes to light woman's hostile bitterness against the man, which never completely disappears in the relations between the sexes, and which is clearly indicated in the strivings and the literary productions of 'emancipated' women."[3] From this perspective, therefore and *on the other hand,* current feminist analysis of the subject would be is anything but silent on the topic of jealousy: on the contrary, jealousy—and nothing but jealousy—speaks loudly there. Yet it is, of course, precisely the imposition of this perspective that has led many to conclude that what is going on in the psychoanalytic account is itself a jealous defense of the privilege accorded the phallus. Thus, when Freud affirms, for example, in the lecture "Femininity," that women are in general more jealous than men and that the reason for this supplemental jealousy is the lack of a penis,[4] with the very performance of that assertion he can be understood as confirming the contrary: men are more jealous inasmuch as they impute to women an envy of the penis. And with this we circle back to the feminist theoretical position already described: man is constitutively jealous (of the phallic privilege and its privileged relation to his own penis), whereas a woman's jealousy is secondary, derived, contingent, historically conditioned. Phallocentrism is structured by jealousy, whereas woman as such, considered before or beyond phallocentrism's rule, is herself before or beyond jealousy. And if feminism is the thinking of woman outside the jealous rule of phallocentrism, then it is not jealous; rather it thinks (masculine) jealousy on the basis of a position without-jealousy.[5]

Can this position or supposition be put in question without giving merely another instance of reversal within the pattern of reversal just outlined? This is what we are asking.

II

But first, we have invoked envy and jealousy as if they were the same or interchangeable. Classically, however, a distinction is drawn between them. One is said to be envious of that which one does not possess, but would like to possess, and jealous of that which one does possess and fears losing. Descartes, for example, in his *Passions de l'âme*, makes this distinction:

> Jealousy is a species of fear that relates to the desire to remain in possession of some good [*quelque bien*]; and it does not arise so much from the strength of the reasons that lead one to judge it might be lost as from the great esteem in which it is held; that is why one examines the least causes for suspicion and takes them to be persuasive reasons.

> [Envy . . . is a species of sadness mixed with hatred that derives from our seeing something good happen to those whom we think do not deserve it; and this can only reasonably be said of goods of fortune since concerning those of the soul or even the body, inasmuch as they are endowed at birth, it is enough to deserve them that they are received from God before one was capable of committing any wrong.][6]

We could remark here that Freud inscribes sexual difference at least in part in this tradition of the distinction between jealousy and envy: Jealousy of what one has and fears losing would describe the boy's castration anxiety, whereas envy for what others have and one does not would describe the girl's penis envy. But this difference is also erased when, as already mentioned, Freud attributes the excess of a woman's jealousy (*Eifersucht*) to an envy (*Neid*) of what she never possessed.[7]

This tendency to subsume all these possible relations to some object—possession, dispossession, non-possession, desire for possession—under a single heading, called indifferently jealousy or envy, has been justified by the French psychoanalyst Daniel Lagache in his monumental clinical study of amorous jealousy. He first notes the tradition we have just cited, quoting both a succinct formulation by d'Alembert—"One is jealous of what one possesses and envious of what others possess"—as well as one of La Rochefoucauld's many maxims concerning jealousy: "Jealousy is in a certain way just and reasonable since it tends only toward preserving something that belongs to us; whereas envy is a frenzy that cannot abide what belongs to others."[8] But Lagache then comments that these distinctions "are difficult to maintain."

> Jealousy does not exclude envy, because I am jealous of that which I possess inasmuch as it can be desired and possessed by others; and the fear at least puts the jealous person *fictively* in the situation of the envious one; the jealous lover is jealous of his mistress and envious of the *real or fictive* success of his rival. Moreover, one is not jealous only of what one possesses, but also of what one desires, of the goods or beings over which desire has already cast the shadow of possession. Inversely, by envying others' possessions, one envisions them inasmuch as they can be desired and possessed by oneself, and it is precisely the impossibility of substituting oneself for others that makes envy intolerable. (Ibid.; my emphasis)

Although Lagache does not proceed to draw the inference here, all these crossings between the two states called envy and jealousy would only be possible if there were no such thing as assured possession or property. Jealousy (or envy) defines a relation to that which one "possesses" in the mode of an always possible, always imminent, and therefore already effected dispossession. One never really possesses what one has. If it can be lost or stolen or expropriated, then to a degree it already has been, if only in a "fictive" projection onto a future rival. Likewise, one can be jealous rather than just envious of that which one only desires to possess, as if the shadow of possession cast by desire, in Lagache's phrase, were already its substantialization or realization. But this is to confirm that between this shadow and this substance, between the "fictional" possession and the "real" one, there is no effective difference: proper or "real" possession is a shadow figure always ready to fade away.[9]

It seems but a step from this insubstantial link that cannot guarantee proper possession (of something or someone else) to the loosening of the tie that binds the self to itself, in a relation of self-possession or "own-ness." From the jealousy (or envy) that marks the relation to some-other-than-the-self, who or which can never be possessed or appropriated beyond the fictive projections of desire, one is led to evoke envy (or jealousy) as a mark within the self or the "own," a mark that accuses therefore a similar space of always possible "dis-ownment" in the very self that would appropriate others to itself. Both Descartes and Lagache, for example, recall the common usage in French (but the same use may be found in English) of the adjective jealous to denote a zealous defense of some abstract quality or attribute.[10] One is said to be jealous of one's reputation, honor, good name, and so forth. "Thus, for example," writes Descartes, "a captain who holds a highly placed position has the right to be jealous of it, that is, to be on guard against any means by which it might be taken away [*surprise*]; and an honest woman is not blamed for being jealous of her honor, that is to say not only for guarding herself from any wrongdoing but also for avoiding even the least causes for gossip" (776). Lagache, for his part, goes to Corneille, La Fontaine, and Bossuet for occurrences similar to the examples given by Descartes (368–69). His citations evoke the zeal with which certain predicates or attributes—honor and freedom—are defended as one defends one's very life by the person who claims them as his or her own. What both these examples recall is a jealous relation of the self to itself, that by means of which it guards itself intact, keeps its own possession of itself but in the mode of an always possible dispossession. "An always possible dispossession": in other words, an irreducible expropriability at the heart of this strange relation to self in which one may be jealous of oneself.

Because Descartes also distinguishes a morally righteous (or as he says, "honnête") jealousy from a wrongful one, he may once again be seen as relaying Freud in a long tradition. Freud too speaks of a normal, as distinct from a pathological, jealousy. "Jealousy," he writes, "is one of those affective states that may be described as normal. If anyone appears to be without it, the inference is justified that it has undergone severe repression and consequently plays all the greater part in his unconscious mental life. . . . It is easy to see that essentially [normal jealousy] is compounded of grief, the pain caused by the thought of losing the loved object, and of the narcissistic wound, *in so far as this is distinguishable from the other wound.*"[11] The wound that occasions normal jealousy may not be distinguishable from the narcissistic wound. This suggestion, planted at the beginning of an essay on jealousy, paranoia, and homosexuality, is not followed up. If it were, would we find that "normal" jealousy is rooted in the narcissism one has always already had to give up, the narcissism one only enjoys in the mode of its loss? And then would one not have to speak of a primary jealousy, alongside and indissociable from the structure of that primary narcissism Freud so tentatively outlined? Following up this suggestion, therefore, would have to take us back to the essay "On Narcissism" that Sarah Kofman has reread so persuasively as a short cease-fire within Freud's prolonged war against the feminine, a kind of cameo appearance put in by the Nietzschean affirmative woman that briefly upstages those three caskets in which Freud reads only death behind each of woman's guises.[12] The question that might be asked is whether the affirmative figure discerned by Kofman is also supposed to be exempt from jealousy or whether this affirmation must be understood altogether differently, as a movement that at once both inscribes jealousy and displaces it—an affirmation, therefore, of self-love *as* other- or object-love that suspends their opposition and retraces their boundaries.[13] Is such a configuration even possible?

This latter question is essentially a reformulation of the one we posed above: Can the position or supposition of a feminine subject beyond a constitutive jealousy—the project of feminist theories of the subject—be put in question without giving thereby merely another instance of reversal within a pattern of reversal? This question is certainly not new: it has defined for some time now the principal stakes of the often fraught relation between Derridean deconstruction and these same feminist theories of the subject. To put it in deceptively simple terms: what has been so long at stake is the very category or analytical term of *subject*, which deconstruction seems so effectively to do without and which feminist theory is largely concerned with preserving *in a certain form.* The latter qualification is central to feminist subjectivist analysis, since it is a contestation of the *generality* of the structure of subjectivity that that analysis undertakes to effect. As a general structure, the subject—whether described in terms of the Cartesian *cogito*, the subject of phenomenology, the Foucauldian subject of power, or the grammatical subject of structural linguistics—can be made to display the more or less violent effacement of difference(s) whereby it lays claim to that very generality.[14] This generality, it is argued, is therefore but a masked particularity; in particular it masks the effacement of the difference that is the feminine. Rather than give up altogether on the generalizing category of "subject," however, much feminist thought has sought to preserve it, albeit in a relativized, particularized, or differentiated form. Hence, the tendency to speak of a feminine subject, a masculine subject, a colonized and a colonizing subject, etc.[15] This kind of particularization, in other words, points to the general failure of the general subject to attain the generality of its concept except as an ideal or ideality. In its material inscription, which is to say wherever a body "lends" its singular articulation to the featureless, mute, pure idea of the "I," the general concept falls back into particularity or specificity.

Feminist subjectivism has been very effective in pointing out the repeated failure of the general subject to inscribe itself beyond the specificity of its material inscription. At the same time, nevertheless, the feminist subjectivist argument preserves the category of subject, understood now as a *limited* generality. One might see in this double gesture a kind of compromise formation: on the one hand, there is recognition of the general structure or ideality of the subject, which necessarily fails to materialize itself; on the other hand, there is a certain disavowal of that recognition, as if the necessary failure could all the same be overcome. This makes it sound like a version of fetishism, the fetishism of the subject who, in saying "I," believes it is fully itself, not "castrated," despite what it knows. It is here that the stakes of a deconstruction of the fetishistic subject become apparent. To return to the terms we elaborated above, what is put in question by this deconstruction is the subject as beyond- or without-jealousy, a subject that can fully appropriate or possess itself. Deconstruction remarks a certain irreducible and constitutive non-return of the subject to itself,[16] an ineradicable force of difference—exteriority, materiality, otherness—within the very relation and the jealous zeal with which the same allies with itself, affects and effects itself in a *movement* of appropriation that is never simply given in the present but must be performed, posed, invented, or traced. Jealousy, then, would be the movement of the same back to itself, a movement ceaselessly driven by the mark of non-coincidence, of impossible appropriation. "They're jealous for they're jealous": the monster of self-begetting returns to a same that is not the same as itself, but already is jealous of a non-appropriable marking or spacing that sends the movement off again.

III

Before considering what it might mean specifically for feminism to affirm (rather than disavow) the inappropriability of its own subject, one needs to say something more about the latter. This because it is too often assumed, not only by feminist subjectivists but by many others as well, that the deconstruction of the subject is based on not much more than a kind of willful play for power within the discursive field loosely called "theory." Rather than get mired in such a projection, however, we can look briefly at an early text in which Derrida most clearly lays out the conditions in which and by which the signifying subject says—or writes—"I."[17]

La Voix et le phénomène, one of the inaugural texts of deconstruction, is a reading of Husserl's phenomenological description of language in the first of his *Logical Investigations*.[18] It opens with an epigraph from that text: "When we read this word 'I' without knowing who wrote it, it is perhaps not meaningless, but is at least estranged from its normal meaning." Derrida's reading of Husserl's theory of the sign will in large measure be oriented by this statement, or rather against it, since, as he writes when he comes to quote the statement again toward the end of his reading, "Husserl's premises should authorize us to say exactly the contrary" (107; 96). That is, an anonymous written "I" is not at all "estranged from its normal meaning"; on the contrary, the condition of anonymity or estrangement is the very soul, so to speak, of the normal meaning of "I" whenever it is spoken or written. Indeed, it is only on the condition of this estrangement that "I" can ever have any meaning whatsoever. How can that be?

It has to do first of all with the structure of the linguistic sign as repetition:

> A sign is never an event, if by event we mean an irreplaceable and irreversible empirical unicity. A sign which would take place but "once" would not be a sign; a purely idiomatic sign would not be a sign. A signifier (in general) must be recognizable in its form in spite of and through the diversity of empirical characteristics which may modify it. It must remain the *same* and be repeatable as such despite and across the distortions that what is called the empirical event necessarily makes it undergo. . . . [I]t can function as a sign, and in

general as language, only if a formal identity enables it to be issued again and recognized again. This identity is necessarily ideal (55–56; 50).

"Identity" here means self-identity, identity to and with itself, the non-diffenence and immediacy of the sign as both formal characteristic (signifier) and meaning (signified). As such, this identity is "necessarily ideal" because no single occurrence, no empirical particular achieves it—only repeats it. By ideality, however, one must understand that which has no existence either in this or some other "metaphysical" world; rather, it is "but the name for the permanence of the same and the possibility of its repetition." The ideality (of the identity of the sign) is but the possibility of the repetition of the same, that is, it "depends entirely on the possibility of acts of repetition. It is constituted by that possibility" (58; 52). This amounts to effecting a reversal of the conventional, metaphysical derivation of the sign as re-presentation of an original presence: as pure ideality, that presence derives from the possibility of repetition and not the reverse. Or rather, as Derrida will put it later, idealization, repetition, and signification "are thinkable, in their pure possibility, only on the basis of one and the same opening" (104; 93). There is, however, a fourth term in this series of possibilities: death. What is opened up, with language and repetition and idealization, is a relation to death, and specifically to "my" death, the death of the one who says "I." How so?

The sense of any discourse depends on the possibility of a repetition of the same, on the movement, therefore, of an idealization that can traverse all the variants of empirical existence, contingency, factuality, and so forth. This sense does not depend on any actual presence; indeed, the condition of discourse is that it be intelligible *in the absence* of its object. The notion that meaning does not essentially imply the intuition or perception of the object of discourse is worked out by Husserl and illustrated by Derrida as follows:

> I say, "I see a particular person through the window" while I really do see him. It is structurally implied in my performance that the content of this expression is ideal and that its unity is not impaired by the absence of perception *hic et nunc*. Whoever hears this proposition, whether he is next to me or infinitely removed in time or space, should, by right, understand what I mean to say. Since this possibility is the possibility of discourse, it must structure the very act of him who speaks while perceiving. My nonperception, my nonintuition, my absence *hic et nunc* are said by that very thing that I say, by *that* which I

say and *because* I say it. . . . The absence of intuition—and therefore of the subject of the intuition—is not only *tolerated* by speech; it is *required* by the general structure of signification, when considered *in itself.* It is radically requisite: the total absence of the subject and object of a statement—the death of the writer and/or disappearance of the objects he may have described—does not prevent a text from "meaning-to-say." On the contrary, this possibility gives birth to the meaning-to-say as such, gives it to be heard and read. (103–4; 92–93)

Up to this point, Derrida has been drawing out to their radical conclusions Husserl's analyses. But with the next step, this radicalization overturns an important and very symptomatic limit that Husserl attempts to place on the possible absence from intuition of the elements of discourse. That limit is the first person pronoun. When "spoken" by the self to itself and referring to itself—in solitary speech or internal monologue—Husserl affirms that "the meaning of 'I' is essentially realized in the immediate idea of one's own personality" (106; 95). In other words, there is for Husserl at least one situation in which the object of discourse is *never* absent from the intuition of the speaker/listener: when the "I" says "I" to itself. The meaning of that speech act is "essentially realized" by the speaker in an "immediate idea of [his/her] own personality." When I say "I" to myself, not only do I know immediately what I mean, but I know the "object" of my meaning to be present in the moment I speak. It is this immediacy of self-presence that Derrida puts in question in the same terms used above for the person seen through the window. This move has as its consequence the uncovering of the essential relation to "my own death" inscribed in the very possibility of discourse. "I," like any other sign, can have meaning only if it "remains *the same* for an I-here-now in general, keeping its sense even if my empirical presence is eliminated or radically modified" (ibid.). Radicalizing from there, Derrida will affirm that if the "I" must be able to function with the same meaning in my absence, then that absence—my death—is structurally inscribed in the possibility of its repetition, the ideality of its meaning.

> My death is structurally necessary to the pronouncing of the *I.* That I am also "alive" and certain of being alive comes over and above the meaning-to-say. And this structure is operative, it retains its original efficiency even when I say "I am alive" at the very moment when, if such a thing is possible, I have a full and current intuition of it. . . . The statement "I am alive" is accompanied by

my being-dead, and its possibility requires the possibility that I be dead; and conversely. This is not an extraordinary tale by Poe but the ordinary story of language. (108; 96–97)

"My death is structurally necessary to the pronouncing of the *I*." This statement not only propounds a rule, it also performs under the imposition of that rule: the phrase "my death" has to have *the same* meaning in the absence of whoever first pronounced it and whoever may subsequently quote it (as we are doing here) or otherwise repeat it. "My death," therefore, does not say *my* death or absence because it says the (necessary) absence of any empirical singularity, my own or anyone else's. Thus, without naming my death and only mine, and precisely because it does not do so, it also enacts my disappearance; that is, the disappearance of the singular, finite instance of its pronouncing. And it does so through the very figure of my finitude, which here assumes the general aspect of "my death." My death, as mine, is structurally absent from "my death," and therefore it is signified as the limit on which I can signify anything whatsoever. That limit inscribes the finitude of meaning as appropriated by any act of signification, the limit, in other words, whereby nothing finally can be signified as mine and only mine, not even or especially not "my death."[19]

IV

Deconstructive thought largely proceeds from this de-propriating force of repetition that is the ground of possibility of meaning. This ground of possibility may also therefore be described as a certain impossibility: the impossibility of a subject that has fully appropriated its own meaning, its own being, in a state—however momentary—of self-presence. Now, too often this latter, critical thrust of deconstruction is mistaken for its principal or even sole "insight"; that is, it is understood as merely a critique of the grounds of meaning and the subject of meaning. This is the version of "deconstructionism" that has been widely consecrated by a certain journalism and has served all sorts of dubious ends, including for some supposedly non-journalist academics. What this version cannot reckon with, however, is an *affirmative* deconstruction for which the critique of presence does not exhaust the resources of thought. On the contrary, for deconstruction the impossibility of a fully self-present meaning is that which opens the possibility of any relation to meaning, indeed of any relation whatsoever to and within difference(s). The impossible reappropriation of the self to itself, the irreducible difference or gap within the relation-to-self is what calls for affirmation and not merely recognition or confirmation. It is not enough, in other words, to offer a critique that demonstrates this impossibility or that negates the possibility of the full presence of the self or the subject. It is not enough because it confirms and leaves intact the valence of negativity that has always attached itself to the inevitable failure of the self to master or appropriate its own meaning, to have the last word, so to speak. Deconstructive practice, on the other hand, affirms the necessary dispersion through repetition of the "I" as the chance and the possibility, not just the negation, of a signifying act or an inscription that, without belonging to or being appropriable by any identity, would nevertheless be marked as *singular* or *idiomatic*.

In an interview published in 1983, Derrida put it this way when prompted by a question about the anxiety aroused by the undecidability of meaning:

> When one writes, one is always trying to outsmart the worst. Perhaps so as to prevent it from taking everything away, but the last word, you know, always belongs to non-mastery, for both the reader and oneself. And it's good that this is the way it is. The living desire to write keeps you in relation to a terror that you try to maneuver with even as you leave it intact, audible in that place where you may find yourself, hear or understand yourself, you and whoever reads you, beyond any partition, thus at once saved and lost.[20]

One could be tempted to see in this brief passage a somewhat off-guard characterization of three essential elements of Derrida's deconstructive practice portrayed in the aspect of its desiring motivation. The affirmation "And it's good that this is the way it is [*Et c'est bien ainsi*]" follows on the constatation of ultimate non-mastery (finitude as necessary limit) and ushers in a possibility: a writing or practice of inscription where perhaps "you may find yourself, hear or understand yourself, you and whoever reads you, beyond any partition, thus at once saved and lost." The impossibility of appropriation is affirmed, which overturns a hierarchical opposition between mastery and non-mastery, self and other, but the desire that had maintained that hierarchy is not thereby negated or denied as desire (there is perhaps no more futile exercise than to attempt to destroy the narcissistic desire in question); rather, it is displaced as the possibility of another *entente*, that of the other, precisely, and of oneself as other. The possibility of being "beyond any partition, thus at once saved and lost," is not a possibility for the self, which is but a figure of its own impossible appropriation, but for an idiomatic singularity, which in the same interview Derrida glosses as follows:

> A property that one cannot appropriate; it signs you without belonging to you; it only appears to the other and it never comes back to you except in flashes of madness that bring together life and death, that bring you together dead and alive at the same time. You dream, it's unavoidable, about the invention of a language or of a song that would be yours, not the attributes of a "self," rather the accentuated paraph, that is, the musical signature, of your most unreadable history. I'm not talking about a *style* but an intersection of singularities, habitat, voices, graphism, what moves with you and what your body never leaves. (119)

This dreamed-of, desired inscription of a singularity, "beyond any partition," would save from ultimate erasure a non-repeatable idiom, but only by losing it for any "self" since "it appears only to the other." Nevertheless, it is as an almost unhoped-for chance that this "loss" is solicited from the other, infinitely desired.

We began by asking what it might mean for feminism to affirm the inappropriable subject. One thing is already clear: it could not mean a simple evacuation or negation of the "I" as instance of the inscription of difference. Rather than that of the subject, however, this instance would be that of a singular force of insistence, a singularity. Singularity is not the subject, which, as we have seen, is but the possibility of a repetition. The singular is not repeatable *as such*, but is precisely the impossible presentation of an "as such." The singular remains in excess of—before or beyond—representation, the difference between the subject and an unpresentable *I*. The latter is finite, determined by the singular events of birth and death, whereas the former is infinitely or indefinitely repeatable, having no origin nor end other than in that repetition.[21] The notion of the singular cannot, by definition, be accommodated by any generality, be it the sort of limited generality we discussed above. Instead, it has to lead us to consider the possibility, the desirability of *something like* autobiography.

That resemblance must immediately be qualified so as not to blur a number of important distinctions that set a recognizable and consecrated *genre* of writing, such as autobiography, apart from that "invention of a language" that Derrida evokes in the passage just cited ("You dream, it's unavoidable, about the invention of a language or of a song that would be yours, not the attributes of a 'self'"). Beginning with the distinction of genre (or gender): the idiomatic singularity in question cannot in any simple sense *belong* to a generality without disappearing altogether, leaving no trace. For it to appear at all (always only to the other), it must remain unrepeatable, ungeneralizable, without genre or gender. At the same time, however, and just as necessarily, for it to appear at all, for it to have even the chance of the other's arrival, it must unfold out of its silence and its secret; that is, it must also be repeatable. Thus, if it is saved in its absolute singularity, then it can never appear before the "last word" of finitude; on the other hand, saved from "my death" through repetition, it is lost as singular idiom. Now, this double-bind structure may be ineluctable, but, in theory at least, there are no limits on the forms of negotiations with its constraints—what Derrida calls above "trying to outsmart the worst."

Which brings up the second reason one should hesitate to invoke the category of autobiography. It is not at all certain that the most "successful" negotiations result in a manifestly "autobiographical" text, according to conventional criteria, nor even, of course, in what we commonly think of as a written text. Practices of the most diverse, infinitely varied kinds, from the moment they appear to the other, including, indeed especially, the most inadvertent gestures, the unreflected corporeality and materiality of a life (that which is the always singular domain of love and jealousy)—all may bear traces of the inappropriable signature, singularity saved and lost, repeated in its unrepeatability.

Finally, however, it is perhaps the "auto" of autobiography that most dissimulates what is at stake in this inscription of singular differences. The "auto" would refer the "-graphy" back to a single life, "bio," and thereby close it up in a circle of self-reference. Not only does this model suggest a closed relation-to-self and therefore an appropriation in place of what "appears only to the other," but in so doing it also leaves wholly unaccounted-for the paradoxical problematic we have been describing: that of repetition of the unrepeatable in a general language. It is this problematic, by contrast, that is brought out, consistently and insistently, in deconstruction. More precisely, deconstruction "happens" because of the necessarily unfinished and interminable articulation of singularity with the structures of repetition of the same. Which is to say that singular differences (material, corporeal, historical, linguistic, sexual, and so forth: the list is, by definition, without end), to the extent they do not disappear without a trace, reserve the possibility for these structures to transform themselves, to deconstruct. Deconstructive thought, and most singularly the work of Jacques Derrida, attempts to formalize *to a certain extent* this possibility held in reserve by the greatest formalizing tradition in the West, the philosophical tradition; it bears down on those places where, precisely, that tradition cannot formalize itself completely or entirely, therefore where it must open itself not only to other traditions or genres (the literary or the autobiographical, for example), but to that which as yet has no tradition, no convention, and no recognizable form: to the force of something other, to the other-than-the-same, to the possibility of invention or the invention of the impossible.[22]

V

"Feminism" and "deconstruction": two terms that designate sites of theoretico-practical intervention. When these terms have been taken up in recent and ongoing "theory wars" in the university, a certain trivialization has worked to prevent an understanding of what is at stake between them. Those stakes are said to be political. And indeed they are: the stakes are political because it is the very sense of the political that is at stake. A deconstruction of subjectivisms (including feminist subjectivism) has necessarily to entail a *different* sense of the political, one that does not project the eventual realization of a fully present (appropriated) subject that would be at the same time fully representative, one which is not itself shaped and determined by the version of the subject as self-presence. To put it in the terms I have so far been using here, subject politics (or "identity politics") is a politics of envy or jealousy; that is, of an appropriating movement driven by the inappropriable finitude of the one who says "I" and "I, we." In its dialectical version, the politics of the subject (which may be a class or a gender) theorizes the political *as* appropriation, as the legitimation/delegitimation of appropriated power. Now, the question we are asking is, What other sense of the "political," beyond or outside this dialectics of appropriation, becomes thinkable once the deconstructibility of its subject is no longer disavowed, but affirmed?

To suggest at least a direction from which a response to that question might come, let us reconsider one of the best-known watchwords of American feminist political thought in the last decades: "the personal is the political." This categorical statement has been understood, in its most general interpretation, to negate the self-evidence of the division between public and private spheres as concerns women (and therefore men). Implicitly or by extension, it accuses the numerous ways in which that putative self-evidence has been used to justify or overlook everything from violence in the "privacy" of the home to the exclusion of women qua women from the institutions of public life. The act of renaming that it performs asserts that there is no "personal" that is not already invested by the "political," that is, by the interests of a power structure that seeks always to perpetuate or legitimate itself even in what are thought to be the most remote or hidden corners of the social fabric. (This thesis is not just that of modern feminism, of course, but one that has characterized revolutionary political thought for at least two centuries.)[23] Now, at the same time as the argument summed up in the watchword has been mobilized in a delegitimizing analysis of patriarchy's division of public domain from private space, it has also been working to legitimate the public or political (in the widest sense) role of women throughout society's institutions. Conversely, and in a consistent application of the "personal-is-political" logic, it has sought political, public recognition and protection of a whole range of concerns formerly relegated to the private domain: child care, family leave, spousal abuse, sexual harassment, and so forth. To a large extent, then, feminist contestation of the social order has undertaken a general *extension* of the public sphere, or rather a recognition and reevaluation of the extension that has effectively been in place for a long time but has been dissimulated beneath the cover of the "personal" or the "private."[24]

There are, nevertheless, significant points at which this contestation takes the opposite form, that is, where it consists in redrawing the limit on this extension of the public domain and in refuting the equation of personal with political against the claims of the state. At those points, the feminist political position stakes out a "personal" space that it would keep free from public purview or regulation. As the increasingly violent confrontation over abortion-on-demand in the United States indicates, however, achieving a *general* consensus to *limit* the extension of the general interest is, as a political aim, a far more divided and divisive matter than achieving a general recognition of women as political subjects. This may suggest that wherever feminism understands its political task in terms of the public, general subject or in terms of the appropriation of that subjectivity by women, then it will advance that aim fundamentally in accord, in alliance, or in complicity with the interests of a sociopolitical order to bring every domain within its purview. Needless to say, if such interests go everywhere unchecked, if the "personal" is everywhere and always the "political" without remainder, then one has entered the dream or nightmare of the totalitarian state. This is not at all to say that some contrary, and ultimately contradictory, politics of the "personal" can be elaborated in terms that will enforce an effective limit on the totalization of the public domain.[25] It is precisely this notion of "effective limit" that is in question.

What both the "public" and the "personal" versions of subjectivist politics discount is the very divisibility of the division dividing one from the other, a divisibility that limits the limiting function of that limit by, precisely, dividing and redividing it.[26] Once again, the confrontation over abortion-on-demand poses significantly the condition of this dividing limit between "personal" and "political." The limit in question does not fall in this case at the apparent boundaries of a personal body or individual life and therefore within the recognized right to personal liberty, but along the uncertain line of division between one body and another, or between a present life and a future one, or finally between a woman and her body/her life, which is at once both hers and not hers, both present and the bearer of a future, another's future, the future as other. This uncertain limit, by definition highly divisible and unstable, cannot therefore reliably set off the political from the personal; it cannot fix the point at which the freedom of individual choice and the right to be free from political constraint is posed unconditionally. It is rather as the inappropriable space of the *other in the one* that this divisible limit becomes the terrain of a struggle for appropriation between the public instance of a plural "we" and the private, singular instance of an "I."

This struggle for appropriation, which has for so long defined the stakes of the political for revolutionary movements on the Right and the Left, movements of liberation as well as nationalist movements, is everywhere driven by the condition of a fundamental inappropriability, what we have here attempted to illustrate with the divisibility of the limit between "personal" and "political." Wherever it is drawn, the limit supposed to separate a personal "I" from a political "we" would be little more than a grammatical or legal fiction, one which the law institutes and to which it refers by way of repetition. The "I" is already a repetition, more than one, always one plus the endless possibility of other ones. That is the condition (the law) of saying "I" and therefore the initial constraint on the freedom or the privacy of the one who says it. From the moment the law of repetition or pluralization is also the condition of "personalization," then one must recognize that, indeed, "the personal is the political." With this recognition or repetition, however, the accent or tone marking that assertion will have itself become divided so as to admit another possible inflection. For in addition to a rallying cry for political mobilization, cannot that phrase now be heard to echo also as an infinite *complaint* that whenever I say or think or otherwise signify "I," a crowd assembles and I am mistaken for everybody else, hence for nobody? And with that, I am expropriated of "myself," "my life," "my person," "my personal life," all of which remain only the most approximate, conventional designators for a singular experience without appropriate name, an experience, therefore, inappropriated by any subject? And isn't this complaint itself made to disappear when it is formulated anonymously and in terms of the greatest generality (not my life, in its most secret intimacy, a secret preserved finally even from me who cannot know it as my own, but the so-called personal in general is the political, that is, everybody's person, every body, and therefore no body's, neither mine nor yours)? Can one hear, then, the phrase as the residue of a jealous movement in the face of the effacement of the "personal"'s property, its proper appropriation of itself? Yes.

—Yes?

—Yes. Yes, not once but twice because it is a matter here of a double affirmation, an affirmation that repeats and that affirms the repetition. Deconstruction follows the path of this double affirmation; it affirms (itself as) repetition.[27] Yes, it says first of all, to the echo or residue, to the *tone* that speaks of and from the place of a singular articulation with the general law, therefore to the repetition of the unrepeatable. This "yes" says: "I hear, come again, again and again. The trace of your voice, its tone (its *ton*, its 'yours,' that is, that by which it belongs to you in this strange mode of not-belonging) is held in my ear and in our tongue, the one we share between us." To the inaccessible, impossible pure tone, to undivided singularity, this "yes" opens a channel, so to speak, allowing a kind of passage at the limit between I/we, a passage, therefore, into repetition, division, plurality; but that passage at the same time carries over an echo or a trace of an inappropriable difference. The difference is inscribed at the limit; it is the difference, or differance, *of* that limit—its division—that holds I-we apart together and thus opens each to the other. The first yes, therefore, is already a repetition, already more than one, already a second yes. And with that it affirms repetition not as the loss of singular truth, but as the chance, the only chance, given by necessity—which is to say by the other—to impossible singularity. It is the chance of difference, and thereby the possibility of transformation of what we mean when we say "we," what we mean by the plural, the public, the political. And not just what we mean, but the transformation of the relation to the other as wholly other, unrepresentable therefore, and finally without resemblance to any political "subject." If this transformation could have a horizon, it would be the singular justice of a "politics" of singularity. By definition, however, no such horizon can be drawn that would limit the transformation, which must remain open to what comes and is coming from the other. In the meantime, the personal *is*... in other words (and in the words of the other), it opens up, divides, differentiates, pluralizes, transforms, deconstructs . . . the political.

—But also vice versa.

—Yes, and it is good that that's the way it is. If, then, we cannot conclude as to what it will mean for feminism to affirm the inappropriability of its subject,[28] it is because any answer to that question will have to come from places that are unheard-of or not yet heard from, which include vast regions of a past that are still before us, that still have a future. At a guess, one might predict that these unheard-of places will not appear, at first, unfamiliar, but will signal themselves with the most common of names, such as jealousy, love, bliss . . .

— . . . pain death, mine, yours

— . . . each time different, each time to be repeated . . .

§ 3   Jealousy Wants Proof

If we ask: What can be known about jealousy? many answers could be gathered from official disciplines (for example, psychoanalysis, whose clinical technique and theoretical framework dictated Daniel Lagache's monumental study, *La jalousie amoureuse*) as well as from "unofficial" kinds of knowledge.[1] And yet to have knowledge of jealousy, official, unofficial, or otherwise, is to know that jealousy has nothing to do with knowledge, or rather (and this is not quite the same thing), what jealousy knows is that it knows nothing. Is it possible all the same, on the subject of jealousy and knowledge, to say something other than that the one knows nothing about the other?

Knowing about the other is, of course, what jealousy wants to do. It has the recognizable form, therefore, if not of a positive knowledge, then of a search for knowledge, a most absorbed and focused form of that search. The searched-for "object," however, that concerning which one seeks certain knowledge, is never a class or species of phenomena, a generalized condition, or a natural law. One seeks, rather, to know fully and without remainder the other in his, in her singularity. Jealousy is "unscientific" inasmuch as what it knows—or thinks it knows—has no validity beyond the singular being on which it concentrates all its efforts. On the other hand, no less than science, with its "objective"—that is, disinterested or indifferent—posture, the jealous desire to know the beloved is constrained by the limits of the phenomenality of the object. The other, the beloved appears; appearing, he or she may also disappear or dissimulate. The rules for judging the reliability of appearance—probability, logic, verisimilitude, reasonableness, and so forth—supply the tools of jealous research, but they are always double-edged since they may likewise have served to create the possibly false appearance jealousy wants to pierce. What is more, precisely because they are rules, that is, because they have a general validity or extension, they are not designed to account for the deviations of singularity, *a fortiori* of *this* singularity and no other, which, as we said, is all the jealous desire seeks to know. That desire to know is conditioned, then, by the impossibility of repeating in a knowable representation the singular determinations of its "object." As Proust's narrator recalls again and again in that monument to jealousy that is the *Recherche du temps perdu*, these singular determinations approach infinity, making of jealousy always an experience of one's own finitude:

> How many persons, cities, roads jealousy makes us eager thus to know! It is a thirst for knowledge thanks to which, with regard to various isolated points, we end by acquiring every possible notion in turn except the one that we require. . . .
> And I realised the impossibility which love comes up against. We imagine that it has as its object a being that can be laid down in front of us, enclosed within a body. Alas, it is the extension of that being to all the points in space and time that it has occupied and will occupy. If we do not possess its contact with this or that place, this or that hour, we do not possess that being. But we cannot touch all these points. . . . Hence mistrust, jealousy, persecutions.[2]

Later, we will have to acknowledge something about the status of such examples. For if jealousy is the "thirst for knowledge" concerning a singular object, made impossible/possible precisely by that singularity, then the experience Proust or another may describe will conform only up to a certain point to a general and thus knowable model, one which may be approximated or illustrated by examples. At some point, that is, every *example* of jealousy will take its form from the infinitely singular being which it pursues and which appears to retreat before it. What we read, then, no longer has the status of example of some larger condition called jealousy, but must be apprehended in a different way, which will have to be specified.

For the time being, however, let us pick up on Proust's suggestion that the jealousy his narrator describes arises from the impossibility of *touching* all "the points in time and space" with which the beloved has come into contact. It seems that it is not exactly the sense of touch that is being invoked with this term; rather touch is standing in for perceptual experience of time and space in general. "But we cannot touch all these points" would mean simply that no one can reproduce the perceptual history of another. And yet, of course, it is above all a matter of touching that concerns the jealous lover, for whom all the sensory experiences of the other may be reduced to the unfaithful touches given and received. Be that as it may, jealousy has its space, as Proust outlines here, in what could be called a perceptual gap wherein the other is never simply perceivable in the *present*, here and now, like a being "that can be laid down in front of us, enclosed within a body." The lover's jealousy is conditioned, therefore, not by a perception, but by the non-presentable and non-perceivable that divides his present by the other's time, past and future, by "all the points in space and time that it has occupied and will occupy."

It is in this sense, perhaps, that one may understand the following remark by Derrida: "Not seeing what one sees, seeing what one cannot see and what cannot present itself, that is the jealous operation. Jealousy always has to do with some trace, never with perception."[3] And yet, perhaps precisely because its operation is not that of a perception but of an unpresentable trace, jealousy seems to keep all the senses on alert, as if through redoubled effort it could close the gap that has been opened in the very sense of the present, and first of all the present of the self, self-presence. This heightened demand on the senses would aim to supply the self with that sense certainty whereby it can once again believe it knows what it knows and knows it to be real. What it wants is proof, proved by the senses, but since the jealous operation subsists on traces, it must work to see "what one cannot see and what cannot present itself." Once again, Proust could supply numerous confirmations of this blinded sight, but before citing again that inexhaustible source, we'll turn to a no less consecrated example of our theme: *Othello*.

What would it mean to say that the jealous operation here has everything to do with the trace, and nothing to do with perception? And therefore that it is not jealousy of anyone in the present or who has been present or can become present, that it is not jealousy of any presence? At first approach, it seems to mean that Othello is jealous of a fiction spun by the jealous and spider-like Iago ("With as little a web as this will I ensnare as great a fly . . . " [II, 1]; "So I will turn her virtue into pitch, / And out of her own goodness make the net / That shall enmesh them all" [II, 3]). But look closer at this web: Othello demands "ocular proof" ("Villain, be sure thou prove my love a whore; / Be sure of it: give me the ocular proof" [III, 3]), to which Iago replies, "It is impossible you should see this." Now, that "impossibility" floats between the sense in which Iago can understand it (impossible to see because non-existent, untrue) and the sense Othello is induced to give it (impossible to see because too well hidden). But it is a third sense of the impossible that holds these two together and makes them interchangeable, much as Iago and Othello are interchangeable, each acting in the other's place, through a kind of dual and diabolical possession. The third sense would be a radical or necessary rather than contingent impossibility, the impossibility of a joining to the other without remainder, of an appropriation of the other's difference without expropriation of the self's sameness: "O curse of marriage!" exclaims Othello, "That we can call these delicate creatures ours / And not their appetites!" Joining and dividing all the jealous couples in the play (Othello and Desdemona, but also Othello and Iago, Iago and Emilia, Iago and Cassio, Cassio and Bianca) is a web of traces of the unpresentable, the "impossible-to-see" ocular proof. Its place is taken—the unpresentable is presented, that is, it is made to disappear in its appearance—by Desdemona's handkerchief.

This highly artful artefact (Othello refers to it as a web) is a veil whose folds envelop the question of Desdemona's true nature—or, simply, the question of truth. When Iago says he saw the handkerchief in Cassio's hand, Othello responds: "Now do I see 'tis true." He sees nothing, of course, for there is nothing to see but a web, a net, a veil, a tissue of illusions and phantasms, the figure and the trace of his own jealousy. And the handkerchief passes from hand to hand: from Desdemona to Emilia, from Emilia to Iago, from Iago to Cassio, from Cassio to Bianca, where it disappears in a fit of the latter's jealousy (IV, 1). This visible trajectory, however, which follows the movement of jealousy in a restricted or determined sense, is itself determined by a point of origin that, precisely, is not a point but a fathomless mystery that recedes beyond the light of reason with its demand for "ocular proof." Othello recounts for Desdemona how this enigmatic object came into his hands (III,4). The handkerchief, he tells her, had been given to his mother by an uncanny Egyptian, and it was said to hold a charm that would, as long as it was kept safe, prevent her from ever having any cause for jealousy. It thus guaranteed the bond between Othello's parents and was the seal, the guarantee of their faithfulness. As she was dying, Othello's mother gave it in turn to her son and bade him to give it to his own wife. Othello repeats what he learned of its provenance: it had been woven in "prophetic fury" by an ageless sibyl from silk spun by hallowed worms and dyed in "mummy, which the skil-ful / Conserved of maidens' hearts." The thing thus inspires in he who re-ceives it a kind of awe or terror ("there's magic in the web of it," says Oth-ello) that he passes on to Desdemona with his gift: "To lose or give't away were such perdition / As nothing else could match." After Othello, in a mounting rage, has pressed her to produce this "ocular proof" and Emilia has asked "Is not this man jealous?" Desdemona replies: "I ne'er saw this before. Sure, there's some wonder in this handkerchief." Her response hits the mark of this jealousy which is tied less to its apparent or present ob-ject, Desdemona, than to the wonder of a trace of that which cannot be, or must not be, looked upon: a mother's union, some uncanny marriage between death and desire.[4]

To quote again from *Glas*, which is perhaps Derrida's most jealously de-signed book, "One is thus jealous only of the mother or of death. Never of a man or a woman as such" (134).[5] By adding to our picture of the jealous operation the elements of the mother, death, and a certain blindness, have we then begun to discern beneath its apparent traits an Oedipal model? Freud's Oedipus, but also *Oedipus Tyrannus*, for as Proust's narrator con-jectures, somewhat disingenuously perhaps: "Jealousy is often only an anx-ious need to be tyrannical applied to matters of love" (86).[6] He then im-mediately goes on to speculate whether his model in tyranny has not been his father. But let us continue to defer this question of jealousy's model un-til we have considered other so-called examples. We will go next to a visual medium, film, which may be able to take us closer, at least in appearance, to the functioning of what the jealous Othello calls "ocular proof." This medium, which is a technical apparatus, a prosthetic supplement for the deficient, or simply finite sense of sight, will also introduce us into the realm of visual or video surveillance with which the jealous operation can begin to dream of finally seeing what cannot present itself.

The film *Proof* (1991) by Australian filmmaker Jocelyn Moorhouse has, besides its title, many claims on our interest, even though one might plau-sibly describe it without any overriding reference to jealousy. Here is my own brief description.

In the first shot, we see a young man, Martin (played by Hugo Weav-ing), walking down the street with a blind man's cane and a camera slung over his shoulder. He soon meets another young man, Andy (Russell

Crowe), in the restaurant where the latter works. Martin takes numerous pictures of Andy at this first meeting and when the photographs are developed, he finds Andy again to ask him to describe each one succinctly. These descriptions are then typed by Martin on Braille tape and affixed to the back of each photograph. Martin and Andy's friendship will develop around this transaction, which Andy agrees to perform on a regular basis. Asked to explain his photographic habit, so peculiar for a blind man, Martin replies that the labelled snapshots are proof. "Of what?" asks Andy. "That what's in the photograph is what was there. . . . This is proof that what I sensed is what you saw, through your eyes. The truth." Once Andy has accepted the task of describing Martin's photographs, the latter says to him: "Andy, you must never lie to me." "Why would I do that?" asks Andy. In place of an answer, the film goes into a flashback: a small boy standing before a window through which streams sunlight. One hears a woman's voice beside him; it describes the sky, a garden, an empty bird-bath. We see the woman, evidently the boy's mother. He asks her if the man is there raking leaves. "Yes. Can't you hear him?" "No," replies the child, "he's not there." The mother then asks the same question Andy asked before this flashback began: "Why would I lie to you?" And the child answers, scornfully: "Because you can." The flashback thus sets up a structure of repetition, in which the honest Andy replaces the lying mother. In fact, this structure has already been put in place through Martin's relation to his housekeeper, Celia (Geneviève Picot), whose persistent sexual advances he takes a perverse pleasure in rebuffing. A similar use of flashback has established a reversed repetition: the same small child tracing with his hand the outline of his sleeping mother's face and neck; she awakes, scolds him, and grabs his hand just as it was descending toward her breast. Reversing and repeating this scene of sexual provocation, Celia responds to Martin's refusal of her explicit offers (she places his hand on her breast, he withdraws it coolly) by a kind of daily petty torture to which his blindness makes him vulnerable. Meanwhile, Celia soon learns of Martin's growing friendship with Andy and, in jealous reaction, insinuates herself between them, which causes Andy to lie to his friend a first time without a very clear motive. This lie concerns a photograph that Martin takes in a public garden; Andy and Celia were caught together by the camera's eye without Martin realizing that either of them were visible in the frame. When asked to describe this photo, Andy lies and says there is no one in the picture. Celia contrives to have the same photo described to Martin by another, and he then learns of Andy's lie. At the same time, he learns that they have been making love together behind his back. In the face of this betrayal, Martin chases both Andy and Celia away. There are two other flashback scenes that align this betrayal once again with the mother's. In the first, she tells him that she is going to die and can no longer take care of him. The child questions her and then accuses her of lying to cover up the fact that she no longer wishes to see him, she is ashamed of him. This is followed by a shot of the child before a closed casket; he touches it, raps on its lid and sides, and then says in a low voice: "It's hollow." At the end of the film, Martin sends Celia away definitively but reconciles with Andy. Their reconciliation is sealed when Martin asks Andy to describe one last photograph, which is in fact the first photo he ever took at the age of ten: Andy looks at it closely and then describes a garden on a sunny autumn day, a man beside an empty birdbath raking leaves. No doubt it is significant that the film's spectator is never shown either this important photograph or its original: the garden described by Martin's mother.

The jealous operation that sustains the interest of this film is Martin's: it is the device of blindness, which is relayed by the supplements that are the camera lens and the seeing eyes of others. The camera is designed to see in Martin's place: literally, he places it before his eyes, it records a scene from what would be his point of view. But its prosthetic function is divided: it replaces Martin's sight but also his mother's voice. The camera does not lie, the mother does, or at least she can. On the other hand, the pictures do not speak, they cannot say "I see" and as a result they have finally nothing to do with sight. The camera does not lie because it does not speak, but it thereby also cannot tell the truth because it cannot see. Sight depends not on an eye but on an "I," on language, and thus on a relation to others. If Martin cannot say what he sees through the camera's prosthesis, it is because he cannot see as the other, he cannot see what the other sees, and yet it is only in his relation to others that he can see at all for himself. In this way, the film isolates what we may call a normal or necessary, rather than abnormal or contingent, blindness as the condition of sight. When I see the other, I do not see what the other sees, I do not see the other seeing but seen; at the same time, I see not because I have eyes but because I have an "I," or rather because I have an "I" always only in the mode of not having it, in the mode of an expropriating-appropriating relation to others. This condition of sight is also the condition of

jealousy, which is classically diagnosed as a reaction of fear before the possibility of being dispossessed of what one possesses.[7]

Here is another exchange between Martin and Andy that goes to the
point of this expropriating-appropriating relation. Martin is recounting to
Andy the scene we have been given in flashback in which his mother describes the garden through a window:

> "Every morning and every afternoon my mother would describe this gar-
> den to me. I saw the seasons come and go through her eyes. I used to question
> her so thoroughly, always trying to catch her in a lie. I never did. But by tak-
> ing the photo I knew that I could, one day."
> "Why would your mother lie to you?"
> "To punish me for being blind."
> "Does it really matter if your mother lied to you about some garden?"
> "Yes. It was *my* world."

"It was *my* world": the actor's intonation of that possessive gives the sense
here. The emphasis floats between a privative meaning—it was all I had,
my world was nothing but the one described to me—and a meaning of
violent appropriation: the world was mine exclusively, it belonged to me
alone, and she had no right to distort it or change the least detail in its
landscape. If one cannot decide between these meanings, between the
complaint of deprivation and the claim of possession, it is because possession here must pass through dispossession, the one relaying the other, supplementing the other, replacing the other just as the mother's sight, her "I
see . . . " relays and replaces Martin's. As he tells Andy, he "saw the seasons
come and go through her eyes," which is to say, his world was also not his
world, and that was the condition of there being any "my world" at all.
This condition, then, is not in itself or not solely, essentially a deprivation,
in the sense, for example, in which Martin is deprived of sight; at the same
time, this constitutive blindness also gives the only possibility of having
sight, of having an "I see" for anyone including Martin, who can also say
without the slightest hesitation or apparent irony: "I saw" as in "I saw the
seasons come and go."[8]

There would be much more to say about this film. I have not touched
at all, for example, on the question of how to read the film as film, and
not just as story or theme. And yet, precisely by its theme, the film is implicated in everything it projects concerning truth and lie, seeing and saying, possession, disposession, and jealousy. Crossing through the fiction's

frame, one might find it significant that the film was written, directed, and produced by women (and thus forms an exception to what is almost an unwritten rule of cinema production). But it is not this fact alone that urges one to look at the film as staging a play about gender. Martin's mother and Celia, who together figure the torment of his blindness, are each the target of his denial or refusal of an affective tie. The film seems to leave little doubt that, in refusing them both, Martin conflates Celia with his mother, and the former's sexual advances with the latter's possible (but never proven) lies and above all with her greatest lie, her own death, that ultimate dispossession that leaves Martin unable to mourn the other in himself, the other who he is himself, his eyes, and his world, leaving him to cling instead to a truth and proof that he, at least, is not dead, that he *is* there. The denial of mourning and the denial of these women are run together in a same denial of the other's traces in the self, that by which we are possessed and dispossessed of the very "I" who says: I am, I am here, I sense, I see, I know. At the same time, this double denial is made to stand as a kind of supporting contrast for the only affection and tie that Martin does not refuse, his friendship with Andy.

There is one scene in which this friendship is cemented most firmly in place: it is, no doubt not coincidentally, a scene at the movies, specifically a drive-in theater to which Andy has brought Martin so that he may have the experience for the first time of hearing someone describe moving pictures to him. The film they see together, and that Andy describes with great delight and exuberant pleasure, is a "slasher" movie: nubile and half-dressed girls are, one after the other, tracked down and killed in some gruesome fashion by a sociopathic villain, man or boy.[9] The friendship that will from then on unite them, however, is owing less to the experience of viewing this film together, through Andy's eyes and captioned descriptions, than to an incidental confrontation with some other, decidedly unsavory movie-goers who mistake the two friends for a gay couple and begin to beat on the car, on Andy, and force them to flee the theater. This leads to a series of highly comic scenes that end with the two laughing uncontrollably together, which is the only time we see Martin laugh in the course of the film. It is a moving sequence. But what exactly moves the viewer in this moving picture? Or rather who moves us, if not the moviemakers with their fictional devices, their "lies," if you will, which give us to see as well the truth of Martin's truth, the masculine bond forged over against the background of the refusal of a woman's always possibly lying words, but also of the denial that this bond of friendship is a homoerotic one, while another screen receives faked images of young women dying for the viewer's pleasure? The two fictions, the two movies—the one we are watching and the one they are watching—frame between them the level of the real, the truth ("the proof that what I sensed is what you saw through your eyes. The truth"), which is depicted as a truth of male friendship, without women, without desire, without jealousy, but not without love or trust or pleasure, and not altogether without death. Yet the screened deaths are visibly faked, which is why they can produce pleasure along with terror; none need mourn what never had any life in truth. But do we see the truth? Can we see the truth? Is the truth what we see? Through whose eyes do we see the seasons change?

By leaving us with such questions, the film does something very rare: it uses visual technology and technique to display the jealous search for truth operating in the blind relay between sense perception and its necessary prostheses or supplements.[10] It shows, that is, the blindness with which one sees and which all the technological supplements imaginable cannot fully correct or overcome. What jealous lover in our advanced technological societies has not dreamed of a total surveillance device, a video *cum* audio *cum* total sensory monitoring apparatus that could somehow faithfully record and relay everything the beloved experiences? That such surveillance, monitoring, and information-gathering technology is also increasingly the dream of many or perhaps even all of our social institutions, not just the police, that it drives an ever-larger sector of the global commercial economy, that it has dramatically heightened the importance of the media in political affairs, all of this might suggest that one should take a far wider view of the question than can be seen from the vantage point of one jealous lover's torment or obsession.

Nevertheless, I will return to Proust for a final example, not least of all because he is acutely aware of the possibilities that new technologies provide for the expanding operation of jealousy.

Marcel, like Martin, is blind. He cannot see the only thing he wants to see: Albertine, in her entirety. "Jealousy, which is blindfolded, is not merely powerless to discover anything in the darkness that enshrouds it; it is also one of those tortures where the task must be incessantly repeated" (V, 195).[11] "I should have liked, not to tear off her dress to see her body, but through her body to see and read the whole diary of her memories and her future passionate assignations" (V, 117).[12] Blind, Marcel must resort to other devices, other means to attempt to overcome the invisibility of Albertine. Or at least it seems that the means he turns to are other. At several points, a distinction is made between knowledge drawn from the senses, and above all the sense of sight, and knowledge that relies on interpreting what others say, on rational deduction. For example:

> The evidence of my senses, if I had been in the street at that moment, would perhaps have informed me that the lady had not been with Albertine. But if I had learned the contrary, it was by one of those chains of reasoning (in which the words of people in whom we have confidence insert strong links), and not by the evidence of my senses. To invoke this evidence of the senses I should have had to be in the street at that particular moment, and I had not been. One can imagine, however, that such a hypothesis is not improbable. And I should have known that Albertine had lied. But is this absolutely certain even then? The evidence of the senses is also an operation of the mind in which conviction creates what is obvious. . . . But still I could have gone out and passed in the street at the moment Albertine said that, that evening (having not seen me), she had walked a short way with the lady. A strange darkness would have clouded my mind, I should have begun to doubt whether I had seen her alone, I should hardly even have sought to understand by what optical illusion I had failed to perceive the lady, and I should not have been greatly surprised to find myself mistaken, for the stellar universe is easier to comprehend than the real action of beings, especially of the beings we love . . . (V, 248, trans. modified)[13]

The phrase "témoignage des sens," which is translated above as "evidence of the senses," occurs four times in this passage. It is first distinguished from "chains of reasoning (in which the words of people in whom we have confidence insert strong links)" and then declared to be a similar "operation of mind in which conviction creates what is obvious." In other words, the senses (or rather the sense of sight, which is the only kind of sense perception invoked here) gives testimony, it speaks, and sets off thereby the same "chain of reasoning" as do the words of others. Like Descartes who can question whether the man one sees in the street is indeed a man and not a specter or an automaton, Proust is led to concede here that "evidence of the senses" must be submitted to an operation of mind no less than the discourse of "people in whom we have confidence."[14] To illustrate or prove his point, he will go on to give two examples of mistaken perception, but appropriately the sense in question in both examples is not sight but hearing, and specifically the hearing or mishearing of words.[15] This brings even closer to the surface the structure of prosthetic supplementarity whereby sight and speech, perception and reasoning, but also what I supposedly see for myself and what others say to me, are changing places. And in the process, it is the very self who sees and hears that seems to be dispossessed of what it can know of itself. I say "dispossessed," but it is by being possessed as one says of someone who hears voices that they are possessed, by some alien influence. And indeed this is what has happened to Marcel in his struggle to possess Albertine, to possess her without remainder, without difference, to possess her as himself and only himself, and thus finally to dispossess himself of her.[16]

> The image which I sought, upon which I relied, for which I would have been prepared to die, was no longer that of Albertine leading an unknown life, it was that of an Albertine as known to me as it was possible for her to be . . . an Albertine who did not reflect a distant world, but desired nothing else . . . than to be with me, to be exactly like me, an Albertine who was the image precisely of what was mine and not of the unknown. (V, 91–92)[17]

But it is Marcel who is possessed and possessed of words, which are spoken by "the evidence of his senses" or by Albertine, either of which may be lying.[18] Albertine speaks, she speaks in him, but also she speaks to others, she is outside, outside him, and thus he is beside himself. Little wonder he prefers her sleeping form: "I felt at such moments that I had possessed her more completely, like an unconscious and unresisting object of mute nature" (V, 88; trans. modified).[19]

The sleeping Albertine is not only mute, she is an immobile body, no longer moving between "all the points in space and time that it has occupied and will occupy," no longer under the sway of the sign of speed. Speed, the speed of movement and communications through space and time, is one of Proust's principal themes in *La prisonnière*: automobiles, airplanes, the telegraph, the telephone. There are, in fact, numerous switching points between the operation of jealousy and the increased speed of communications technology, as if Marcel were suffering from a new form of the *mal du siècle* at the dawn of the new telecommunications era. Albertine torments him by the speed with which she can be transported elsewhere, by the fact that her voice and her words can be carried many miles away even as she apparently remains in his presence, and these effects of teletechnology are no less dismaying when they occur through the relays of her memory or her desire than when they pass through the technical pathways of the telephone or automobile. The one apparatus plugs into and relays the other. Albertine's mobility, her transformations, her multiplicity, all are read under the sign of the speed and even the speed of light: "O girls, O successive rays in the swirling vortex wherein we throb with emotion on seeing you reappear while barely recognising you, in the dizzy velocity of light" (V, 77); "To understand the emotions which they arouse . . . we must recognise that they are not immobile but in motion, and add to their person a sign corresponding to that which in physics denotes speed" (V, 113–14).[20] More troubling than the speed of light perhaps, though less quick, is the speed of sound, and the relays of the telephone, that instrument that Marcel approaches with trepidation, each time invoking the "irascible deities" whose handmaidens are the switchboard operators, those girls whose disembodied voices pronounce the fate reserved for his communications. I will take just one example of this telephonic relay of jealousy.[21]

On the phone with Andrée, Albertine's more or less trusted chaperone, Marcel has let his mind wonder off into its jealous obsession, a distraction provoked by his own pronunciation of the name of his beloved. Having said her name over the phone, he is reminded of the envy he once felt when he heard Swann say Odette's name to him, an envy for the "entirely possessive sense" that the name had on Swann's lips. But rather than experiencing what he imagined to be Swann's pleasure at possessing the beloved so totally, Marcel utters Albertine's name only to find himself chasing its bearer in his mind through all the relays of a vast worldwide telecommunications network, stretching backward and forward in time. Recall the passage at the beginning of this chapter, where Marcel laments the impossibility of making contact with all the points that Albertine has touched in her other lives, in her life as other. Read in context, one can now hear the stress of its distress placed on the impossibility of retrieving all the calls made in Albertine's name over that network; but it is also the distress of a voice that, rather than venture out over the lines that stretch infinitely into the distance, keeps to itself and thus risks losing contact altogether:

> And I realised the impossibility which love comes up against. We imagine that it has as its object a being that can be laid down in front of us, enclosed within a body. Alas, it is the extension of that being to all the points in space and time that it has occupied and will occupy. If we do not possess its contact with this

or that place, this or that hour, we do not possess that being. But we cannot touch all these points. . . .

But already one of the irascible deities with the breathtakingly agile hand-maidens was becoming irritated, not because I was speaking but because I was saying nothing.

"But see here, the line's free! I've been holding it for you all this time; I am going to cut you off."

However, she did nothing of the sort but, evoking Andrée's presence, en-veloped it, like the great poet that a damsel of the telephone always is, in the atmosphere peculiar to the home, the district, the very life itself of Albertine's friend.

"Is that you?" asked Andrée, whose voice was projected towards me with an instantaneous speed by the goddess whose privilege is to make sound more swift than lightning. (V, 125; trans. modified)[22]

—You have put forward what seem to be two very different explana-tions of the jealous operation. On the one hand, and to begin with, you said that jealousy is driven by the impossibility of knowing the only thing it wants to know: the other in his, in her infinite and unrepeatable singu-larity. On the other hand, you've shown at some length, with *Proof* and Proust, that the prosthetic or supplementary structure of the perceptual or technical apparatus itself, and its consequent blindness, will always pre-vent the sort of proof or certainty that the jealous lover pursues.

—These two impossibilities cannot finally be kept separate from each other. The condition of blindness is the condition of the other's opacity. Or to put it in terms that are not still those of Othello's demand for "oc-ular proof," the "testimony of the senses" is the trace of the other's speech in me, and thus the possibility of my speech, of my saying what I see. A condition of impossibility that is also the condition of possibility: the text of jealousy is the trace of the one in the other, the one as the other.

—But do we or can we know any other kind of text?

—No. Every text is jealous, and jealous finally and first of all of its own operation (for we should be left with little illusion about having "un-locked the secret" of our three sample texts). This is not to say, however, that we have discovered a model. Jealousy, rather, would seem to take and to give shape according to an even more classical device, that of the muse. Among the nine goddesses who presided over official knowledge, there is not, of course, one whose name and gifts were dedicated to jealousy. If, then, one were to identify any name with the liberally jealous art, it could only be in an unofficial capacity, on a one-time basis, and not as a general or generalizable figure. The tenth muse would not have just one name, but innumerable names, both masculine and feminine, feminine or masculine, as well as neither one nor the other: innumerable, indeed infinite, the name of the infinite as the name of the other.[23] For Proust or for Marcel, *for example*, the name was Albertine, a feminized masculine name, the one that calls him on a search for lost time:

> Then beneath that rose-pink face I felt that there yawned like a gulf the inexhaustible expanse of the evenings when I had not known Albertine. . . . I felt that I was touching no more than the sealed envelope of a being who inwardly reached to infinity . . . urging me with cruel and fruitless insistence in search of the past, she was, if anything, like a mighty goddess of Time. (V, 520)[24]

—"For Proust, for example," but the example is infinite.

§ 4   The Other Sexual Difference

> What will the index be? On which words will it rely? Only on names?
> And on which syntax, visible or invisible? Briefly, by which signs will
> you recognize his speaking or remaining silent about what you
> nonchalantly call sexual difference? What is it you are thinking
> beneath those words or through them?
>   —Derrida, "*Geschlecht*: Sexual Difference, Ontological Difference"

The expectation for this chapter is that it talk about gender in the company of Derrida's thought.[1] The point would be to see how such a companion or accompaniment might influence the direction taken by talk
when it turns to the subject of gender. Naturally, one should try to meet
this expectation as far as possible. To do so, of course, one will need to
write in some particular language, preferably a language in which talk
about gender can be understood, in which the word "gender" is in common use. Even if the choice of language were not already limited by other
conditions, this expectation to talk about gender would limit the choice
to English. One can write "gender" only in English.

Such a limitation is only reasonable. It does, however, complicate the
task at hand. Because Derrida does not write in English, he does not write
in the language to which the word "gender" belongs. It is thus highly
probable that he has never written that word as such or even intended the
ordinary meaning it has in English through the use of the related French
word "genre." In French, words, more specifically nouns, have a *genre*,
masculine or feminine; there are *genres* in a specialized literary historical
sense, and there is *genre* in general (genus, kind, manner, fashion). But
genre is not gender if one means by that a sexual classification. The French
noun "sexe" is the closest translation to what Anglophones have generally
intended by the word gender, especially in recent times. "Genre" and
"gender" form a pair of what translators commonly call "faux amis" or
"false friends," the kind that betray each other and part company.[2]

At the very least, this means that one cannot begin responding to the expectation by indexing all the occurrences of "gender" in Derrida's very considerable oeuvre. On the contrary, one must assume that there is none and that Derrida has literally had nothing to say about gender, at least nothing to say about it by that name. It also means, therefore, that to speak on the subject in Derrida's company, without leaving our companion in the lurch like a false friend, one can only do so at the conjunction of more than one kind of difference: gender or sexual difference, but also language difference, which makes for the differences between "gender" and "genre," "gender" and "sexe," "sex" and "genre," and so forth. The complication seems inevitable, and with it comes the risk that a discussion of language difference and the consequent problems of translation have to lead one off the subject of gender difference. After all, what does the one have to do with the other?

As we shall see, Derrida would most probably say that they have everything to do with each other. That assertion is likely to sound surprising and not only in an English-speaking context. Before we attend more closely to this surprising notion, and before we thereby risk losing track of the theme of gender, against all expectation for this chapter, let us try to hear how that theme is playing in English alone.

Consider, for example, the distinction often made in English between sex and gender. What is the difference invoked by this subsisting distinction in our language? To begin to outline an answer, we can turn to one of the most frequently cited authorities on the question. Judith Butler, perhaps more than anyone else currently writing in English, has raised general awareness of the problems inherent in the supposition that sex can be reliably distinguished from gender and vice versa. In a book devoted essentially to contesting that supposition, Butler writes: "Originally intended to dispute the biology-is-destiny formulation, the distinction between sex and gender serves the argument that whatever biological intractability sex appears to have, gender is culturally constructed. . . . Taken to its logical limit, the sex/gender distinction suggests a radical discontinuity between sexed bodies and culturally constructed genders."[3] When she goes on to point out, however, that this distinction must itself in fact be discursively produced, Butler is able to make appear a continuity in the place of the supposed "radical discontinuity" between the two terms: the seemingly prediscursive, "natural" domain of sex, since it is produced by and as discourse, is above all cultural, which means that the prediscursive is first of all discursive. With that, Butler is able to show how the distinction collapses: "Perhaps this construct called 'sex' is as culturally constructed as gender; indeed, perhaps it was always already gender, with the consequence that the distinction between sex and gender turns out to be no distinction at all" (7). The distinction turns out to be no distinction. Within a certain *discourse*, one may now quite correctly use "sex" to mean gender and "gender" to mean sex.

Yet, in speaking of "discourse," "discursive production," and so forth, Butler is clearly not making an argument about the *language* in which she can write both "sex" and "gender" and maintain a distinction between them. Indeed, the clarity of this argument depends altogether on being able still to distinguish between them without risk of confusion. In other words, the collapse of the *discourse* of sex/gender depends on the *language* of "sex" and "gender" upholding the distinction *against* collapse. It is impossible to say, therefore, which of these movements—the collapse or the maintenance of the distinction—is more essential, more necessary to the understanding afforded by her argument. And consequently, one cannot say for certain that some notion of gender (or sex, there being no difference finally) is dependent on a discourse rather than on a language. Nor can one affirm with any certainty that an argument such as this one has moved beyond the discourse of sex and gender rather than merely reinscribing the very terms of the opposition it sought to displace.

That reinscription, without any significant displacement, may be in fact the overall effect (if not the intent) of Butler's argument here seems to be confirmed in the passage with which it concludes and which proposes other differentiating terms in place of the collapsed distinction. Butler writes:

> It would make no sense, then, to define gender as the cultural interpretation of sex, if sex itself is a gendered category. Gender *ought not to be conceived merely* as the cultural inscription of meaning on a pregiven sex (a juridical conception); gender *must also designate* the very apparatus of production whereby the sexes themselves are established. (7, emphases added)

The added emphases bring out one apparent connection made between what is still being called "sex" and "gender" despite the demonstrated uselessness of that distinction. The connection seems to be a mere addition: gender is not only this but also this. However, with this dual definition of gender, Butler is adding a discursive operation, which is called an operation of production, to another operation, which is here called inscription ("the cultural inscription of meaning"). While this addition follows as a consequence of the collapse of a discursive distinction (between sex and gender), it also *makes* a distinction between what is being called inscription and what is being called production. These terms would be related otherwise than by simple addition or repetition: they are, it is implied, in a clear relation of difference, which must therefore be marked by two different terms. "Gender ought not to be conceived merely as the cultural *inscription* of meaning on a pregiven sex (a juridical conception); gender must also designate the very apparatus of *production* whereby the sexes themselves are established" (emphases added). If one follows the logical relations implied by this choice of differentiating terms, it would seem that gender as production produces the sexes, whereas gender as inscription receives them pregiven from this other productive apparatus. This means that the conception of gender as "cultural inscription" on the received sexes is being thought as secondary and dependent on the operation that is here being called production. Thus at one level what is formulated as a simple addition (not merely this gender but also this gender) is at another level (but within the same syntax) formulated as an order of priority that makes gender as inscription a phenomenon secondary to and dependent on gender as production.

The move just retraced in Butler's analysis raises a number of questions. For example: Why is "inscription" the term chosen to distinguish the secondary, derived (sense of) gender from the other, the first, the "apparatus of production" as it is called? And then, likewise, why is "production" the term chosen to distinguish the more powerful, more originary (sense of) gender? These terms, one must suppose, have certainly not been chosen at random. This choice, then, raises further questions: What is one doing when one displaces the binary distinction of the sexes and the genders (male/female or masculine/feminine or man/woman, which are implicated with every other binary known to man or to woman) into this other distinction between production and inscription? What trait or traits make(s) the distinction between these terms more reliable than the collapsed distinction between sex and gender? And in making such a distinction is one doing something that is more like a production or more like an inscription?

To address this last question, one would have to take into account what has already been noted: the fact that Butler's analysis cannot dispense with *inscribing* a terminological or lexical difference between "sex" and "gender" even as it works to produce a collapse of that difference. Because, therefore, this argument requires both the collapse and the maintenance of its distinctions, because it must describe the collapse of terms in a language that clearly holds them apart, because, in other words, it can seem to *produce* something like an idea or concept of *no* difference between its terms only by *reinscribing* the difference between them, the new distinction would have to be no less collapsible than the one it has displaced. The assertion of the priority of production over inscription must be inscribed to be produced.

As I said, in order to notice this effect, one must pay attention to the specific language in which it is being produced or inscribed. (Which does not mean that, if it goes unnoticed, the effect is any less effective or even productive, that is, *reproductive* of its own terms, a fact that finds confirmation perhaps in the frequency with which this argument is referred to or otherwise repeated. Judith Butler is, as I said, unquestionably one of the most cited authorities on the question we are examining.) The argument, however, seems quite deliberately designed not to call attention to its own language in this way.[4] This distraction from what one could call the scene of inscription in a particular language is the very doubtful ground on which Butler seeks to establish the priority of what she calls, following Foucault, "the apparatus of production" over inscription. And in fact, the priority asserted in the above passage will never again be put in question in the analyses that follow in the rest of this book.

That this ground is indeed doubtful may be gauged by recalling the principal argument of Derrida's *Of Grammatology*. Moreover, his analyses there allow one to suggest provisional answers to at least some of the questions in the swarm of those we have just asked about Butler's move from the collapsed sex/gender distinction to the clear priority of production over inscription. What her terminological choice repeats or reproduces is the tendency Derrida identified and analyzed to figure inscription as a secondary operation, a writing, which is itself produced by something else, some other, more originary operation. Because this gesture has been so regularly and persistently repeated, Derrida was able to isolate it as an identifying trait of what he called, in *Of Grammatology* and elsewhere, the metaphysics of presence. This phrase, which has come to function as something like deconstruction's watchword (meaning what one is *on watch for*, if not against), economically designates the mode of thinking from a self-present and undifferentiated origin. What Derrida shows is that, however else such an origin may have been represented throughout the Western tradition, it has been most constantly characterized as *prior to* writing. There is thus the metaphysical tradition of a certain writing about how writing (or inscription) is always a secondary operation. Butler's choice of the term "inscription," which she wants to make secondary to "production," seems therefore still to belong, at least in part, to this tradition.[5]

But just as clearly Butler's gesture is more complex, if only because, in another sense, it also resembles or imitates Derrida's. More specifically, her marking of the collapse of the sex/gender distinction repeats a recognizable procedure of deconstruction that Derrida worked out, and, once again, very thoroughly in *Of Grammatology*: the hierarchized terms of a binary opposition are reversed, the secondary or derived term is generalized as differance, which will have "produced" the opposition in the first place (although Derrida would not describe differance as "producing" differences or oppositions and still less as an "apparatus of production"). Likewise, in Butler's analysis, the distinction of sex from gender is said to be "produced" by the discursive condition identified with the second term; gender is thereby generalized as something like differance. Nevertheless, the generalization that Butler performs also leaves intact and undeconstructed the trait of secondary inscription. Thus, despite a certain recognizable outline of the deconstructive procedure, of which Butler makes such good use, a distance is also inscribed from the kind of thinking one associates foremost with Derrida.[6]

I am suggesting that this distance can best be measured as the one traversed—or not—between sexual/gender difference and language difference. When gender as discursive production is said somehow to precede gender as inscription, then this "productive" differance is explicitly encoded as *not* originally a kind of writing. The point is not whether this dismissal of writing holds up or even whether Butler wants it to hold up; the point is rather that the argument rests finally on a mode of *exclusion* of inscription and therefore of what it itself is doing when it writes "sex" and "gender" in a particular language. For that is indeed what can be said to differentiate inscription from production as they appear to be used here: production is chosen to be the more general or powerful term because it seems not to be tied to any language and therefore to any language in particular, a language of inscription, this one, for example, in which however often one describes the collapse of the binary couple of either sex or gender, one is, uniquely perhaps, able to inscribe it again in those same terms, as I have just done.[7] Uniquely, in your or my idiom of English, another pair is reiterated.

It is in the engagement with this necessary inscription that Derrida's thinking of "gender" (although inscribed by other names) plots some paths across the distance between sexual difference and language difference, between generality/genderality and its marking, which takes place in a particular language. If, then, this chapter began by pointing out that, in all probability, Derrida has never written the word "gender," it was in order to call attention right away to the inscription of *something other*, perhaps an other (than) sexual difference on the body of his language. Instead of a general reproduction of gender, by that name and therefore only in one particular language, there would be the inscription in a different language of another "generalization." But if gender is indeed being generalized *in other names* by that writing, then this leaves open the possibility that anything or everything Derrida has written can be taken to refer its reader somewhere or somehow to (a) sexual difference.[8] That probability is even a certainty if one takes as seriously as one should *dissemination* as Derrida has described it. This term can still be heard in its so-called sexual (that is, genital) sense: a dis-semination, where the prefix has a privative value. It would be a non-semination, a non-generative non-reproduction of the seed and the semen, which is the masculine essence. But the word has not just a privative sense, because it also says *dissemination*, the scattering of the semantic or semiotic value of signs. Between these levels, between the body of signs and the genitally sexed body, the act of semination is itself dis-seminated, meaning it does not reproduce itself, no "itself" can reproduce itself.[9] This important term for Derrida has therefore also to be heard as a calculated, strategic displacement of the term "reproduction," above all sexual reproduction, and *a fortiori* of the term Butler privileges: "production," as in "apparatus of production." As a descriptive name for the movement and transformation of meaning, dissemination explicitly detaches that process from the transmission of a father's seed, which would be reproduced only in sons. Indeed, as Derrida has used it, it makes detachment from the original "seed" of meaning, or from the kernel of an original intention to mean, the condition of the transfer. If it retains a mark of gendered, genital sexual difference, that is also so as to scatter the mark in a generalization without gender, a generalization of gender's mark. As we have just described its double operation, "dissemination" emulates several other strategically deployed terms in Derrida's texts where once again a genitally sexual sense gets remarked.[10] Such a deliberate sexualization of the general language of philosophical or analytic discourse is a strategic move as well against or at least in tension with the kind of neutralization of sexual difference that has traditionally characterized it. I will return below to this tradition and its affinities for a neutralized sexuality.

To admit such a generalization, a sexualization of differance, is also to admit as an ongoing possibility that sexual difference will not always be marked or inscribed by its most common or general name in a given language. This is yet another reason it would be strictly impossible to recognize the limits of a theme of gender or sexual difference running through Derrida's text. The possibility of thematizing this difference, and all the difference it makes, is throughout put in question there, explicitly in innumerable places and implicitly at every stroke with which the text imprints itself. The problem, therefore, in attempting to meet the expectation to talk about gender in Derrida's company, is that one is left with no clearly or certainly pertinent way to proceed. There is no one thread to follow; instead there are the innumerable threads of "sexuality's" thematic name disseminated through every other term. One has only to choose.

For the sake of simplicity, however, let us choose to follow the thematic name of "sex" a little farther into Derrida's text. Perhaps, in this way, we'll be led to glimpse a place or a space of its dissemination. We can begin with the title of an essay, since a title is one such thematic marker. If we are looking for our clearly marked theme, then the title "*Geschlecht*: Sexual Difference, Ontological Difference" cannot be a bad place to start since it names or cites sexual difference twice, in two different languages.

The essay is a reading of Heidegger and what he had to say about sexual difference. But the question one must immediately entertain is whether indeed he had anything at all to say about it. For Heidegger apparently referred only minimally, if it all, to sex, sexual difference, or gender. In this way, at least, Heidegger's thought seems worlds away from, for example, Butler's preoccupations.[11] But what if it could be shown that the gesture with which the one silences sexual difference is essentially the same as the gesture with which the other speaks apparently of little else? What happens when the difference collapses between naming and not naming "sexuality" by whatever name it is given in a language? Is there then even still a word, one word, with which to name, rather than silence, sexual difference? And if not, does that mean sexual difference will have been disseminated somehow beyond the binary mark of gender, the +/-

marking of the two and only two? I will take up these questions again in conclusion, after first having followed closely this reading of Heidegger's silencing of sex.

This silence is remarkable if only for the fact that Heidegger's contemporaries are Freud and psychoanalysis, for whom sexual difference is presumed to be speaking everywhere. In that contrasting light, the silence calls attention to itself; indeed Derrida suggests it may even sound rather "haughty, arrogant, or provoking in a century when sexuality, commonplace of all chatty talk, has also become the currency of philosophic and scientific 'knowledge,' the inevitable *Kampfplatz* of ethics and politics."[12] Derrida's note of sarcasm here, which mocks "the commonplace of all chatty talk [*lieu commun de tous les bavardages*]," seems to be reserved for one feature of this scene of our century of psychoanalysis: the name of "sexuality."

This is made clear when the essay continues by questioning Heidegger's silence, in the sense of questioning whether he *did* indeed maintain silence on "sexuality." In order to assert this with certainty, one would have to be able to index everything Heidegger ever wrote. And yet, were one to propose drawing up such an index, one would first have to decide how to answer certain questions. In the passage from which the epigraph of this chapter has been drawn, Derrida lists these questions as follows:

> What will the index be? On which words will it rely? Only on names? And on which syntax, visible or invisible? Briefly, by which signs will you recognize his speaking or remaining silent about what you nonchalantly call sexual difference? What is it you are thinking beneath those words or through them? . . . What measure would seem to suffice to allow that silence to appear as such, marked and marking? Undoubtedly this: Heidegger apparently said nothing about sexuality by name in those places where the best educated and endowed "modernity" would have fully expected it given its panoply of "everything-is-sexual-and-everything-is-political-and-reciprocally." (396; 381)

If, on the other hand, rather than asking such questions, one were just to follow the common nouns already found in any index, then one would try to track down every mention of "sexuality" in Heidegger. But, of course, one would have to look for it in another language, German, where it more or less translates into the word "Geschlechtlichkeit." Only more or less, however. This difference of language is naturally not insignificant, since it is also a difference in the possibilities for the dispersion of some sexual sense or the sense of the sexual that occurs in German as in no other language. These possibilities are held in reserve by *Geschlecht*, of which sex, in the sense of one sex or the other, is only one possible translation: "genre, family, stock, race, lineage, generation" are others.[13] In other words, what in English we call sex or sexuality is inscribed in German with a word that also serves to gather up a family group, a generated line of descent. Essentially Derrida's essay titled "*Geschlecht*" is going to be concerned with following the double movement that scatters or disseminates "sexuality" through this term that *marks out* belonging to one *Geschlecht* and not another, that is, one family, stock, kind, gender, sex, etc.[14] He's interested in tracing the movement of a dissemination that gets gathered up under the mark of *Geschlecht*. *Geschlecht* derives from the verb *schlagen*, to strike a blow ("one of the most prevalent senses of *schlagen* is to mint or stamp a coin").[15] This also clearly suggests that with *Geschlecht*, unlike the term "gender," there is as much reason to speak of its *inscription* as of its production.[16]

Despite these initial and unavoidable complications, Derrida proceeds as if one could rely on an index to check Heidegger's references to sexuality. He is thereby taken to a page on which Heidegger invokes the term *Geschlecht*, in the plural *Geschlechter*. It occurs in a passage where Heidegger is explicitly negating that Dasein can be said to have a sex or to be one of either of the two sexes. Because Dasein must be thought of as neutral, then, as Heidegger writes: "That neutrality means also that Dasein is neither of the two sexes [*keines von beiden Geschlechtern ist*]" (400; 386). First let us recall that Dasein is the name chosen, in Heidegger's great work *Being and Time*, for the kind of being concerned with its own existence (Dasein, being-there, existence) in the world with others. One reason this name is chosen is its neutrality. The existence called Dasein is, for example, neither that of a male nor female being, neither man nor woman. Yet, as Derrida remarks, this neutralization does not mean to say that Dasein is asexual, without sexual existence; it is a neutralization only of the sexual duality, of *sex-duality*, if you will, rather than *sexuality*. It is the binarity of sexual difference and not sexuality as such that for Heidegger must be neutralized. Moreover, suggests Derrida, this might at least partially explain why, when he is led to specify the neutrality of Dasein, Heidegger thinks first of sexual neutrality: the neuter is neither one of two (*ne-uter*), and the binary division of "man" that most quickly comes to mind is the sexual division (401; 386).

One should thus understand Heidegger's negation of Dasein's belonging to either of two sexes as above all not a negation of a more general sexuality, more general than the classification by *Geschlecht*: a pre-dual, non-binary sexuality. On the contrary, this negation would be necessary to open the thinking of Dasein to a sexuality freed from its determinations by metaphysical binarity. It would be a more general "sexuality" before or beyond the logical division by two; a sexuality not yet or no longer *according to binary reason*. And thus in some sense more powerful than reasoned sexuality. Heidegger makes this clear as the passage Derrida is quoting continues: "But such asexuality is not the indifference of an empty nullity, the feeble negativity of an indifferent ontic nothing. In its neutrality, Dasein is not just anyone no matter who, but the originary positivity and power of the essence" (402; 387).

As this language clearly indicates, the neutralization of sexual difference is a movement that adopts the path of a negation ("neither of the two sexes") in order to bring out the positivity and the power, or one could say the potency, of Dasein's non-dual sexuality. The problem, however, is how to neutralize Dasein's belonging to one of two sexes without neutering its sexual power. This is a problem for Heidegger in his language, the language of Dasein, which means both the language to which the term Dasein belongs (German) but also the language as spoken (or rather written) here by Dasein. Dasein seems to be proper to some one language, someone's language. Indeed, the fact that Heidegger's English translators most often leave this term in German suggests that it has the force of a quasi-proper name.[17] Dasein is not a proper name in the common sense, of course. On the contrary, it is a very common name for existence in a certain language. Nevertheless, this effect of properness must be related to what Heidegger wants us to understand about Dasein, that it is, as he puts it, "in each case mine."

With this figure of Dasein's properness or "mineness," there is another face put on the problem of articulating its neutrality without negating the force of its existence and its sexuality. To ask the question of the meaning of Being or to analyze existence from the place of Dasein that is in each case mine is to turn inside out, as it were, the space of neutral objectivity, to reinscribe objectivity within its "subject," who is therefore not a subject inquiring as to or into objects but a mode of being that relates to itself by questioning its own, each time my own, existence. Heidegger's bold deconstruction of the space of the metaphysical subject requires that he negate the neutrality of Dasein in the sense of the neutrality supposed to detach the inquirer from the inquiry. Dasein, which is each time mine, is defined, we could say, as that which is above all not neutral toward its own Being, its own *being there* or *da sein*. As Heidegger puts it in the opening of his treatise:

> We are ourselves the entities to be analysed. The Being of any such entity is *in each case mine*. These entities, in their Being, comport themselves towards their Being. As entities with such Being, they are delivered over to their own Being. *Being* is that which is an issue for every such entity. [*Das* Sein *ist es, darum es diesem Seienden je selbst geht.*][18]

We have just identified two modes of Dasein's neutrality or non-neutrality. On the one hand, Dasein is neutral, for example, with regard to belonging to either of the two sexes. On the other, Dasein is in each case mine because it is not neutral as regards its Being, which, as we just read, is said to be "an issue for every such entity." These two modes, however, are also thought by Heidegger to be in a certain relation of subordination. The neutralization of Dasein's belonging to one of two sexes *follows from* its non-neutrality as regards its own Being in the world with others. With this ordering, Heidegger means to recall the priority of ontological difference, the difference of Being, over every other difference; before Dasein can be said to be, for example, of one sex or the other, it is, or we might say in a more Heideggerian tone, it must be or even it *bes* the Being that it is. Since, therefore, Heidegger wants to speak principally of the ontological difference of Dasein, he will naturally have little to say about sexual difference, which is a secondary phenomenon.

What one may remark, however, along with Derrida, is that this subordination reproduces one of the oldest gestures of the philosophical discourse Heidegger is attempting to deconstruct. This discourse, as dictated by "the most traditional philosophemes," is one that derives, deduces, or distances sexuality "from every originary structure," and it is repeated, in Derrida's phrase, "with the force of a new rigor" when Heidegger neutralizes the mark of sexual difference in order to proceed with the analysis of Dasein (410; 397). With this rigorous repetition, in other words, Heidegger stiffens up the reasons for maintaining the ban on speaking of Dasein as essentially *Geschlechtlich*, belonging to one of two sexes or, as we say, having a sex. The strongest or most rigorous reason Heidegger provides is to recover the power of "sexuality" before or beyond sex-duality. Derrida thus aligns this aspect of Heidegger's thought with what he himself has shown to be constantly at work whenever a philosophical discourse subordinates the difference made by sex to a more general difference. One has reason to suspect that this structure of thinking, which defines the limits of the pertinence of sex-duality, also reproduces within those limits the enforced subordination of one sex to the other. This latter effect of Heidegger's ontological discourse is among those that Derrida's essay is engaged in undoing.

He does so principally, as we will see, by calling attention to gestures taking place in a space of inscription. These gestures describe a "kind of strange and very necessary displacement" (402, 388), and the space of their inscription would be in fact a "transformation or deformation of space."[19] Like non-neutral Dasein that is in each case mine, this transforming, deforming displacement does not align with the space of an interiority, an enclosable space bounded by some fundamental distinction of inside from outside. The displacement occurs wherever some such distinction is made since it can only be made at the limit of Dasein, where the self-relating mineness of Dasein in itself, in its "interiority," is put in relation to some not-self, some exteriority. The transformed space of Dasein, then, is inscribed, strangely but necessarily, as a relation to some other, some other Dasein, but also perhaps some other *than* Dasein.

This space of Dasein, then, would be that of deconstructing relations to some other than itself. One can always ask to know if these relations are sexual, that is, if Dasein is having sexual relations. But to whom would such a question be addressed? From whom would an answer be expected? Is that not a question Dasein can only answer for itself? For who can presume to say that Dasein has this or that sex, in other words, that Dasein is having sex, or what sex is for a Dasein that is in each case mine? If it is always mine, then it is only for me to say. But, on the other hand, if it is only for me to say, then to whom or to what do I say it, which I must if in fact there is a relation to some other that is, as we say, sexual? Such questions begin to sound unbearably indiscreet.

Since we have been led to invoke our sense of discretion, let us go back to the way in which Derrida is reading Heidegger's apparent silence on the sexuality of Dasein. The silence is perhaps to be heard as discretion, a "transitive and significant silence (he has silenced sex) which belongs . . . to the path of a word or a speech he seems to interrupt" (397; 382). Silence is aligned here with interruption of speech, the active non-saying of something, the secreting of discretion. What is interesting and important to note, however, is that Derrida's reading does not follow the trace of some secret, which it would work to reveal, but the trace only of the secreting, of the *active* non-saying, which is to be traced as the displacement of a non-said through a discourse. The protocol of reading here is therefore not first of all a hermeneutic, but a remarking of written gestures whereby some sexual body discreetly covers itself. Thus, the questions guiding the reading do not amount to the necessarily indiscreet one: what is the secret that is being hidden? Rather Derrida asks: "What are the places of this interruption? Where is the silence working on that discourse? And what are the form and determinable contours of that non-said?" (397; 382). These questions, in other words, do not ask the discreetly covered body to bare itself; rather they propose that one follow the determinable contours of a form that has given body to a textual corpus.

These determinable contours, however, belong to no naturally given body that we think we know. Instead, the outlines of a textual body are difficult to trace and cannot be modeled as an object in space or a substantial body. That it does not represent an object does not mean, however, that it corresponds to nothing real. These are the real gestures of a strangely different corpus that is neither body nor object but a *relation* between at least two. It is the relation realized in the act of reading, which is prerequisite to encountering the gestures of a text. As we have already remarked, Derrida's reading of Heidegger follows the traces of such gestures.[20] More precisely, it *re-marks* these gestures in the course of its reading, the reading it is doing or performing. We will take a few examples of these re-marks.

The next occurrence of *Geschlecht* that Derrida isolates is found in a passage that once again neutralizes sexual difference. This time Heidegger adds quotation marks around the word *Geschlechtlichkeit*, but he also adds an *a fortiori* that, as Derrida remarks, "raises the tone somewhat." This tonal remark concerns the *a fortiori* reason one must hold Dasein to be sexually neutral. The term Heidegger in fact uses here is not the logical Latin term, but a German adverbial phrase that invokes, albeit from some distance, the law: *erst recht*, literally "first by law" but usually translated as "with all the more reason," "all the more so." What is properly, rightly, or by law first is the stronger reason, the more forceful reason, that which has all the more reason, or as one says in French "plus forte raison."[21] Heidegger is speaking of a *Selbstheit*, selfhood, or (to use a more technical term) ipseity of Dasein that is neutral with regard to any being-me or being-you, any egoism or altruism, an ipseity "not as yet determined as human being, me or you, conscious or unconscious subject" (404; 390). With regard to all of these divisions, the being-a-self of Dasein is neutral, asserts Heidegger, "and with all the more reason [*erst recht*] with regard to 'sexuality' [*'Geschlechtlichkeit'*]."

About this insistence on the *a fortiori* or stronger reason, Derrida remarks quite simply: If the reason is so strongly obvious, then why insist on it? Why does it not go without saying? He then points out in strictest logic that the

> movement of this *a fortiori* is logically irreproachable on only one condition: It would be necessary that the said "sexuality" (in quotation marks) be the assured predicate of whatever is made possible by or beginning with ipseity, here, for instance, the structures of "me" and "you," yet that it not belong, as "sexuality," to the structure of ipseity, an ipseity not as yet determined as human being, me or you, conscious or unconscious subject, man or woman. Yet, if Heidegger insists and underlines ("with all the more reason"), it is because a suspicion has not yet been banished: What if "sexuality" already marked the most originary *Selbstheit*? If it were an ontological structure of ipseity? If the *Da* of Dasein were already "sexual"? What if sexual difference were already marked in the opening up to the question of the sense of Being and to the ontological difference? And what if neutralization, which does not happen all by itself, were a violent operation? (ibid.)

If indeed there is violence here, it subsists in the traces of the invoked law or order of reasons, in the structure of derivation from a first ipseity presupposed as without sexual difference in itself. Invoking the greater, stronger, or more powerful reason as that which necessitates this neutralization, one has perhaps covered over a weaker reason, a reason that is rather a nagging suspicion or even a fear, which has not yet been banished and perhaps can never be banished: perhaps "sexuality" already marks the most originary being-self and is an ontological structure of ipseity. For if, following from the *a fortiori*, the only logically correct or faultless order of reasons here means that "sexuality" *must* be the predicate of everything made possible by the being-a-self of Dasein, but does not, itself or as itself, belong to what it makes possible, then a strange displacement of the ordered derivation or predication has been effected. "Sexuality" would have to be said to *participate without belonging* to everything made possi-

ble beginning with ipseity, and thus ipseity itself would have to be inscribed already within a strange sexuality without "sexuality" or
"Geschlechtlichkeit."[22]

The problem is quite clear. The ipseity or self-relation that Heidegger
wants to mark out as that of a Dasein not indifferent to its own being
would be, as Derrida phrases it, a "minimal relation to itself as relation to
Being, the relation that the being which we are, as questioning, maintains
with self and with its own proper essence. . . . Neutrality, therefore, is first
of all the neutralization of everything but the naked trait of this relation
to self" (399; 384). But if it is said to be first of all or above all (*erst recht*)
sexual neutrality, then this implies that some *other* sexual non-neutrality,
some *other* sexual difference has first of all to be neutralized, reduced, or
withdrawn *so that* one may isolate the "naked trait" of self-relation. For
Dasein properly to name such a naked self-relation, this other sexual difference must be withdrawn and, by withdrawing, *give* one the possibility
of thinking something like a self, the being-a-self of sexually neutral Dasein. Dasein itself and as a self would be something like a gift of the other
sexual difference, the one that withdraws just as every other sexual couple
or coupling does, behind some folded tissue: curtain, veil, venetian blind,
rideau, jalousie, and so forth.[23] The problem, then, is this gift, whereby
Dasein is given (a) sex, and at the same time—and this is what we call
birth—given all that is made possible by being a self. If the self-relation is
thus given, then it cannot be thought of as *first of all* a self-relation, but
necessarily as a relation to something other than the self it is given. One
cannot think the self beginning with itself.

The question remains why this impossibility should be thought to create a problem. In other words, why does the necessity of the non-self-relation seem to make for a problem rather than a gift? This question can
only be pursued by the more specific one: for whom does it make problems? Derrida is isolating the problems it makes for Heidegger, quite singularly, but at the same time he is opening up the possibility for thinking
non-self-relation in terms *also* of gift and not just of problem. We will
later propose at least one consequence of this for the notion of sexual reproduction as that which gives life.

Like the problem of Dasein's sexual neutrality with which we began, the
problem just alluded to is also one for Heidegger's language, the language
in which he would inscribe "Geschlechtlichkeit" so as to neutralize it,
erase it, or withdraw it. This is where the tissue of his text must fold back

over its own inscription. As Derrida points out, the appearance of the quotation marks on "Geschlechtlichkeit" should not be overlooked (Heidegger writes: "with all the more reason with regard to 'sexuality' ['*Geschlechtlichkeit*']"). And as Derrida often does when analyzing this punctuation, he cites in passing the distinction made in speech act theory between use and mention.[24] According to that distinction "the current sense of the word 'sexuality' is 'mentioned' rather than 'used'" (405; 390). There is, however, some reservation regarding this distinction, signaled here by Derrida's own use of quotation marks on the terms "mentioned" and "used." Is not Heidegger's mention of "Geschlechtlichkeit" also a kind of use, and does not this neutralizing "mention" of sexuality also have the allure of a not-indifferent and perhaps even violent "use," the operation of quotation, a citation to appear, *erst recht*, before the law? In that guise, "sexuality" would be, Derrida suggests, "cited to appear in court, warned if not accused" (405; 390). The bracketing of "sexuality," its furtive appearance under citation could suggest some scene of guilt, a fault that the court of ordered reasons *must* contain at the risk of contaminating the original structure of ipseity and of Dasein. Derrida suggests that this is perhaps what is at stake here for Heidegger: "For in the end, if it is true that sexuality must be neutralized *a fortiori*, *erst recht*, why insist? Where is the risk of misunderstanding? Unless the matter is not at all obvious, and there is still *a risk of mixing up once more* the question of sexual difference with that of Being and ontological difference" (404; 390; emphases added). Or, put in somewhat different terms: "Above all, one must protect the analytic of Dasein from the risks of anthropology, of psychoanalysis, even of biology." That is, *Geschlechtlichkeit* is a thematizable, representable object for these sciences, but not for the fundamental ontology that Heidegger wants to adumbrate and that he wants to protect from contamination by these other disciplines. One way he does so is to avoid thematizing sexuality in that name. *Geschlechtlichkeit*, therefore, will be set aside or rather withdrawn behind the curtain set hanging between the quotation marks placed around the word.

At this point, then, Heidegger's text exposes an order of forced reasons. This exposition follows a strictly logical path, but in so doing it also exposes (itself to) a certain risk. And this risk is determined *erst recht* as the risk of mixing or contamination. But an exposition, in addition to the senses of philosophical or logical argument and of exposure to risk or to contamination, also remarks a spatial movement, an ex-position, a transformation or deformation of positioned, oppositional space. There is thus a fold in the order of reasons that exposes itself here, in other words, makes itself visible or phenomenalizes itself. The phenomenon of this exposition, however, occurs as the ex-posing of a *text*, rather than an object in conventionally lighted oppositional space. How does Heidegger's text expose itself in all these senses at once? And how does this irreducible semantic plurality come to displace and reinscribe the figure of a contaminating sexual duality?

If Heidegger's "all the more reason" is a blow struck in the name of a certain non-contamination of Dasein's ontological difference by sexual difference, then this *coup de force* or forced neutralization, by raising the tone, also calls attention to what "does not happen all by itself" but must be forced to happen, *performed as perforce*. Above the surface of the text's argument, a gesture juts out and can be remarked: it puts sexuality in its place, but the same gesture cannot prevent the appearance of the strange displacement whereby sexuality, by not belonging to ipseity, nevertheless belongs to everything it makes possible. Only a *coup de force* here can decide that this non-belonging of "sexuality" does not indicate a more general structure of sexual difference rather than a more restricted one, a contaminated structure of ontologico-sexual difference rather than one that determines sexual difference to be logically dependent on the being-a-self of Dasein, which would only thereupon receive the predicate of sexual. This latter order of implication or derivation, whereby a contaminating sexual difference is contained, would be what has to be preserved by the strategy of neutralization.

And yet, it is the movement of neutralization itself that brings out or allows to appear in this strange, non-phenomenal light a sexual difference that contaminates all others. Or rather, since this language of contamination signals already the decision by the court of forced reason, let us resume the language of gift introduced above. As we were saying, there would be a sexual difference, an *other* sexual difference, that *gives* all others or that *gives* itself in the guise of all other differences. This general space of the other sexual difference would thus also be the possibility of transformation or deformation of a certain engendering power of "sexuality." One touches here, in other words, on the limit of the determination of sexuality as it has always been understood: reproduction, engenderment, genital sexuality. As that which "gives life" to this deformed space, that is, puts it in motion, sexual difference has now also to be heard in another sense, before or beyond this limit that defines the most general sense of "life" as sexually engendered life, this life here. "Sexual difference" would then also have to be heard without this general sense, without a generalizable sense of the "life" it gives.[25] This other sexual difference invokes an unheard-of sense, its tones muffled as it were within parentheses: (sexual) differe/ance.

The textual gesture just retraced is not that of some body but of a covering or silencing of the body, its withdrawal from discursive space. For all that, the sexed or sexual body is not simply absent. Rather it is withdrawn but into the folds of a text. Because it is folded in this way, a text does not lay itself out flat or in a straight line. But also because it is folded, a text somewhere exposes the manner in which it still harbors the force of whatever sent it into waves for a start (call it the *sextual* drive). That is why, when he comes to formalize this structure, Derrida briefly sketches the outline of a form that is not stable but rather a movement that is being somehow driven. This movement in discursive space can be traced through the displacement of a *pair* of terms, always a pair or at least a duality. The paired duality functions something like the negative and positive terminals of a battery that charge and discharge the *dynamis* driving the movement. Here, then, is the brief sketch Derrida draws of this drive or transmission system:

> By a kind of strange and very necessary displacement, it is sexual division itself that leads to [*porte à*] negativity; so neutralization is at once the effect of this negativity and the effacement to which thought must subject it to allow an original positivity to become manifest. Far from constituting a positivity that the asexual neutrality of Dasein would annul, sexual binarity itself would be responsible, or rather would belong to a determination that is itself responsible, for this negativation. To radicalize or formalize too quickly the sense of this movement . . . we could propose the following schema: it is sexual difference itself as binarity, it is the discriminative belonging to one or another sex, that destines or determines (to) a negativity that must then be accounted for. (402–403; 388)

This is a formalization of what Heidegger does when he negates sexual binarity in order to retrieve an original positivity of sexuality. The formalized schema will be taken a little further, but first let us remark the initial strangeness in this movement. Sexual division or sexuality "leads to" negativity: that is, it carries toward, it puts in motion (*porte à*), but it also carries that motion in itself against itself since the movement is toward a negation of itself as binarity. A fold is created here when sexual difference carries within "itself" its own limited determination as binarity. Binarity with its negative and positive poles, in other words, is at once the determination to be negated and that which determines, makes necessary, or destines to the negation. This effect of an implicated fold within the movement, which, moreover, folds or doubles around binarity, is marked at the articulation of negative and positive terms: neutralization. That "neutralization," we read, "is at once the effect of this negativity and the effacement to which thought *must* subject it to allow an original positivity to become manifest" (emphases added). In other words, the neutralization must submit to the double necessity to inscribe a negativity and efface it, to inscribe it by effacing it. And since the neutralization is itself but the movement through this inscription and effacement of negativity, it carries toward and away from "itself," toward and away from this strange ipseity marked already by sexual division. Sexual difference is "itself" divided, it divides its own location.

It is this power system driven by positive and negative poles that Derrida remarks when he takes the formalization a step further. What he traces is the implied or enfolded negative term corresponding to the positive pole of power in Heidegger's language ("In its neutrality, Dasein is not just anyone no matter who, but the originary positivity and power [*Mächtigkeit*] of the essence"). The enfolded, withdrawn structure is drawn out by means of Derrida's translation of Heidegger's term into its implied opposite: powerlessness, or, depending on how one wants to hear it, impotence.

> Going still further, one could even link sexual difference thus determined (one out of two), negativity, and a certain "impotence" [*"impuissance"*]. When returning to the originality of Dasein, of this Dasein said to be sexually neutral, "originary positivity" and "power" [*"puissance"*] can be recovered. In other words, despite appearances, the asexuality and neutrality that must first of all be withdrawn from the binary sexual mark, in the analytic of Dasein, are in fact on the same side, on the side of *this* sexual difference—the binary—to which one might have thought them simply opposed. (403; 388; translation modified)

If we follow Derrida's example and remark the use of quotation marks, then we see the terms "impotence" and "power" being both used and mentioned here. There is mention or citation (but also translation) of

Heidegger's term "Mächtigkeit," in the phrase "Mächtigkeit des Wesens," the power (potency) of the essence, of originary positivity. "Impotence" ("impuissance," with the always possible sense of "impossibility") is the word Derrida unfolds out of the implied system of Heidegger's discourse. The term, therefore, is not a quotation or "mention" of what actually appears as the discourse is written. But neither is it simply being used in some context, a context that would serve to determine whether or not we hear the term in its strictly sexual sense (genital impotence) or in any one of its many other possible uses: powerlessness of whatever sort, impossibility in general. (But what would that be, "impossibility in general"? We'll leave this question suspended for the moment.) The quotation marks around "impuissance" signal a suspension of all these senses and all possible contexts of the term's use. But the quotation marks, because they cite only an implied term in Heidegger's discourse, also point very precisely to the contours of an active silencing, the withdrawal of the sexual mark. Derrida remarks that Heidegger "will never directly associate the predicate 'sexual' with the word 'power,' the first remaining all too easily associated with the whole system of sexual difference that may, without much risk of error, be said to be inseparable from every anthropology and every metaphysics" (403; 389). But also no doubt Heidegger avoids this association because the sexual mark invariably reiterates the link between positive and negative poles, potency and impotence. Despite that, however, insofar as non-dual sexuality is recovered as a positivity, the power one strives to withdraw from the binary poles of negative and positive is also, still, once again getting its charge from that binary system. That is why one can say that the "asexuality and neutrality that must first of all be withdrawn from the binary sexual mark . . . are in fact on the same side, on the side of *this* sexual difference—the binary—to which one might have thought them simply opposed." The binary opposition is therefore both withdrawn and redrawn. This back and forth describes the movement of its displacement through a system, its repeated inscription and effacement.

In addition to placing quotation marks around the interpolated term "impuissance," Derrida traces another typographical gesture in the same passage. There is also a use of italics that marks out "*this* sexual difference" for special emphasis. I would suggest that the deictic "this" receives its emphasis by force of dissemination. I would also therefore be tempted to read this device as something like a *coup de force* that is both analogous to and a displacement of Heidegger's "with all the more reason." Specifically, it re-marks difference or division at the site of the deixis, which is the index of a gesture, the possibility of any reference to *this here* and of any relation of this "this" to itself. It thus situates the dividing limit at which every ipseity, every "this, here, now," is posed and exposed, displaced into another "this," into another's here and now. In other words, "*this* sexual difference" carries toward an immediate multiplicity of senses, illimitable by any two; but it also continues to signal *this* singular sexual difference here, in all its impossible binarity. This "this" uncannily appropriates and expropriates the ipseity of every "myself" when it divides its mark, on the page, and splits its location, deforming the former space of binary opposition. The italicized deictic "this" imprints, inscribes, or strikes sexual difference ("*this* sexual difference") with the force of its dissemination.

Would not such a *coup de force* have to reinscribe the whole machinery of "puissance," power, potency, or *Mächtigkeit*? Perhaps, but only on the condition of remaining strangely powerless in itself, only on the condition that it be suspended in advance—disseminated—from the other to which or to whom it is consigned as a sign to be read, or not, in *this* text *here*. "*This* sexual difference," which is to say, at once, the other (and the other's) sexual difference. Sexual difference divides—itself. It thus divides its proper meaning, and this division inscribes (itself as) a text. The general name of humanity's gender deconstructs.

Nothing is perhaps less certain of success than the project to recapture the originary power of "sexuality" by neutralizing sex-duality. Whether in Heidegger's discourse or, very differently, in a discourse like Judith Butler's, that gesture has to remain implicated without neutrality in *this* sexual difference, which thereby also reinscribes its binary trait. No power of sexuality that does not also, at the same time, get transmitted as an im-power, an impotency. Heidegger's discourse perhaps sought to dissimulate or discreetly silence this inscription of "impower" by, in one of those gestures Derrida re-marks, "never directly associat[ing] the predicate 'sexual' with the word 'power.'" He would thereby have wanted to avoid falling back into a strictly binary sexual domain, but perhaps he was also secretly re-connecting sexuality to an absolute power, a power without implication in im-power. Butler's discourse would seem to make this connection without dissimulation, in the open: it is overtly a discourse of sexual politics, rather than always only potentially or in secret. That is, sexuality is connected by its discursive arguments to a system it calls the "apparatus of production." But we have also seen that, as the condition of its identifying a source of production that is not yet an inscription, such a discourse attempts to hide in plain sight its own articulations, there where it must draw on the binary trait and reinscribe it. Such an attempt, if it could ever succeed, would dissimulate the text *as* text, that is, as both more and less than the vehicle of a discourse's conceptual generalizations. It would thereby also spell the end of whatever can still come to be inscribed of the other sexual difference, beyond, before, or within the binary, and thus the end of any transformation of the relations held in place by sex-duality.

If such a transforming inscription is still possible, however, then oddly enough it can announce itself in the figure of impossibility, of that impower Derrida unfolds at the point at which his reading, we might say, poses another signature on Heidegger's text. When we earlier suspended the question "What is impossibility in general?" it was this scene of a signature that we were anticipating. For would not impossibility *in general* have to include the impossibility of that very generalization? If so, then it is always somewhere being restricted in the general sense, specified as the impossibility of this or that, of this one or that one. It is this necessary limitation of impossibility that allies it with the restricting effects of signature on generalizing discourse, *a fortiori* discourse on gender. Such effects are re-marked everywhere in the gender-less texts signed "Jacques Derrida."[26]

Somewhere closer to the beginning of this essay, it was asked: "What if it could be shown that the gesture with which the one silences sexual difference is essentially the same as the gesture with which the other speaks apparently of little else?" Perhaps what happens in that eventuality is that terms like "gender," "Geschlecht," "sexe," and so forth will indeed have come to be neutralized but in another fashion. They would have been neutralized for use as reliable markers of the *general* theme of sexuality inscribing discourse in a language.

—By "neutralized for use," do you mean that these terms have been put out of commission, rendered useless, and therefore discourse has to drop them? Or, on the contrary, do you mean they have been shorn of whatever would make them useless, such as the necessity to translate between languages, and turned into conceptual tools with which a discourse can construct itself?

—Whichever. In either case and in all cases, the theme plays only when some non-concept, some impossible concept, something like a proper name, picks it up as an instrument of quasi musical inscription. And begins to write in more than one voice, more than one language, more than one sex, and therefore more than two.

§ 5   The Sacrifice of Sarah

The fearsomeness of imminent and inevitable death has been called up or appealed to only rarely, it seems, through the figure of a woman. In the West, the heroic effigy has had its most memorable and oft-repeated incarnation as a man: from Achilles, Hector, and Socrates to Billy Budd and Terminator 2, popular or classical literature has recorded the ultimate moment of these singular lives, all lived within men's bodies, even if, as in the case of Terminator, that body is a simulated one, indeed, doubly simulated. The counter-examples of heroic women standing before death or sacrificing their lives are far fewer in the general cultural imagination. Obvious exceptions—Antigone, Joan of Arc, Rosa Luxemburg—are exceptions, moreover, in more than one sense, which complicates this apparently simple calculation: it is as exceptions that they were put to death by men, for example, by a man like Creon who, when he pronounces sentence on Antigone, seems to fear that she will prove to be more of a man than he is: "This girl, already versed in disrespect / When first she disobeyed my law, now adds / A second insult—vaunts it to my face. / O, she's the man, not I, if she can walk / Away unscathed."[1] It is as if by standing up to the death warrant, Antigone had acted as a man, not a woman, and this act is her crime for which she must be made to stand before a death warrant as the mere girl that she is. It is hard, in other words, to prevent this status of exception from working to confirm the rule. One might thus conclude that Antigone dies like a man, which is to say, not as a mere girl but also as something greater than herself and that is why it is a memorable death, a sacrifice of her mere life for a greater good or a higher law. As something greater than herself, she is not just a girl whose death would be of little account. As one may quickly see, the logic that distinguishes "mere" from "greater" by means of the distinction of girl from man could work to efface from view and thus from memory any death that is not a "man"'s death. There is a fatal reversal afflicting this rigorously binary and hierarchical pattern, and with every reversal it seems to exact the sacrifice of the greater term. The greater term is even greater in its demise.

Nicole Loraux, in her stunning book *Tragic Ways of Killing a Woman*,[2] has shown how the language of the Greek tragedies in fact recorded the deaths of women characters in remarkably consistent terms according to patterns that can be reconstituted as the codes governing heroic and non-heroic deaths, the deaths of men and women. Women die, more often than not, by their own hand and by hanging, which is an ignominious death. They do not die by the noble sword, unless it is the instrument of the sacrifice to which, like Iphigenia, they are forced to submit, its victims or tokens.

(But what is sacrifice? How do we conceive the memory of sacrifice? Under what guise is sacrifice commemorated and kept sacred? Is the sacred law given to memory the same or different when this guise is feminine? These questions will be left hanging for the moment.)

As for the biblical or religious figuration, as distinct from the classical heroic one, there seem to be no sacred deaths—to be remembered, revered, or worshipped—except those of fathers and sons. One could extend the references in several directions in order to track the ways in which a woman's death is most often represented non-heroically, which is to say as non-exemplary.

The death of Socrates, on the other hand, is exemplary. Setting out from this example, philosophy has sought to speak non-finitely, infinitely, of finitude. Not too surprisingly, then, it could also be heard speaking of infinitude, of the immortality of the soul. This discourse that would be infinite, without limit, has traced its history as a struggle to think itself as infinitely finite. Which has also meant to overcome finitude. This history reaches a certain culmination with Heidegger's attempted *Destruktion* of metaphysics, a metaphysics that, among other things, has bequeathed us the figure of the immortal or resurrected soul. In his existential analytic in *Being and Time*, Dasein assumes and affirms the finitude of its being *zum Tode*: toward death, for death, in view of death. The existential analytic is the name of the discipline with which Heidegger proposes to speak with infinite resonance of Dasein's own finitude, that which is each time Dasein's own, my own. Heidegger's own. *Being and Time*, like Hegel's *Phenomenology of Spirit*, Plato's dialogues, Descartes' *Méditations*, Augustine's *Confessions*, and so many other great works of the Western philosophical tradition, can also be read as something like autobiography. The resonance such works continue to have for us, in our and their finitude, has to do with this autobiographical lining or allegory of the philosophical discourse. It is this lining or *doublure* that Heidegger attempts to formalize as existential analytic, by which he names what will have been his own autobiographical performance. His reason for doing so is quite simple, actually: we must begin from wherever we are, where each *Dasein* "is," however briefly.

Heidegger famously argued that "Dying is something that every Dasein itself must take upon itself at the time."[3] That is, every death is irreplaceable and no one can die in the place of another. One may indeed sacrifice one's life to or for another, but sacrifice is not substitution and the other will still have to die his or her own death in time. Heidegger, of course, would not write, as I just did, "his or her" since the other is the other Dasein and Dasein is neutral, which above all means it belongs to neither of the two sexes.[4] From these premises, one could deduce that for Heidegger there is simply no point to questions about death and sexual difference, or about exemplary death.

But the question of sacrifice is still open and perhaps still suspended from that of sexual difference.

Consider a certain paragraph from *The Gift of Death*, one of the essays in which Jacques Derrida concerns himself most closely, among other things, with Heidegger's analytic of *Sein zum Tode*. The paragraph follows an analysis of Kierkegaard's famous reading of the sacrifice of Isaac in *Fear and Trembling*, from which Derrida has just drawn some parallels to Melville's "Bartleby the Scrivener." The final parallel put in place concerns the place of woman in these stories of sacrifice, or rather her absence there:

> It is difficult not to be struck by the absence of woman in these two monstrous yet banal stories. It is a story of father and son, of masculine figures, of hierarchies among men (God the father, Abraham, Isaac; the woman, Sarah, is she to whom nothing is said; and "Bartleby the Scrivener" doesn't make a single allusion to anything feminine whatsoever, even less to anything that could be construed as a figure of woman).[5] Would the logic of sacrificial re-

sponsibility within the implacable universality of the law, of its law, be altered, inflected, attenuated, or displaced, if a woman were to intervene there in some consequential manner? Does the system of this sacrificial responsibility and of the double "gift of death" imply at its very basis an exclusion or sacrifice of woman? A woman's sacrifice or a sacrifice of woman, according to one sense of the genitive or the other? Let us leave the question in suspense.[6]

A question is left in suspense. To "suspend" a question, an interrogative sentence, is to do, possibly, several things: (1) the interrogative process of question-response is interrupted, leaving, as we say, a question unanswered; but also (2) a question is suspended from a certain point, it is made to depend or hang on some point in space, or in the discursive space of an argument; but also (3) a question is suspended when it is adjourned, when the parliamentary session is over and discussion adjourned to a next meeting. The question that Derrida suspends, in one or more of these three senses, is formulated, in fact, as three different, but related questions. To repeat, these are first: "Would the logic of sacrificial responsibility within the implacable universality of the law, of its law, be altered, inflected, attenuated, or displaced, if a woman were to intervene there in some consequential manner?" Second: "Does the system of this sacrificial responsibility and of the double 'gift of death' imply at its very basis an exclusion or sacrifice of woman?" And finally, a supplemental question to this sacrifice: "A woman's sacrifice or a sacrifice of woman, according to one sense of the genitive or the other?"

The "question of woman" has been posed (and suspended) repeatedly in Derrida's writings and at many different points of articulation with a larger cultural text. Here the articulation is plotted at a specific intersection where Bartleby crosses the path of Abraham as the latter ascends Mount Moriah. At that intersection woman is absent. The suspended questions concern this absence from the stage on which a certain Western sacrifice is played out—the sacrifice in which the act commemorated is not a tragedy but a gift or grace, given by God. In this great scene of God's gift of death, what does it mean that woman is not represented or is represented as absent? To ask what this absence means is also to ask, as Derrida puts it in his first question, whether the whole scene would be "altered, inflected, attenuated, or displaced, if a woman were to intervene there in some consequential manner?" In order, however, to even imagine that difference, the difference that a woman's intervention might make in this scene, one must confront another question: "Does the system of this sacrificial responsibility and of the double 'gift of death' imply at its very basis an exclusion or sacrifice of woman?" Exclusion or sacrifice: these two determinations of woman's absence, which are metonymies of that absence and thus metonymies of each other, also speak of that absence, inscribe it in the scene being figured here. In other words, if we say "yes, the system at work *implies* at its very basis an exclusion, a sacrifice of woman," then by *implication*, that is, by a folding back of the terms constituting the scene, woman already figures in the sacrifice, her exclusion is also an inclusion of an occluded sort, although she is not addressed and she does not show herself there. If the scene of sacrifice is constructed by the sacrifice/exclusion of woman, then woman is not simply absent there; it is also *her* sacrifice, the sacrifice *of her*. Her absence is not a pure and simple absence, but rather something like a ghostly presence. The question then becomes: what is the role of a woman's ghost in sacrifice?

A ghost is a kind of double or doubling, a shadow or shade, in itself neither present nor absent, living nor dead. A doubling of life, the ghost imprints its "presence" on the doubled syntax of the phrase "sacrifice of the woman." And this leads to the third question that will be suspended: "A woman's sacrifice or a sacrifice of woman, according to one sense of the genitive or the other?" In French: " . . . sacrifice de la femme. *De* la femme, selon tel ou tel génitif?" The ghost of a woman's presence is implicated in the scene of sacrifice, but in more than one place. Grammatically at least, woman can double all three of the principal roles in the scene: the one who commits the sacrificial act, the one who commands that this act be committed, and the one who is sacrificed there.

Of these three possibilities, it is the third, the role of the victim, that seems easiest to map onto the implicated but unrepresented sacrifice of woman in the scene: "the sacrifice of woman," then, would be woman as victim offered up at another's command; woman as the absent victim, she whose sacrifice is figured by Isaac's. Isaac's sacrifice *within* the story would be put in place, preceded and displaced by the sacrifice of (the) woman *outside* the story. But the division just evoked appeals to an outside that cannot be represented since it is outside, precisely, representation, a radical "outside," therefore.

From that unrepresentable space, "the sacrifice of woman" imprints a double on another's role in the scene, the one who *commands* the sacrifice of Abraham, the one to whom Abraham listens, that *other* radical, unrepresentable other who is called God in the represented, representative story.

It would thus be the sacrifice of the woman in the sense that one sacrifices *to* her, *for* her, at her command, according to her law. This possibility is very disturbing in its implications, for it doubles or ventriloquizes the very voice of God.

However, perhaps just as disturbing is the third possibility of the shifting genitive: "the sacrifice of the woman" cannot exclude from its possible implications that the woman's sacrificial act in this scene is the one played out by Abraham in the theater of the three Western religions that trace their common commemoration, their common memory to Abraham the patriarch. Behind Abraham would stand Sarah, just as the proverb says about every good man. She stands behind him, or even beside him, seconding his act, her arm raised with his in the split second of decision that is demanded of her, of him. In that split second, Abraham as Sarah, Sarah as Abraham sacrifices what he/she loves most to the other.

To speak, then, of the sacrifice of Sarah is to engage this triple scene in which all the roles are doubled. The doubling occurs as a marking of sexual difference, here in a proper name. Sarah's proper name, absent in the scene of sacrifice, in its very absence traces a doubled mark: sexual difference. But something disturbing arises when one considers all the possible doublings, which are sexual doublings, in this scene. A disturbance need not be merely negative, a principle of disorder or destruction. A disturbance can signal the interference or intervention of some other order—or dis-order, according to this tracing law of sexual difference. This is indeed a way of taking up again the first question posed and suspended by Derrida. That question asks about something like a possible disturbance: "Would the logic of sacrificial responsibility within the implacable universality of the law, of its law, be altered, inflected attenuated, or displaced, if a woman [e.g., Sarah, the doubled name of sexual difference] were to intervene there in some consequential manner?" "Altered, inflected, attenuated, displaced" are modes of disturbance. We are asking if the intervention of a woman in the sacrificial economy—a woman herself, as herself, not as a ghost of herself or the other, but as woman *and not* man, as woman *without* man—would disturb it, inflect it in a significantly different sense, alter or even interrupt its trajectory.

If, however, that is the question, then the answer has already begun to suggest itself. Woman *herself*, properly herself and not someone's ghost or spirit, is a figure of sacrifice, a figure of exclusion, woman constituted by the concept of not-man. Thus, the disturbances set off by the shifting genitive may be profound but perhaps not so profound as to clear the stage for a wholly different act, an act of love or gift without sacrifice, without the demand for sacrifice. Whether woman commands this sacrifice or obeys the command, whether we hear her name behind God's order or Abraham's response, the play repeats and the scene multiplies. This is disturbing in another sense because the place of woman's implication in the scene, whether God's or Abraham's, is a place of *responsibility* for this repetition. And that is disturbing for the "good conscience" of whatever or whoever would seek to reclaim the place of woman at this scene of inaugural sacrifice. "Good conscience" can only arrest the ghostly possibilities of that place in the sole position of innocence, apparently: the position of victim. That is, "good conscience" is bought with the bad faith assertion that neither God nor Abraham is Sarah's double, but only Isaac, herself in her child alone. "I too, Sarah, the woman, am the victim, I too am but a child, *without* responsibility. Yet." To the question of woman's apparent absence from this scene, the answer of good/bad conscience is not yet a response, a responsible response. It leaves still suspended the question of whether a woman's intervention can disturb or displace the repetition of the sacrifice in Sarah's name. Which is also the name of Abraham, Isaac, and, finally in all its secrecy, God.

It is thus a different law of responsibility, different from the sacrificial responsibility inaugurated by God's command to Abraham, that we obey in suspending these questions, that is, in *opening them up again* to the future from which they have come to us. The question is asked in the hypothetical mode of the present conditional: "Would the logic . . . be altered, etc. . . . . *if* a woman *were* to intervene there in some consequential manner?" This conditioned hypothetical is in the mode of a suspended judgment. If a woman were to intervene in a determining manner, which is always possible, would it be the fact that it is a woman, and not a man, who intervenes, would this fact in itself be finally determining, determinant? Or can woman intervene at all qua woman, rather than as already doubled by man, just as man is already doubled by the excluded woman? To ask whether sexual difference is a *determining* difference is to ask whether it makes a difference *in the end*, in function of the end, in function of finitude. To put the question more in Heidegger's terms, if Dasein as being-toward-death is each time mine, *jemeinig*, then is Dasein toward death differently by being mine, a woman's, rather than yours, a man's?

—That sounds like a different question than the one with which you began.

—It does, but in fact, look, we have merely continued to formulate interrogatively what it is we think we all know by knowing something like necessary finitude. But now we are asking whether sexual difference divides this possible knowledge or this possible trajectory toward death in an irreducible way. And if so, in what way.

For Heidegger, for Levinas, and for Freud as well in his speculation on a death drive that would be phylogenetic, no such division or difference is marked. For them, the question is not even posed or suspended there. Derrida once again reads in this silence a certain absence and wonders whether it goes without saying or whether, on the contrary, some ghost of sexual difference is lingering over the final scene. In the same essay, *The Gift of Death*, the marked suspension of this question, which is closely related to the question of woman's sacrifice, is put in place some pages earlier. Derrida has just cited Heidegger: "Dying is something that every Dasein itself must take upon itself at the time [*Das Sterben muss jedes Dasein jeweilig selbst auf sich nehmen*]." He then comments:

> The question becomes concentrated in this "oneself," in the identity [*le même*] or oneself [*le soi-même*] of the mortal or the dying one [*le mourant*]. "Who" or "what" gives itself death or takes it upon himself or herself? Let us note in passing that in none of these discourses we are analyzing here [i.e., Heidegger's, Levinas's, Freud's] does the moment of death give room for one to take into account or mark sexual difference; as if, and it would be tempting to think this is so, sexual difference no longer counted in the face of death: it would be the ultimate horizon, namely the end of sexual difference. Sexual difference would be a being-*up-until*-death. (45; 49)

—Why would it be *tempting* to think that "sexual difference no longer counted in the face of death"?

—Perhaps because one could then imagine the death of desire, the end of life as the end of the desire to live in the caress, the folds, the hidden orifices of another's life, another's body? If the dying one has no sex, then will it not be easier—for him? for her? for "it"?—to relinquish this life, to accept death, as we say?

—It would be tempting to think so, perhaps one may even hope that it is so.

—What Derrida seems to be interrogating here, however, is also the consistent and persistent posing of this figure of death (in Freud, Heidegger, or Levinas) without sexual difference. That question is not merely a skeptical one, posed about an experience that can never be experienced or known in the present as my own. Rather than a radical skepticism, there is the certainty of the experience of death as always also the death of another to whom one is addressed in particular and thus in function of sexual difference, sexual differences.

This is the essence of a dispute or a *differend* between Heidegger and Levinas that, in his own way, Derrida is arbitrating. Specifically, Levinas objects to Heidegger's existential analytic of *Dasein* that it gives priority to my own death over the death of the other. And, recalls Derrida, "Levinas wants to remind us that responsibility is not first of all responsibility of myself for myself, that the sameness of myself is derived from the other, as if it were second to the other . . . " which is why Levinas can write: "I am responsible for the death of the other to the extent of including myself in that death. . . . It is the other's death that is the foremost death." Arbitrating this dispute, in effect, Derrida hears Heidegger and Levinas saying virtually the same thing. Or rather, he hears that the one cannot say what he says without the other. They are hostages to each other, at once each the hosts and ghosts of the other. The secret agreement between Heidegger and Levinas, but also with Freud and Patočka as well as so many other thinkers of finitude, is the agreement concerning sexual difference as a non-ontological, reducible difference, which therefore reaches its term before death, sexual difference being only up-until-death.

But there is another, perhaps more fundamental reason that it "might be tempting to think" that, before death, sexual difference no longer counts, no longer differentiates or determines Dasein's being. With the reduction of sexual difference, another reduction becomes possible or another suspended question gets decided: "'Who' or 'what' gives itself death or takes it upon himself or herself?" In French: "'Qui', 'qu'est-ce qui' se donne ou prend la mort sur lui ou sur elle-même?" The question of "who" or "what" is suspended from the possibility of a difference within the apparent "subject" of the dying one that each of us is. Sexual difference is not only the difference between generic sexes but first of all the difference made by being-sexual, by the finiteness and specificity of sexual being with others. It differentiates every mortal "who" or "what" as a himself, herself, itself. As Derrida here reads Heidegger, for whom death is each time my own, for whom my death can never be exchanged for another's, either given or taken, the whole possibility of giving and taking is suspended from and in the death that is each time *jemeinig,* my own. Drawing out this point, he writes: "Death would be this possibility of *giving and taking* [*donner-prendre*] that actually exempts itself from the same realm of possibility that it institutes, namely, from *giving and taking*" (44; 48). To insist, as Heidegger does, that death can neither be taken nor given, that it is each time properly my own, exempts it from the giving-to and taking-from *others;* that is, it says that death can only be given to and taken on by *oneself,* by a self, who or which is properly itself, without difference, without other selves.[7] By being toward death, *Dasein* is always being toward this proper event of itself. This is not to say, however, that *Dasein* only realizes in the moment of death its "irreducibly different singularity" (45; 49), that which makes its irreducibly different from any other "itself." For if that were the case, then it could not be *toward* death as its own death, that death which it can only give to or take from itself. The problem that Derrida detects here, and that he will work out in its most far-reaching effects in another related essay, *Aporias,* is "concentrated in the *même* or the *soi-même*" of this irreducibly different singularity of Dasein that must give itself or take on its own death. "Who" or "what" can the "soi-même" be if it is "soi-même" only by virtue of *giving or taking* its own death? For Derrida, this giving-taking remains irreducibly marked by an interval, by a difference that cannot be self-contained.

To rephrase, then, Derrida's "concentrated" question: Can we ever *know,* simply and without remainder, *who or what* dies when a mortal being—man, woman, or other finitude—ceases to be present among the living, as we say?

—Excuse me? Did I hear you correctly? For if indeed that can be a question, if it does not come with a self-evident answer, then what does it mean to die, to have to die?

—Precisely. And even to have to give oneself death.

Not without some trepidation, I ask the question of another Sarah, Sarah Kofman. Not of Sarah herself, alas, for she took her own life in 1994. But one can still ask the question of her name.

In the last text Sarah Kofman herself saw published, *Rue Ordener, rue*

Labat, the doubling of the mark of a name gives the text its own title, its own doubled name. *Rue Ordener, rue Labat* is also a book of names, names given and taken, hidden and unknown. The names are recalled from the childhood of a naturalized French Jew, a rabbi's daughter, in Paris during the deportations, her father among them, to Auschwitz, leaving six children who had to be hidden for the duration of the Occupation. As each child passes into the hands of Catholic hospitality, he or she is "rebaptized," given a new Christianized name behind which to hide. "Isaac ('christened' Jacquot) . . . Rachel (transformed into Jacqueline), Aaron (now Henri), and I . . . "[8] "I," Sarah, does not say at this point with what name she was "christened." Later, however, when she is hiding with her mother in the apartment of "the lady from la rue Labat," Sarah comes to be called "Suzanne." She is given that name by "the lady from la rue Labat" whose actual Christian name, Claire, is mentioned, I believe, only once; everywhere else, this woman is referred to metonymically through the name of the street on which she lived, rue Labat, a small street in a northern section of Paris not far from rue Ordener where Sarah and her family were living when the deportations began: "the woman who henceforth asked me to call her *mémé*, while she christened me Suzanne because that was the name closest to hers (Claire) on the calendar" (39). "Suzanne" also called her "*mémé*," and it was to *mémé* that, in transferring such a name, she also transferred the affections that should have tied her to her own mother while the three of them were living together. The mother's suffering and making-suffer an insufferable daughter. Sarah who had a brother named Isaac. Sarah who, as her father prepared himself with prayer to be taken away, watched his every gesture, fascinated. At that moment, an image-memory "touches" her mind, like the very finger of God: "The memory of the sacrifice of Isaac (whose depiction in an illustrated Bible, my Hebrew textbook from early childhood, had often worried me) fluttered through my mind" (5–6). Sarah's child was there at the sacrifice, as the daughter; she could take no responsibility for it, just a child, a child who was saved because she had two mothers, her own and another. A child who learned to read her father's language in an illustrated Bible, which touched her mind like the troubling image of another sacrifice.[9]

We have been asking whether and how the intervention of woman in the scene of sacrifice could change its law, the sacred law of a father-God. That is still the suspended question. The sacrifice of woman, by radically standing outside our representation of sacrifice, is perhaps the name that best comprises it, sums it up, brings it to a close, and therefore can respond to another command: to sacrifice sacrifice *itself.* To sacrifice that which woman *herself,* in the name "woman," has represented from a certain outside. The question is still suspended because one must decide that there is indeed a difference to be made between the sacrifice of sacrifice and the sacrifice of "woman." Between what would be a gift and what would be a sacrifice.

—But a gift, if it is truly a gift, cannot also be a sacrifice.

—It can be a name, however; perhaps indeed it can only be a name. The saving gift of names that can be given away to the other without sacrifice. They stand before *and after* what we call death, subject to a different mortality, a death that is also not what we now know it to be.

§ 6 To Give Place: Semi-Approaches to Hélène Cixous

First Approach

A matter of some gravity: that which pulls toward the earth, the lowest level, below ground even, the weight and volume with which heavier substances displace air or water. One says a matter is grave as a reminder to ponder it, to weigh it carefully, to exercise acute ethical vigilance: all the moral senses alerted to those imponderables that at every moment risk being swept aside or, worse, trampled underfoot by the ponderous march of gravity's law. If the matter is grave, then, by definition, it should not be taken lightly. Moral seriousness, it seems, requires that weight be given.

Approached from another angle, however, the scales tip in an apparent paradox: what is wanted is lightness, not weight or gravity. And it is above all a question of approach, approach to the other, under the gravest imperative to let the other escape the force of our gravity, the inertial wave that can level everything in its path, crush whatever does not have time to get out of the way. The most responsible and most serious approach advances carefully and slowly, but above all lightly—which may mean obliquely, or imperceptibly, or even not at all. For there is perhaps no more careful approach than a stillness that would let the other come out of her own, his own movement.

How to approach stillness stilly enough, lightly enough, and yet seriously enough to make some advance into the distance holding me at such a remove from the other's encounter? The question is placed here at the brink of this approach to the writing of one who could imagine the following exchange between two voices on the subject, precisely, of writing:

—Because the secret dream of writing is to be as delicate as silence.
—But is there a writing of such delicacy?
—There is one, but I don't have it. Because in order to write delicately about delicacy, one would have to be able not-to-write.
—One would have to be able to write effacement. But can one "write" effacement?[1]

This question arises for the writer who would send a first letter of love, while fearing that her words will ensnare, entrap, and finally crush the beloved beneath their law. A fear presides over this "first letter" or first approach to the other in writing: "How can I do things so is free? Concern: Fear that loving her will impose a law on her" (21).[2] Slowly, lightly, she approaches the "last sentence" and the "Ultimate Book" for which this book will have been a sort of prolegomenon, a writing-toward the "melodical cell of an entire book" (275).

If, then, the task proposed is to "write on" a writing that itself wishes secretly to approach silence and effacement, at every turn the risk, or rather the certainty, is that one will displace that delicate stillness with the volume—both the noise and the weight—of one's own descriptions. Such "writing on," the more serious and pondered and concrete it becomes, the more it flattens the intricate retreats of the other's effaced discretion into recognizable or familiar patterns, general molds, one-size-fits-all patterns of thought. The question is, then, how to write *on* without ruthlessly crushing beneath the weight of discourse that to which one wants above all to grant the chance of a certain lightness on the page, the chance of flying to meet the other, of touching her or him without touching.

Toward the beginning of the same text, the unnamed "she" who throughout will seek the "Ultimate Book" and the last phrase, recalls her earlier attempts at sentences, all of which had been discarded for making too much noise, for being "too long, too narrow, too cold, not carnal enough, much too timid, meager, and heavy as lead." She is then portrayed thinking:

> Lightness also weighs down. What I have to say is lighter than lightness or else it is not. The word "lightness" is already a weight. There is no word light enough not to weigh down the lightness of lightness.
> And what I have to say is of the realm of lightness proper. (Ibid.)[3]

The predicament "she" begins to uncover here—that "lightness proper" is itself improperly named, too heavy—and the predicament that is ours as we approach the serious lightness of this writing are not, of course, encountered uniquely in the vicinity of texts signed by Hélène Cixous. Indeed, as I will try to make clear, it is the very generality of the dilemma that accounts for its inextricableness and inevitability. Which is not to say (but this too will have to be shown) that these texts display any less singularly the marks of this general problem. There is, however, another circumstance dictating an especially circumspect approach to the writings of Hélène Cixous if we would not crush them under too much critical weight.

It is the circumstance of Cixous's reception as "French feminist theorist" in certain Anglo-American circles. Much has now been written about the imprecise, hasty divisions that this label has fostered as commentators struggled to justify its application. This hastiness or heaviness has been especially evident with regard to the writings of Cixous despite the fact, or, perhaps, rather *because* of the fact that, for a long time, and to a certain extent it is still the case, the "theorist" characterization was constructed on the basis of a very few English translations of Cixous's work.[4] For most intents and purposes, it was based on the translation of two essays in the journal *Signs* in 1976 and 1981.[5] It is indeed one of the more remarkable aspects of this reception that so few translations had appeared and yet Cixous's name was almost always included whenever the "French-feminist-theory" construction got called up.[6] Perhaps this oddity says something about such a construction's potential disregard for what happens in the encounter between languages or idioms, and more generally in the encounter with the other that is given a space in writing. In any case, we will be led to examine more closely below the reluctant relation Cixous's writing maintains to translation, not only in the narrow or "proper" sense, but all forms of transportation or transmutation—beginning with the transmutation into a "theory," French, feminist, or other.

First, however, consider how the construction of Cixous as theorist has not hesitated to dismiss or merely disregard this reluctance. One of the most symptomatic examples of such commentary is Sandra Gilbert's "Foreword" to the American translation of *La jeune née* [*The Newly Born Woman*] in 1986, which is titled "A Tarantella of Theory."[7] The symptom it exhibits is in fact double, for Gilbert seems undecided whether to try to make the "French feminist theory" label stick or, on the contrary, to dispute its pertinence. The result is a version of the "kettle logic" that Freud immortalized in his famous joke: all of this French stuff is very foreign to us American feminists; besides, our English-speaking women writers already invented it; and what they didn't invent is probably bad for you anyway. On the one hand, Gilbert insists on the strangeness of Cixous's "dazzling tarentella of theory" for the typical American readers whom she supposes for this purpose. Inadvertently, no doubt, her descriptions of this encounter manage to call up comic images: provincial American tourists squirming with disapproval as they watch some Mediterranean peasant festival in which the women, really, get far too carried away with the rhythms of the dance. On the other hand, however, Gilbert also manifestly wants to domesticate and reappropriate "French feminist theory" by comparing (and postdating) its tenets, procedures, or assertions to those of some of the Anglophone world's most respected "madwomen in the attic," Emily Dickinson or Virginia Woolf. This side of the strategy leads Gilbert to try to purify the "Dickinsonian" strain in Cixous by denouncing its admixture with a decidedly less savory association (at least for Sandra Gilbert and her imagined "typical American readers") to Lady Chatterley. "Didn't D.H. Lawrence . . . begin to outline something oddly comparable to Cixous's creed of woman before she did? . . . This often misogynistic English novelist defines an 'orgasm' whose implications, paradoxically enough, appear to anticipate the fusion of the erotic, the mystical, and the political that sometimes seems to characterize Cixous's thought on this subject. . . . " (xvii). Despite the hedging ("appear to," "sometimes seems to"), Gilbert's tactic here is unmistakable: appropriate the "good things" in Cixous by assimilating them to respected English-speaking precursors and, once the technique of comparison is in place, switch the poles to a negative, "often misogynistic" association to repel whatever cannot be assimilated.

Whereas commentary like Gilbert's seems simply not to have noticed the resistance Cixous's texts pose to this kind of appropriation, elsewhere the elaboration of the French-feminist-theory construct has shown greater awareness of the forcing required to make the mold of "theory" fit. Here is how another commentator, Toril Moi, makes her approach to what she calls "Cixous's textual jungle":

Between 1975 and 1977, [Cixous] produced a whole series of theoretical (or semi-theoretical) writings, all of which set out to explore the relations between women, femininity, feminism and the production of texts. . . . The fact that many central ideas and images are constantly repeated, tends to present her work as a continuum that encourages non-linear forms of reading. Her style is often intensely metaphorical, poetic and explicitly anti-theoretical, and her central images create a dense web of signifiers that offers no obvious edge to seize hold of for the analytically minded critic. It is not easy to operate cuts into, open vistas in or draw maps of Cixous's textual jungle; moreover, the texts themselves make it abundantly clear that this resistance to analysis is entirely intentional. Cixous believes neither in theory nor analysis . . . [8]

One may be intrigued by the slight hesitation betrayed at the outset between "theoretical (or semi-theoretical)" to qualify the so-called "whole series" of writings in question; nevertheless, the potentially interesting notion of the "semi-theoretical" is simply dropped as Moi proceeds to dismiss the "abundantly clear . . . resistance" to the kind of analysis (or semi-analysis) she wants to perform. The principles of that analysis are themselves made clear in this initial paragraph and they derive from the familiar set of distinctions that includes expression vs. thought, style vs. substance, metaphoric vs. literal, and poetic vs. theoretical. All of the first terms in these pairs designate or describe what makes it difficult for this "analytically minded critic" to seize and to cut. Difficult, perhaps, but not impossible as long as one remains confident that, whatever the complications and implications, expression, style, metaphor, and poetry may finally be treated as incidental adjuncts to thought, substance, and so forth. And, most important, they are considered to be without relevance to what interests Moi above all: politics. Given the more or less unquestioning assumption of these conventional analytical categories, the fact that Moi goes on from there to find little good to say about Cixous's "whole theoretical project" (105) cannot come as too much of a surprise.[9] Things would perhaps look different if one pursued the less predictable category or the non-category of the "semi-theoretical." For her part, however, Moi is intent on nailing down "the *kind* of feminist theory and politics [Cixous] represents" (104).[10]

The pairing of "theory" with "politics," here in Moi's phrase but also in the title of her book, may be read as confirming a widely shared axiom: a literary theory, which is to say, a theory of meaning and value, is necessarily a theory of politics, even or especially if it does not explicitly claim to be so. The axiom is the distilled result of an intense exploration, over several decades (in fact, ever since Nietzsche), of "theory"'s limits. We now call "theory" the practical demonstration of how and why theory is not in fact possible as an act of thinking uncontaminated by contingency, particularity, or experiential differences.[11] Because it cannot avoid putting these differences materially and practically into play, "theory" is political: it is implicated necessarily in the very process of signification and symbolization it describes, the process by which some differences are made to represent difference in general. And in this sense as well, "theory" is always semi-theory.

It is not easy to reckon with this insight. If theory is always semi-theory, then there is no telling absolutely when and where the semi-theoretical and semi-political may shade off into the semi-poetic or semi-fictional or some other semi-recognizable mode since such distinctions are rendered rather dubious by the contaminating non-category of the "semi-." Nevertheless, the "semi-"is not, as some may want to claim, an excuse for renouncing literary theory, which is to say, a thinking about written texts that seeks a certain generality. On the contrary, and this is the difficulty, such thinking opens onto a responsibility to that which is only glimpsed beneath the effacement of the prefix "semi-" on all names and general concepts. A semi-name is not altogether there, it does not name a presence, nothing that *is*; rather, it calls for something to present itself otherwise. If semi-theory responds to, is responsible for, this semi-effacement that carries so little weight in the present, it is because it gives place to that which as yet has no name: a future.

Cixous is one of our age's greatest semi-theoreticians. And as such, she will disappoint whoever supposes that theory's political responsibility begins and ends in a present "reality," by which is meant that which is fully present to itself rather than disseminated by the semi-. Moi's critique, for instance, is inscribed by that supposition:

> It is just this absence of any specific analysis of the material factors preventing women from writing that constitutes a major weakness of Cixous's utopia. Within her poetic mythology, writing is posited as an absolute activity of which all women *qua* women automatically partake. Stirring and seductive though such a vision is, it can say nothing of the actual inequities, deprivations and violations that women, as social beings rather than as mythological archetypes, must constantly suffer. (123)

The motive and the endpoint of this critique is to be found in the phrase "women, as social beings rather than as mythological archetypes. . . . " The term "mythological archetype" is not Cixous's, of course, but has been chosen here to qualify the "women" of whom Cixous speaks in (a few of) her semi-theoretical writings. Such so-called archetypes have no social being, which is not to say they are false, or that the evocation of these nonbeings is in error. In this, Moi agrees with Catherine Clément when, in her exchange with Cixous in *The Newly Born Woman*, she said: "Your level of description is one where I don't recognize any of the things I think in political terms. It's not that it's 'false,' of course not. But it's described in terms which seem to me to belong to the level of myth or poetry . . . " (124). The politics invoked by Clément or Moi implies first of all an ontology. Which means that the "women" to whom they would refer are those beings classified (and restricted) as such, that is, "social beings." This is, ultimately, but a tautology of reference: "women" means (those beings who are called) women. And "women"'s sociality is understood here as that which is named by the fundamental social convention of a stable referential language.

Cast in its starkest terms, the distinction Moi (or Clément) invokes is between a politics and a poetics of "women." The former, it is supposed, cannot do without a stable reference to the "actual" experience of social beings (in Moi's phrase above, "the actual inequities, deprivations and violations that women, as social beings . . . must constantly suffer"). The latter, on the other hand, dispenses not with reference but with referents; it is a practice of what has been called reference without referent.[12] But once again as regards such distinctions, are we not obliged to have recourse to the notion of the semi- in order to account for a politics that must also be a poetics? For indeed what kind of politics would be possible given a stable referential system, in which tautology stands in for ontology? If in fact "women" were confined (but on whose order? by what law?) in the tautology of reference, in the actuality of the present, if one could name with that term only an ontologically pre-determined being (the "social being" in question for Moi), then could there even be a politics of women, a feminist politics? The term "woman" is a political term because it can be expropriated from any "actual" referent, turned aside from a given coded function. Just like any other term, and still differently. A politics is possible only to the extent that the referential tautology can be expropriated, indeed, has already expropriated itself, which is to say, it is possible only to the extent that, between "women" as "actual, social beings" and women as *something else, something other* than this apparent actuality, the distinction is unenforcable because unlocalizable. This possible politics is that of semi-reference, or of reference without referent, which names the impossible "thing which is not."

A practice of semi-reference like Cixous's will, therefore, require one to read this expropriability at work within texts that appear to be making theoretical statements about "women." To illustrate, one may recall any one of a number of frequently cited passages from "Sorties" in *The Newly Born Woman*, for example:

> I will say: today, writing is women's. That is not a provocation, it means that woman admits there is some other. In her becoming-woman, she has not erased the bisexuality latent in the girl as in the boy. Femininity and bisexuality go together. . . . It is much harder for the man to let himself be traversed by some other. Writing is the passageway, the entrance, the exit, the dwelling-place of the other in me—the other that I am and am not, that I don't know how to be, but that I feel passing, that makes me live—that tears me apart, disturbs me, changes me, who?—a feminine one, a masculine one, some?—several, some unknown, which is indeed what gives me the desire to know and from which all life soars. This peopling leaves neither rest nor security, always disturbs the relationship to the "real," produces an uncertainty that gets in the way of the subject's socialization. It is distressing, it wears you out; and for men this permeability, this nonexclusion is a threat, something intolerable. . . . It is true that a certain receptivity is "feminine." One can, of course, as History has always done, exploit feminine reception as alienation. . . . But I am speaking here of femininity as keeping alive the other that is confided to her, that visits her, that she can love as other. . . . Through the same opening that is her danger, she comes out of herself to go to the other, a traveler in unexplored places; she does not deny, she approaches, not to do away with the space between, but to see it, to experience what she is not, what she is, what she can be. (85–86; trans. modified)[13]

There is a potentially vertiginous effect set off by the series of semi-referential turns negotiated here. It begins with the first assertion, "today writing is women's," which advances its sense only on the condition of a reciprocal untying of "writing" and "women" from their ordinary, or "actual," referents. The assertion consists of a coassignment of each term's meaning to the other: hence (and henceforth: "aujourd'hui") I will say "writing" is that which is given over to "women" and, with the same gesture, that a "woman" is whoever is given to "writing." The coassignment in question, however, is less something to be asserted or described than forcefully put in play by the very practice that writes "writing" and "women" as each given over to the other, as the site of the admission "that there is some other." It is, however, a *coup de force* against near insuperable odds, against the resistant logic of opposing names. For Cixous here would rename "women" with the name of the other even while retaining the same name. The text thus advances through *contradiction*, countering logical diction with force, which precipitates more than one difficulty.

For example: "Femininity and bisexuality go together. . . . It is much harder for the man to let himself be traversed by some other." If "femininity" is the welcome given to the other "that I am and that I am not," then linking it to or renaming it "bisexuality" appears to accommodate that welcome. Yet, the "bi-" also indicates a duality, one whose other face is recognizable by its symmetrically opposed features: man or masculinity, that which does not easily let itself be traversed by the other. There would thus seem to be a limit posed on the "bisexual" welcome given to the other, and it is the limit setting off "masculine" exclusion from the "feminine" welcome. But this limit determines a "bisexuality" that in effect excludes the "masculine," or, what amounts to the same, a "bisexuality" that is exclusively "feminine." Which is to say, a "bi-" that is precisely not dual or, still less, pluralized, but gathered up within a single and same concept, "femininity," even as the latter is being rewritten here as the mark of a certain plurality. It would seem that the intractable logic of opposition has played its formidable hand to counter the text's pluralizing movement. In so doing, that logic uncovers a seemingly paradoxical *identity of the plural* constructed over against the identity of the same, "masculine" identity. But that is not all. For if, finally, a logic of identity prevails here over its pluralization, tracing a limit that falls between "feminine" and "masculine" along a division that remains in place despite the nominal introduction of "bisexuality," then there will have been all the same a crossing of the border between the two, a kind of contamination of the feminine by its masculine other. This crossing occurs less as a welcome laid out for the other, however, than as an unadmitted admission, when admission is refused to that which is defined as refusing admission to the other. But what is refused is thereby admitted since "femininity," if it wants to keep its name, must admit that for which the other is named "masculine": the desire, precisely, to keep its name and with that an identity. "Femininity" cannot name only itself precisely because it would name itself to the exclusion of the other name, the name of exclusion. And in that sense, which is the sense in question here, the "feminine" is "masculine." The price of keeping the name is losing it.

At the same time, with the same gesture, drawn here and crossed over is the limit of a possible theory of the "feminine," that is, of a certain concept of "woman" posed, or imposed, by its name. In the construction of "French feminist theory," is it not this limit that has to remain unremarked? Perhaps, however, in the appropriation of Cixous's writings for that construction, the limit has been translated, so to speak, into the limit of translation. That is, perhaps the fact that this appropriation has relied on limited translations can itself be interrogated for its theoretical import.

With its very name, "French feminist theory" presumes that the theory in question is translatable. And indeed what kind of theory could ever presume otherwise? Tied to an idiom, to a particular, singular, linguistic site of formulation, theoretical concepts would be prevented from posing their universal, generalizable validity. Which is why, by "theory," one always understands also a certain theory of translation, in fact the necessity of a translation without remainder or resistance. "French feminist theory" is theoretical to the extent it is translatable. This explains in part why the construction could occur, or even had to occur, as a phenomenon in a language other than the original. (And given the presumption of translation, the "French" label, which cannot be the mark of linguistic particularity, ends up thematizing some unspecified cultural difference and provoking the sort of uneasy and defensive recuperations we saw in Sandra Gilbert's commentary.) By remarking the apparent resistance of Cixous's texts to translation in the ordinary sense, I am pointing once again to the notion of the semi-theoretical. Here "semi-" would mark the tie to a language or idiom, at the same time as it works to loosen the referential link, to open meaning's construction to the future's deconstruction. Translation, in effect, has to reverse this process, at least in part: it reasserts referential value in order to sever the relation to the other language. The point, however, is not to reiterate this limit on translatability, and thus on theory, but to advance always under the necessity of thinking, in terms that are as rigorous as possible, the semi- (semi-theoretical, semi-translatable, semi-referential, semi-fictional), there where a difference crosses with the generality of the concept.

This necessity has been made more apparent than ever by the impasse into which a certain thinking of difference (gender difference, but not only gender difference, of course) seems to have been led in recent years. Naomi Schor is certainly not alone when she insists on "the urgency of rethinking the very terms of a conflict which all parties would agree has ceased to be productive."[14] The "conflict" is understood here as that between essentialism and anti-essentialism, one which Schor and others want to rethink in a way that will preserve an essential unity of the feminine without which feminism, as a theoretical construct and political position, seems incoherent. But whether one adopts the terms essentialism/anti-essentialism or others to qualify the nature of the opposition, the rethinking that is called for must finally rethink, which is to say displace, opposition itself as the structuring concept of difference. This is the condition of marking a difference that does not return, like a debt to be paid, to the concept of the same.

In a note to the same essay, Schor writes: "The question that arises is: how to theorize a subjectivity that does not reinscribe the universal, that does not constitute itself by simultaneously excluding and incorporating others?" (56 n. 5). If indeed that question arises, has it not be given its impetus by the experience of a certain impossibility at the heart of such a theorization? An experience that is inscribed in the very terms of the question as posed here? It asks: what would a subject be that excludes exclusion and yet at the same time avoids incorporation of what it does not exclude? But this question soon begets others, for example: How can such a subject exclude exclusion without excluding itself as nonexclusive? And what would be the difference finally between this wished-for subject-in-theory and the classical subject described as "simultaneously excluding and incorporating others"? Each is consigned to an *essential* impossibility of reserving the subject exclusively for itself and no other. Each is delivered over to the experience of the impossibility of being its own subject, of presenting itself to itself without difference, without delay, without others. The wished-for theorization is, moreover, the very form in which this impossibility imposes its limit at every moment on my experience of a subjectivity that is never "mine." For the subject in question is already theorized, that is, it has the form of a general concept, and this theorization or generalization is the condition of its impossible appropriation by anyone, any *one*. A call to retheorize the subject, in order more properly to take account of the differences that remain uninscribed by the universal, must set out from this limit on appropriation, rather than from the wishful desire to lift it so as finally to overcome the exclusion of exclusion.

It is as the site of the experience of the impossible that the "subject" in all its difference from "itself" can be rethought otherwise than as a new inscription of the exclusive universal. An experience of the impossible, which is to say, of the other. This task for an active thinking cannot be reduced, however, to a theorization of the limit or the impossible appropriation: at some point, it will have to encounter that limit *in itself* as the limit posed, each time differently, to the theorization it would perform. Of necessity, the theory in question, if it is to be rigorous, must affirm itself as semi-theory. What is needed and what is called for is not, therefore, a new theory of the "subject," for that project always lures one with the promise of appropriation, of a finally appropriate concept of difference in all its difference. Rather, it is to the possibility of the semi- (the possibility, if you will, of an impossible name) that the excluded other of the subject calls.

"The semi-" would be here an impossible name, a semi-name for that which each time must be addressed differently. With its hyphen, or *trait d'union*, it signals the space within the name of a heterogeneity, that for which there is no common measure other than the minimal mark of co-appearance—minimal, almost weightless as it waits for the other's approach. A spacing . . . that which gives place to writing.[15]

Second Approach

Toward the end of *Limonade tout était si infini*, the writer recounts a remarkable event. It is a *grazing* encounter, which nevertheless has the force of a tremendous explosion. A man (F.) was taken by his friend (M.) to meet a third (O.) who was blind. When the two were presented to each other, standing face to face, F., the visitor, silently executed a bow of the head to O. in acknowledgment. This gesture, unseen by the one to whom it was addressed, nevertheless managed to touch him because when the visitor, who was Franz Kafka, lowered his head, his hair *grazed* the blind man's forehead. Neither Kafka nor his friend, Max Brod, seemed to have realized what had happened, but the third man, the addressee, consigned his experience the next day to a typewritten account, which Cixous transcribes in part as follows:

> It was as if lightning had struck me. At the contact of that hair, I felt a pain which I could not confess to my friends, but that pain caused me *a joy*; I could not hold back my tears. They seemed to flow directly from my heart. Then, as if by the violence of the flow, a veil of night was torn from my pupils: I thought I saw—I am lying—I did see, with certainty, with my eyes as if I were suddenly seeing the light. (245–46)[16]

"For the first time," he wrote, "someone considered my infirmity to be a fact that concerned only myself" (244).[17]

The writer of *Limonade* recounts this extraordinary event with infinite caution so as not to crush its diaphanous miracle with words. "What gives this scene its fragility, which could be broken by a word, is the fact that it almost does not take place, so to speak, because it happened in the invisible. The unsayable delicacy of the gesture: to make a sign for sight in front of a blind man, and thus not to deprive him of the most diaphanous respect" (241).[18] "Each word casts more shadow" (ibid). "Perhaps I have used words that are too gross, too visible?" (240). Like Kafka, she would bring an extreme discretion to the encounter with the other. Called upon to render a silent gesture and an invisible touch, words are too loud, too visible. And yet, the grazed forehead also touches the dream of an impossible address for the Cixousian writer, "the secret dream of writing," which is to be "as delicate as silence." To write of this scene is to dream of reproducing it, to take it as the model of writing. But it is an ungraspable model, or rather, it is the ungraspable as at once model and without model, at once a generalizable, repeatable mark and an unreproducible singularity. This doubled mark is the mark of a dreamed-of writing. How so?

Kafka bows his head to the other. He executes, that is, a highly conventional gesture signifying respect, assent, greeting, or obedience, but which, precisely because it belongs to the code of polite address, does not address his interlocutor specifically. Instead, it is a general address, and the respect it signifies is a function of this generality. It addresses the other as, in effect, the same as all those to whom one owes respect, all others, regardless of any and all difference. More precisely, it acknowledges the other as other than him- or herself, as more than or greater than a contingent, finite self, and finally, it addresses its respect to no one in particular, but to a concept of the other as that to which respect is owed.[19] This is the condition of the iterability of any mark, here the mark of respect. While it is usually buried beneath the very convention it makes possible, this condition of repetition is made to appear in a singular manner in the event recounted by Cixous's writer. It appears, so to speak, in its invisibility to the blind man for whom the conventional address seems most inappropriate. But because the mark is inappropriate with regard to his blindness, because it addresses him without respect to this contingency but in the mode of respect for a general concept of the other, it is able to close a gulf where a different, though no less general mark (grasping the hand, for example) would have had no such effect.

This is not all, however, for it does not yet account for the effect of the doubling of the mark. Kafka bows his head to the other. He touches his interlocutor with the same gesture that repeats a general address. This other mark is accidental, contingent, inadvertent, and therefore singular, but also indissociable from the conventional, deliberate, and general mark. The stunning effect of the episode derives, finally, from this indissociability, from the fact that the same gesture does and does not address the other in his singularity, does and does not address the other as general concept. The one and the other indissociably, and thus effectively. If the accident had not accompanied the execution of the gesture, then the blind man most likely would not have known he had been addressed as he was, which is to say, not as himself but as a general other. But precisely because he did perceive the mark it was no longer simply the general mark he perceived, but that mark doubled by its singular address.[20] What has occurred, no less by chance than by convention, is an implication of the singular in the general and vice versa, the one made possible by and given to the other: difference literally grazes, crosses its general concept.

In what sense is this event an event of writing? In the sense that its sense is disseminated, and therefore there can be gift, something given without return and without reappropriation. Cixous is here thinking through the paradoxical non-economy of the gift, more powerfully and consequently even than in the semi-theoretical terms advanced in *The Newly Born Woman*. In the earlier essay, what is called gift does not give without taking, without reappropriating what is given in a return to the giver. Nevertheless, a distinction is made there between two kinds of "giving-for," which are in turn aligned with masculine and feminine economies of identity:

> in the movement of desire, of exchange, he is the en-grossing party; loss and expense are stuck in the commercial deal that always turns the gift into a gift-that-takes. The gift brings in a return. Loss, at the end of the curve, is turned into its opposite and comes back to him as profit.
>
> But does woman escape this law of return? Can one speak of another spending? Really, there is no "free" gift. You never give something for nothing. But all the difference lies in the why and how of the gift, in the values that the gesture of giving affirms, causes to circulate; in the type of profit the giver draws from the gift and the use to which he or she puts it. . . .
>
> She too gives *for*. She too, with open hands, gives (to) herself—pleasure, happiness, increased value, enhanced self-image. But she doesn't try to "recover her expenses." She is able not to return to herself, never settling down, pouring out, going everywhere to the other. (87; trans. modified)[21]

Once again, the practice of semi-reference is set to work detaching "woman" from an actual referent and reattaching it to another, here to the gift that does not return to the giver, reattaching it, in other words, to dissemination. But as we saw in the earlier passage, the logic of identity is also working to counter the effort to pluralize or de-propriate the "proper" of femininity. The consequence is a return of the feminine to itself, which finally gives itself the gift of its own generosity, an "enhanced self-image." Unlike in the passage cited above from the same text, however, this consequence is conceded at the outset when Cixous writes, "Really, there is no 'free' gift. You never give something for nothing." As these categorical assertions ought to make plain, it cannot be a question of distinguishing between gift and nongift, but rather only between two ways of taking back the "gift," two ways, therefore, of taking what one gives. If, however, there is no gift that is not already a gift-for, that is, a giving-in-order-to-get-back, then what can it mean to write of "woman," as Cixous does here: "She is able not to return to herself, never settling down, pouring out, going everywhere to the other"? And then to add, in another attempt to contradict the stated law of identity and of the non-gift, "If there is a 'proper' trait of woman, it is paradoxically her capacity to de-propriate herself without calculation"?

What it *can* mean is a certain possibility of *thinking* the gift (and thus a woman "able not to return to herself") beyond or despite its impossibility in fact or in reality, beyond and despite the fact that "there is no 'free' gift." This fact or reality of the nongift comes down to and comes back to its subject, whether giver or receiver. So long as the gift is considered only in the form of gift-for/from-a-subject, then it can only be a matter of more or less taking, a matter of degrees of the nongift. In this regard, the "masculine" nongift would be but a version of the "feminine"—or vice versa. What would be a gift that returns to neither, to no subject, to no instance of appropriation? An impossible gift since, as Derrida has argued in *Given Time,*

> For there to be gift . . . it is thus necessary, at the limit, that [the donor] not *recognize* the gift as gift. If he recognizes it *as* gift, if the gift *appears to him as such*, if the present is present to him *as present*, this simple recognition suffices to annul the gift. . . . *At the limit, the gift as gift* ought *not to appear as gift; either to the donee or the donor.* It cannot be gift as gift except by not being present as gift.[22]

The gift can never be (a) present, a gift as such, that is, it cannot present itself *for* a subject. As Cixous had intimated when she wrote "you never give something for nothing," the gift cancels itself out in the "gift-for" by which a subject capitalizes its loss. Derrida works through this aporia to the point at which the gift disappears with the very appearance of this subject. The gift is annulled

> as soon as there is a subject, as soon as donor and donee are constituted as identical, identifiable subjects, capable of identifying themselves by keeping and naming themselves. It is even a matter, in this circle, of the movement of subjectivation, of the constitutive retention of the subject that identifies with itself. . . . The question of the gift should therefore seek its place before any relation to the subject, before any conscious or unconscious relation to self of the subject. . . . One would even be tempted to say that a subject as such never gives or receives a gift. (23–24)]

This "place" of the question of the gift, "before any relation to the subject, before any conscious or unconscious relation to self of the subject," is what Derrida has been calling trace, differance, writing in the general sense: "there is a problematic of the gift only on the basis of a consistent problematic of the trace and the text" (130). For a subject, the gift is impossible, but the *thinking* of this impossibility is opened up where an economy of the proper can only turn in its own circles:

> For, finally, if the gift is another name of the impossible, we still think it, we name it, we desire it. We intend it. And this *even if* or *because* or *to the extent that* we never encounter it, we never know it, we never verify it, we never experience it in its present existence or in its phenomenon. The gift *itself*—we dare not say the gift *in itself*—will never be confused with the presence of its phenomenon. Perhaps there is nomination, language, thought, desire, or intention only where there is this movement still for thinking, desiring, naming that which gives itself to be neither known, experienced, nor lived. (29)

It is to this possibility of the impossible, to the movement of thought, desire, and naming in the absence of an apparent phenomenon of gift, that Cixous's writing is given over. In *Limonade*, the writing finds an emblem in Kafka's gesture. His is an effacement that nevertheless inscribes itself with the lightest of touches. "What is ineffaceable in the story is F.'s effacement: in order to make such a delicate gesture, one has to have become as transparent as a dragonfly [*libellule*], as light as a grasshopper [*sauterelle*] . . . " (241).[23] In rewriting this ineffaceability, Cixous transports the desired qualities of transparency and lightness on the syllabic wings or *ailes* of two names: *libellule, sauterelle*. It is a most delicate operation for it would disseminate the ineffaceable effacement throughout a text woven with the repetition of "ell."[24] Ell, as in the name of the beloved Elli, to whom the writer would send a first letter of love. But with that name, one reads—or rather she reads—the letter's forwarding to a general address: *elle (qui) lit*, she (who) reads. To Elli, to elle-lit, she would send, that is, give, with a gesture that repeats the transparency and the lightness of the grazing dragonfly and leaping grasshopper. A double gesture in one: addressed to Elli alone, but comprehended in a general address to every "elle (qui) lit."

But, still, how to give without weighing down with debt?

> How can I say to her "I want you to know you are free" without the sentence catching her between its paw-like words, if only to caress her, and in its desire to confide in her its good intention, obliging her to slow down? . . . And the question is: can one give without taking part? How to let something be known without words? Silence is also speech. . . . For to think the mysteries of giving, which are as delicate as butterfly wings, required a delicacy of exactly the same nature. Just thinking about it made her feel her own heaviness. (18–20)[25]

In contrast to this heaviness, there is Kafka's effacement, his address to the other that manages to give without incurring debt. But how so, exactly? "The marvelous thing about this story is how F. manages to give, even if O. is not up to receiving." And yet "the gift has indeed been received" (243). It is indeed received, and well received, "il est bien reçu," because an incalculable difference opens up within the address, which sends it off beyond any possibility of return: "The miracle had already begun to take place. Remains the additional trait: the unexpected effacement of F.'s effacement" (ibid.). The effacement of the effacement, what one might call the splitting between its two faces, is a mark of which there is no author, no one to whom a debt is due. It is the uncalculated, incalculable chance whereby the general gesture is split by the grazing touch of a singular address. In that split moment, there is a gift that calls for no return, no gratitude, no recognition. The splitting cuts across, so to speak, the two sides to the encounter, as each is divided by the incalculable address; neither coincides with himself in that moment and from that moment, and this noncoincidence is the space of the encounter with the other.

For Cixous, this space of encounter, of writing, or of dissemination of the gift remains *impossible* not because it is wholly imaginary as some would have it, but because the noncoincidence with the other cannot be made present to a subject. Nor does this impossibility signal toward some utopian escape from the gravity of the world's affairs. For the gravest of questions in that world is still: what *takes place* in the approach to the other? Or, to put it in other terms, what gives there? What gives beyond the calculations of exchange, the taking grasp of appropriation? What place is *given* that is not already taken back?

—But "to give place" is not an idiomatic English expression.

—No, which is why in order to think its necessity one must approach the idiom of the other, the untranslatability of the *donner lieu*, that place-less place in which the impossible encounter takes place as a giving of place beyond or before any give-and-take. A place-less place or a silent word, unballasted of even the slightest weight, a breathless word, perhaps, *hors d'haleine*, extenuated from its effort of leaping at the impossible, à la *sauterelle*, of understanding (as one reads in a phrase I will leave untranslated so as to give place to the other's breath and the other's name) "non avec des phrases de haute voix mais plutôt avec l'haleine du sang d'âme" (189).

Fictions of Address

§ 7   "Fiction" and the Experience
of the Other

For Derek Attridge, in answer to a question

How can we take fiction seriously? The question may be either serious or
not-so-serious, an urgently real question or a dismissively rhetorical one.
In this form and without any context, it sets up an undecidable oscillation
between its grammar and its rhetoric, as Paul de Man might have noted.[1]
On the one hand, it asks, seriously, to know how to take fiction seriously,
thus also implying that this is something we must or should do, while, on
the other hand, it says that we cannot take fiction seriously, that it is not
to be taken seriously, that it is even the name of everything which must
not be taken seriously.

Let this undecidable grammar stand for the doggedness of the problem
we have taking fiction seriously. The question (or statement) resonates to
its full, oscillating extent perhaps only in the place where it is already supposed that one *can* take fiction or literature seriously: in that wing of the
literary institution housed in the university. Throughout its brief history,
academic literary studies will never have had all that much difficulty
achieving its standing as a serious undertaking in that institution.[2] In the
last decade or so, however, it appears that the discipline of literary studies
has begun to negotiate a transition or a displacement into the almost unlimited domain of cultural studies, media studies, communications, and
so forth. This development may well indicate that a growing number of
practitioners in this domain has renounced the project of taking literature
seriously, at least under that name. In any case, it signals some displacement there that affects literature as the name of something to be taken seriously, in a disciplined manner.

This development might be seen as the most recent outcome of the long-standing misunderstanding between the university, as a project of knowledge, and literature, that object about which no essential knowledge is possible. Literature's inclusion among the divisions of knowledge has always been highly ambivalent and incomplete. This ambivalence is such that it can never be finally resolved, only provisionally relieved.[3] A construction that provided some relief for a time was what came to be called literary theory—a misnomer if there ever was one. But the misnomer was no accident; rather, it satisfied the requirement of the discourse of knowledge. And for a while it seemed to bury the ambivalence in a title (and in innumerable course titles in university catalogs), one whose ambiguity could then be forgotten. For the title "literary theory" may be understood grammatically in at least two ways: as a theory *of* literature, and as literary theory, that is, theory *qualified as* literary or *modified by* the literary. In the first sense, the phrase implies that literature is an *object* of theoretical knowledge like any other, while in the second sense, it implies some qualification or modification of theoretical knowledge itself, perhaps even a transformation of its whole basis. "Literary theory" was thus able to absorb the fundamental ambivalence into these two, not necessarily compatible ideas. Eventually the *malentendu* would have to resurface and would do so in the obvious place, around the question of the literary qualifier or modifier. For indeed, what is literary about literary theory?

This is, as always, a very good question, but it is also irresolvable as soon as it is posed as an ontological question—*What is*, e.g., the literary, literariness, literature? Literature is essentially nothing, essentially nothing but its name. The name of literature has always been peculiarly full of emptiness. This has something to do with why it will have been so easily displaced. But precisely because it is empty of substance, literature is also tied to and dependent on its name. It exists in name only, we could say. This does not mean that the particular name literature, itself, is irreplaceable. Of course it is not, as its history could easily confirm. The name is replaceable; it is even effaceable, at least in theory, although one has to concede that, for quite practical reasons, "literature" is not about to be effaced from the general archive any time soon. Which is fortunate, because that means we still have time to figure out what, if anything, should be saved from the ruins.

I am going to argue here that it is a certain notion of *fiction* or the fictional operation that, above all, ought not to be dispensed with. In the inaptly named literary theory, it is the irreducible possibility of fiction that is brought to bear in such a way as to shift the ground on which any theoretical discourse may claim validity. Essentially, literary theory takes *fiction* seriously. By this I mean simply that it prizes literature's display of the fictional operation and isolates it as a lever with which to shift a number of familiar theoretical assumptions. Although these have classically found their place in a strictly philosophical tradition and have even defined that tradition to a certain extent, they are certainly not confined to formal philosophy. Philosophy, however, in order to formalize its system, has had to rely on certain assumptions concerning what the fictional operation is or does, assumptions that not coincidentally allow one to proceed *as if* the possibility of fiction had been eliminated, *at least in theory*. It is thus assumed that one need not take fiction or the possibility of fiction into account in order to construct a valid theory of how truth is to be made, known, or recognized. On the contrary, one of the most consistently recurring gestures of philosophical discourse makes out literary fiction in particular but all so-called representative art in general to be essentially dependent or parasitical on, therefore secondary to the whole presumed realm of "non-fiction."

Let us take an example, which will be familiar to many. In *How to Do Things with Words*, J. L. Austin writes that, when spoken on stage or in a poem, language is "in special ways—intelligibly—used not seriously, but in ways *parasitic* upon its normal use—ways which fall under the doctrine of the *etiolations* of language." This determination is meant to set up and indeed to justify the exclusion that the next sentence performs: "All this we are *excluding* from consideration."[4] In his reading of this passage, which would figure prominently in a subsequent dispute with the philosopher John Searle, one can see how Derrida executes very precisely with a series of questions what I described above as a shift of the theoretical ground:

> What is the status of this *parasitism*? In other words, does the quality of risk admitted by Austin *surround* language like a kind of *ditch* or external place of perdition which speech could never hope to leave, but which it can escape by remaining "at home," by and in itself, in the shelter of its essence or *telos*? Or, on the contrary, is this risk rather its internal and positive condition of possibility? Is that outside its inside, the very force and law of its emergence? In this last case, what would be meant by an "ordinary" language defined by the exclusion of the very law of language? In excluding the general theory of this

structural parasitism, does not Austin . . . pass off as ordinary an ethical and teleological determination?[5]

These questions are provoked by Austin's easy acquiescence to philosophical doctrine as regards the status of the literary or fictional object. By defining that status as parasitical on ordinary language use, the doctrine Austin uncritically endorses encloses theory, for example the theory of speech acts, within the limited and finally untenable space from which its own conditioning possibility has been excluded. Instead of elucidating the theorized object's real possibilities, the theory truncates them so as to uphold an "an ethical and teleological determination" of the object. At this juncture at least, it closes the door on a general theory that can account in the same terms for all speech acts, without recourse to a prior determination of what constitutes "serious" or "non-serious" speech.

Thus, the shift onto a more general theoretical terrain has to put in question what Austin calls here the "doctrine of the etiolations of language." Doubtless this doctrine would identify many kinds of "etiolations" other than the literary. Yet, it is certainly not by chance that, to illustrate the sort of utterance he has in mind, Austin goes to the storehouse of literature, as broadly defined: "a performative utterance will, for example, be *in a peculiar way* hollow or void if said by an actor on the stage, or if introduced in a poem, or spoken in soliloquy" (ibid; Austin's italics). Theater and poetry are cited precisely because they are exemplary of the hollowing or voiding of utterance that we recognize as the consequence of fiction's operation. Although, as Austin acknowledges, such hollowing out can happen to utterance anywhere and not just in a poem, on a theater's stage, or in a novel, these more or less generic categories serve to *announce or mark* the work of fiction by calling it poem, play, novel, story, soliloquy, and so on. In this way, the categories *marked out* as fiction seem to offer themselves as example, whenever one needs one, of a *general* operation of fiction that, as Austin puts it, can "infect *all* utterances" (21; Austin's italics).

What, however, is literature exemplary of, exactly? What does the fictional operation do? Before going much further trying to take fiction seriously, shouldn't one be clear at least about what it is that solicits such serious concern? Or rather, not what it *is* but what it *does*? The question concerning fiction is not: what is it? but rather, what does it do? This form of the question is dictated at least in part by the word itself, deriving as it does from the Latin past-participle root *fict-* of the transitive verb *fingere*:

to shape, fashion, make, feign, contrive, invent; (cf. *fictor, fictoris*: a fashioner, counterfeiter). Fiction would be a kind of doing, then, even though the word is most often used now as a noun. As a substantive, however, it names something without substance, hollow, false, or, as Austin preferred to say, void. ("Is not a statement," he asked, "which refers to something which does not exist not so much false as void?" [20].) A fiction refers to nothing that exists. It refers, but to nothing in existence. Thus, the fictional act or operation consists in making reference but also in suspending the referent. It is a referential operation that does something with or to reference.

Let us try to specify further the nature of this referential operation. As we've just seen, literary fiction, because of its peculiar hollowness, is left out of consideration by Austin in his elaboration of a theory of speech acts. Despite that, he shows persistent interest in the general question of how the referent may be, as he calls it, voided by a statement, that is, by a constative utterance. He takes up this question in a section of the second lecture, right before the passage already cited, where he is wondering whether the sort of "infelicity" that can characterize performative utterances can also affect the way a *statement* does what it is supposed to do, which is to refer, reliably, to a true or real state of affairs.

> Lastly we may ask—and here I must let some of my cats on the table—does the notion of infelicity apply to utterances *which are statements*? So far we have produced the infelicity as characteristic of the *performative* utterance, which was "defined" (if we can call it so much) mainly by contrast with the supposedly familiar "statement." Yet I will content myself here with pointing out that one of the things that has been happening lately in philosophy is that close attention has been given even to "statements" which, though not false exactly nor yet "contradictory," are outrageous. For instance, statements which refer to something which does not exist as, for example, "The present King of France is bald." There might be a temptation to assimilate this to purporting to bequeath something which you do not own. Is there not a presupposition of existence in each? Is not a statement which refers to something which does not exist not so much false as void? (20; Austin's italics)

When Austin specifies that a statement may be outrageous without being either false or contradictory, he makes clear that such infelicity is a matter neither of faulty logic, nor of some kind of falsehood: a lie, a misstatement, or a misapprehension of facts. It thus has some other source that he will proceed to elucidate, first by assimilating or equating the sample statement to an infelicitous performative and then by transferring the infelicity of the performative utterance to the constative one.

One sees that Austin is interested above all in the way in which, like a performative, a statement may also do something. Yet, it is difficult to determine, in the analogy he makes between the "The present King of France is bald" and a false promise, just how far one can take the assimilation of constatives to performatives. Does it go so far as to transfer moral outrage to the statement for referring to what does not exist? This is unclear.[6] According to Austin, the statement's outrageousness arises from a "presupposition of existence" that one makes upon hearing such a statement, no less than one supposes a benefactor to own what he promises to bequeath. In the case of the promise (provided, of course, it is a "serious" speech act), the presupposition is easy enough to grant: because the promise will have been made in some situation of address, the presupposition takes the form of a presumption of the other's good faith. Moreover, the addressee and potential legatee has every interest in presupposing the existence of the other's property, since he or she stands to inherit it. But in the situation of the so-called statement, why does Austin suppose that it presupposes existence?

This would seem to be because the utterance "The present King of France is bald" is understood as uttered here, now, by someone addressing me, or else it is a statement that I, or some "I," have just now made to another. Yet, the situation of present address is only one among an incalculable number of others imaginable in which the same statement might be said, even in all seriousness, without necessarily appearing outrageous One does not need to invoke theater or poetry (for Austin would have us consider only serious speech) in order to imagine many other contexts in which the same statement, "The present King of France is bald," would be altogether banal, hardly outrageous, without being either false, contradictory, or fictional, at least in the literary sense: if made, for example, in the memoirs of a royal wigmaker. Austin thus supposes that the utterance is made fully in the present, where a speaker is present to a listener, in time if not in space. This presence of the speech situation is the condition of the particular presupposition of existence that Austin makes here. Under that condition, a statement, to be fully felicitous, ought to be full of this presence, rather than the empty vehicle of a voided referent. That is the outrage. It is an outrage to presence, to the present reference, because it voids or suspends it.

This presupposition of presence has everything to do, of course, with the exclusion from serious discourse of fictional modes of speech, where all "speakers" are radically absent, that is, with an absence that has never been present. And yet, Austin's analysis of the "statement which refers to something which does not exist" situates quite precisely the standing possibility of fiction as a suspended or voided relation to the referent. He has not, however, in the least foreclosed that possibility (for how could he?). He has, however, limited the scope of the question "what do such speech acts do?" He looks for an answer there where language does something other than state what is the case, but he ends up assimilating fiction to a moral (or immoral) action. This is what Derrida identified, in the passage cited above, as "an ethical and teleological determination."

Yet, clearly Austin's fictional example of a fiction also exceeds this determination. That is, it does something more (or less) than that to which it is being compared. It also *marks and lets be remarked* the voiding of the referent, which is why it can be taken as an example of an outrageous statement in the first place. Such marking is not at all necessary for the false promise; indeed, if it wants to achieve rather than annul the effect of a promise, the speech act will have to avoid remarking and thus making known the non-existence of the referent.

Fiction, the excessive mark of fiction, suspends the sign as sign of a referent, which otherwise, without the mark, would be presupposed. As such a mark, it has its "being" only by virtue of an act of reading, whereby its mark gets remarked. It is thus less the name of an entity than the name of an *experience*. What does it mean to call fiction, literature, experience?

This term can be used here only with considerable caution, for one must take care not to understand, as one commonly does, the "lived" or "life" experience of a subject, the sum of adventures or occurrences to which some subject will have been present as conscious witness and participant.[7] It is true that literature, in the modern sense, has been massively assimilated to this notion of experience, hence to the subject. The appropriation by the subject has been mounted from at least two directions. First, when it is thought to record, represent, or report the lived experiences of a writer, literature, and above all lyric poetry, is made to stand for or refer to the full presence to itself of this subject's consciousness. Secondly, and this is above all the case for narrative fiction, when literature is thought to make available the experience of "characters," which can be assumed vicariously or virtually by the reader as his or her subjective experience for the duration of the reading. I wish to evoke, however, an experience of literature, fiction, or poetry that, on the contrary, takes place outside and before any subject, an extreme experience, therefore, because from beyond the circle within which the subject appropriates experience as its own. The extreme experience of literature recalls, as both Jean-Luc Nancy and Philippe Lacoue-Labarthe have done, that the Latin *ex-periri* at its root associates crossing with danger, risk, *periculum* at the perimeter.[8] Fiction, poetry, would be experience only on the condition that one understands: experience of the other.

But is there any other kind? What would an experience be without any intervention of difference? How could there be an experience of the same, an experience without experience, in sum, because without any difference from itself? This is the serious question that fiction keeps open, on the condition that one continues to take seriously the ways in which its excessive, extreme mark resists assimilation to and appropriation by a subject's "own" experience of presence to itself.

It is this resistance that would be remarked by "literary theory," that is, by a thinking that does not enclose itself within the presupposed existence, to recall Austin's language, of its objects or its referents. At the edge of the philosophical thesis of existence, literature offers philosophy the experience of the suspension of that thesis, which is why it can in no sense be simply opposed to the experience of philosophy that it also makes possible or even provokes. This "force of provocation" is discerned by Derrida in what he calls a neutralized or neutralizing "'philosophical'" experience:

> Even if they always do so unequally and differently, poetry and literature have as a common feature that they suspend the "thetic" naivety of the transcendent reading. This also accounts for the philosophical force of these experiences, a force of provocation to think phenomenality, meaning, object, even being as such, a force which is at least potential, a philosophical *dynamis*— which can, however, be developed only in response, in the experience of reading, because it is not hidden in the text like a substance. Poetry and literature provide or facilitate "phenomenological" access to what makes of a thesis a *thesis as such*. Before having a philosophical content, before being or bearing such and such a "thesis," literary experience, writing or reading, is a "philosophical" experience which is neutralized or neutralizing insofar as it allows one to think the thesis; it is a nonthetic experience of the thesis, of belief, of position, of naivety. . . . But it is true that . . . the phenomenological language in which I'm presenting these things ends up being dislodged from its cer-

tainties (self-presence of absolute transcendental consciousness or of the in-
dubitable *cogito*, etc.) and dislodged precisely by the extreme experience of literature, or even quite simply of fiction and language.[9]

Literary experience is a neutralized or neutralizing "philosophical" experience inasmuch as it suspends thetic referentiality, thereby allowing
one to think that thesis as such. But this neutralization is never completely
effective—it is, in a sense, itself neutralized—since, as Derrida goes on to
remark, the suspension of the referent is also, irreducibly, a suspension
from or dependence on the referent. Literature, that is, does not effect an
absolute suspension of the referent, which would destroy its structure ("a
literature that talked only about literature or a work that was purely self-
referential would immediately be annulled" [47]). Thus, whereas "literature's *being-suspended* neutralizes the 'assumption' which it carries," this
capacity remains "double, equivocal, contradictory, *hanging on* and *hanging between, dependent* and *independent*, an 'assumption' both assumed
and suspended" (49). That which I am calling the experience of fiction,
then, would be essentially equivocal, hanging as it does between the suspension of the referent, as signaled by fiction's mark, and the persistence
of the assumption of referential language, whereby fiction also always exceeds itself toward something other.

Derrida's analysis of this equivocation presents a problem, however, for
our own reliance on the term "fiction" up to this point. For fiction itself is
an equivocal term, indeed a "terribly equivocal" one, as we are reminded
here:

> The terribly equivocal word *fiction* (which is sometimes misused as though it
> were coextensive with literature) says something about this situation. Not all
> literature is of the genre or the type of "fiction," but there is fictionality in all
> literature. We should find a word other than "fiction." (Ibid.)

The point is certainly well taken and one would do well to recall the terrible equivocation "fiction" shares with the Greek *pseudos* (both poetic fiction and falsehood, lying), which Plato, for example, exploits to the full in
books 2 and 10 of *The Republic*. This equivocation can always superim-
pose itself on the necessarily ambivalent suspension of the fictional operation. And because this double suspension is irreducible, the equivocation
really is terrible, that is, terribly equivocal. Fiction is also terrifying, ter-
rorizing, or terribilizing so long as it can be taken to name those acts

called lying, perjury, misleading statement, or, as in Austin's example, false promise. That is perhaps why one should try to find another name and reserve it for "fictions" that we consent to experience as neither true nor false, innocent nor guilty, "beyond good and evil," the interpretation or, more exactly, the experience of a world without substance and without subject.

To call for another name for this "fiction" does not, however, call for the end of the equivocation as such. Rather it would displace that name with and to another name. In other words, it cannot be a matter of putting an end to equivocation, but of calling upon a plurality of names, and thus a plurivocity, more precisely a *heteronomy*. Heteronomy—the law of more than one law—preserves equivocity in another name, the name of the name, "Literature" or "fiction."

One is tempted to call out, as Juliet did into the night: Oh be some other name! The cry would echo that of every reader whose experience takes place at the limit, the extreme limit of this heteronomy. It calls into Being, it is the calling of being at the limit of everything that is, the whole world as it is presumed "to be," in Hamlet's phrase. Derrida, who has also been known to recite both *Romeo and Juliet* and *Hamlet*, puts it in these terms in the interview we've been following:

> Experience of Being, nothing less, nothing more, on the edge of metaphysics, literature perhaps stands on the edge of everything, almost beyond everything, including itself. It's the most interesting thing in the world, maybe more interesting than the world, and this is why, if it has no definition, what is heralded and refused under the name of literature cannot be identified with any other discourse. (47)

Almost beyond everything: this is the equivocation and it is irreducible. "Fiction" remains irreducibly suspended between the world of presupposed referents, which it can never fully suspend, and this same everything-of-the-world, everything-in-the-world from which it hangs suspended. It suspends the world: everything hangs from it. It is the possibility of world, of possible, virtual, fictional worlds, of other worlds.

As to finding a word other than fiction, one might look to the recurrence in this analysis of the figure of a certain neutralization. Reference is made to a "neutralized or neutralizing" philosophical experience. Neutralization is said to be the effect of the literary or the fictional on philosophy. Rather than an experience of fiction, then, would one do better to evoke an experience of neutralization, neutrality, the neuter, or the neutral? "The neutral": this term (if it is one and only one, without equivocation) has perhaps a certain force to dislodge what philosophy poses as thesis, which is always the thesis of some subject. What would be neutralized by "fiction" is the thesis, the position of the subject.

In a section or fragment of *The Infinite Conversation* in which, unless I am mistaken, the word "fiction" never occurs, Maurice Blanchot deploys a notion of "the neuter" or "the neutral" as what it becomes possible to read in the wake of Kafka's writing:[10]

> In the meantime Kafka wrote. . . . What Kafka teaches us—even if this formulation cannot be directly attributed to him—is that storytelling brings the neutral into play. Narration that is governed by the neutral is kept in the custody of the third-person "he," a "he" that is neither a third person nor the simple cloak of impersonality. The narrative "he" [*il*] in which the neutral speaks is not content to take the place usually occupied by the subject, whether the latter is a stated or implied "I" or the event that occurs in its impersonal signification. The narrative "he" or "it" unseats every subject, just as it disappropriates all transitive action and all objective possibility.[11]

Notice that Blanchot is describing here an experience that is undecidably one of writing and reading. It is an experience of narration governed no longer by a subject and an organizing subjective point of view, all of which has been neutralized from somewhere outside the circle of narrated/narrating subjects. This narration, in other words, is governed in all its aspects by the neutral, which, because it is external to language, can receive no simple name. Characterless, featureless, it is consigned or, as Blanchot writes, "kept in the custody of the third-person 'he,'" that is, of the neutral pronoun *il*, not only "he" but "it," and thus "neither a third person nor the simple cloak of impersonality." Blanchot here is signaling an essential difference with the impersonal narration achieved by Flaubert, where "the ideal is still the form of representation of classical theater" (382) and where impersonality is that of aesthetic distance. Flaubert's achievement of impersonal narration, in other words, leaves altogether intact, according to Blanchot, the Kantian, disinterested subject of aesthetic contemplation and enjoyment. It is this subjective theater of visibility and disinterested distance that Kafka's writing displaces, and displaces definitively for whoever now takes "fiction" seriously.

With Kafka, "fiction" takes itself seriously, that is, it takes seriously the demands made by an exteriority that can no longer be seen as set up for the subject's pleasure, indeed that can no longer be *seen* at all. But Kafka's writing of "the neutral, the 'he/it'" also comes after a long sequence of displacements of the passage from "I" to "he/it" that, as Blanchot recalls near the beginning of the essay, he had earlier identified as the essential gesture of writing: "If, as has been shown (in *The Space of Literature*), to write is to pass from 'I' to 'he' . . . " (135). For Blanchot, this pronoun shift marks all writing; it is even what writing essentially is or does. Literature, "fiction," is the space, however, in which this gesture is remarked in and as narrative. The narrative possibility will have been repeatedly affirmed, throughout literary "history," by the different displacements of the "he/it." Through these displacements, the neuter pronoun can be traced as the marker of "the unlighted event that occurs when one tells a story" (381). If the event is "unlighted," *inéclairé*, that is because what is taking place is a telling and not a showing, a writing and not a pointing to objects as they already are in the world. Blanchot will quickly sketch here some of these displacements: from epic story, to the disenchantment of story in *Don Quixote*, where the neutral "he/it" becomes "everyday life without adventure: what happens when nothing is happening, the course of the world as it escapes notice, the passing of time, life routine and monotonous." And, he continues, it is through this "banality of the real" that "realism seizes on the form of the novel that for a long time to come will be the most effective genre of the developing bourgeoisie." This ideological seizure finds a sturdy handle in the "he" to the extent it also

> marks the intrusion of the character: the novelist is one who foregoes saying "I" but delegates this power to others; the novel is peopled with little "egos"— tormented, ambitious, unhappy, though always satisfied in their unhappiness; . . . the novel's narration, that of individuality, is already marked . . . by an ideology to the extent that it assumes that the individual, with his particular characteristics and his limits, suffices to express the world: it assumes, in other words, that the course of the world remains that of individual particularity. (381)

It is this whole ideologically marked construction of narrative that yields, deconstructs, when, in the meantime, Kafka wrote. In Kafka's texts, as already noted, the "'he' of narration in which the neutral speaks is not content to take the place usually occupied by the subject, whether this latter is a stated or implied 'I' or the event that occurs in its impersonal signification." There is thus a shift of the essential "fictional" gesture, whereby "I" passes into "he."

As Susan Hanson has remarked in the introduction to her translation of *The Infinite Conversation*, this text should be read as continuing but also breaking with Blanchot's thinking of the "space of literature" in the earlier work by that title. She remarks:

> The break is signaled most clearly by the emergence of the problematic of *autrui*—by the *address* of *autrui* as Blanchot responds to it throughout the text. While the carefully worked through terms of the question of reflection that Blanchot brings out in his earlier critical writings in fact prepare the space of encounter with *autrui*, the thematization of *autrui* in this collection signals the intrusion of otherness with an urgency that is not heard [earlier]. (xxv–vi)

One may find a confirmation of this observation at the juncture we are examining, where, after recalling his own earlier formulation of the essential gesture of writing in the pronoun shift, Blanchot goes on to raise a fundamental question and to take it as the one to which this essay will endeavor to respond:

> If, as has been shown (in *The Space of Literature*), to write is to pass from "I" to "he," but if "he," when substituted for "I," does not simply designate another me any more than it would designate aesthetic disinterestedness—that pure contemplative pleasure that allows the reader and the spectator to participate in the tragedy through distraction—what remains to be discovered is what is at stake when writing responds to the demands of this uncharacterizable "he."

That is, what is at stake when writing no longer portrays or relays the interests of subjects? Or when it no longer pretends to *show* a spectacle to the reader's disinterest? When the question is later addressed specifically to Kafka's texts, the notion of subjective interest/disinterest is going to be displaced into the strange figure of a concern with what does not concern one and indeed concerns no one directly. But already here in this general formulation of the question, what is said to be at stake and in play is writing (or reading, still undecidably one and the other) as possibility of *response* to demands that come from some other who or which is radically uncharacterizable: the neutral. Blanchot's articulation of the stakes is very precise: "what remains to be discovered is what is at stake *when writing responds* to the demands of this uncharacterizable 'he.'" Writing responds, to the demands of the neutral other. Perhaps, then, it is simply the possibility of response—to what concerns me without concerning me—that is at stake?

This is suggested when the vocabulary of the stake, of what is *en jeu*, recurs a few pages later. The passage in question is describing the marked austerity of Kafka's narratives, which should not be confused with the austerity of Flaubertian impersonality and distance. Kafka's distance, in effect, puts something altogether other in play, *en jeu*.

> The distance—the creative disinterestedness (so visible in Flaubert inasmuch as he must struggle to maintain it)—which was the writer's and the reader's distance from the work and authorized the contemplative pleasure, *now enters into the work's very sphere in the form of an irreducible strangeness* . . . this distance is the medium of the novelistic world, the space in which the *narrative experience* unfolds in unique simplicity—*an experience that is not recounted but that is in play [en jeu] when one recounts*. This distance is not simply lived as such by the central character, who is always at a distance from himself . . . this distance keeps him aloof from himself, removing him from the center, because it is constantly decentering the work in an immeasurable and indiscernible way, while at the same time introducing into the most rigorous narration the alteration occasioned by another kind of speech or of the other as speech (as writing). (383–84; emphases added).

Although the emphases added to these sentences ought to suffice for commentary, since Blanchot's language is, as always, so precise, let us nevertheless attempt, not paraphrase, but something more like another, looser translation. It is a matter of a distance that no longer holds the work at a distance, from writer or reader, because it now *enters* the work as "irreducible strangeness." Distance is, as it were, brought closer. What does it mean to say distance enters the work? It means that distance is now in play, at stake, *en jeu* in what the passage calls the narrative *experience* (the word is repeated), which is glossed as "the experience that is not recounted but that is in play [*en jeu*] when one recounts." This description, then, is of the *entry* of distance or something distant into the experience involved "when one recounts." And what enters alters, for distance introduces "the alteration occasioned by another kind of speech . . . " Narrative experience puts in play the experience of distance and alterity.

As the description continues into a new paragraph, the term "enjeu" (now used as a compound noun) will recur once more, indicating that one is still endeavoring to respond to the question of what is at stake in this writing. But shouldn't the question also be: How can anything come to be at stake there at all? What has happened to turn writing, that space of the disinterestedness of aesthetic distance, into the space of an *enjeu*, and even perhaps (upping the ante),[12] the space of all possible *enjeux*? I continue the citation:

> One consequence [of this sort of change], immediately evident, is noteworthy. As soon as the alien distance becomes the stake [*enjeu*] and, in a sense, the substance of the story, the reader can no longer be disinterested in it; he who up to now has been identifying from afar with the story in progress (living it, for his part, in the mode of contemplative irresponsibility), *can no longer take a disinterested pleasure in it*. What is happening? What *new exigency has befallen the reader?* It is not that this concerns him: on the contrary, it concerns him in no way, and perhaps concerns no one; it is in a sense the *non-concerning* [Blanchot's italics], but with regard to which, by the same token, the reader *can no longer comfortably take any distance*, since he cannot properly [*d'une manière juste*] situate himself in relation to what does not even present itself as unsituatable. How, then, is the reader to set himself or herself apart from the absolute distance that seems to have taken all distance up into itself? Without any bearing, deprived of the interest of reading, *he is no longer allowed to look at things from afar, to keep between things and himself the distance that belongs to the gaze* . . . (384)

This time the added emphases bring out all the ways these sentences are defining a heteronomous law to which reading is submitted once distance enters into the narrative experience, once distance can no longer be kept at the comfortable distance of a disinterested distraction. It is this relation of aesthetic distance that will always have been irresponsible; more precisely, it irresponsibilizes the reader, who has no call to respond to anything set before him or her because distance remains the distance between the reader and the object of contemplation. But when distance *enters into* the narrative experience, when it involves that experience in the stakes of distance, when distance, as we've just read, "becomes the stake and, in a sense, the substance of the story," thereby displacing the narrative "substance" or substrate that is the subject, well, then, something happens to the reader and to the reader's experience. Remarking Blanchot's language closely, one reads that the reader *falls under* a new demand or necessity. This affirmation comes in the form of a question: "Sous quelle exigence nouvelle [le lecteur] est-il tombé?" The experience of reading is governed here by a law of distance, a heteronomy, which both falls upon it, compels it, and touches it but *as* distance. The experience of the reader thereby comes to involve a new exigency that befalls it. Above all, what is new is the possibility of response that this exigency or demand confers upon this act—reading/writing—which, up until then, has been left to its disinterested irresponsibility. The narrative experience enters the age of its responsibility and this is marked by the necessity of somehow *responding* to distance. The description insists on the new constraint that falls upon the reader, who "can no longer take a disinterested pleasure in it," who "can no longer comfortably take any distance," and who is "no longer allowed to look at things from afar." This new demand, in other words, demands what, for the self-interested subject, can only seem to be a paradoxical response: to concern oneself with the non-concerning. More precisely, not to keep one's distance from it, even as one has no longer any measure with which to determine the proper distance. The reader's response to this demand cannot take its bearings "since he cannot properly [*d'une manière juste*] situate himself in relation to what does not even present itself as unsituatable."

There is thus demand and impossibility of responding to the demand "d'une manière juste." What is now impossible is any calculation of the *proper* distance in one's relation to the other, since the other's distance is such that it does not present itself as situatable or even unsituatable in a space no longer oriented by vision or point of view, that of some subject or other. It does not come from a subject, yet the demand remains a demand, the necessity to respond to the other "d'une manière juste": *in a proper or correct way,* but also *in a just manner,* which is to say, to respond justly, in the manner of justice.

Nothing less, therefore, than the demand of justice is at stake in the narrative experience, which is the experience of a distance and a strangeness, the experience of a relation that is *not yet* or *no longer* between subjects. Justice is at stake in this relation because it alone would speak, *if that were possible,* the neutral or neutralized language transcending language, from somewhere outside language, as other than language. What is at stake and in play in the narrative experience is always the *possibility* of the relation to the other who *just is* different from all the concepts and names by which language situates otherness within its own limits.

The concern with the justice of the *récit* confirms that one of Blanchot's principal interlocutors in *The Infinite Conversation* is quite evidently Levinas. In *Altered Reading: Levinas and Literature*, Jill Robbins concludes her very fine study with a brief section devoted to Blanchot, whose narrative writing earns it the status of exception, along with very few others, to Levinas's otherwise consistently negative judgment concerning the ethical force of literary discourse. She points out that

> Levinas acknowledges very precisely the possible convergence and the limits of such a convergence between the alterity of the ethical and the alterity of the literary when he describes the literary work of art in Blanchot as "an impersonal speech, without a 'you,' without interpellation, without vocative, and at the same time distinct from 'a coherent discourse' manifesting universal Reason, both discourse and Reason belonging to the order of the Day." This is to say that at issue in the literary work of art in Blanchot's analysis is not an ethical speaking but nonetheless a kind of speaking that is distinct from the totality. It is the outside or an exteriority that speaks.[13]

Robbins underscores "a certain circularity" in the thought of Blanchot and Levinas, which must be kept in mind when one reads the one beside the other. Thus if a certain *récit* of Blanchot's can be read as "an instance in which a literary work is genuinely commensurable with the level of Levinas's ultraethical discourse," it is no doubt because Blanchot's text has "relayed itself through Levinas's ethical philosophy" (152). And vice versa, of course, although Robbins will not argue that Levinas's ethical philosophy relays itself through Blanchot's *récit*. She is doubtless correct when she concludes that "on the basis of reading Blanchot, Levinas has modified somewhat his understanding of the work of art," but then adds: "any question of how much Levinas may have learned from Blanchot in the interim must also acknowledge that Levinas remains unconvinced about the capacity of art to signify transcendence" (154).

It is, nevertheless, the possibility of a relation to radical difference that is carried or borne by the form of writing Blanchot calls *récit*, the word that can be read as displacing, with great economy and precision, the term "fiction."[14] This displacement is very closely traced in the final pages of the fragment we're reading, which ought to be cited *in extenso* and commented upon endlessly, were there world enough and time. But as we're nearing the reasonable limit of this chapter, let us once again resort to the silent commentary of italics on a long final quotation from "The narrative voice, the 'he,' the neutral." I will simply underscore, in these rapidly telescoped lines, certain active verbs or phrases indicating an action, be it the strange "action" of *attraction* or of *tendency*, or yet again, a certain force of *obliqueness* that turns language toward an outside, if not inside out, emptying or voiding it, as Austin might have said, of its power to pose or express being, to do what is called, in the final sentences I'll cite, the work of being. It is this kind of action or attraction (the attraction not of sameness nor finally of strangeness, but of the neutral that withdraws from even this difference), that, we read, *may be* at stake in *récit*, that is, "in recounting (writing)." Although there is no further recurrence in these lines of the term "enjeu," the mode of this "might be," "may be," or "maybe" locates all the same something that is still in play and therefore at stake in *récit* or writing. It is the mode of possibility, which neither affirms nor negates but, as Blanchot writes, *donne à entendre*, gives to be heard the possibility of all that can be understood through affirmation and negation. The neutral *récit*, then, would be—might be, maybe—the possibility of putting anything at all at stake in language. As such, it has an irreducibly *critical* function, in an almost Kantian sense of the term. It criticizes, one might say, all that language presumes to name; that is, it both sets and lifts the limit of language, keeping thus *at stake*, in possibility, the opening to the other.

> The narrative "he" [or "it," *il*], whether absent or present, whether it affirms itself or hides itself, and whether or not it alters the conventions of writing—linearity, continuity, readability—thus *marks* the intrusion of the other—understood as neutral—in its irreducible strangeness and in its wily perversity. The other speaks. But when the other is speaking, no one speaks because the other . . . is neither the one nor the other, and the neutral that indicates it withdraws it from both, as it does from unity, always establishing it outside the terms, the act, or the subject through which it claims to offer itself. The narrative (I do not say narrating) voice derives from this its aphony. . . .
>
> Although it may well borrow the voice of a judiciously chosen character, or even create the hybrid function of mediator (the voice that ruins all mediation), it is always different from what utters it: it is the indifferent-difference that alters the personal voice. Let us (on a whim) call it spectral, ghostlike. Not that it comes from beyond the grave, or even because it would once and for all represent some essential absence, but because it always *tends* to absent itself in its *bearer*. . . . Tacit, the narrative voice *attracts* language indirectly, *obliquely* and, under this attraction of an *oblique* speech, allows the neutral to speak. . . . [I]t may be that recounting [*récit*] (writing) *draws language into a possibility* of saying that would say being without saying it, and yet without denying it either. Or again, to say this more clearly, too clearly: it would es-

tablish the center of gravity of speech elsewhere, there where speaking would neither affirm being nor need negation in order *to suspend the work of being* that is ordinarily accomplished in every form of expression. In this respect, the narrative voice is the most critical voice that, unheard, might give to be heard. That is why, as we listen to it, we *tend* to confuse it with the *oblique voice* of misfortune, or of madness. (385–87; italics added).[15]

Although commentary must break off here, a few words in conclusion about this last remarked tendency, the tendency to *confuse* narrative voice with another voice. Given that both are said to be "oblique," it cannot be a matter so easily of avoiding the confusion between the one and the other, between narrative voice and the voice of "misfortune, or of madness," between, that is, a neutral other or exteriority, which knows neither fortune nor misfortune, reason nor madness, and the other who will already have come to stand before me suffering from all the marks these differences make. Therefore, one should not read any simple admonition here to distinguish what we tend to confuse. *Perhaps even*, and on the contrary, it is through the inevitability of this confusion that one can still hear the call to respond to the other, in other words, the call to or toward justice.

Perhaps—a final perhaps—this call for response brings its answer to the terribly equivocal question with which I began: How can one take fiction seriously? For now we might even be able to reply, after Derrida, Blanchot, Kafka, and quite a few others have written: there is nothing that could or should have a more *serious, critical* claim on our attention than "fiction."

—"Fiction"?
—No. No "fictions," never again.
—Oh, be some other name!

§ 8   The Experience of Deconstruction

The title of this chapter might strike many as odd, even somehow at odds with the fundamental grammar within which it can make any sense at all. Just to read "the experience of deconstruction" is already something of a jarring experience. It shakes up everything we thought we could rely on by experience, as experience, from experience. It bids us to imagine the absolute event of experience, a perilous crossing of the perimeter from beyond oneself, beyond the same, beyond all that which repeats as the experience of self.[1] An experience without self, from outside self, an experience without experience itself. Is such a thing even possible? For whom?

If deconstruction can be experienced or an experience, then it seems that this possibility would have to deconstruct some essential notion we have of what experience itself *is*. If there can be an experience of deconstruction, if such a thing is possible, then that possibility makes for a deconstruction of experience itself. Of our notion of experience but also of our *experience of experience*. The experience of experience, in other words, the place of a certain repetition, where the singular, one-time experience, which is unlike any other, begins to repeat by means of a figure of sameness. Deconstruction, insofar as it deconstructs such repeating figures, retrieves the traces of some singularity of experience, which is *also* being remarked through repetition. Repetition, in effect, can be seen to con-figure singularity, give it a name, a name that is a figure—face, voice, gaze. Someone's. Some one's. The experience of deconstruction, if such a thing were possible, would be the singular experience of a repeating singularity, always someone's. But whose? Whose experience is it? To whom does it belong?

These questions ("to whom?" "to whom does it belong?" "to whom does it return properly as (a) property?") have been at the focus of deconstructive thought. This thought has entailed a radical displacement of all the presuppositions implied by the very form of these questions, and hence of the answers to them that have tended to recur. This displacement, I venture to say, is precisely what would have to be jarring about the experience of deconstruction. If it were possible, it would have to be an experience in which the very question of *whose* experience it is, to whom it belongs or returns, has to remain suspended.

Such a suspension shakes the perimeters of a grammar in which, for example, the noun "experience" is apt to occur most readily in clauses with the verb "to have" or its cognates, either explicit or implicit. One *has* experience(s). Experience is something someone, anyone *has, acquires, comes to possess*. This is a virtual presupposition of the grammar of experience. Experience is presupposed to be that which is appropriated, thus appropriable. Yet, as an appropriable thing, experience is to be considered fundamentally different from other kinds of things that can be had. We maintain (or rather, presuppose) that having (an) experience is not like having a car, brown eyes, or a job. These are had, owned, possessed as some kind of property or by legal title. When one has experience, however, one does not necessarily end up owning anything or having title to anything. If I say "I had an experience," I mean that something happened to me and not that something came into my possession. And even though one may be said to possess experience, we still make a distinction from other kinds of possessions one may have. So experience is not itself properly what we call a possession; rather, it is that which comes to be appropriated as a self, a self-possession, the self one is or has—in other words, repeats.

Experience repeats, we believe. Repeating itself, we further believe, it coheres and becomes continuous over time. Hence, we say of someone "she has experience," and we usually wish to understand thereby that she has accumulated experiences, over and over, and that through repetition of the same or similar experience, she is now qualified to be called "experienced." This set of beliefs permits a certain level of reliance on technical expertise and on experts who can produce the model of fully experienced discourse in any technical field. Likewise, if one is reassured by the idea of experienced technicians—surgeons, pilots, auto mechanics—it is no doubt because one can call up an image of repeated acts in the course of which the actor has learned to minimize the chance of error or accident. Experience as cumulative through repetition, as constituting a continuity over time (which continuity is called the subject), is the distinguishing trait in play in the difference between experience (abstract singular), and experiences (plural). Yet, what does it mean to say that one experience repeats another and then another and then another, and that each time it is also the same experience, a *repetition* of the same? What about this *trope* of repetition whereby plural experiences are said to add up to experience?

By recalling that repetition is a trope, I mean to indicate one place in which to look for a deconstruction of this trait, which accumulates experiences, plural, into experience, abstract general singular. The trope gathers disparate events so that they cohere as a subject unified over time. The unification of the subject happens as an appropriation of a plurality of experiences into (its own) experience. The instrument, so to speak, of this unifying appropriation, which also reduces plurality to a general singularity, is the trope—or the fiction—of repetition. To call repetition a fiction, however, points us as well to a narrative structure, to narrative as a mode of repetition.[2] It also raises the question of *literary* fiction, of fiction in the sense of a written literature. Narrative repetition occurs in literature, of course, but we hold the kind of experience one may have *reading* such narrative literature to be essentially different from the experience(s) of repetition that happens in reality. There is, we believe, a fundamental difference between the experience of fictional repetition and an experience of repetition "in real life."

It is this belief that Freud, in his essay "The Uncanny," sets out to test, in his own best quasi scientific manner. The etiological question of the essay is: what causes the experience of the uncanny? But Freud, it seems, can approach this question only by dividing the experience he's investigating into fictional and real occurrences, which he will then attempt to compare so as to determine if there is more than one origin or cause of uncanny sensations. In the rest of this chapter, I propose to consider, once again, this argument concerning the uncanny experience of fiction, which Freud persists in wanting to distinguish from real experience. Despite that will, which is the will of empirical, experimental science (the science of real as opposed to fictional experience), "The Uncanny" goes a considerable way toward deconstructing the trait of the difference between the real and the fictional moments of a same experience, and therefore, between my own, someone's "own" experience and the inappropriable experience of another, who may be a fiction. In the following pages, I will accompany Freud's essay for a certain distance as it goes about this—quasi scientific, quasi fictional—work of deconstruction.

As is well known, Freud ends up associating the quality of feeling called the "das Unheimliche" or uncanniness with "something repressed which *recurs*."[3] The essay, in effect, traces the process of the "discovery that whatever reminds us of this inner 'compulsion to repeat' is perceived as uncanny" (215). It thus has an evident affinity with another text of Freud's, concerned apparently more directly with the repetition compulsion, *Beyond the Pleasure Principle*. "The Uncanny," however, is noteworthy because in it Freud also attempts to specify differences between the real and the aesthetic experience of uncanniness, between experience that can be submitted to what he calls "reality-testing" and experience for which no such testing can be performed. By aesthetic experience, Freud seems to have in mind the experience of reading narrative fiction because his examples are all taken from this realm. The essay, then, and for good reason, has repeatedly attracted the attention of literary theorists, since it appears to address head-on the area of their concern and to make connections between that concern and the sort of psychic phenomena investigated by psychoanalysis.[4] It is indeed perhaps the only attempt Freud made to come to terms with the specifics of the psychic experience of reading fiction.

It is not at all clear, however, that he really meant to get into such questions. Very near the conclusion of the essay, after having considered "the possibilities of poetic license and the privileges enjoyed by story-writers in evoking or in excluding an uncanny feeling" (228), that is, all those possibilities that belong to fiction, he concedes that he has "drifted into this field of research half involuntarily." This is an odd remark to find at the end of an essay that begins by announcing its subject to be aesthetics.

> It is only rarely that a psycho-analyst feels impelled to investigate the subject of aesthetics, even when aesthetics is understood to mean not merely the theory of beauty but the theory of the qualities of feeling. . . . But it does occasionally happen that he has to interest himself in some particular province of that subject; and this province usually proves to be a rather remote one, and one which has been neglected in the specialist literature of aesthetics. (193)

These are the first lines of the essay. With these initial sentences, Freud seems to understand clearly that he is preparing to enter into the subject of aesthetics, albeit a remote province of that subject, and that, however exceptionally or reluctantly, he is doing so deliberately. That is why it is odd to find him musing at the essay's close about how he has drifted "half involuntarily" into the "field of research" that studies the devices of story-telling. It is as if, by the end of the essay, he had forgotten that it had been his announced intention at the outset to take up this province of aesthetics.

There are, however, at least two notes struck at the opening of the essay that will resonate with the later image of involuntary drift: a psychoana-lyst, writes Freud, only rarely "feels impelled" to investigate the subject of aesthetics [*verspürt nur selten den Antrieb zu ästhetischen Untersuchungen*]; and it occasionally happens "that he has to interest himself" in it (*dass er sich für ein bestimmtes Gebiet der Ästhetik interessieren muss*). The essay "The Uncanny" describes itself, then, as having been put into motion un-der some coercion or compulsion: a feeling-impelled and a having-to-in-terest-himself. If these marks of coercion manage to sound rather innocu-ous, it is because Freud has couched them in the third person of scientific discourse. He does not write "I, Freud, feel impelled to speak of the un-canny"; or "I, Freud, have to interest myself in these questions." It is the psychoanalytic investigator, the scientist, the researcher who must do these things, and if he must, it is because science demands it; it is the will of science. But this use of the third person is also a transparent discursive screen for the first person signatory of these lines, for Freud himself, for the one who chooses, for apparently scientific reasons, not to write "I," "I feel impelled," or "I have to interest myself." Such a confessional mode would be most out of place, unscientific, and above all, it would prompt questions as to who or what is impelling me, the writer, to write about uncanny feelings, and by what necessity I have to interest myself in them. As it stands, the opening of the essay is designed to avoid all such ques-tions since their answer is already implied: science makes me do it, I do it for the reasons of science.

Despite the appeal to a strictly scientific proceeding, it is possible to re-vive the buried question about the force under whose impulse or coercion Freud approached the notion of the uncanny and was attracted to it in the first place. Indeed, Freud's own psychoanalytic procedure encourages one to lift the lid of scientific discourse that he frequently clamped tightly into place in order to secure a place for his discoveries alongside those of as-tronomy or neurology.[5] He himself just as regularly dispensed with that cover, and this essay is no exception. The investigator, the psychoanalyst, the scientist is also going to acknowledge or confess his own uncanny feelings, although at first he continues to do so under cover of the scientific third person. This device, however, now begins to sound altogether stilted and artificial, a purely conventional manner in which to talk about oneself in all one's peculiarity or singularity. A few paragraphs into the essay, he writes:

> The writer of the present contribution, indeed, must himself plead guilty to a special obtuseness in the matter, where extreme delicacy of perception would be more in place. It is long since he has experienced or heard of anything which has given him an uncanny impression, and he must start by translating himself into that state of feeling, by awakening in himself the possibility of experiencing it. (194)[6]

This highly self-conscious language is also rather complex in its pragmatic function or performative force. On the one hand, confessing in the third person to "a special obtuseness in the matter" can be a somewhat coy fashion to qualify oneself for this investigation. It suggests that, because he is largely immune to uncanny feelings, one may rely on this investigator to keep a cool, scientific head when speaking of them. On the other hand, the same confession discourages readers from pursuing the possibility that the coercion or compulsion under which he is writing could have any resemblance to the kind of uncanny experience he is describing, because, we read, it is "long since" the author has experienced such a thing. So, if one had begun to follow the thread of this possibility from the opening lines, from the feeling-impelled and the having-to-interest-himself, it gets broken off here by Freud's frank acknowledgment of his insensitivity.

With the passing, rhetorical mention of guilt or accusation, however ("The writer of the present contribution, indeed, must himself *plead guilty* to [or charge himself with, accuse himself of] a special obtuseness in the matter" [*sich einer besonderen Stumpfheit in dieser Sache anklagen*]), one may pick up again the thread of the uncanniness that Freud swears he has not felt in many years. At the very least, the association of uncanniness and guilt may suggest one motive he has in declaring so forthrightly his lack of uncanny experience. This suggestion gathers some force a few pages after the mock self-accusation, when he introduces a brief narration of an uncanny experience of his own. There will be two more such personal experiences of the author recounted in the course of the essay, one of which is consigned to a footnote while the other concerns an experience of reading to which we will return in a moment. Of these three, only the first, which I am about to cite, is offered as a firsthand, real experience of the uncanny as distinct from, as Freud puts it, "the uncanny that we merely picture or read about" (224). Here is the well-known narrative:

> As I was walking, one hot summer afternoon, through the deserted streets of a provincial town in Italy which was unknown to me, I found myself in a quarter of whose character I could not long remain in doubt. Nothing but painted women were to be seen at the windows of the small houses, and I hastened to leave the narrow street at the next turning. But after having wandered about for a time without enquiring my way, I suddenly found myself back in the same street, where my presence was now beginning to excite attention. I hurried away once more, only to arrive by another *détour* at the same place yet a third time. Now, however, a feeling overcame me which I can only describe as uncanny, and I was glad enough to find myself back at the piazza I had left a short while before, without any further voyages of discovery. (212–13)

Given what Freud has earlier said about his particular obtuseness to uncanny feelings (and thus his lack of firsthand experience), one may suppose he recounts here one of the rare occasions when his obtuseness was overcome, and perhaps even the only occasion. In any case, it is given this status in the essay and if only for that reason it has the force of not just any example. Instead, it is the only example of what the subject of this investigation *himself* refers to when he speaks of an uncanny feeling experienced in real life, one he felt without having to translate himself into that state of feeling, as he says he must now do given his acquired insensitivity. It is also, of course, an example of uncanniness that owes nothing to fiction, since it really did happen to someone real and not just in fiction or by means of a fiction.

Or so Freud appears to believe.

He offers no commentary on the episode, which is introduced to reinforce the point about "the factor of the repetition of the same thing," a notion that he fears "will perhaps not appeal to everyone as a source of uncanny feeling" (212). Having concluded the account, and without pausing for commentary, he goes on to list similar but generic experiences: being lost in a mist and returning to the same spot or wandering in a darkened room and repeatedly bumping into the same piece of furniture. Neither of these generic examples, however, share the feature that makes Freud's narrative so telling: the feature of the sexually marked character of the place to which he returns under his compulsion to repeat. It is almost as if, by putting his experience on such a list, he were distracting attention from this feature, which he has nevertheless placed in clear view, as clearly in view as the painted women seen at the windows of the small houses. Or, put another way, it is as if Freud were pointing to the repeated involuntary return to the same place as in itself uncanny, which is manifestly insufficient to account for what he experienced in an unfamiliar provincial town in Italy.

I am not suggesting, of course, that Freud missed the most obvious thing about his own anecdote; rather, I want merely to underscore that he appears to cite it (that is, repeat it) solely because it illustrates the involuntary repetition of an action. Doubtless he considers the connection to go without saying between his uncanny experience, on the one hand, and, on the other, the psychoanalytic account he offers of uncanniness: that it is "something repressed which recurs," that it "proceeds from something familiar which has been repressed" (224), or that it "proceeds from repressed infantile complexes" (225). All of these formulations could no doubt account for the way in which the specific features of Freud's experience produced a feeling of uncanniness. In other words, the theory conforms well to the experience and finds confirmation there that the uncanny is not just a repetition but a repetition of what *ought to have remained hidden* or repressed (hence guilt), so that the act of repetition is itself the means whereby the repressed returns. Despite, however, this excellent fit between Freud's theory and his experience (which, of course, is anything but surprising), there remain some features of the experiential anecdote that may not be altogether compatible with the theoretical framework of the essay. I will try to spell these out briefly.

As already mentioned, one of Freud's aims in this essay is to distinguish the uncanny *aesthetic* experience from the uncanny *real* experience. A general theory of the uncanny would have to account for both but it would also have to be able to locate the dividing line of their distinction. For Freud, this line seems to fall in an entirely conventional way between literary fiction and lived, real experience. More generally one could say it falls between, on the one hand, fictions, which we experience in a fashion that must fail the test of reality, and, on the other hand, any experience that passes the reality test for the subject of the experience. This distinction is never questioned by Freud; it is simply taken for granted. In this, he seems to rely on a stable category of fiction, which is defined, analyzed, and studied by the discipline of aesthetics. This is the domain he drifts into half involuntarily when he tries to work out the specific differences between an uncanny experience produced by real life and one produced by fiction. Just as he did in that unnamed provincial town in Italy, at some point in the course of the essay he crosses over the line separating aesthetics from real life (which suggests that not only the experience of reading but the experience of writing as well can produce uncanny effects on a subject).

Despite all that, despite the fact that the essay begins its drift into the "subject of aesthetics" from its very first words, the theory has no difficulty, apparently, maintaining the distinction of the real and the fictional. But can we say the same for the real experience and the experience of the real that this theory is meant to account for? Does that experience *as recounted* remain altogether within the category of real versus fictional experience of uncanniness? What if the so-called "real" experience had to remark within itself the "unreal" from which it is to be distinguished? In what sense would it still be, through and through, a real experience?

These questions come down, perhaps, to wondering at what point, in his aesthetic wanderings through a provincial Italian town, Freud crossed over from the province of the beautiful into the area of the uncanny. As a tourist, he has no doubt gone to Italy for its many beauties, the beauties of its plastic arts. He did so often in his youth, and then later he would be repeatedly drawn to these arts of the beautiful in his writings. Thus, despite what the psychoanalyst says at the beginning of the essay, it is more than "only rarely" that he has felt impelled to investigate the subject of aesthetics.[7] In these investigations, moreover, he showed a marked predilection for Italian art: the Moses of Michelangelo and the painting of Leonardo, not to mention all the mythological lore and sculptural remains of Pompeii, Signorelli, etc. Now, the anecdote in the unnamed provincial town will have most likely occurred under the impulse of attraction to these monuments to beauty where they reside in Italy. In the course of one of his tourist walks, he came upon some painted women, only they were not the painted women of Signorelli or Leonardo, they were not the Virgin and St. Anne, they were not even representations of the artist's grandmother or stepmother; rather, these women were painted artlessly, vulgarly, and did not reside in museums or churches but in small, mean houses, houses of the *vulgum pecus.*

At what point does the uncanny experience with the painted women *re-*

ally begin? The narrative suggests that it is at the point at which he returns for a second time to the ill-famed quarter; the first time he wanders into this part of town, he sees quickly that he has deviated from his aim, which is to look at beautiful art; right away he sees that the painted women are not painted artfully, but with the bald-faced urgings of sex. "Nothing but painted women [*geschminkte Frauen*] were to be seen at the windows of the small houses, and I hastened to leave the narrow street at the next turning." The second time, and the first repetition, he *does not see just the women but sees himself also seen by them*; what is more, they see his desire, they see what has carried him back their way: "I suddenly found myself back in the same street, where my presence was now beginning to excite attention." This is not yet uncanny, just embarrassing, too revealing, like being in one of those dreams where one walks about in public half dressed. (And, indeed, immediately before launching into his anecdotal example, Freud has noted that this sort of uncanniness "recalls the sense of helplessness experienced in some dream-states.") It is not until his third passage through the same street, and the second repetition, that Freud is overcome by the uncanny feeling. Because this experience is cited to reinforce his point about the repetition of the same thing as source of uncanny feeling, the narrative marks clearly the onset of uncanniness at the point of the second repetition, the repetition of what is already a repetition.[8]

All of this supposes, however, that the series of repetitions begins when Freud first enters the ill-famed quarter. That is, it begins with the first sighting of the painted women. But can one in fact make such a supposition?

The serialization of the repetition poses problems, which are to a certain extent strictly logical problems. If one supposes that the first sight of the painted women begins the series, then one must also assume that this is the point at which Freud begins to cross from the region of his aesthetic tourism to the nether region of the uncanny. But if he only *begins* to cross here, that means he has not yet fully entered into the region of the uncanny; it is not yet an uncanny experience. Nevertheless, in order to experience the uncanny sensation in the third moment as he does, he will also already have had to cross over the line into the series without realizing it. When he realizes it, it has already happened. It has already happened in the first moment, without happening yet as an event for consciousness. Consciousness will come only after the fact, after the experience. This means that the experience will not have been *anyone's* properly conscious experience. The beginning of the series will

never have been a beginning in consciousness until it has already been repeated. The beginning is constituted only after the fact, after it has been
repeated. Which means that at the beginning, from the first, there will
have already been repetition, Nothing here begins by beginning but only
by repeating.

Another way to put this would be: the narrated series has or is given a
beginning only as a fiction. The episode that Freud recounts as a real experience depends on this fiction to constitute it as experience, and as the
experience of a series that has a beginning (as well as an end). In *reality*,
the reality as experienced, nothing began until it began to repeat; in the
fiction, however, it began as a narrative would begin: from the beginning,
its first words signal the impending event of what will only later be the
first of a series: "As I was walking, one hot summer afternoon, through the
deserted streets of a provincial town in Italy which was unknown to me, I
found myself in a quarter . . . " What begins here is a fictional experience,
not because it never happened, but because the one who is portrayed as
the subject of the experience, the one who was walking without knowing
where he was going and found himself in a certain quarter of the town,
this subject never existed in any present moment of the past that was also
present to itself. In the phrases "As I was walking" and "I found myself,"
the "I" is a *figure of the narration*, that is, of the device whereby experiences are made to begin repeating each other. As such, the "I" corresponds
to no one and nothing but this narration. It is a fiction.[9] The point is that
the narration simply *is*, that is, constitutes or invents the experience as real
and really lived. Which is also why the uncanny sensation arises at the
same moment as the possibility of narrating a series of repetitions, the
moment of the second repetition. It arises, that is, when, between the reality of an experience and a fiction, the distinction can no longer be
strictly made.

So, essentially, the feature unaccounted for by Freud's theoretical mod-
eling of the uncanny here would be this irreducible reliance on the fiction
that narrates an experience no one present to himself in the real ever had
as such. This is not to say, of course, that Freud discounts fiction as a
source of uncanny feeling. On the contrary, he speaks at length about fiction in general, and about several fictional works in particular; one such
text is even cited as having been the occasion for him of a quite remarkable experience of the uncanny. This is the only other example from his
own experience of uncanniness that Freud cites in the essay. It concerns

his reading of a "naïve enough story" out of a magazine that just happened to fall into his hands:

> In the middle of the isolation of war-time [*Mitten in der Absperrung des Weltkrieges*] a number of the English *Strand Magazine* fell into my hands [*kam eine Nummer des englischen Magazins 'Strand' in meine Hände*]; and I read a story about a young married couple who move into a furnished house in which there is a curiously shaped table with carvings of crocodiles on it. To-wards evening an intolerable and very specific smell begins to pervade the house; they stumble over something in the dark; they seem to see a vague form gliding over the stairs—in short, we are given to understand that the presence of the table causes ghostly crocodiles to haunt the place, or that the wooden monsters come to life in the dark, or something of the sort. It was a naïve enough story, but the uncanny feeling it produced was quite remark-able. (221)[10]

It would be tempting to analyze this passage in the light of what has just been discovered about such uncanny narratives. Once again there would be questions to ask about its beginning. Does the uncanny experi-ence begin only after Freud has begun to read it in the magazine or al-ready when the magazine "fell" or came into his hands? Why does he note the circumstances of his coming to read this story? Perhaps he merely wanted to waylay any derogatory judgments of his taste in reading; it was "[i]n the middle of the isolation of war-time," he notes, as if to explain that one had to read whatever came into one's hands. But, if that is the reason for beginning this way, the explanation it implies is far from evi-dent. On the other hand, there seems to be little doubt that Freud as-sumes that the quite remarkable uncanny feeling produced by the story had nothing to do with reality for the story's reader. This he does when he mocks the premises of the fiction: "in short, we are given to understand that the presence of the table causes ghostly crocodiles to haunt the place, or that the wooden monsters come to life in the dark, or something of the sort." In other words, it was a wholly artificial production, possible only in fiction, although the uncanny feeling it produced was quite remarkably real. Because the premise of ghostly crocodiles or "wooden monsters come to life" is so absurd, Freud refers the uncanniness produced by the fiction to primitive animism, that is, "to modes of working of the mental appa-ratus that have been surmounted" (221). While residual animistic beliefs can also produce uncanny sensations in real life, at least for the most primitive among us, fiction is better able to exploit these beliefs because, once again, it cannot be submitted to reality-testing; hence "there are many more means for creating uncanny effects in fiction than there are in real life" (226).

Freud's argument, of course, is indisputable as long as one understands the term "fiction" to have only its most conventional reference to a coded genre of narrative, to fictions published and presented as such. Because he intends this conventional reference, he can confidently invoke a distinction between fiction and real life. But we have seen that things are not quite so simple when, in order to account for and give an account of so-called real life, he must have recourse to the fictional device that is his own narrative. Here the distinction cannot be made; "real life" gets remarked as a fiction and suspends the simple opposition. When the suspension or, more precisely, the deconstruction of this distinction happens, as it did to Freud in Italy, one receives the sort of jolt he calls the uncanny.

Perhaps, however, this simply is the uncanny experience; wherever it occurs, it simply is the experience of the deconstruction of the distinction between fiction and real life. If so, then it would be pointless to try to differentiate uncanny effects in fiction from the same effects in real life. Yet Freud presumes it is necessary to do so. Why? Well, principally, it would seem, to save the scientific theory, to save it *as* scientifically valid. To do so, one must be able to answer all contradictions of the hypothesis being put forward. And as Freud notes, nearly all these contradictions arise from the possibilities realized only in fiction: "nearly all the instances that contradict our hypothesis," he writes, "are taken from the realm of fiction, of imaginative writing. This suggests that we should differentiate between the uncanny that we actually experience and the uncanny that we merely picture or read about" (224). We should so differentiate, in order to answer the contradictions, but can we? If uncanniness arises from somewhere on the site of the deconstruction of that distinction, then it is one of the possible names we can give to the *experience* of that deconstruction. It is the experience we think we saw happening to the subject of the so-called real-life uncanny experience in Italy; but also to the reader of a strange story that just happened to fall into his hands.

We have not yet, however, shown how such a deconstruction may also leave its traces in the experience of reading fiction, as it is conventionally represented. True, we have wondered, with regard to the haunting crocodile story, whether the quite remarkable uncanny feeling it could produce in its reader had something to do with the real circumstances of that reader's life at the moment, the isolation of wartime. One can entertain such questions about the anecdote but they cannot lead anywhere since Freud himself saw no reason to raise them. What is more, the example, at least as Freud presents it, appears to reduce fiction to its most conventional, even primitive, level.[11] The reading experience there is a self-described naïve one, merely a device, perhaps, to distract oneself from isolation in the midst of war. But there is, of course, another reading experience recounted in this essay, one which apparently bears little resemblance to the kind of naïve reading Freud indulged in, perhaps out of some haunted desperation. It is his reading of the story by E. T. A. Hoffmann, "The Sandman," which also presents the essay's most extended analysis of an uncanny experience. To conclude, then, let us turn briefly to this famous reading.[12]

It is introduced into the essay by way of Freud's disagreement with Jentsch. Jentsch had argued some years earlier that the uncanny effect produced by Hoffmann's tale can be traced to uncertainty about whether a character in a fiction is a human being or an automaton. Thus, for Jentsch, the uncanniness in the tale arises from Nathanael's having taken the doll Olympia for a living girl, which allows the more naïve reader (or the reader who reads the tale only once) to do the same. Freud is going to argue that the uncanniness produced by "The Sandman" has quite another source in addition to the ontological or intellectual uncertainties about Olympia. This other and more important source of the uncanny is also its main theme, the theme named by its title.

> But I cannot think—and I hope most readers of the story will agree with me—that the theme of the doll Olympia, who is to all appearances a living being, is by any means the only, or indeed the most important, element that must be held responsible for the quite unparalleled atmosphere of uncanniness evoked by the story. Nor is this atmosphere heightened by the fact that the author himself treats the episode of Olympia with a faint touch of satire and uses it to poke fun at the young man's idealisation of his mistress. The main theme of the story is, on the contrary, something different, something which gives it its name, and which is always re-introduced at critical moments: it is the theme of the "Sand-Man" who tears out children's eyes. (202)

It is doubtless correct to say that the Sandman theme is the main one of the story, and that Olympia's appearance to Nathanael is episodic and brief, compared to the repeated sightings he has of the Sandman or his avatars. With Freud's remark about the "touch of satire" accompanying the Olympia episode, however, he all but dismisses it entirely as a source of uncanniness for the reader, who is meant to pick up enough of the satiric hints to be able to laugh along with the author at a young man's "idealisation of his mistress." This sensitivity to satire, one must suppose, is the trace of Freud's own experience of reading the Olympia episode. It implies that, because of the satiric tone, the episode did not arouse, in his experience, an uncanny feeling, or at least nothing to compare with the uncanny feeling associated with the returning theme of the Sandman. The same reader who can, along with the author, mock Nathanael's idealization receives no such hints to laugh off his idea or *idée fixe* concerning the Sandman as likewise an idealization, that is, an idea, a fiction, even a madness. Freud's argument concerning the source of the reader's, that is, first of all his own, uncanny sensation is that as readers we "know that we are not supposed to be looking on at the products of a madman's imagination" when we, along with Nathanael, look at the Sandman; hence, for this reader, that is, for Freud, no less than for Nathanael, "Coppola the optician really *is* the lawyer Coppelius and also, therefore, the Sand-Man" (206). This is the premised reality of both the fiction and the reading of the fiction.

Rather than try to paraphrase this argument any further, I will cite at some length Freud's explanation for his own and therefore any reader's uncanny sensation, which concludes the refutation of Jentsch.

> Uncertainty whether an object is living or inanimate, which admittedly applied to the doll Olympia, is quite irrelevant in connection to this other, more striking instance of uncanniness. It is true that the writer creates a kind of uncertainty in us in the beginning by not letting us know, no doubt purposely, whether he is taking us into the real world or into a purely fantastic one of his own creation. . . . But this uncertainty disappears in the course of Hoffmann's story, and *we perceive that he intends to make us, too, look through the demon optician's spectacles or spy-glass*—perhaps, indeed, that the author in his very own person once peered through such an instrument. For the conclusion of the story makes it quite clear that Coppola the optician really *is* the lawyer Coppelius and also, therefore, the Sand-Man.
>
> There is no question therefore, of any intellectual uncertainty here: we know now that we are not supposed to be looking on at the products of a madman's imagination, behind which we, with the superiority of rational minds, are able to detect the sober truth; and yet this knowledge does not lessen the impression of uncanniness in the least degree. (205–6; emphases added)

When Freud writes "we perceive that [Hoffmann] intends to make us, too, look through the demon optician's spectacles or spy-glasses," he is taking, that is, *repeating* a significant figure from the tale in order to characterize the conditions under which the reader reads it. Like Nathanael, the tale's reader, claims Freud, is made to see that Coppola really *is* Coppelius, really *is* the Sandman, and that therefore the Sandman really *is*, that he really is not just a fiction or figment of anyone's imagination. There is this ontological certainty because the reader, like Nathanael, looks through a particular instrument. But in Freud's borrowed metaphor of the spyglass as the instrument of reading, what exactly in the act of reading corresponds to the instrument? In other words, what allows Freud to *appropriate* this instrument as a figure of the reader's perception, that is, of his experience?

Let us recall that the "demon optician's spectacles or spy-glass" refers in "The Sandman" to the wares of the optician Coppola, in whom Nathanael sees the return of his childhood nemesis, Coppelius, alias the Sandman. It therefore refers as well to the specific spyglass or pocket telescope Nathanael buys from Coppola and through which he immediately proceeds to look at Olympia. It is the same telescope Nathanael has in his pocket when he ascends the tower with Clara in the tale's final scene. He looks through it and sees Clara in a way that causes his own eyes to roll and precipitates his unsuccessful attempt to throw her over the parapet before he does succeed in throwing himself to his death. Nathanael is never described as looking at anyone or anything other than Olympia and, briefly, Clara, through Coppola's telescope. Now, can one tell whether this fact is at all significant in Freud's choice of the figure? Is it, in other words, a feature that, in his own description, corresponds to some feature of the reader's own experience? I think we must say it does not and even that Freud takes up the instrument only in order to *turn it away* from Olympia and point it instead at Coppola/Coppelius.[13] It is on their troubling identity and reality that he trains the figurative power to collapse the difference between what Nathanael sees and what the reader must also see, which is likewise its power to telescope encounters with different characters, therefore different experiences, into Nathanael's experience with solely the Sandman, the figure who threatens to tear out children's eyes. The links are thus put in place that will lead Freud from this telescoping figure to what he designates as the "substitutive relation between the eye and the male organ" (206) and thus to the dread of castration portrayed as a fear for one's eyes. This is the source of the strongest uncanny sensation produced by the tale, insists Freud; it is what recurs that ought to have remained secret, hidden, *heimlich*, repressed. It is not merely a residual animistic belief, like some wooden monsters coming to life, such as may be provoked in a naïve fiction. It is an uncanny sensation aroused by "repressed infantile complexes," which recur in the form of a repetition. As such, it is exactly like what can happen in real life, and Freud even suggests that the story may be a transposition of the author's experience, the blinding oedipal experience of having himself "in his very own person once peered through such an instrument."

This figurative pattern, installed by the borrowed telescope, easily confirms Freud's reliance on the instrument of castration, which is both a theory, a theoretical instrument that can cut through to "repressed infantile complexes," and an instrument that cuts or threatens to cut flesh, and thus (into) the real; it would cut *for real* and cut into the real. The telescope cuts by collapsing the apparent distance between seer and seen, subject and object, but also, as an instrument of reading or writing, between reader and character, character and author, and so forth. Furthermore, one could show that the instrument Freud borrows from Hoffmann's tale gives the focus to all of his cutting operations throughout the essay, and principally to all those concerned with the differentiation of "fiction" and "real life." It is as if all these distinctions were being made under threat of what will happen if one doesn't clearly make the separation. "[W]e should differentiate between the uncanny that we actually experience and the uncanny that we merely picture or read about." Yes, we should, it is a duty, a debt owed, we ought to do so. Otherwise, not only is our theory weakened but the very eyes with which we try to see clearly are threatened, the eyes of the one Nietzsche called "theoretical man."[14] In order to see anything at all, we theoretical men (sic) must see the difference between real experience and experience happening to some other which "we merely picture or read about."

—If this differentiation is ultimately impossible, then perhaps the uncanny records the experience of that non-differentiation and therefore the deconstruction of the distinction between "real life" experience and fictional experience.

—Yes, but also and therefore between "my own" experience and that of another who, for example, waits at the window of a small house and there catches sight—not once, not twice, but three times—of someone walking blindly "one hot summer afternoon, through the deserted streets of a provincial town in Italy . . . " So begins the fiction of "my own" experience, which is immediately not only mine but also another's. It is uncannily like the experience of deconstruction, that is, the deconstruction of experience.

—What is it, finally, about "The Uncanny" or about its problematic that can come to function virtually as another name for deconstruction, and for deconstruction as experience?[15]

—Notice that, with its very title, "The Uncanny" displays the uncanny doubling it would attempt to analyze, for it names at once the essay itself and the theme of the essay, its object. Like any title, it splits its reference, putting forever into an abyss the one and only one named. This is what Freud also describes as his real experience of uncanniness. Self-reference, the very experience of self, must come to depend on a fiction, a narrative wherein the trope of repetition can stand in as a figure for the self, which is not self-present but absent from itself. By insisting that this uncanny repetition may be read right away in the title, one would be trying to account for the experience of reading such a text, which *calls itself* "The Uncanny," and thereby names whatever one encounters in the experience of reading it. (Or in the experience of writing it, for as we noticed, Freud seems to have been uncannily drawn to his subject.) For Freud, however, it is axiomatic that such an uncanny reading experience is not real experience, and this axiom will be left standing even though his reading of "The Sandman" turns on the moment in which the reader uncannily is made to see exactly what Nathanael sees: the identity of the Sandman figures. This is the significance of his turning the viewing/reading instrument away from Olympia, who is unreal, a mere fiction or simulacrum of a girl. Even when we merely "picture or read about" it, the uncanny is experienced as real.

—And yet, for Freud, reading, and above all the reading of fiction, is to be distinguished from real experience.

—Yes. This is where his "deconstruction" of experience, which he calls the uncanny, confirms and accepts a limit that later deconstructive thought will not leave intact. Still, he will have done more than just glimpsed, through his own fictional looking glass, this further deconstruction on the limits of real experience. In some very real sense, he will have experienced its necessity.

§ 9 Deconstruction Reading Politics: Democracy's Fiction (Everything, Anything, and Nothing at All)

As anyone may read it, the title "Deconstruction Reading Politics" allows for at least two grammatically distinguishable readings, and several possibilities within each grammar.[1] The difference between these readings, moreover, turns on the way one reads the word "reading" in the minimal context of this title. The first and more obvious possibility is to read "reading" as a present participle, in which case it designates the transitive act of a subject (deconstruction) on or toward a direct object (politics). In this reading, the phrase points to that action by that subject on that object. It could thus remind one, although rather incongruously, of the grammar of snapshot captions in photo albums: Jack making breakfast, Diane playing checkers, Dad watching television, deconstruction reading politics.

But of course, that grammar is unfigurable and instead of sending us to the photo album, our title announces acts to come; more than that, it calls for them to take place even as we speak, in this context, and to take place as acts of reading. The act of reading, even in the most ordinary sense, does not occur in a world of visible, sensible phenomena. Which is why even if I saw someone training his attention on the open pages of a book, I would still be unable to affirm with any certainty that he or she was reading. Here I'm reminded of the passage near the beginning of Maurice Blanchot's *Thomas the Obscure* where Thomas is described as "reading in his room." We are directed to picture him sitting before an open book, with forehead supported on his two joined hands and so absorbed that he was absolutely still. Nevertheless, others who entered the room "seeing his book open always to the same pages, thought that he was pretending to read." They cannot see that he is reading; indeed, they cannot see that, as we readers are told, "he was reading with an unsurpassable minuteness and attention."[2] Reading, when it occurs, happens beyond what any observer may see, since it consists less in the act some subject performs on an object, than in an act of utter passivity, if one can say that. In the same passage from *Thomas the Obscure*, there occurs a very striking analogy for this passivity: "He was, in his proximity to each sign, in the situation of the male when the female preying mantis is about to devour him." The description of this passivity continues for another two pages and would demand the same level of "unsurpassable minuteness and attention" if one undertook to read it now, which we will not do. Suffice it to say that the act or activity of reading, as it is understood in this most abyssal passage, operates a reversal whereby the reader is read, indeed devoured by the words, more than he or she reads.

If, however, one takes the term "reading" not as a participle, and thus a verb, but as a gerund, and thus a nominative form, the title can be read as the accretion of three nouns: deconstruction reading politics. True, one would ordinarily expect commas or some other punctuation to indicate that the terms were being aligned in this serial fashion. But it is not at all improbable that whoever devised the phrase "Deconstruction Reading Politics" could have had in mind another title, "Signature Event Context," that likewise dispenses with serial commas and perhaps provides a model for this particular syntactic solecism. One could even show in some minute detail how the title "Deconstruction Reading Politics" has been derived term for term from this other three-noun title: "Signature Event Context." One could, that is, rehearse a reading of this latter essay by Derrida that would transpose, translate, or transfer that signature, that event, and that context into this one here. And because Derrida's essay marked in a certain way deconstruction's major engagement with speech act theory, with the Austinian notion of performative, and in general with the ideas of act and event, then it is easy to imagine that the author of "Deconstruction Reading Politics" wanted to invoke Derrida's disseminal essay with his own title. Perhaps he believes, as I do, that it is among Derrida's most affirmatively political writings, an *exemplum* of deconstruction reading politics, and he wanted to cite it as such.

I will add that I have a slight preference for the second reading of "reading" in our title. It places something apparently more substantive between the other two nouns, which may therefore better resist collapsing into each other too quickly. In other words, reading introduces between deconstruction and politics an interval that is not nothing, even though it is nothing that can ever appear *as such* in the world of phenomena, even though the verb or gerund "reading" can designate no visible action by an actor. Remember that Thomas was absolutely still as he read, so that his visitors assumed he was only feigning to read: they assumed, that is, something like an anterior, interior, and invisible scene that the visible, exterior appearance of reading—he had, after all, his eyes trained on the open pages of a book—would be meant to hide. Reading is apparently the most insubstantial act; that is how it is seen by many, which is to say, how it is not seen.

The problem with this reading of "Reading" as a substantive, then, is that, precisely, it substantializes the nothing-visible, nothing-to-be-seen of reading. When we try to name reading as a thing, with a noun, the *act* of reading at that precise moment becomes invisible, which means invisible to itself, to reading. In other words, to become visible as substantive thing, it must become invisible to itself as act or event without substance. Which is why I am going to give up, finally, reading this title and will turn, abruptly, to literature, to the question of literature.

By "literature" I invoke simply the name under which reading has been most fully substantialized, instituted as a thing and not nothing. It is well known in what ways the history of this institutionalization has both forged and followed the path of at least European political events since the introduction of the process by the German Romantics, who were in part responding first to the French Revolution and then to the Napoleonic wars of conquest. What Lacoue-Labarthe and Nancy have called "the literary absolute" is also this position of an absolute, transcendental subject taking substantive form in and as literature. Nancy, Lacoue-Labarthe, but also many others have given us to understand the importance of letting this institution and this thing of literature deconstruct, and even of helping it along in whatever small ways we can.[3] Certainly deconstructive thought has maintained from the outset a major engagement with literature and the literary. But this engagement has also provoked deconstruction's critics to dismiss out of court any claim it could make to serious, political thought, as if to engage with literature, that is, with the reading act insofar as it appears in a substantive form, is to short-circuit the political or else endlessly to defer it. It is this dogma that will be in question, at least implicitly, in the rest of this chapter, which begins by rehearsing very briefly the deconstruction of one familiar figure of the "literary absolute."

The figure I have in mind is that of literature as a totality. It is not difficult to understand why this figure gets invoked as necessary in the course of the substantialization of literature to which I've just alluded. Doubtless one could find the totalizing trait to have been at work from the outset of that process, if we go along with Lacoue-Labarthe and Nancy in situating this at Jena in the late eighteenth century and then recall their analyses, for example, of the role of the fragment in the project of the Jena romantics. Nevertheless, I am going to draw on a much later avatar and direct descendent of the figure: it is the notion of literature as totality already in question in the title of Wellek and Warren's monumental *Theory of Literature*, first published just over fifty years ago.[4]

The figure is explicitly mentioned for the first time when, in an early chapter, the authors take up the question of comparative literature and find themselves right away obliged to invoke what I will call the "continental limitation." The continent in question is, of course, Europe, and the passage (which I will paraphrase and comment on briefly) is a classic in the grand discourse of comparative literature as essentially European.

There is a conception of "comparative literature," they write, that identifies it "with the study of literature in its totality, with 'world literature,' with 'general' or 'universal' literature." As for world literature, it is often taken to imply something "perhaps needlessly grandiose," namely "that literature should be studied on all five continents, from New Zealand to Iceland" (48). Qualifying this as a needlessly grandiose ambition, they suggest that one continent ought to suffice to contain the idea of literature as totality. And so it does for, one may notice, even as the notion is convoked of more than one continent, continents, therefore, *other* than Europe, this pluri-continental world remains contained within the figure of Europe. The world they name is finally a European one because it goes as they put it, "from New Zealand to Iceland," invoking thereby two insular European outposts beyond the strict geographic borders of Europe. Europe can thus still figure as horizon of the concept of even this pluri-continental world, which will have managed to remain flat, with just one horizon line. The grandiosity Wellek and Warren suspect, however, concerns less the notion that literature is not contained by any one continent, and more the idea that pluri-continental and therefore dis-continental literature should be studied by any one, any one subject who is a scholar, a theorist of comparative literature. Only a grandiose subject, a subject who is more than a continent, if not a whole world of continents, could contain knowledge of the literature that presents itself beyond continental borders.

Yet, one may well ask whether Wellek and Warren's knowing subject is not even more grandiose. After dismissing world, general, and even comparative literature, after rejecting all qualifiers of literature ("Possibly, it would be best to speak simply of 'literature,'" they write [p. 49]), they easily move on to asserting a notion of literature's totality. "Whatever the difficulties into which a conception of universal literary history may run, it is *important to think of literature as a totality* . . . " (ibid.; emphases added). To do otherwise is to fall into the error of believing that literature must be understood as essentially contained by national or linguistic borders. If we know this to be a manifestly false conception, it is because we can cite the example, "at least," of Western literature. "Western literature, *at least*, forms a unity, a whole" (emphasis added). This "at least" signals that the minimal condition for falsification of a proposition has been met. There is at least one of the world's literatures that forms a unity, a contained whole, despite the plurality of languages in which it is written and the various national cultures to which it belongs. Hence, one must attend to the possibility that all literature is part of some greater totality. Western literature, from New Zealand to Iceland, from Greece to Hawaii, is both one example, at least, of unity in the case of a plurilinguistic literature and the reason to think of an even greater totality. Europe, the idea of the West or of Western literature, commands or teaches us to think in terms of totalities; by its example, it consigns how we are supposed to think about literature: "it is important to think of literature as a totality."

Wellek and Warren were writing at the end of the 1940's. Surely there were still many echoes in the air from the last European war, the total war, and a war between totalitarianisms over which system would pacify and unify the world's continents. These echoes were recent enough, in other words, to have found a sounding board in the totality evoked by *Theory of Literature*, more precisely by what I would call their totalitarian method, meaning the method they follow and the fact that the figure of totality, European *par excellence*, is their principal signpost along this path. It points them to their object, which they call literature as a totality. (As we shall see, they also speak of the importance of seeing the individual work "in its totality," which for them is not only possible but necessary.) It is not at all clear, however, that they were listening for these echoes, even if we think they ought to have done so. Perhaps they had no ear for them. Or perhaps they even sought to close out the sounds totality makes when it induces war, so that they could better hear the sound Western literature makes when it forms its unity and gives us the idea of literature's totality, a unified totality, therefore a totality without war. It would be the sound of a continent at peace at last. They wanted to hear, they wanted us to hear and understand one totality, or continent, and not the other. But such discrimination is difficult because it is a matter, precisely, of totality, of that which is without alternative, without other. Totality is a totalizing term, if you see what I mean. Even for Wellek and Warren who, as we already remarked, cannot speak of a pluri-continental world without assimilating it to the totalizing concept of Europe.

Now, at this point you may be wondering: Has not the continental limitation long been apparent and one of the most obvious limitations of the theory of literature as inherited from Wellek and Warren, which they in turn inherited largely from the German romantics? Surely the critique of this limitation does not need to be repeated for comparative cultural theorists today, for whom Eurocentrism has become anathema (although there are still many who mistakenly believe it suffices to denounce Eurocentric totalizations in order to avoid their totalizing effects). At least the chorus of comparative literature has long agreed on the necessity of thinking its object without recourse to the figure of totality, which is the legacy of Europe and of the idea of a unified Western tradition. Certainly no one needs to be reminded how this figure has accompanied a uni-horizonal concept not just of world literature, but of the geopolitical world.

But let us hesitate all the same to reshelve *Theory of Literature* without one last glance at the figure of totality which they call the work, the individual work. Something seems to linger in this figure, something that can still animate it in a way that no longer happens (or at least more and more rarely) with the European idea of literature as a totality. That is, whereas literary comparatists now generally claim to have dispensed with the model of "literature as a totality," they continue regularly to rely on the figure or pre-figuration of each work of literature as a totality, as if they were quite confident that these two figures are unrelated. Perhaps the reason for their confidence is that, unlike the former idea, which Wellek and Warren are able to advance only because they can cite the example of Western literature, the idea of the "work in its totality" can be asserted virtually as a tautology, every work being an example of such a totality by definition. This is at least suggested when they invoke, as they write, "the obligation to see the work in its totality." This obligation, they imply, is put in place by the work itself, by the nature of what it is, which is a totality. One calls work, work of art or of literature, something which maintains itself and has existence as a totality. They warn, however, that the totality of the work is not to be understood as a unity of parts in a whole, an organic unity, or anything that simply follows from asserting the identity of content and form. This latter notion in particular is facile and "encourages the illusion," as they write, "that the analysis of any element of an artifact, whether of content or of technique, must be equally useful, and thus absolves us from *the obligation to see the work in its totality*" (pp. 27–28; my emphases). The work in its totality: that is what must be seen.

Doubtless when Wellek and Warren invoke the obligation to *see* the totality of the work, this is just a manner of speaking. The entity they call the totality of the work is not, strictly speaking, something that can be seen; it is not, in other words, to be confused with some object of perception, for example, the assembled pages of a book. It is therefore not perceivable as such. (If there were any doubt about this, one could read their later chapter titled "The Mode of Existence of a Literary Work of Art," where they endorse up to a point Roman Ingarden's phenomenological analysis principally because it determines the work's mode of existence with reference to what Husserl called an ideality, which is not sensible but only intelligible.) This notion supposes a subject or a subjectivity who or which is able to represent to itself the idea, the ideality of totality. Given that this totality is not an object of so-called ordinary perception, the subject that has to be supposed by this idea of the work is not an ordinary perceiving subject. It is rather a subject capable of representing to itself the work as totality, thus, of seeing what is nowhere to be seen *as such*. Therefore, when Wellek and Warren invoke the obligation to see such a thing, when they write of "the obligation *to see* the work in its totality," they are indexing first of all this subjective capacity to figure an ideality, namely "the work in its totality," to "see" it figuratively in the manner not of perception but finally of theorizing. In theory, for theory, and for the theorizing subject, the work is a totality.

There is then a necessity, or an obligation, to suppose such a subject. Wellek and Warren, however, confuse this necessity, in effect, with the work itself, which they insist must be seen as a totality by this subject. The phrase that seems to point to some lingering problem with totalities still today occurs in the final lines of chapter 3, titled "The Nature of Literature." The nature of literature and the nature of the work of literature is to be a totality, so they conclude. But this conclusion has been drawn, it would seem, simply from the necessity of figuring a subject capable of conceiving such an ideality. If so, then although one may be able to say something about the nature of this subject, aren't we as much in the dark as ever about any putative "nature" of literature or of the work of literature? How can a phenomenology of the theorizing subject ever yield an ontology of literature or its works? Does not a phenomenology of literature necessarily have to produce a theory of literature as the self-knowledge or self-consciousness of the reading subject?

There is something in this confusion, it seems to me, that lingers on long after the totalizing effects of the idea (or the ideality) of Western or European literature have been largely exposed, made obvious, even if not necessarily thereby dispelled. What lingers, I believe, is less some figure of literature as totality (despite our being in "a global age," there are as yet, as far as I know, no departments of global literature) than endless possible figures of whatever can obligate one to continue to read, for example, literature. What lingers is the force of an obligation, although not necessarily, as it was for Wellek and Warren, the "obligation to see the work in its totality." For the remainder of this chapter, I will consider another possible response to which this obligation can give rise, another "theory of literature," if you will, although inasmuch as it tries not to confuse the (necessity for a) seeing, theorizing subject with the structure of the literary "object," it is anything but a theory, anything but a theory of literature, and certainly not a theory of comparative literature. Instead, there is response to what I will call, for the occasion, literature without comparison, which is a thing not to be subsumed too quickly to an ideality, that is, to something whose "mode of existence," as Wellek and Warren put it, is as "a system of norms of ideal concepts which are intersubjective."[5] Indeed, as we can quickly verify, the obligation this thing carries with it is tied, inextricably, to its material mode of existence, to its "materiality," to use this currently much-favored word.

An obligation to literature: I would prefer to speak of fiction, the fiction that is at the heart, if you will, of literature. The obligation I want to isolate, if possible, is to that essential fictional movement whereby the one who does the writing can never be simply equated with the poetic voice, character, narrator, and certainly not with what Blanchot calls the "voix narrative." Fiction, then, understood as whatever may arise from the essential possibility of saying "I" and meaning another, or alternatively of saying "he" or "she" without being able to exclude a reference to self. When Rimbaud reported in one of his "lettres du voyant" that he had recognized himself as a poet, it was as one for whom, in his famous phrase, "I is another" (" . . . il faut être fort, être né poète, et je me suis reconnu poète. C'est faux de dire: Je pense: on devrait dire on me pense. . . . JE est un autre").[6] But this is to evoke an obligation, and a responsibility, to a structure whereby the responsibility of the legal signatory, the author him- or herself, is suspended, evacuated, or at least rendered null before any law that supposes a responsibilizable subject who can be held accountable for his or her acts. How is one to construe an obligation to that which begins thus by untying obligation from the legally responsibilized subject? How indeed is one to construe it in a way that would not be simply irresponsible?

We can refer these questions first to a book titled *On the Name*, which is signed Jacques Derrida. This book obeys what seems to be a thoroughly different obligation from that which may be incurred by a theory of literature that must posit its object for the subject. Derrida evinces an obligation to the irreducible possibility of fiction, which obligation is incurred by what we call democracy; it is even an obligatory condition so that there may be democracy. What he argues here quite forcefully is that the possibility of democracy, the possibility of justice is indissociably bound up with an unlimited, unregulated, uncensored possibility of fiction. In the pages from which I am going to quote some passages, it is also possible to hear an argument about the essentially fictional status of our democracies as well as about the essentially democratic institution we have called literature in the West:

> Literature is a modern invention, inscribed in conventions and institutions that, to hold on to just this trait, secure in principle its *right to say everything* [le *droit de tout dire*]. Literature thus ties its destiny to a certain noncensorship, to the space of democratic freedom (freedom of the press, freedom of speech, freedom of opinion, and so forth). No democracy without literature; no literature without democracy. One may always wish away either of these, and under all regimes, there has been no shortage of those ready to get along without one or the other; one may well consider neither of them to be an unconditional source of all that is good or to be indispensable rights. But one cannot, in either these ways or others, dissociate one from the other. No analysis of them would be capable of that. And each time that a literary work

is censured, democracy is in danger, as everyone agrees. The possibility of literature, the authorization that a society grants it, the lifting of suspicion or of terror with regard to it, all of that goes together—politically—with the unlimited right to pose all questions, to suspect all dogmatisms, to analyze all presuppositions, even those of the ethics or the politics of responsibility.[7]

Although this passage does not speak of obligation, one nevertheless reads it as itself placed under obligation, specifically the obligation to grant literature, what we conventionally call and institute as "literature" or fiction, the right to say everything, in French, *le droit de tout dire*. Fiction is that which arrogates to itself, gives itself, requires, demands, and puts us under obligation to grant it *le droit de tout dire*. The word "tout," which is here a pronoun but which also has uses as an adverb or a noun, is, one notices, of the same family, the same Latin family (European and Western, therefore) as totality. There is, one could say, a lingering family resemblance among the languages that have drawn words from the Latin *totum* or *totus*, which does not mean, of course, that they form a totality. In French, there are still many such words, whereas English has made do with forms of totality, total, totalize. Hence, we must translate *le droit de tout dire* as "the right to say (or tell) everything, anything, all, or anything at all." Certainly, however, we cannot translate it as the right to some totality, the right to be or to appear as a totality. The *tout* of *tout dire* does not translate as totality but as anything at all, for example. The right to say anything at all, which is the unquestionable right of literature or fiction, does not carry with it, therefore, the obligation, as Wellek and Warren put it, "to see the work in its totality." One is under obligation, rather, to grant literature an unlimited right to say *tout*, anything, everything, all it chooses to say. No containing borders, limits, or definitions can be set in advance on what it has the right to say. By this right, which we are obliged to grant it, it cannot be contained within any legal limits; it figures no totality that can be represented to the subject capable of idealization. On the contrary, *tout dire*, saying everything and anything, would figure a force that deconstructs this representation. That is, because it carries with it "the unlimited right to pose all questions [*toutes questions*], to suspect all dogmatisms [*tous dogmatismes*], to analyze all presuppositions [*toutes présuppositions*]," the *tout dire* reserves the right to deconstruct the idealized limits on what is possible, on what it is possible, for example, for literature to say.

So, literature as *le droit de tout dire* and literature as totality, despite some family resemblance, are not to be related except insofar as the former deconstructs the latter. But there is another sense of *tout dire*. The same phrase can also be used in expressions that would be better translated as "tell all," as when one means to say that someone has told all his or her secrets. In this sense, *le droit de tout dire* would carry an implication of the right to tell all, to keep no secrets, to hold nothing back. Are we not also obligated to understand literature's unlimited and inalienable right in this fashion?

The answer, it seems to me, must be at once yes and no. Yes, to the extent that no act of censorship can ever be allowed to limit the kinds of "secrets" divulged by literature, meaning once again, fiction and works of fiction. But as soon as one specifies literature as fiction, then this right it has to divulge secrets is also emptied or suspended in a peculiar way. Therefore, no, we are not obligated to understand literature's, that is, fiction's right as the right to tell all, to keep no secrets. This is because the I-is-another structure of fiction will forever leave open to question whether fiction is even capable of divulging secrets at all. What it would seem unable to do, however, is *confess* the secrets of a subject, just one subject since it is structured by the fundamental sharing of all the secrets of one subject, one "I" with another. This secret sharing of fiction (and one may think of Conrad's novella *The Secret Sharer* as in effect narrativizing the fiction's own condition of possibility) happens, however, in the open; indeed it is the opening up of fictional space. No secrets can be bared in fiction because nothing can keep itself hidden in that opening, which is not at all a figure of depth—the opening of a door, of a tomb, or of a mouth—but the opening of a space between all depths, an open spacing, not even flat, where everything comes to be articulated with anything, even its supposed opposite, according to an effect of the *tout dire,* which leaves nothing concealed in the opened space it arrogates to itself. Yet, at the same time, this structure of fiction also imparts itself as a seal on whatever is placed under the protection of the right to say all, tell all, or write anything. It is protected speech also in the sense that none can wrench from it the confession of its truth; none can make it speak in the mode of true confession before the bar or in an interrogation room. The right to *tout dire* is thus *at the same time* the right of absolute non-response to whatever or whoever would propose to make it tell all. For that reason, the right to say anything and everything would be indissociable from the right to say nothing at all.

This makes the space of fiction, of the *tout dire*, the space, paradoxically, of a certain inviolability of the secret.

This inviolability, the absolute secret that remains sealed by fiction, brings out a contradiction inherent in the democratic concept of responsibility, as responsibility of a subject before the law. Here is how Derrida lays out this contradiction in *On the Name*:

> This authorization to *tout dire* . . . acknowledges a right to absolute nonresponse, there where it cannot be a matter of responding, of being able to or of being obliged to respond. This nonresponse is more originary and more secret than the modalities of "being able to" or "being obliged to," because it is fundamentally heterogeneous to them. There is here a hyperbolic condition of democracy that seems to contradict a certain determined and historically limited concept of the said democracy, the one that links it to the concept of a subject that is calculable, countable, imputable, and responsible, a subject having-to-respond [*devant-répondre*], having-to-tell [*devant-dire*] the truth, having to testify on sworn faith ("the whole truth, nothing but the truth"), before the law [*devant la loi*], having to reveal the secret. . . . (29; trans. modified)

The formulation of what Derrida calls here the hyperbolic condition of democracy is of enormous importance, it seems to me, for any discussion of politics today. I am going to try to demonstrate this very briefly in conclusion by reviewing a recent chapter of political history in the U.S. I propose to submit this event to the scrutiny or the test of democracy's hyperbolic condition.

The event in question concerns democracy as it has been put to the test in the U.S., which very much likes to think of itself as the world's leading democracy and as leading the rest of the world to democracy American-style (largely if not solely the style of the capitalist market). This test via the hyperbolic condition of fiction will consider the democratic credentials of the American political process, to the extent that that process can be distinguished from the working of the interests of capital. If indeed there are politics in America (which is a serious question), then somewhere, in some discourse or other, they have to be distinguished from the interests of capital. The discourse that performs or that would perform this distinction in the U.S. is above all the discourse of democratic law, and of the principle of equality under the law. It is not surprising, therefore, that the trial case to be considered takes the form of a legal procedure conducted fully in public view: the impeachment of a President. This event, which entirely

absorbed public political discourse in the U.S. for a full year, consisted
solely in making public a private matter, indeed of making public the very
privates of the President, his penis and even his semen. The relation between public and private, as already shown, is precisely what is in question
in fiction's *droit de tout dire* inasmuch as this right may be construed as the
right to publish all secrets. This is why it would perhaps be apt (or at least
interesting) to submit this whole affair to the action of deconstruction via
the hyperbolic condition of democracy.

To begin this brief experiment, let us recall the contradiction Derrida
identifies in the limited concept of democracy. This concept is limited because tied to the concept of the responsible subject obliged "to tell the
truth . . . to reveal the secret" and therefore in contradiction with the
more originary right of absolute nonresponse. It is this contradiction that
surfaced in a massive way throughout the impeachment process. In order
for perjury regarding private sexual relations to be put forward as evidence
of high crimes and misdemeanors, the notion of nonresponse to the demand to tell the truth has to have been equated with an essential threat to
democracy itself. And so it was countless times on the floor of both houses
of the U.S. Congress, principally, of course, by Clinton's political oppo-
nents, who wished to see in the President's nonresponse the grounds for
conviction on the impeachment charges. But there were likewise none
among his defenders, as far as I know, who spoke in defense of any right
to absolute nonresponse. The consensus was and remains that under the
rule of law, democracy always requires that the truth be told, the whole
truth [*toute la vérité*] and nothing but the truth.[8] What is thus exposed is
the contradiction between democracy instantiated and producing its effects as the rule of law, on the one hand, and what Derrida refers to here
as "the hyperbolic condition of democracy," the nonresponse that is "ba-
sically heterogeneous" to the modalities of power and obligation [*pouvoir*
and *devoir*].

In the events leading up to Clinton's acquittal, there was, I believe, one
very specific moment at which this contradiction came into play most
critically, the contradiction between democracy's instantiated rule of law
and its hyperbolic condition in absolute nonresponse—or even absolute
secret. It is a point at which one might be able clearly to "see" the contradiction at work if it were not for the fact that the event in question concerns the condition of non-revelation and it does so under the cover or
force of law. As is well known, Monica Lewinsky's initial deposition by the

Office of the Independent Counsel and all of her subsequent testimony before juries and grand juries, before committees of managers or the upper house of Congress, was made under an agreement of immunity from prosecution on any charges that might arise from her telling all, the whole truth and nothing but the truth. There was, however, a very surprising clause included in this agreement as drawn up by Kenneth Starr's Office of Independent Council. Under the terms of this clause, Lewinsky was explicitly forbidden from revealing the circumstances under which she was initially interrogated by the prosecutors and investigators of the OIC. In other words, she was expressly prohibited by this agreement, under penalty of revocation of her immunity and liability to prosecution, from discussing, describing, leaking, or otherwise breaking the seal on whatever happened when, apparently against her will, she was made to testify as to the whole truth of all her most intimate relations with another human being. To be quite precise, these circumstances, and whatever degree of coercion or force they brought to bear on her reluctance to be made to speak before the law, were not to be discussed or described by her with journalists or in any legal proceeding. They were thereby placed under the seal of secrecy by law, which covers itself (but by what right?) with a veil of secrecy. Such a veil would seem to function solely to hide the self-instituting figure of the law as always possibly lawless force or coercion. So, for instance, her first interview on television, after Clinton's acquittal, was preprogrammed by this prior restraint; hence no questions were allowed on the subject of her initial interrogation by the OIC. Nor could she, by force of this condition on her immunity, reveal this condition. In other words, she had to silence the fact that she was keeping silence. The spectacle thus created in effect concealed the other scene in which the force of law forces its own concealment as force without law.

In exchange for her compliance or docility in this regard, in exchange for keeping the law's secret, Lewinsky got to make her debut on national television as a tell-all heroine in the perverse romance of democracy as ruled solely by truth insofar as truth can be determined by law: essentially this is the truth of witnesses who take an oath before the law. I call this romance perverse because, as we see, at some point it turns aside the movement of tell-all truth before the bar of the law. When a figure of the law demands to remain hidden, the tell-all movement is perverted, turned aside, as if it had been infected with a kind of auto-immune disease. It turns against itself, or against the only available figure of itself, which is tell-all revelation. I mention auto-immunity because when this perverse effect of law seeks to limit danger to the legal system of truth, it grants what it itself calls immunity. Derrida's analysis, at the very least, gives one a way of understanding why this perverse effect occurs. It happens when the democratic rule of law and of legally established truth becomes cut off from its hyperbolic condition, the right of absolute nonresponse. It is important to note as well how the media played a role in covering (and covering up) the law's contradiction. The media in general, inasmuch as they would cover everything, that is, leave nothing to be uncovered, with their demand for the totality of truth, the whole truth, are the media of this perversion to the extent that they are supposed to have a truth-telling, journalistic function.

I mentioned that the conditioning limitation on Lewinsky's immunity agreement extended only to journalistic or judicial contexts of truth-telling. What is interesting is that the Office of the Independent Council did not or could not enforce its gag rule on the book in which Lewinsky "tells all" to Andrew Morton. This is interesting because it seems to indicate that the force of law remains somewhere obliged to yield to the structure of fiction, the "I is another," or "I" as told to another where everything stated, described, asserted, declared to be the whole truth will have been submitted first to the fictional opening that seals it as inviolable secret. One does not need even to read *Monica's Story* to have little doubt about one thing: Kenneth Starr would be among the first to want to label it a fiction, especially, no doubt, those pages in which she recounts the violent and violating circumstances of the initial interrogation to which she was subjected by Starr's henchmen.[9] But Starr was also apparently the first who was obliged to grant the book the right to appear in print, and therefore immediately in every other media.

And to appear in any guise it chose. Monica could even choose, if she wished, to make it appear that she was everyone's victim, not just Starr's. She must not be prosecuted for imagining herself in the role of romance heroine, who, like a Jane Eyre from Beverly Hills, deserves to be rescued from her unfortunate life and given a lot of money or at least a great job. That is her fiction. And even if, in some real court or the court of some reality, she might reasonably be held responsible for having put in motion, with this fiction, the whole event of impeachment, that would only confirm our sense from the beginning that this was not *really* happening, that it would not and could not happen that the U.S. President would be removed from office on such *fictional* grounds, thereby threatening to annul a supposedly democratic election. But because these grounds got authorized by the machinery of a legal system, which had been placed in the service of an Office of Independent Council, they were endorsed as having a general truth. Once the fiction was authorized as general truth, the event had too many authors to hold any one of them responsible. Responsibility, as the responsibility of individual subjects under the law, was suspended.

Unless responsibility lies there where our democracy would attempt to sever the connection to its own hyperbolic condition, to the absolute right of nonresponse. But how to take responsibility for this nonresponse and this nonresponsibility? And who can take it?

—It is strange how, having set out from some pages in Wellek and Warren's *Theory of Literature*, you have ended up between the sheets or under the covers of *Monica's Story*, as if it were the greatest example of fiction in our time, and the greatest representative of literature in the post-impeachment U.S.[10]

—Strange indeed. This strangeness accompanies the experience of deconstruction, which is always somewhere the deconstruction of the totalities (and totalitarianisms) under which or with which we still live, either in memory or here in the present (in fact, however, always both at the same time). The deconstruction of totalitarian or totalizing systems produces this strange experience of "life" doubling itself in fiction, and it does so with uncanny effects. I may have just demonstrated this uncanniness with a deconstruction of any possible theory of literature, which is by nature comparative literature, that is, literature as a totality. Rather than a totality, the right to *tout dire* articulates with the contrary right, the right *not* to say or tell all, the right to withhold the truth *from* the truth, from the law of truth. The right to say not all, not yet all, so that one may still say everything or anything at all.

—So that *one* may still do these contradictory things? Who or what is this "one" who/that can suspend the totality of truth's regime?

—If you have followed the demonstration, this "one" would be what we are still calling literature, the one in whose name—which is no one's proper name—the right is granted to say all and not all at the same time. As such a "one," however, literature has never been a subject. It is no one who could come before the law and swear to tell the truth. Rather, it is that which can speak or tell all while leaving inviolable the secret of its nonresponse. It is such a one who or which is capable of producing such an event, at least in principle. Literature, that is, fiction, is always the possibility of events, events that can happen, that could happen, that could have happened. This possibility is infinite, but only so long as we recognize its absolute right to nonresponse. Democracy, if it is possible, has somewhere to resist the terror of its own law, its own demand for truth without shadow. No democracy without an absolute obscurity, which is not just the absence of light, the obscurity of what would otherwise be visible and that can be brought to light; rather, it is the obscurity, the absolute non-visiblity I began by invoking with the initial approach to reading, and to reading "Reading" in our title. It is what happens, obscurely, when anyone reads.

—Which is to say: everything, anything, and nothing at all.

§ 10 The Other Fiction

The pretext for this reflection is the question: what effects, if any, has deconstructive thought had on new narrative writing?[1] For reasons that I hope will become clear, I am obliged to redirect the question toward a place where the deconstruction of its terms can begin. Without leaving these terms behind, I would like to situate them in a more general field, the field of the possible relation between deconstruction and literary fiction or narrative. This relation is anything but simple or obvious. It would thus be far too ambitious to attempt to give a summary account of it. I have chosen, therefore, to insist on certain features that seem most pertinent in this context. It is likewise these features that can help me explain why I must back up or back off in order to approach the question as posed.

I back up, first of all, from the notion of a relation between two heterogeneous forms of discourse, of which one would be theoretical, scientific, or descriptive and the other fictional, inventive, or creative. Such a schema is altogether inapt to characterize what ought to interest one most about this relation. First, because it assumes that deconstruction is a kind of discourse. Although there has been over the last thirty years an effort toward a new theorization that has given itself or let itself be given the name deconstruction, this name was forged at the outset to indicate precisely that which prevents any discourse from presenting itself without fault or remainder. That is why this work of theorization has never put itself forward as a method or even a theory, that is, as a totalizing or systematizing view on some object. Deconstruction, rather, is what happens at the limits of any discursive or conceptual construction, what makes for opening at the limits of such constructions. With this name, Jacques Derrida and then others who have followed him on this path have attempted to get theoretical leverage on what is already, always underway and what does without any proper name, being the possibility of the name before the name. It turned out that this provisional, improper, and ambivalent name of deconstruction offered itself like a handle with which diverse institutions could grab onto what was showing up in this work, and thereby constitute it as a thing or an object—like a pitcher or a jug—having a certain usefulness for and within these institutions. It is not deconstruction as such that is thereby institutionalized (for there is no deconstruction as such), but the possibility of reference to forces that are destabilizing reference.

These distinctions need to be underscored because they are indispensable, I believe, to any rigorous consideration of the proposed theme: the relation of deconstruction to literary invention. To take the term "deconstruction" too much in the sense in which the institutions of literary or journalistic criticism have appropriated it is to renounce at the outset the possibility of finding anything remotely pertinent to say about this relation. Even in the limited context of our question, deconstruction can interest us only as a force working at the borders of all institutions, as the space of their casting and recasting, of their invention and their history.

There is a second reason to refrain from giving a description of this relation that begins by supposing some fundamental distinction between deconstruction and writing called literary, that assumes we are talking, if not about two kinds of discourse, then about two clearly distinct categories of work in and on writing. Once again, such a supposition seems to me difficult to maintain; what is more, by staking out the field of our interrogation in this way, one prepares it to dissimulate the very thing one is looking for. There are at least four reasons for this.

1) Deconstructive thought has demarcated itself from the philosophical tradition to which it is heir in several ways, one of the most important being its way of taking into account the givens of writing called literary. This is, of course, one of the reasons for which "deconstruction" in the insitution of the university has so often been assimilated to literary disciplines, whereas, with few exceptions, the academic discipline of philosophy, especially in the Anglo-American university, has preferred to ignore it. One needs to recall these well-known conditions so as not to give refuge too quickly to the traditional reflex in our manner of interrogating the relation between deconstruction and literature. This reflex finds support as soon as one supposes an effective division there where deconstructive

thought has constantly questioned such a simple divisibility. This supposition has taken several different forms, of course, since Plato sought to expel a certain practice of mimesis in order to preserve intact the regimen of truth, a gesture that has been relayed by Aristotelian rhetoric, the great aesthetic theories of Kant and Hegel, down to the different "sciences" of literature in our day. There is, nevertheless, a constant feature throughout this history: this feature, which has been remarked by deconstructive thought, is the house arrest of fiction as a genre that is dependent on, secondary to, or derived from philosophical or scientific truth. Literature has always been thought according to this feature or trait that makes of it a domain over which philosophy has purview, a domain already *comprehended* by philosophy. By remarking this trait, that is, by remarking the gesture whereby philosophy subsumes to itself, in the phrase of a current practitioner, "the logical status of fictional discourse,"[2] deconstruction situates the place of an opening onto another thinking of fiction that would not be the contrary of truth, but rather the possibility, in differance, of this very distinction.[3] At the same time, the figure of philosophy comprehending fictionality within itself is retraced by deconstructive thought to quite different effect when what is thereby brought out is the irreducible metaphoricity—*or writing*—of any discourse of truth.

2) With this thinking of differance before or beyond the distinction truth/fiction, one is set before a reconfiguration of the field in which literature or fiction no longer occupies the place of simply one circumscribed object among others. By fiction, then, one must understand that which traces and retraces the borders of the field, crossing them in all directions and pluralizing them endlessly. What is called deconstruction brings this crossing and pluralization to bear in the case it makes for literary writing as that which has an original, rather than just derived or secondary, force of thought. But deconstructive theorization is also traversed by the fiction of which it speaks and in several ways. In Derrida's writings, the fictional crossing sometimes gets remarked in an altogether patent fashion, for example in "Envois" in *The Post Card*, which may be read as an epistolary novel that exposes and overrides many of the conventions of the genre. Or in numerous polylogued texts by the same author, in which there are the minimal outlines of "characters," of narrating voices, and so forth. These are but the most obvious narrative procedures one may encounter in just this one writer-thinker, but one whose writings are naturally at the center of this discussion. As for "poetic" procedures, the think-

ing of the language in the language, as for fiction in the sense I alluded to a moment ago, their share in this work cannot be identified as easily, for it would situate the very place of the opening of this writing. As such, fiction is irreducible and leaves its fundamental mark—that of a groundless ground—on all the movements of "non-fictional" writing.

3) Is this, then, to say that there is no distinction to be made between writings called literary and those we tend to read as theoretical, philosophical, historical and so forth? The answer to this question is double. On the one hand, one must reply: no, quite obviously, but it is just as obvious that such distinctions always arise out of provisional determinations on which depend at the same time all sorts of institutions. On the other hand, therefore, a paradox appears, the very paradox I am trying to isolate and that is brought together in the obviousness of these distinctions. This paradox is made to appear as soon as one poses the question, as we are doing here: what is happening that is new in, for example, novelistic writing? Such a question invokes a genre or a category of writing but so as to ask right away if the limits of the genre have not been displaced somewhere. Yet, how is one supposed to recognize that which does not resemble any model if the instrument guiding this search—here the notion of the novelistic genre—must prove to be the one most apt to provoke a *misrecognition* of the thing sought? I will return to this problem in some detail below. For the moment, let us insist merely on this first observation: the notion of genre, here a literary genre, must itself be susceptible to radical suspension in order for the sought-after transformation to even be possible. This is to say that this transformation cannot take place within the given limits of a genre but only on the condition of a possible effacement of those limits—and thus of the genre. If one wished to take this observation to its extreme—and why not?—one would have to say that the condition of a genre is the suspension of whatever distinguishes it from other genres, from other genres of genres (for example, genres called non-literary), and from genres without genre. Genre as such, by itself, well contained within its limits: that is what there has never been and this "never" is the condition for new genres to arise. This condition is also what is called deconstruction, which is perhaps first of all and above all the deconstruction of "genre."

4) There is a last feature to be added to this portrait of writing in deconstruction. It is the most difficult one to sketch rapidly for it concerns the phantom that has incessantly haunted any reflection on writing: the

distinction form/content. It reappears, at least implicitly, in our question that seeks to determine the relation between a thinking of writing and a certain practice on the basis of that thinking. I have just suggested why deconstruction cannot be reduced to either a discourse, a theory, and thus still less to a content, as it is called; the pertinence of the couple form/content is overrun at every point by the movement of deconstruction. And is it not just such an overrunning or exceeding that must take place in order for something other to appear, that is, something that would be neither a simple putting into form of an already given content, nor a simple change of themes that leaves the form intact?

This is where we need to have recourse to another term that signifies neither form nor content and yet both form and content at the same time: the term "force." When one is led to speak of the force of a writing, what is one talking about if not that which has no possible measure in a content to be represented or a form to be repeated? Force forces the form to give up its content and the content to think its form; it is thus the force of a conjunction of the other with the same, a conjunction whose powerful reserve can be redeployed many times and always otherwise without being easily exhausted. Such force arises neither from a thinking without form, a pure thought, nor from a form that would be beautiful in itself, a pure aesthetic object. There is no aesthetics of force. And I would add: there is also no aesthetics of deconstruction.

(How to go on after such a *coup de force*? Especially when I am writing, as I did for the original occasion of this essay, in a language that is not mine and in which, therefore, force is what I lack? I will never be able to invent anything in French; my "inventions" will always run the risk of being taken for errors, even for barbarisms. This is merely to make explicit the confession of a desire: to write or speak correctly the other's language, without giving oneself away too quickly as the foreigner that one is to that idiom. Such a desire pulls me into the fiction in which I would now be writing and another would be reading *as if* . . . as if I were inventing my language instead of submitting to a double constraint, namely, the laws of its system and the fact that I understand these laws across several levels of translation. [And this is no less the case here where I am ostensibly translating French "back" into English, my first and finally only language.] I could never explain this strange desire without launching into many stories—family histories, love stories—that, in the end, would explain nothing at all, that would only put some additional phantasms into play in the scene enacted, and that would thus be more than ever out of place here. Up to this point I have chosen to imitate an "objective" discourse, as it's called, which invents nothing and whose only possible and very limited interest would be in the correctness or precision of its assertions. If, nevertheless, I have inserted this parenthesis, it is as a sort of warning or reminder that nothing is perhaps more "false" than this objectivity, that it covers over innumerable stories and endless novels, that its objective remains the impossible language, at once inventive and invented, that would know how to speak to the other without detours or translations. To invent one's language as the language of the other: is there any other fiction worth dreaming about?)

Is invention another name for force? And are we doing anything else here but wondering whether deconstruction invents and how so? In particular, has it invented any new stories, any new narrative possibilities? Formulated in this way, our question forms a fold around the apparently irreducible element of narrativity: what is called an event. The event is that which allows one to identify a writing as narrative and, when taken in the sense of that which happens for the first time, it is the criterion of invention, here the invention of a new writing. The figure of the fold is inevitable because we are attempting to speak, in effect, of literary invention as invention of invention or event of events. Let us try, therefore, to unfold somewhat this doubled syntax.

To begin, one can take the term "event" in the sense it is given in narratology. Didier Coste, in *Narrative as Communication*, provides a succinct definition of this sense: "1. narrative discourse is the genre of discourse whose minimal unit, the NARRATEME, (re)presents an EVENT; 2. an EVENT is a comparison between two states of a single entity separate in time and differing by at least one feature other than their temporal situation."[3] For reasons no doubt of clarity and simplicity, the first example Coste proposes of an event in this sense is an increase in the price of a pound of beef. Indeed, such an example makes one thing clear: what interests the narratologist are the necessary and minimal traits that will permit him to identify narratemes and thus a narrative discourse, so as to determine subsequently the place this discourse occupies in a text. What is of less interest to him is a certain event structure that is not simply part of the narration, that does not constitute it either as uttered or utterance.

Narratology sets aside or disregards any event that does not present itself as "a comparison between two states of a single entity separate in time." No narrateme represents the event in the sense of the first time, of that which happens only once and that happens less in time than to time. Representation will always repeat the "only once"; it will always bring everything that happens to it under its regime of repetition. Following other narratologists, Coste thus points to what he calls the narrative paradox, namely: "In order to understand 'X has changed,' I have to accept that X remains X whether p or -p is true about it" (9).

By isolating this paradox, which both affirms and negates a change to X (an algebraic designator that Coste will quickly identify as a subject for the reader) and by making the paradox into the crucial test of its own pertinence, narratology installs itself within the limits of representation. Which is why it can never be a question there of what happens *to* representation, of what happens at its limits, of its de-limitation, and still less of that more-than-paradoxical "event" that is the repetition of a first time and the first time of repetition. If, therefore, we want to pursue any further these questions—in general, the question of invention—we will have to abandon narratology here and tack in another direction.

An essay by Jacques Derrida takes precisely this question of invention as its principal theme. What the author says there about the circumstances in which this theme imposed itself on him seems very pertinent to our context here:

> why is the word "invention," that tired, worn-out, classical word, today experiencing a revival, a new fashionableness, and a new way of life? A statistical analysis of the occidental *doxa* would, I am sure, bring it to light: in vocabulary, in book titles, the rhetoric of advertisement, literary criticism, political oratory, and even in the passwords of art, morality, and religion. A strange return of a desire for invention. . . . To invent not this or that, some *tekhnè* or some fable, but to invent the world, a world . . . a novel world, another habitat, another person, another desire even. A closer analysis should show why it is then the word "invention" that imposes itself, more quickly and more often than other neighboring words ("discover," "create," "imagine," "produce," and so on). And why this desire for invention, which goes so far as to dream of inventing a new desire, on the one hand remains contemporary with a certain experience of fatigue, of weariness, of exhaustion, but on the other hand accompanies a desire for deconstruction, going so far as to lift the apparent contradiction that might exist between deconstruction and invention.[4]

The pertinence for our context of these observations can be stated in a few words: a desire for invention has shown up across a vast cultural field; our question about narrative or novelistic invention is part of this phenomenon, which has been explicitly inflected here with a demand addressed to deconstruction, despite the "apparent contradiction" that Derrida signals between deconstruction and invention. This contradiction has nothing to do with the fact that, habitually and mistakenly, deconstruction is apprehended in exclusively negative forms, which would thus be destructuring and, so it would seem, non-inventive. Rather, the contradiction resides in the wearing down and using up of the very concept of invention, which it would then be a matter of re-inventing by elaborating the deconstruction already at work in the concept and that has begun to make its effects felt. But here's the question: deconstructed, is invention still invention? Is it not the word and concept "invention" that needs to be replaced by another, for example the word "deconstruction"?

In the course of the essay in question, Derrida does not propose such a substitution; he even refuses it explicitly when he writes: "I am not trying to conflate the problematics of invention with that of deconstruction," but then right away adds, in the next paragraph, "Deconstruction is inventive or it is nothing at all" (ibid.). This would lead one to understand something like an inventive *essence* of deconstruction if it were possible to speak here of essence. Perhaps, however, it is merely the word "invention" that is being preserved here, and this is an instance of the deconstructive practice of paleonymy. For it is a word that says the coming of something other as unparalleled event, as the arrival of an "avenir" or future and of what can overcome or "survenir" the convention of repetition of the same.

Such a coming of invention, however, lends itself to misrecognition when its identifying features are made to conform to the figure of man, himself the inventor and the inventor of himself as the same. What if the *force* of invention did not belong or return to whoever holds the patent or signs the book, even though it is precisely these positions that are recognized and maintained by our invented institutions of invention? To allow to appear that which does not return to the same in a movement of thinking or invention: this is what is called deconstruction. What, then, would be an invention that does not return to the same, that is not already programmed by the institutions that grant it its status of invention?

This is one way to translate the terms of our question—and all the difficulty such an undertaking involves. This difficulty has already been flagged: How does one recognize that which has no previously recognized model? How does one recognize what is by definition unrecognizable? Posed in this way, the problem does not seem to admit of any solution. But perhaps this is because we are invoking a simplified notion of invention, according to which invention has to break with whatever might confer on it a recognizable status. Let us examine this notion briefly with Derrida:

> we have at least the feeling that an invention ought not, as such and as it first emerges, have a status. At the moment when it erupts, the inaugural invention ought to overflow, overlook, transgress, negate (or, at least—this is a supplementary complication—avoid or deny) the status that people would have wanted to assign to it or grant it in advance; indeed it ought to overstep the space in which that status itself takes on its meaning and its legitimacy—in short, the whole environment of *reception* that by definition ought never be ready to welcome an authentic innovation. On this hypothesis (which is not mine, for the time being) it is here that a theory of reception should either encounter its essential limit or else complicate its claims with a theory of transgressive gaps. About the latter we can no longer tell whether it would still be theory and whether it would be a theory of something like reception. (41)

This hypothesis of transgressive invention, which Derrida will refer to as the "common-sense hypothesis," leads strictly to the precise contrary of common sense: if an invention must transgress everything that institutional space can envision as possible, then the invention of what is merely possible is not an invention; the only possible invention would be the invention of the impossible, which is not possible. Impossible invention is the only possible invention (60). In the face of such a suspension of decidable grammar, the problematics of invention call for the deconstruction of the figuration of a *same* space, which cannot hold together these absolutely contradictory assertions. As a result, the concept of invention is opened up to another movement, which is no longer merely that of transgression and of its reception or nonreception. The limit between these two moments or these two loci of invention is displaced and, through this displacement, divided and repeated. Invention begins by repeating, which is why it is impossible. But from out of that impossibility is traced the nonrepresentable, unrepeatable other, the other of invention.

It is, then, the whole field of literary (but not only literary) invention that would have to be rethought, reinvented. On one side (to continue to use this language of simple division), what has been called invention might be revealed as a particular mode of reception, a very elaborated fashion of receiving the other movement and letting it be inscribed. At the end of his text, Derrida will speak of the necessity of "the most genial inventiveness . . . to prepare to welcome" the coming of the other (60). On the other side, then, what has been called reception, rather than an arrival and arrest at destination, would be the locus of the apparently contradictory movement, a putting-into-motion. This rethinking, therefore, would also call literary criticism, history, and theory to another task than the one that has traditionally fallen to those discourses: the other task would be the literally endless one of receiving without arresting literature's a-destinality.

—Has not this thing called the novel always required, since its invention, an improbable, even impossible "milieu of reception"?

—No doubt, and doubtless as well it is only on the condition of not granting it a fixed status, a duly registered patent, that this milieu can promise the genre-less genre a future in which it will continue to resemble itself even as it defies us to find any resemblances there. Such an improbable milieu would itself be a space of great inventiveness to the extent that it is constantly testing its own receptivity, and not only as regards the most recent writings, but with the immense anachronistic resources of the genre that is nevertheless supposed to be the most historical of all. Has there ever been, is there still *a* milieu of reception, just one, for *Tristram Shandy* or *Jacques le fataliste*, to name only these two texts that are at the same time without genre and of many genres, all the genres? Like every invention, the novel will have begun by repeating itself, narrating itself, citing and reciting itself, even parodying itself.

—So, the question would not be whether and how deconstruction contributes to narrative invention, but rather, how, without this invention, we could even call upon something called deconstruction.

§ 11 Syringe (at the point)

I am going to try to write of and from an untenable, even painful place: the point of sharpest contact with certain texts of Jacques Derrida's, at the tip of the pointed instrument of a writing, there where a common language and remnants of an idiom cut into each other and words split apart.[1] This will be all the more painful, or simply beside the point, in that the point in question articulates itself in another language and I am therefore going to have to translate. A repeated shibboleth effect, marking this linguistic frontier, will at every turn threaten to divide the tongue.

To begin, a few questions: What is it that cuts a text in this fashion? What is it in literature in particular or at its edges that cuts, or perhaps that stabs like a sword or stings like a syringe with "a sharpened point"? Next, what is this blood by which one recognizes the passion of literature, in literature, and as literature? Why is it that the literal mark of literature is blood, a bleeding passion that is quickly cooled by the drying ink, which is the cut's strange survival? "Il faut que ça saigne," "It has to bleed": Is this the watchword of the letter, the letter of literature that is cut out and marked off as something other within writing in general?

Jacques Derrida has at several points identified this "something other" with the features of the "tout-dire," the "say-everything" that arrogates to itself the right to put everything into language and, by means of a particular, singular signature, to appropriate to itself all possibilities of speech: referentiality, performativity, but also truth, what is said to be truth, the truth one makes by saying it to another.[2] "To make the truth," says Saint Augustine, whom Derrida reprises and repeats in another text that I will approach only later. Between the "say-everything" of literature and the "do-everything" of the truth (for if one can "make the truth" then one can do everything), the relation must be a cutting one, sharpened to the point at which it bleeds: this watchword is also to be heard as an order given to literature, which would therefore be not what *corresponds* to some description or definition, but what *responds* to this order or this law of blood.

Of course, this cut cuts two ways. Beneath the sign of the two, the passion of literature is associated with the passion of love, with the alliance of two beings of flesh and blood who, precisely, by mixing their blood together, make the pact to have but one destiny, whatever may happen. With the sign of this double life, of the one in the other and each apart from the other, literature had its beginnings and the topos of *courtly love* will have shed a lot of blood in the meantime. When Shakespeare puts it on stage in the names of Romeo and Juliet, he is prolonging a long theatrical (but also, of course, romanesque) tradition, one whose survival his *Trauerspiel* will guarantee. In the aphoristic text he wrote for a French production of the play, "Aphorism Countertime," Derrida in turn stages a certain *analysis* by means of which the lovers cut themselves off and separate from one another precisely at the point at which they are trying to dissolve into a single life, the life of the one *and* the other beyond all names. A life beyond the separate and separating names, which is to say, a survival or living on, that can only be the living on of names. The analysis submits to the trial of irony. The text is composed as thirty-nine aphorisms, of which the second recalls the cutting vocation of this form ("aphorism separates, it marks dissociation [*apo*], it terminates, delimits, arrests [*horizo*]. It brings to an end by separating, it separates in order to end—and to define").[3] This analysis is first of all Juliet's who, in the famous balcony scene, attempts to introduce between Romeo and his name a blade sharpened by her desire for that which cannot be named:

> What's a Montague? it is nor hand, nor foot,
> Nor arm, nor face, nor any other part
> Belonging to a man. . . .
> . . . Romeo, doff thy name;
> And for that name, which is no part of thee,
> Take all myself.

Derrida will call this analysis "implacable" because it separates from the proper body everything that in any case is not a part of it and that should therefore be able to come off like a piece of clothing. Nevertheless, the analysis proceeds only by cutting into the flesh of the beloved: "She knows it: detachable and dissociable, aphoristic though it be, his name is his essence. Inseparable from his being" (426). Like a chemical analysis, of blood for example, Juliet's desiring analysis would separate into its elementary components her living lover from this death borne by the parasitic name, but implacably the analytic separation runs into the inseparability of the name and the life, that is, the death, that is, the final separation of the lovers in their shared finitude. Behind the loving traits of Juliet, one is forced to recognize the "ironic consciousness" that "analyzes, analyzes, and analyzes." It is because Juliet, with her name, already bears the death of Romeo, who will also bear that of his beloved in that impossible essential contretemps in which each survives the other. Here is how Derrida concludes his analysis of the unanalyzable ironic analysis of the two lovers:

> And they state this clearly, they formalize it as even a philosopher would not have dared to do. A vein, through the sharp point of this analysis, receives the distilled potion. It does not wait, it does not allow any time, not even that of the drama, it comes at once to turn to ice the heart of their pledges. This potion would be the true poison, the poisoned truth of this drama. (432; trans. mod.)

It is as if all the poignancy of this literature of impossible love, of love of the impossible, were tapered down toward this pointed tip with which the two lovers take each other's lives or give each other death. But this sharpened point is nevertheless not an indivisible point. It remains double-edged, like the double death and the double survival of the two lovers. Piercing them both, the point sharpens without ever reducing the gap between their names, that is, their deaths. By means of a simulacrum, she dies before *and* after him, the second time "for real," but between this real death and the simulated death, the theater makes no difference. It stages the staging of death as real death, death that arrives through its simulacrum, that is, to the other and through the other before it finally arrives "for real." This is the vein that is found in the play, and all this literature: the potion distilled by the analysis signed Juliet Capulet Montague Shakespeare is introduced right into the spectating of the spectacle, into the capillary veins of the eyes and the ears.

In this first and unavoidable slice of its history, then, literature sounds death in two moments, which are nevertheless irreducibly singular, each time doubled by what one loves most of all, the *simul-* of the same, the other same: *l'autre même*. Represented, put on stage in its simulacrum, the same becomes other in what has been called the irony of fate. The figure of irony, put forward by the first literature—by Plato or Sophocles—and the reigning figure of the Romantics, would have served perhaps only to blunt the point through wear and repetition. To resharpen its blade, Derrida passes Shakespeare's instrument over the honing edges of his aphorisms. On its most worn surface, which is the balcony scene where the irony of the name injects itself into love, he must bear down with particular force so as to bring the analysis out of the torpor of its ironic consciousness. This he does with pointed economy when he remarks that they are two: "And *they* state this clearly, formalize it even . . . " They are the two edges of the blade that no consciousness, not even that of speculative philosophy, can contain in itself. "And *they* state this clearly, *they* formalize it as even a philosopher would not have dared to do." The force of the clear statement, of the formalization of the impossible comes back to them, that is, to their always plural names of which literature is the guardian.

When the "sharp point of this analysis" finishes off the contre-tempestive reading of *Romeo and Juliet*, with the figuration of the instrument of a death that is double because it has already happened, one is reminded of the furtive and fleeting appearance of a certain "sharpened point" [*pointe acérée*] earlier in the text, in the twelfth aphorism, which is the longest in the series. The two words are in quotation marks in a sentence that reads in part: "the singularity of an imminence whose 'sharpened point' spurs desire at its birth—the very birth of desire" (420; trans. modified). The indicated quotation is in fact double: at its nearer edge, it comes from the title given in French to a poem by Celan, "A la pointe acérée," which happens to be the first poem cited in Derrida's *Schibboleth for Paul Celan*, a text that appeared in French the same year as the original version of "Aphorism Countertime"; at its farther edge, Celan's quotation, as we are reminded in the first note to *Schibboleth*, comes from the third of Baudelaire's prose poems in *Paris Spleen*, "The Artist's *Confiteor*." Here is the poem's first paragraph in which the two quoted words occur:

> How penetrating the late afternoons of autumn! Ah! penetrating to the verge of pain! For there are certain delicious sensations whose vagueness does not exclude intensity; and there is no sharper point than Infinity.[4]

Between Baudelaire's prose poem and *Romeo and Juliet* as sharpened by Derrida's reading, there are points that touch or wound each other across their different languages and their split tongues.[5] Because of the quotation marks, the Baudelairean arrow even sticks up a little in Derrida's text, as if it were already pointing toward "the sharp point of this analysis," which finds the vein finally in the frozen dream of the double death/double survival. But two arrows that touch at the tip can also be read as contrary indications, that is, as signs pointing in opposite directions; or yet again, they may look like swords drawn against each other in a duel—one which takes place not at dawn but in late afternoon. At the risk of being sent in the wrong direction, we'll nevertheless take a detour through Baudelaire's text that follows the sharpened point of its directional arrow or its dueling weapons.

The prose poem can indeed be read as the account of a duel.[6] As we have just seen, it opens with a penetration "to the verge of pain." An initial sally by the "late afternoons of autumn," that is, by days in their infinite repetition, is going to be parried in a first moment of the reverie by the next paragraph:

> Sheer delight to drown one's gaze in the immensity of sky and sea! Solitude, silence, incomparable chastity of the azure! a small sail trembling on the horizon, and whose smallness and isolation imitate my irremediable existence, monotonous melody of the swell—all these things think through me or I through them (for in the grandeur of reverie, the *self* is quickly lost!). They *think*, I say, but musically and pictorially, without quibblings, without syllogisms, without deductions.

This is what I'll call the positive face of this reverie (for there is a negative face and in its duel the text swings between these two aspects), the dream of a musical and picturesque thought, which would be launched from some point between all these infinitely immense or tiny things and the speaking subject, a thought that is both without subject and also (and therefore) "without quibblings, without syllogisms, without deductions." This dreamed-of thinking would not even be spoken, "I say"; it is I who say and repeat to you that "they think," these things, without using a used-up language; rather they think "musically and pictorially," I say, with these adverbs that are neither one nor the other. Even though the parenthesis insists on this loss of the "self," the *moi* ("for in the grandeur of the reverie, the *self* is quickly lost!"), one cannot fail to notice on the horizon an imitation of "my irremediable existence" that saves from loss and keeps a place for the "me" in this tableau: "a small sail trembling on the horizon, and whose smallness and isolation imitate my irremediable existence." This small sail sticks up on the horizon, and it is by its size that the artist claims he recognizes an imitation of himself. Irremediable, then, is this thinking of the "me," of my existence, which does not manage to lose itself altogether in the immensity, but still sticks up however minimally, for a moment, and can therefore still receive blows from the infinitely sharpened point. In its acuteness, thinking hurts.

In the next paragraph, "these thoughts" begin the swing toward the negative face of the experience:

> However, these thoughts, whether they emerge from me or spring from things, soon grow too intense. The force of voluptuous pleasure creates uneasiness and concrete suffering. Then my excessively taut nerves produce nothing but shrill and painful vibrations.

The reverie is on the point of pivoting. Suspended between me and all these things, in an undecidable and indifferent direction of movement— either come out of me or sprung up from things—the "too intense" thoughts cause the musical and the picturesque, that is, artistic beauty, to turn into "shrill vibrations." This intensification or sharpening happens under the pressure of a certain force, the one the artist applies to the work or else the one he applies to himself in order to make a work, as if he were also the instrument for rendering sounds, a lyre, but an unnerved, discordant lyre. A lyre broken in two, or even into so many pieces that it can never be reassembled. What comes out of me or, indifferently, out of things, this infinite thinking of the infinite, is *at once* the endless or timeless time of the general "me," the me without me, so to speak, the me of no one in particular that loses itself in the immense grandeur, *and* the finite time of me now, here, who sticks up briefly at the horizon before disappearing. The discord would be between these two times, a lack of accord, or rather a duel of one time with the other, a division into two that, to finish things off, will organize itself into a bruising, disfiguring, murderous face-off. It is with this opposition, by making itself into opposition and opposing itself, that the work is determined and represented as a failure: it fails to realize itself without doing itself harm, without doing itself badly (in French, one could say: *sans se faire mal*), without activating against itself that which tears it apart.[7]

Distributed between the positive and negative moments of the reverie, the difference of time, the difference in time, gets sharper as the prose poem approaches its end. Having observed at the outset the infinite repetition—time without limits, the timeless time of "the ends of autumn days"—the text will *soon* get around to measuring the time that is passing: "these thoughts . . . *soon* . . . grow too intense." The movement of intensification passes by way of this sharpening of the time that is measured and limited, the irremediably finite time of my existence.

This acute movement will be carried to its extreme point in the final paragraph, which is launched from the punctuality of a "now":

> And *now* the sky's depth fills me with dismay; its limpidity exasperates me. The sea's insensitivity, the scene's immobility appall me . . . Ah! must we suffer eternally, or else eternally flee the beautiful? Nature, sorceress without mercy, ever victorious rival, let me be! Stop tempting my desires and my pride! Studying the beautiful is a duel in which the artist shrieks with fright before being defeated. (Emphasis added)

This "now" is the punctuation of the self that recovers itself and withdraws; it withdraws its little boat out of the sea's insensitivity. The "self" nevertheless comes ashore pierced by the hole this "now" makes in time, for it is now this "now" that ends up driving home the sharp point of infinity: a point that is not one, it divides and gets carried away right away, that is, without waiting and without any possible measure of time, it is carried beyond its time, beyond the measure of time given to me, here, now. "It gets carried away" also means it becomes the vehicle of a sense that can carry as far as us, now. This division of the point of time, of the *stigmé*, would thus be the immutable condition of my being able to say, myself, "now."

It is against this very condition of possibility that the Baudelairean artist rails, and it is this condition that he, the artist of the beautiful, dreams of chasing or feigns to chase from his horizon, before conceding, in a final sentence, his inevitable defeat in the duel. The classical rhetoric projects onto this condition the feminine features of Nature the sorceress, temptress, and rival, an immense castrating Gorgon. The auto-division of the artist's self, that by which the work would make itself beautiful by doing itself harm and doing itself badly, is covered over or crossed over in this dual portrait of the "me" that opposes me to the other, always or at least too often in Baudelaire a feminine, threatening other.[8] The whole rhetoric of the sexual division, that is, of their duality and their duel, as well as the rhetoric of beauty (and the one is interminably relayed by the other), is gathered up and put in place around the dividing and divisible point. It is as if a wound had opened up only in order to close itself again in that which codifies and embellishes suffering.

Although I have quoted it from one end to the other, this reading will not even have begun to come to the end of this text. In particular, I have said nothing about its title. A title is always a kind of arrow that indicates with a nod or shake of the head a path to be pursued by the text that follows it. Baudelaire's title is no exception. "The Artist's *Confiteor*" tells us the mode in which the poem is proferred. It is that of prayer, as signalled by the Latin word which names one of the so-called "usual" prayers of the Catholic liturgy, the one that begins: *Confiteor Deo omnipotenti, et vobis, fratres*, and in which the supplicant accuses him- or herself according to the consecrated formula: *mea culpa, mea culpa, mea maxima culpa*. With this effect of quotation, the poem plunges into the abyss of an undecidable speech act, here a prayer, by means of which it names itself but with a name that is also a kind of quotation. To cite the famous distinction of speech act theory (to which Derrida has so often had recourse), are we to see here a *use* or rather a *mention* of the cited act?[9] In other words, would this "Artist's *Confiteor*" be a prayer of confession/confession of prayer, or would it merely cite what is already a citation and thereby imitate or simulate instead of pray truly or confess in truth? Is it literature or truth?

Whichever, the mode of the text remains that of address. Right from the title, there is an understood address: to God and to you ("I confess [to almighty God and to you my brothers . . .]"). In the body of the text, the mode of address is repeated, marked off according to the standard rules of grammar and with emphasis: "Nature, pitiless sorceress, ever victorious rival, let me be! Stop tempting my desires and my pride!" That it is impossible to discern or to separate the use of address from its mere mention, that Baudelaire's formidable irony raises to an even higher level the doubling of the speech act he either performs or imitates, none of this can overcome the fact that there is address, whether it be mentioned, cited, simulated, or turned against itself. None of this can obviate the necessity whereby every text, like every speech act, constitutes itself out of the possibility of address to and by some other. This doubling, however, should dissuade one from concluding too quickly that the address here finally comes down to this command or prayer spoken to Nature, for the latter is only the consecrated but desacralized figure of another always possible addressee.

And yet, having taken this precaution, one will still have left this text under the impulsion of the imperative tone that asks this figure, or prays that this figure will, "let me be and stop," that is, in French, *laisser* and *cesser*. The prayer, the demand, or their simulacrum is thus emitted in this hissing tone of the frightened animal, who has been hunted and cornered (the translator has transferred the effect somewhat to "sorceress without mercy," but "pitiless sorceress" would have done likewise). It is the hissing that one can still hear, now, as the sound emitted by this "thing" that would think "without quibblings, without syllogisms, without deductions," here before us and between us and it. Hissing his last word, which is not a word but a tone, a speech act of the sort that all animals are capable of, even poets, Baudelaire's artist seals it in the envelope of the final sentence, and sends off to the reader's address the shriek of terror with which the artist cries out before being defeated, just before the end, therefore, the penultimate breath that says nothing less, nothing more than all the pain he has at the thought of his own death.

If it now seems appropriate to turn to that other animal with the hissing name, the *hérisson*, which, like its English cousin the hedgehog, is covered with pointed spines and spikes, it is because Derrida gave this creature the role of responding to the question: *Che cos'è la poesia?*, what thing is poetry?[10] But after dueling so fiercely with Baudelaire, I'm a little afraid of spooking that text into a retreat behind spiky defenses. Steering around it, carefully, I will recall merely that the arrows of Derrida's *hérisson* keep at a distance only so as to signal the other to approach, so as to appeal to the stranger, to him or to her. Its points have been sharpened on a "passion of the singular mark," which addresses a command or a prayer: "Eat, drink, swallow my letter, carry it, transport it in you, like the law of a writing become your body."[11] But the hospitality of the poematic *hérisson*—the one it gives and the one it asks of the other—extends no less to Baudelaire's prayer of confession, the one that is said to the other but also *in* the other and thus always as a secret for whoever confesses. The prayer that hisses in conclusion "laisse-moi," leave me, by being confessed or confided to the other, would let itself be inhabited by the opposite command: "come." The *hérisson* once again: "no poem that does not open itself like a wound, but no poem that is not also just as wounding. You will call poem a silent incantation, the aphonic wound that, of you, from you, I want to learn by heart" (233).

A text, a poem, that, opening like a wound, is no less wounding: it is called as well *Circumfession* (1991). Right away, it is a question of blood, the cruelty of blood spilled in *his* tongue, *his own*, which is also

> the other one, the one that has always been running after me, turning in circles around me, a circumference licking me with a flame . . . cruelty above all, blood again, *cruor, confiteor* . . . a sentence came . . . scarcely a sentence, the plural word of a desire toward which all the others since always seemed, confluence itself, to hurry, an order suspended on three words, *find the vein*, what a nurse might murmur, syringe in hand, needle upward, before *taking blood* . . . at the precise moment at which by the point of the syringe there was established an invisible passage, always invisible, for the continuous flowing of blood . . . the quite complicated apparatus of the syringe being introduced in that place only to allow the passage and to disappear as instrument . . . without the now brutal intervention of the other who, deciding to interrupt the flow once the syringe, still upright, was withdrawn from the body . . . the blood could still have flooded, not indefinitely but continuously to the point of exhausting me, thus aspirating toward it what I called: the glorious appeasement.[12]

To quote a text is always to cut into it and interrupt its flow. That action here ends up miming the gesture of an imagined nurse who inserts a syringe to draw blood and then stops up the opened vein. If the syringe can thus turn around in the reader's hands, it is because its pointed tip is a "quite complicated apparatus" that serves to aspirate as well as to eject or inject— blood, but also a drug or a medicine, but also a poison or a virus, a contamination. It is as if one could not touch it without getting stung, without also risking some contamination. And yet, it is this syringing operation that translates the dream of a non-contamination of the written, a pure aspiration toward the outside, without the machination of writing by interposed instrument. A pen, a stylus, or a style can seem to aspirate but it is only by force of calculation: "I always dream of a pen that would be a syringe, a suction point rather than that very hard weapon with which one must inscribe, incise, choose, calculate . . . once the right vein has been found, no more toil . . . " (12–13). *Cruor, confiteor*: to let the blood of the confession be drawn toward the exterior by this instrument for taking blood, an instrument manipulated by the other, always the other, it must be always an other.

The *disappearance* of this "quite complicated apparatus" would form a key element in the dream of *cruor, confiteor*: it would be "introduced in that place only to allow the passage and to disappear as instrument." This sentence fragment is arresting because it shows a considerable resistance to its own disappearance: in calling for the disappearance of the instrument, it succeeds in calling all the more attention to the instrument that it is "in that place." By aspiring this disappearance toward itself, by filling up its form with this signified content, the phrase thus seizes the contrary or the counter-example of what it means to say.[13] It cannot but act therefore as a contaminated syringe. Hardly its first sentence begun and the confession is already contaminated in its desire to say what is most proper to it, the blood which no instrument should touch except to allow its passage. Catastrophe of confession, the very thing one is supposed to avow without detours, without lyricism, without literature. And for that, it needs the instrument of its own disappearance.

Without lyricism, without literature. This is the "without" [*sans*] without which the confession does not shed blood [*sang*]. A confession must give its dates, real, non-fictive dates. The date of November 29, 1988, for example, the day on which, we read, the syringing phrase arrived. Who knows who pronounced it first, for it came "from further away than I could ever say . . . an order suspended on three words, *find the vein*, what a nurse might murmur, syringe in hand . . . " Everything that follows is going to happen under the at least triple sign of this phrase-event,[14] which nothing allows us to take as anything less than the truth: the truth that is to be made here, in *Circumfession*, and not the truth that anyone can recite or fabricate or imagine.[15] In other words, it is a matter of doing something other than a literary confession, of confiding oneself to this something other that has as yet no proper name, just this monstruous name of circumfession, which presents itself as the last offspring of a marriage between a Jewish mother who is a little too Catholic and a Church Father who likes to dress up as a Jew from New York or Los Angeles.[16] Behind the features of this monster of the improper there advances the desire for a wholly *new*, as yet unknown propernesss, and which sets one to dreaming for long sentences that stretch to pages at a time. The dream of a new invention, but which is anything but a novelty; on the contrary, it is perhaps the most ancient thing in the world, "come from further away than I could ever say." The invention of a whole past without a single false note, without the least literature.

To do this, and since it is, I quote, "up to the other to invent me," take the instrument that this book puts in your hands; her proper name is Syringe, a distant descendant from Syrinx, the nymph whom Pan pursued with his desire; perhaps, like her ancestor, from out of her furthest withdrawal, Syringe will transform herself also into a musical instrument, not a lyre—do not speak ever again of "lyre" without hearing also the name of one of the traditional instruments of circumcision, a sinister tool of torture, whose lyric shape is reproduced on p. 67—not the lyre, therefore, but the "carved and hollowed out reed, whence the country flute or the Pan flute." This dreamed-of transformation, the lyric cry transformed into the song of a demi-god, is also capable of sowing panic. No sooner named, Syringe risks reintroducing literature by its most banal or at least most outdated door, the bucolic door of some shepherd's longings for the shepherdess. Thus, the instrument will be called upon to disappear, and the name Syringe, unless I am mistaken, will not again appear in the course of this circumfession to which it opened the door.

If only it were enough to silence a name or a word. Or to put the word "literature" under arrest for too many crimes against the truth. Obviously, this will not suffice because the literary contamination is not carried just by its name. Nevertheless the greatest risk taken by *Circumfession* is that of the contamination by literature, precisely because it is not a matter of this name or of what it may still signify. Taking up a finely honed blade, one must cut oneself *off* from literature, being careful not to cut oneself *with* literature, for there is a risk that each time the blood is set flowing it will be contaminated by this lying other from which one must protect oneself at all costs: "I write with a sharpened blade, if it doesn't bleed the book will be a failure" (130). In a writing that proceeds only by letting itself be contaminated in its most proper desire, a writing in which it is above all a matter of affirming the desire of contamination even if it is lethal ("better AIDS than lose you"), the cutting oneself off from/with literature would be what draws this writing forward, taut as a cord, and makes of it a cutting instrument.[17] At stake is how a word or a phrase can want to bleed before it signs or *signifies*; in French, the difference between *saigner* and *signer*, to bleed and to sign, is the slim difference of a letter. At stake is the symptom of blood, by means of which the circumfessional saying delivers itself over to the other who holds the book like a large syringe. It is up to the other to invent me, that is, to tell me if I have said the truth—or not. This is the large risk taken: to exhibit the symptom whereby the writing cuts itself off from/with literature and its secretive little games.

The syringe-phrase dreams of turning itself over to what it calls "the glorious appeasement," a dream which is, therefore, euthanasic. As appeasement of all wounds, given and received, it would pardon everything by calling for the Great Pardon for everyone and for all those living dying within him. The reigning tone of appeasement throws into stark relief a fit of anger unleashed in period 12, against Proust, or rather against a sentence of Proust's that someone has quoted with approval in a book from the same collection in which *Circumfession* will appear with its French publisher, the series called "Les Contemporains." The passage begins by mimicking the famous first line of Proust's *Recherche du temps perdu*:

> and then I remember having gone to bed very late after a moment of anger or irony against a sentence of Proust's, praised in a book in this collection "Les Contemporains," which says: "A work in which there are theories is like an object on which one has left the price tag," and I find nothing more vulgar than this Franco-Britannic decorum, European in truth, I associate with it Joyce, Heidegger, Wittgenstein, and a few others, the salon literature of that republic of letters, the grimace of a good taste naive enough to believe that one can efface the labor of theory . . . to believe that one must and above all that one can efface the price to be paid, the symptom if not the avowal, I always ask what the theory is a symptom of and I admit that I write with the price on, I display, not so that the price be legible to the first-comer . . . (62–63)

The anger is set off by a phrase that, from a certain angle, recalls the dream from which arose the first taking of blood, the first confessed symptom, where it was a question of a syringe that would disappear once the vein had been found. True, the resemblance seems rather slight: to see it, one must tolerate a similarity of theories and instruments, prices to be paid and syringes. But the fact remains that between the dreamed-of phrase, with its cleansing, appeasing effect, and the detested, contaminated sentence, something seems to be *exchanged*, a point or a tip at which they secretly communicate. There is something like an element of possible confusion between them, and it is there that everything is put at risk. So as not to get mixed up in the mechanics of literary confession, one dreams while writing of causing to disappear the instrument that receives the blood in small specimens, but not at a small price. But it is precisely at that moment that one risks finding oneself on this detestable stage where everything is told, everything is sold, everything is exchanged without anyone having the bad taste to display the price tag.

The worst kind of contamination thus circulates in this element of nee-
dle/pen exchange, and it is this contamination that will be vigorously de-
nounced further into the passage with words like "blasphemy," "simulacrum," "imposture," "perjury." First, however, the element of the word
and the idiom will be remarked, in particular, the idiom of the word
"prendre" or of the syllable "pri-," which is the idiom above all of *Circumfession*, where "prise" (as in "prise de sang," blood sample) and "price,"
but also "prie" as in "I pray," and here for once even the name of Proust
get all mixed together. It is thus at the price of making this idiom bleed,
of passing a "sharp blade" down the middle of the same untranslatable expression, which cannot be grasped only by its meaning, that the pe-
riphrastic period attempts to operate its own circumcision of/from
(*d'avec*) literature. I take up the quotation once again:

> one writes only at the moment of giving the contemporary the slip, with a
> word, the word for word, you'll see . . . that's the condition for it to take [*pour
> que ça prenne*], untranslatable locution, losing its head between two values, on
> the stage where it takes because one believes in it, one has believed in it, in
> blasphemy, simulacrum, imposture, supplement of perjury called avowal, but
> also on the scene where it takes, just now, like that chaos of red lava that hard-
> ens to put itself to work, only by not coagulating [*ce chaos de lave rouge qui
> durcit pour se mettre en oeuvre sauf à ne pas coaguler*].

Since there is risk of contamination between the two values, the two
scenes distinguished here, one must cut; but it's precisely at the point of
the cut that one risks contamination, one risks getting taken up on that
stage or in that scene where everything exchanges with everything else.
This latter contamination is transmitted by the blows of an unclean knife
or syringe, one that has passed from hand to hand, like so many repeated
credulities. In filigree, then, there is a reprise of the dream of the syringe
that disappears as an instrument, having served only once to create the
passage. But this "chaos of red lava" comes along to recall an operation of
the work without instruments, as that which would have presented itself
as the work of all terrestrial scenes, without contaminating intervention,
"sauf à ne pas coaguler" (a phrase that I will not even try to reduce to its
possibilities of meaning, so as to leave its passage open). To hear in this
way a reprise or repetition of the initial blood-letting is not to denounce
an already used instrument, but on the contrary to restore to it if possible
its belonging to the idiom of this text without example, which is made up

of counter-examples of itself. It is to take the text in its very phrase, its sy-ringe-phrase. It is to repeat with it, on its counter-example, that the syringe is *his* or *her* instrument, always his or hers, the other's.

This phrase could have been that, for example, of a nurse; it is "what a nurse might murmur, syringe in hand . . . " However hypothetical this murmuring nurse, another, some others are indeed there taking words the way one takes blood. They are numerous, at least two, but one can easily imagine three or four or more, without counting the one who is writing and who doubles all the roles. I take up again the initial period near the end:

> when for example in my childhood, and I remember that laboratory in the rue d'Alger, the fear and vagueness of a glorious appeasement both took hold of me, took me blind in their arms at the precise moment at which by the point of the syringe there was established an invisible passage, always invisible, for the continuous flowing of blood, absolute, absolved in the sense that nothing seemed to come between the source and the mouth, the quite complicated ap-paratus of the syringe being introduced in that place only to allow the passage and to disappear as instrument, but continuous in that other sense that, with-out the now brutal intervention of the other who, deciding to interrupt the flow once the syringe, still upright, was withdrawn from the body, quickly folded my arm upward and pressed the swab inside the elbow, the blood could still have flooded, not indefinitely but continuously to the point of exhausting me, thus aspirating toward it [*vers lui*] what I called: the glorious appeasement.

Glorious appeasement, that is, absolution. Which can be given only by another, who or which is perhaps indicated by the pronoun "it" [*lui*] in the last words of the phrase. The antecedent of this pronoun cannot be easily sorted out from the flow of the phrase: "the blood could still have flooded . . . aspirating toward it . . . " (At this point, I want to acknowl-edge Geoff Bennington's admirably scrupulous translation of this text.) Is "it" my blood or the other, that is, whatever interrupts the flood but which could also have aspirated the blood toward it "to the point of ex-hausting me"? In a phrase that dreams of the continuous flow of my blood, without my perhaps deceitful intervention and thus without pos-sible mixture or mistake as to the source of this blood ("nothing," we read, "seemed to come between the source and the mouth"), there is right away the other that introduces itself, like the mouth or the embouchure that as-pirates the flow. Is it my blood or the other? In other words, is it a true specimen or some contaminating counterfeit? Just try to figure it out, begin the analysis.

A confession should not be literature. Whoever says "I," "I confess," "I admit," "*confiteor*" must not borrow the mask of another, must not hide behind another in order to say it. He or she must not calculate what is said, what is written, but let the confession be determined by the sole truth of his/her being, life, blood. In this sense, he should not even be present to his saying, his writing, his blood, but turn himself over, absolved, into the hands of the other who will calculate when to interrupt the operation. In other words, in order to confess my truth, which is both mine and true, without admixture of fiction or lie, it is necessary that the other do it for me, in my place. It is necessary that it be the other who holds the syringe, who plunges it into my arm after having found the vein (with luck and inspiration), who measures the flow of blood, and withdraws the instrument at the right moment. Which is to say, it is the other who must write me and this is the condition for it to be me who is written and given to be read. The syringe is *his* (or her) instrument, not mine, and the calculation of the blood comes back to him (or her).

Repeated, "The syringe is his instrument" becomes a quotation. This syringe has already been used and first by Derrida in his essay on the painter Valerio Adami, "+ R." The phrase occurs at the moment attention is being called to all the machines, tools, and devices that Adami has scattered throughout his drawings:

> It goes or goes off almost on its own.

> Drive or penetrating projection (catapult, rifle, but also the syringe of *Sequenza*), attraction, aspiring introjection (fishing weapons, the vacuum cleaner of *Scena domestica*, the syringe again with sharpened point but disjointed from itself). The syringe is his instrument: drawing with an incisive point, penetrating the skin, sharp style/stylus removing and then, after mixing, injecting the colors, irrigating and revealing the unconscious body; it's done in music: Syrinx, panic.[18]

"The syringe is his instrument": rediscovered in a quotation, the possessive pronoun seems to point in a single direction, toward the first one, the first man, Adami, who draws as if with an incisive, penetrating, aspirating, injecting point. But that it is a question here solely of him, this other, Adami, and no other other—nothing is less certain. That is, it is not at all certain here that between him and the other a chiasmatic syringe has not intervened, like the *chi* in the painting that Derrida baptizes *Ich*, thereby crossing an "Etude pour dessin d'après *Glas*" with the text he has himself signed—*Glas*, which is taken up and cited in "+R." To show this uncertainty with certainty, one would have to reread the latter text closely, but I will take merely some very small samples.

Derrida approaches "Etude pour dessin d'après *Glas*" by anticipating "the point of a text that interests me" and then adds right away: "At the point of this text (general text, I'm not going to define it again in all the cog wheels or energies of its apparatus), the angular signature of Adami was waiting for me. . . . So I yielded, even before knowing it, as if I were read in advance, written before writing, prescribed, seized, trapped, hooked" (156). In the center hangs a fish from a hook through its mouth. The vertical fishing line intersects the upper edge of the drawing, suggesting the whole apparatus of a pole and reel just above the frame, which leads Derrida to write: "the fish drawing which I shall baptise *Ich*: without the author's authorization, in order to take it from him in turn and hold it at the end of my line, with an apparently simple line, without a reel, without the interposed machine turning and fishing all by itself . . . " (157). It is no doubt interesting that the mechanical device noticed in so many of the other drawings is here left outside the frame, making itself invisible. As for what might be motivating such a drawing "after *Glas*," Derrida takes some samples from his own text, which has now become the other's catch, prize, or *prise*, as one says also of a blood sample: *une prise de sang*. Such sampling is an infinite task since "it is possible to describe ad infinitum the instantaneous capture [*prise*] of *Glas* by *Ich*, *Ich*'s hold [*prise*] on *Glas*" (161). Here is one sample (I quote Derrida quoting *Glas*, hence a quote within a quote): "'we do not comprehend here the text named Genet's, it does not exhaust itself in the pocket I cut, sew, and bind [here then, folded in like a pocket, is another scene of taking a sample or a specimen, and the abyss sinks out of sight—PK].'" It is his text [Genet's] "'which pierces a hole in the pocket, harpoons it first, looks at it; but also sees it escape, carrying its arrow toward unknown neighborhoods'" (162).

There is all the same an arrow, a pointed tip, a very small spot in Adami's drawing that Derrida does not pick up, at least not in detail. Indicated with a tiny trait, the barb of the hook extends beyond the muzzle of the fish: it points upwards, toward the machine that cannot be seen interposing itself in the drawing.

—But now you must cut, interrupt, stop the flow. How are you going to do that?

—I will try to find a phrase, just one phrase, to sum up the itinerary pointed out by all these arrows that carry off toward some unknown vicinity, that is, "des parages inconnus," thus toward the title of a "book" still to come, *un livre à venir*, already summoned to appear.[19] The unknown vicinity stretches beyond the limits of any known language, it summons something like translation even as it defies one to carry over sense from one idiom to another. What sense might there be—perhaps none—in confiding this final phrase to the most used up and worn down of words, in either language, the word "new" or "neuf"? There is no counting the number of times it has passed from hand to hand, but the same syllable is also reprised in one language as, precisely, a number, *le neuf*, the number nine, any nine, *tout neuf*. And then one may remark that, for no apparent reason, this pointed itinerary has in fact unfolded between the thirty-nine aphorisms of "Aphorism Countertime" and the fifty-nine periphrases of *Circumfession*.[20] So let us call it, between our known languages: the peripeteia of the *neuf*, of the one who/which repeats for the nth time and thereby *se remet toujours à neuf* (untranslatable, so we must translate: "always renews himself/always returns to nine").

Public Address Systems

§ 12 The Ghosts of Critique and Deconstruction

By grammar alone and without much context, one cannot decide whether to read the plural in this chapter's title as the two ghosts of critique and deconstruction, each having or being its own ghost, or whether to read a plural plurality: both critique and deconstruction having—or being—more than one ghost and even more than one kind of ghost. Both of these plurals are possible, which means that there is yet another kind of plurality to be reckoned with in the title's phrasing: a plurality of kinds of pluralization other than the pluralization of separable, identifiable ones. There would be a possible plurality of not just the more than one but also a plurality of modes of plurality: the other than one.

In French, an expression says at the same time more than one and other than one: *plus d'un*. Depending on whether or not one pronounces the "s": *plu(s)/plus*, the expression shifts registers from that of counting by ones to that of counting without number one, or of taking account of the other than one. In French, then, it is possible to say all that at once, or rather to write it, because this pluralization of the same time has its effect only if voice itself is muted so as to suspend the final "s" of *plus/plus* between its two possibilities.

Jacques Derrida has frequently made use of this fortunate possibility in the French idiom, to the perpetual torment, perhaps, of his translators. But it is also the chance his texts give to the work of translation between languages and idioms: the chance of pluralization of another language. Here it is the chance of posing at the same time the other time that is not counted by beginning with one. For example, in *Specters of Marx*, which deploys Derrida's most concentrated reflection on a certain plurality of ghosts, the phrase "plus d'un/plus d'un" regularly rhythms the opening pages. When these conjunctions occur, translation encounters or makes apparent a sudden pluralization of the features it must attempt to project into the other language, with all its idiomatic differences. There is immediately more than one translation called for.

I should explain why I thought a conference titled "Critique and Deconstruction" offered the best opportunity I would likely ever find to revisit the opening pages of *Specters of Marx*, and to read them as if for the first time.[1]

For me, "critique" has always shaded quickly into the indistinct area of "criticism," and thus into what is called "literary criticism." There is, of course, no more indistinct "thing" than literary criticism; just about anything and everything written in the vicinity of the literary can and has been called criticism. As for the boundaries of the "literary," these are, of course, even more imprecise than the boundaries of criticism. But I do know this much about critique in the Kantian sense: it is all about setting down clear boundaries between things.[2] Hence, I must assume that critique should not be equated with criticism, and certainly not with literary criticism.

So, although the topic of critique and deconstruction sets up some strict, philosophical questions, I'm going to invoke the altogether looser discourse of criticism. This discourse, however, has at least the advantage of being somewhat more familiar, since it is not confined to the publications or classrooms of formal philosophy but spills over into mass-circulated newspapers, for example in the form of supplemental Sunday "Book Review" sections. Moreover, that deconstruction has been frequently assimilated to the discourse of criticism is something anyone in these very broadly defined intellectual circles may easily observe. It has been repeated over and over that deconstruction is a kind of literary criticism, even a discipline of reading, which is why, we are told, it has been most extensively imported by departments of literature in our universities. As anyone can tell you who has had some recent experience in these departments, such an assertion is neither simply true nor false. But by force of repetition, it seeks to authorize itself as true, to perform and to produce its truth. The performing assertion predicating deconstruction as criticism is almost invariably accompanied by the manifest pronouncement that the said deconstruction is now dead and buried in these same departments of literature, or wherever else one wishes to locate its grave. Because, however, this performing/predicating discourse continues to be neither simply true nor false, which is to say not definitively or solely constative but performative as well, it also induces its own repetition, the necessity of repeatedly performing what otherwise has no certain truth. It is a matter, one might say, of having to reassert, reaffirm, or re-verify the death of deconstruction.

One way to understand this necessity is to invoke a logic of spectrality. That is, there would be a haunting effect observable in the discourse of deconstruction-as-criticism. It is as if criticism repeatedly had to exorcise a ghost, and even one that it seems to recognize as its own ghost. Take the example of the *New York Review of Books*, a journal in which a certain discourse of criticism materializes on a bimonthly basis, like some ghost that regularly returns. In an issue dated June 25, 1998, the *NYRB* printed the report of one of its hired guns who had been sent out to read some recent books by Derrida so as to put to rest rumors that the ghost still walked. Mark Lilla, the ghostbuster-for-hire, did so very dutifully, although without much originality. Anyone who took the time to read this routine report would quickly see how it strings together almost all the known incantatory formulae of the critical exorcism of deconstruction, including the *de rigueur* "deconstruction-as-criticisim-confined-to-literature-departments-where-it-is-now-dead." Lilla thus earns his fee by confirming that deconstruction remains buried in these departments, the graveyard of the university. But if one had access to the archives of the *NYRB*, one would also notice that this magazine has had to print similar articles, which do more or less the same job, at regular intervals of every four or five years. On these occasions, it has called in all the best exorcisors, political philosophers, and even philosophers of speech acts, but the thing keeps reappearing somewhere, rumors get back to New York, the capital of speculative capital and skeptical criticism, that "this thing has appeared again tonight." For twenty or twenty-five years at least, the *NYRB* appears to have been haunted by it knows not what.

It would be a kindness to put it out of its misery, if anyone had the power to do so. Perhaps, however, the power needed is not the exorcist's, with which to rid criticism of the deconstruction that haunts it, but the power of a *possibility* made available by the logic of ghosts, more precisely, by what *Specters of Marx* calls *hauntology* and which is not an ontology precisely because it does not begin by posing the ontological existence of ghosts. The notion of hauntology would allow one not only to account for the phenomenon of the *NYRB*'s repetition compulsion, but to address the haunting figure without succumbing to the paralyzing fear that the figure really exists somewhere.

It might thus be an act of kindness to submit Lilla's *NYRB* article to a hauntological analysis, but it would also be rather tedious. This particular representative of critical discourse too often resembles bad journalism. And however loose the common notion of literary criticism may be, we still think we can distinguish between journalism and scholarly criticism. It is this category of the "scholarly" that is going to permit the return to *Specters of Marx* and to the plurality of ghosts. First, however, it is necessary to take one more and longer detour through the very vague terrain of criticism, this time scholarly criticism.

By scholarly criticism, what is generally understood? Perhaps nothing more than criticism practiced from within the school, criticism, therefore, that accompanies or is accompanied by an injunction to teach and to study. Whereas journalistic criticism performs under a different compulsion (in the example above, it is the compulsion to exorcise deconstruction, either to kill it or to pronounce it dead), scholarly criticism, at least in theory, performs under the injunction to teach or to study—for example, deconstruction, or not. It would be fairly easy, however, to locate many places where the scholarly and journalistic injunctions cannot be radically distinguished from each other. That is why it is best to try to formalize the distinction in a strictly minimal fashion: scholarly criticism, let us say, is criticism that is supported by the apparatus of the "school," which includes the classroom and the seminar room, sites of scholarly publication, research, and so forth. The school apparatus would be that which, like a prosthetic body, houses the spirit or the idea of scholarly criticism. Like any body, this prosthetic apparatus can be interpreted as displaying its symptoms on the various surfaces that support critical writing. The innumerable entries through which this body writes its symptoms come to be ordered and ordered like a body, from head to toe or from the top down. That is, the "school" apparatus, the prosthetic body of scholars or of scholarship, is also—and this is something today's university "scholars" are constantly told to take into account—ranked from the top down. The school embodies itself in a more or less rigidly hierarchized differentiation, a trait that can therefore never be strictly excluded from the scholarly criticism produced or supported by the apparatus. How this trait of hierarchical ranking gets remarked in the work of scholarly criticism would be a vast area of study, and would even be very interesting if undertaken without the presuppositions of Bourdieu-style sociology, which disallows any spectral possibility from the analysis.[3] A hauntological analysis, on the other hand, would have to address also the possibility that the hierarchy of the school's prosthetic body is the effect of a haunting by some *spirit* of scholarly criticism.

But which spirit? Whose spirit? And is this spirit a ghost?

Like the journalistic criticism of the *NYRB*, scholarly criticism has to do with the specter of spirit. But if indeed it is a specter or a ghost, that is, if it indeed materializes in the world of phenomena, then the body it assumes is also *someone's body, the body of some one.* That is the difference commonly assumed between spirit and specter.[4] The spirit has no one's body, no one body, which is why it can be the spirit of all in a collectivity: a spirit of nation, of language, of literature, of history, of philosophy, of criticism, and so forth. One even speaks of a school spirit. If, however, scholarly criticism acknowledges that, first of all and perhaps even above all, it has to do with the *specter* of spirit, then it is put to work on the question: whose specter is it? That is, whose ghost haunts the critical spirit?

Specters of Marx, as I'll try to show in a moment, has taken up this task of criticism as one that requires a deconstruction of the spectral spirit by which criticism has let itself be guided. The deconstruction of criticism occurs in this text not as a discarding of criticism's ghosts but as their inheritance. Which means that there is an affirmation of the necessity to inherit and to inherit affirmatively, that is, by selecting and differentiating that which presents itself to be inherited, in all the different forms it may present itself. One of Derrida's fundamental gestures here is to demonstrate the necessity to inherit from criticism the question: whose spirit? whose body? whose ghost?—but then to undertake to inherit it affirmatively, that is, deconstructively, by transforming the presuppositions of the question. Because the question "whose ghost?" implies that there is only one of them, it presupposes the singular unity of the one at the origin. But Derrida will wonder whether it is not possible to *speak to ghosts, always more than one, and to speak to them without questioning them.* I have tried to analyze elsewhere the significance of this suspension of the interrogative in *Specters of Marx*.[5] For my purposes here, I will simply underscore once again that a suspension or bracketing of any question to the ghost is the final gesture of the book. The last line of *Specters of Marx* quotes yet again the words spoken by Marcellus (in act 1, sc. 4 of *Hamlet*) to the scholar Horatio, as both stood on the rampart before the apparition. He turns to Horatio and enjoins him: "Thou art a scholar; speak to it, Horatio." In the play, Marcellus adds: "question it," but Derrida cuts short the quotation and does not repeat the injunction to question it.

Now, anybody can quote *Hamlet* and millions do so every day. So there's not necessarily any significance to be noted when another scholar selects the same phrase, truncated at the same point, to conclude an essay on a certain ghost of literature, for example, the Ghost of *Hamlet*. However, the essay in question, Stephen Greenblatt's "What is the History of Literature?" exhibits many other potential parallels with Derrida's, at least with its interest in haunting and conjuring as modalities of our relation to literature. For example, both set out from the recognition that this relation is spectral and not just spiritual. And yet, although Greenblatt's brief essay was published subsequently, it makes no reference to Derrida's book. The omission is disappointing for whoever may have wished to understand in Greenblatt's own terms what difference he would make out, if any, between the ghost of literature he is talking about—or to—and the ghosts or specters Derrida entertains in his book. The ghosts they are talking about (or to) seem at once altogether other and yet oddly conjoined in spirit. Someone might thus be led to conclude that they haunt each other's analyses.

Greenblatt's omission is puzzling since it seems unlikely that it could have been accidental and therefore utterly without intention. This absence, when one might have reasonably expected something else, raises at least the possibility that, whatever else he wanted to do in this essay, Greenblatt sought to dissociate his discourse from that of Derrida or of deconstruction. He therefore took no risk of misunderstanding on this score and went so far as to silence any reference to *Specters of Marx*, even though he would no doubt have found much there to fuel his own thinking, both positively and negatively, about ghosts, literature, *Hamlet*, history, the difference between spirit and specter, and so forth and so on. Every literary scholar knows how distressing it can sometimes be to discover that another's research covers the same terrain as one's own, or is framed by a similar set of questions posed perhaps to the very same texts one is also investigating. In that situation, one is usually impatient to read the results of the other's work, an impatience laced with trepidation. When the work one is impatient to read is that of someone like Derrida, one may even have to arm oneself in advance against the power of his arguments or his readings. Perhaps this is what happened to Greenblatt, but the chronology of publication suggests that he had more than two years to read what he didn't want to have to read. Since Stephen Greenblatt is no slouch, it is hard to believe he simply forgot to do his scholarly work. That is why one is left trying to puzzle out the sense of this marked absence of reference to the book that he all but quotes when he ends his essay with the same line from the play truncated at the same point: "Thou art a scholar; speak to it, Horatio."[6]

One is thus left to determine the significance of the omission by the way it is inscribed on the surface of the scholarly apparatus, the apparatus of the school as this gets defined itself through competing schools of criticism. It is on this apparatus that his gesture is able to signify in a minimally differential way: not-deconstruction. That is, it is for the school in which "deconstruction" is the name of a school of criticism that there can be something significant about omitting its name or the name of the one most associated with it.

I will take advantage of Greenblatt's omission in order to talk about this negative thing that is positioned as criticism-but-not-deconstruction. It is doubtful that Stephen Greenblatt would accept to describe what he is doing as "criticism," but what matters for my purposes is that he quite pointedly removes what he is doing from the purview of deconstruction. More specifically, I would suggest that he removes it, attempts to set it out of view of, Derrida's reading of *Hamlet* and of Marx in *Specters of Marx*. The conjunction of *Hamlet* and Marx, a certain Marx or a certain Marxism that one wishes to inherit from Marx, is a vein that has been deeply mined by criticism labeled loosely New Historicism or, as Greenblatt himself prefers to call it, cultural poetics. It is in the spirit of a certain Marx that Shakespeare critics, first of all and above all, have set about to reinherit or reinvent the inheritance of the whole of literature in English.[7] By the criterion of the school's body-prosthetic and its ranked system of value, New Historicism or cultural poetics is to be differentiated as a competing school within the one school of the critical spirit, as one of the schools competing to define the terms of this critical spirit.[8] The omission marking Greenblatt's essay is thus perhaps the trait of this competition, which would play itself out as a competition for the conjoined inheritance from the very heady spirits of Shakespeare and Marx. At stake would be the position at the head of the body of scholars. But to reach the head, the essay does not undertake crudely to try to "kill" its chosen adversary or to announce, once again, that deconstruction is dead. Rather, it proceeds in a more *scholarly* fashion, even though it thereby runs the risk that someone might remark the omission and fault its scholarship. For if some such competitive urge were indeed dictating the silence, then precisely it cannot be avowed, or can only be disavowed, in the spirit of scholarly criticism.

At this point, one might observe that this structure of differential marking seems to affect Derrida's text no less than Greenblatt's. *Specters of Marx*, in other words, likewise makes no reference to anything Greenblatt has written, notably anything he has written on Shakespeare, which is quite a lot. But it also makes little or no reference to Shakespeare criticism before or since Greenblatt, which is quite a lot more. It will take some space (and a little patience) to explain why these omissions should not be understood as mirror reflections of each other, a mutual disavowal and dismissal of two competing schools of criticism. The difference in question, however, resembles nowhere a clear line of demarcation. Nevertheless, I will try to make apparent a difference between these two mobilizations of the ghost of *Hamlet,* and therefore of literature, that cross at the point of their disjointed inheritance. In brief, what I will be attempting to show is this: whereas criticism, with its undeconstructed question as to the identity of the ghost, keeps alive a certain spirit of competition or dispute over the ghost's property, deconstruction moves to pluralize the spirit by pluralizing the ghost and therefore the possible scenes of inheritance. In order to describe criticism and deconstruction as two different or even opposed and competing ways of inheriting (which would amount to assimilating them to the same critical spirit), one has to dismiss the possibility that the pluralization in question in deconstruction comprehends, or at least *wishes to comprehend,* the critical inheritance that it would not therefore oppose. Moving to pluralize the spirit from which, or in (the name of) which one inherits, deconstruction also displaces this comprehension out of any totalizing unity or identity and onto multiple stages.

Let us proceed, then, to reread some scenes from *Hamlet* with Greenblatt and Derrida.

A certain logic of exemplarity, which cannot be summarized here,[9] leads Greenblatt in the final pages of his essay to the supreme example of *Hamlet* and to the ghost in *Hamlet,* who is the chief or head ghost of English letters. When this subtly argued essay acknowledges its crowning example, two pages before its close, it does so in startling terms that strike with great force. After having quoted the line with which the Ghost begins his apostrophe to Hamlet in act 1, sc. 5, "I am thy Fathers Spirit," Greenblatt writes: "There is no more powerful claim in literature to an absolute attention, a complete investment of uncritical belief, than the dead king's horrific tale of his death."[10] This is a striking, indeed a doubly striking affirmation. The striking, almost paralyzing force of the statement comes from the impossibility of deciding which of the two claims it contains is the more powerful one. Is it the claim said to be made by "the dead king's horrific tale of his death" or is it rather the claim being *performed* here, which claims that the other claim, the claim made by a ghost and then repeated by the critic, is the most powerful claim "in literature to an absolute attention, a complete investment of uncritical belief"? Is it even possible to separate the two claims or the two performances? Since what is claimed is that this tale of the dead father has the power to suspend our disbelief, then the extraordinary thing that is claimed is that we cannot but believe both claims as having absolute sway over our attention, which is powerless to resist its call or its claim.

Greenblatt, of course, will not let this absolute claim stand unchallenged. He proceeds immediately, in the next sentence, to take apart the rhetorical basis on which the Ghost grabs our attention. The essay carefully unpacks the line with which the king's ghost explains his restless appearance among the not-yet-dead-and-buried. He was, he still is, as Shakespeare phrased it, "Unhous'led, disappointed, unanel'd," that is, buried without communion, without confession, and without an element or anointing of the seven places of his dying body, according to the sacrament of extreme unction. Greenblatt retrieves the historical, non-rhetorical use of these terms in Church rituals governing the passage into the realm of the dead, which would be the realm of the spirit and not of ghosts only on the condition of the proper burial of bodies. He then remarks: "The rituals that governed the passage of a person from the living to the dead had been changed, and the words that signified these rituals had been unmoored, making them the objects of a prolonged and murderous struggle. In *Hamlet* they have become a piece of spectral poetry, a weird pentameter line, voiced by a 'questionable shape'"(478). The scholar of the English Renaissance, who knows to read the line against the background of the "prolonged and murderous struggle" called English history, questions the "questionable shape" as to the bona fide claim made by a doctrine of religious faith. His philological exercise dismantling the

Ghost's assertion is performed in the very best tradition of enlightenment, even Kantian enlightenment. Greenblatt himself describes this philological commentary as "a form of conjuration" (481) that dispels or exorcises the ghost by disputing the faith to which it appeals.

However, this post-Enlightenment, post-Kantian criticism does not only evacuate the claims of religious faith; it also reaffirms the claim of what Greenblatt calls here "the imagination's power." As a result, this literary criticism or literary historicism (for it is not certain that this scholarship would differentiate them) sets itself up in a certain way to inherit the ghost and from the ghost called literature. I quote Greenblatt's exorcising conclusion to this reading of the Ghost in *Hamlet*: "The Ghost in *Hamlet* is the *genius literarius* come to excite the literary historian's wonder at the imagination's power to invent and unsettle the real and to cross the boundary from death to life" (481). The power of ghosts is attributed to or appropriated by the power of what is called imagination, which is to say a specular structure. It is this structure that governs or watches over the scene of the strictly *filial* inheritance of literature that Greenblatt is recalling and calling upon us to renew.[11]

But cannot this inheritance also be enacted otherwise, more critically, more affirmatively, more deconstructively? And even, one might add, more historically? For one may easily be struck by the way in which Greenblatt's own appeal to the power of imagination seems to be carried forward by the history (that is, the legacy) of romanticism, with the result that it has little or no leverage on that history. It inherits above all from romanticism and the romantic configuration of literature as power of imagination, and it does so automatically, as it were, without questioning the very scene in which it is inscribed as son and heir to romanticism's realm. Criticism is unhistorical to the extent that it is not urged to question the scene of its own inheritance, for example, its inheritance from the figure of the romantic imagination. If it is not urged to do so, then perhaps that is because the interests of criticism, in body or spirit, are best served by leaving fundamentally unquestioned or unchallenged the provenance, the origin, or the identity of the ghost whose inheritors it would be or claim to be.

Whereas Greenblatt, the historical, philological scholar, easily disputes the king's claim to have been buried "Unhous'led, disappointed, unanel'd," what he does not question is the king's claim to be "thy Fathers spirit." It is because that claim to the identity of spirit is accepted *at face value* that it has the force Greenblatt remarks and repeats, performs by repeating: "There is no more powerful claim in literature to an absolute attention, a complete investment of uncritical belief, than the dead king's horrific tale of his death." The striking force of this double claim, one may now see, is the force of a son's belief that he is addressed by the spirit of his father. The historical, philological apparatus the scholar will immediately deploy to counter this belief appears to have above all an apotropaic function. That is, it serves to remind the one who wields it that the father is indeed dead and buried; hence his son need not fear the spirit that he sees, or reads, before him. Not only need he not fear it, but it is a sign of his own power, the power of his own imagination, for the fearsome father is not a castrating agent but an agent of his own excitement: "The Ghost in *Hamlet* is the *genius literarius* come to *excite* the literary historian's wonder at the imagination's power to invent and unsettle the real and to cross the boundary from death to life."

I am suggesting, then, that this historical scholarship is *not yet* historical, *not yet* historical enough because it raises its shield against the *impossibility* of knowing whose ghost addresses us. This impossibility is set at the limit of history understood as historical knowledge, that which it is possible to know. When historical scholarship is limited in this fashion to what it is possible to know, one renounces for it any thinking of the possibility of history itself, the becoming-historical of that of which one can have no knowledge until it happens. One renounces, that is, the necessity of thinking a certain *impossibility as also possibility*, as that which shelters possibility and gives it its chance. When the shield of scholarship is raised, when the whole armor of the prosthetic body is wielded, it is also wielded against the necessity of thinking this other possibility, the possibility of other histories, in all their plurality, and even the possibility of other pluralities. The fundamentally apotropaic gesture of scholarship is put in place as a protection against the *trope* of plurality, against the *more than one* but also the *other than one*.

The question, then, is whether there can be another scholarship, if not another scholar, one which or who would deploy a different shield that, unlike Jason's, did not immediately deflect away the effects of looking into the face of plural possibility, so to speak, and that did not therefore have the same power to reflect back only the image of the one who wields it. A shield that is not a mirror, a shield that could shield, protect plurality, a shielded plurality and thus plural shields. What would such a body of scholarship look like? In what kind of body could it appear that would be able to hold together or stand up as a body has to do? Whose body? The ghost of whose body or of whose spirit?

Early in the first chapter of *Specters of Marx*, after Derrida has quoted for the first time Marcellus's injunction to Horatio the scholar, he wonders about the possibility of this other scholarly body. He has just rehearsed the scene between Marcellus and Horatio, while putting the reader on guard against what he calls the Marcellus complex whereby credulous eye witnesses to an unheard-of event call upon a scholar to verify, as only scholars know how to do, what the non-scholars like Marcellus think they have seen. Their claim to have seen "the same figure, like the King that's dead" is what needs to be authenticated by the scholar who is enjoined to "speak to it," and more specifically to "question it." The presumably illiterate Marcellus calls a witness who can ask the Ghost to identify himself. This implies that literacy is the capacity to speak with the ghosts of the dead. In other terms, to be able to hear oneself being addressed by the dead would be the mark of the scholar.

Horatio's scholarship, however, consists in charging the Ghost to speak its name before the court of reason. Here is how *Specters of Marx* describes the scene:

> "Thou art a Scholler—speake to it, Horatio," [Marcellus] says naively, as if he were taking part in a colloquium. He appeals to the scholar or to the learned intellectual, to the man of culture as a spectator who better understands how to establish the necessary distance or how to find the appropriate words for observing, better yet, for apostrophizing the ghost, which is to say also for speaking the language of kings or of the dead. (12)

It is tempting to read these lines, or indeed the whole of *Specters of Marx*, almost as stage directions for a representation of this scene in *Hamlet*. If one gives in to that temptation, however, then one must also recognize that Derrida's analysis takes part in the scene it describes, as director but also as actor; it even plays all the roles, a plurality of roles. What the Scholar is called on to do by his naïve compatriot Marcellus is to verify that this plurality comes together under one, under one body, the body of the "the king that's dead." But as soon as this scholar comes on stage, the scene embeds another one within it, another play within the play being performed. Marcellus speaks, remarks Derrida, "as if he were taking part in a colloquium," and we recall that *Specters of Marx* first took part, played a part in a colloquium.[12] Horatio, who is only one of the scholars being represented here, finally speaks to the thing when it returns, but he speaks to it by charging it, by commanding it to speak so that it may speak its own name: "By heaven I charge thee speake!" This scholar, in heaven's name, conjures the Ghost to identify itself and to arrest the frightening plurality of possible ghosts, the crowd of ghosts that comes on stage under the trope, or the figure of the King: "the same figure, like the King that's dead." As enacted by Horatio, the scholar's function is to question the Ghost so as to be able to identify it. Again, Derrida's stage directions are very precise: "By charging or conjuring [the Ghost] to speak, Horatio wants to inspect, stabilize, *arrest* the specter in its speech" (ibid.). And then the line is quoted in which Horatio vainly tries to arrest the departure of the Ghost—"Stay and speake"—before he turns back to Marcellus and commands him to intervene: "Stop it Marcellus."

"Stop it Marcellus": in Derrida's staging of the scene, this imperative gives the command to intervene with force so as to arrest the retreating Ghost. It would probably be somewhat perverse to hear it any other way. And yet this re-staging also tempts me at least to wonder about another possible intonation. What if Horatio, or someone in Horatio, had meant to say, with a certain annoyance in his tone: "Stop it, Marcellus. You are getting on my nerves with your credulity concerning the power of father-kings to rule even from beyond their graves. Not every ghost that walks before or beside you is the ghost of a father-king. Get that through your thick skull. Learn that, learn how to live with that, learn how to live with all the other ghosts, your own ghosts; learn that every ghost is altogether another and another's ghost. This is what I would have to teach you, for you are not yet literate and therefore cannot see the difference between a body and its prosthesis, a body and a body of letters."

This scene of an irascible scholar faced with his thick-headed illiterate student is not, however, the only one that Derrida's re-staging allows his readers to envision. For he asks whether it is not also possible to hear Marcellus, in his very naïveté, calling for another scholar to come, other than the irascible, charging, arresting, conjuring, exorcising scholar who is Horatio. Marcellus, to whom Derrida, like Greenblatt, is going to leave the last word of his lecture, would have thereby anticipated, as he puts it,

> the coming, one day, one night, several centuries later, of another "scholar." The latter would finally be capable, beyond the opposition between presence and non-presence, actuality and inactuality, life and non-life, of thinking the

possibility of the specter, the specter as possibility. Better (or worse) he would know how to address himself to spirits. He would know that such an address is not only already possible, but that it will have at all times conditioned, as such, address in general. In any case, here is someone mad enough to hope to *unlock* the possibility of such an address. (Ibid.)

As he has done elsewhere in a similar way, Derrida is signaling here to the situation of someone giving what is called the "keynote address" at a conference or colloquium. He thereby signals once again his own inclusion in the scene he is describing or anticipating. But one should not rush to conclude that there is some kind of facile self-reference here—or there. With the phrase "here is someone mad enough" the translator was translating "voilà en tout cas quelqu'un d'assez fou . . . " "Voilà" can always be translated as either here or there, but more often one hears it as "there," as a deictic that points not to the place from which one speaks, and therefore not first of all to oneself, but to another place and to the place of another over there. By translating it as "here," the translator perhaps *wanted to make believe* that Derrida was speaking about himself and announcing his own arrival as this other scholar, mad enough to believe he brings the key to unlock the possibility of all possibilities of address. If so, this may be a serious fault of the translation, because it once again arrests under one figure the plurality of ghosts and therefore the plurality of scholars who are speaking to ghosts here and there.

But where, here or there? So many scenes and acts are embedded at once, at the same time, as soon as a ghost can come on stage like any one of the other actors. And even if one now tried to own up to this faulty translation, the only way to do so would be to appeal again to an original one, thereby essentially repeating the fault whereby plurality, the plurality of possible translations, is referred back to just one. One would end up by doing nothing but multiplying all the scenes of the fault, and therefore all the stages on which a ghost may walk with the other actors. Perhaps, however, that is the point of doing what we call deconstruction: to end up doing nothing else but multiplying the scenes. The deconstructive scholar, the scholar whom Marcellus may have anticipated, for better or worse, is one who, we read, "would know how to address himself to *spirits*." The translation here cannot make any mistake about this plural. The scholar would know how to address himself "aux esprits." This pluralization of address, of the scenes of address, is altogether what deconstruction is, that is to say, what it does, what is done, and what happens. There is always more than one scene in deconstruction because deconstruction deconstructs the stage on which only one scene can be played at any time, the stage on which there is only one time in play.

This would be the point at which to recall Derrida's very *scholarly* reading of Hamlet's phrase after the Ghost has left the stage: "the time is out of joint." The phrase is made to resonate, in particular, with and against Heidegger's rendering, in "The Anaximander Fragment," of *adikia* (commonly translated by injustice) as disjunction, out-of-jointness. *Specters of Marx* is placed under the surveillance of "the time is out of joint," which, in its English version at least, is printed as a separate epigraph to the book as a whole. Hamlet's complaint thus commands, overlooks, and determines everything put forward between the book's covers, including everything Marx is made to think or to say when he comes back on stage later. The book is thus not only a staging of the play but a prolonged translation into French (and a few other languages) of the event that Hamlet names "time-out-of-joint." With this translation, the phrase can be heard naming something like the event of history itself, and not just history repeating itself as either farce or the tragic call to vengeance.

Now, any critic who has the good fortune to be able to encounter Shakespeare in English may very well conclude that if indeed *Specters of Marx*, as I have just claimed, essentially retranslates bits of *Hamlet* into another language, then he or she does not need any such intermediary to read this scene. Perhaps that is what Stephen Greenblatt concluded; perhaps that is why he proceeded headlong as if he were a son listening without any intermediary to the voice of the father's spirit, giving no heed to another's warning that the ghost is always more than, other than one: *plus d'un*. If, however, he had allowed himself to take account of this new version of Shakespeare's play, he might have noticed the effect of what is translated there as the "visor." It is the effect of that piece of the armor which allows someone to see without being seen. Noticing this effect, he would possibly not have been so ready to take the phrase "I am thy Fathers Spirit" at face value, meaning to *take it for* a face, in the place of the face one cannot see. All of that is possible. But it is also possible, of course, that Greenblatt did not notice this effect when he read Derrida's translation, or that he did notice it and decided he did not have to take account of it. Or that he simply decided he did not have to take account of anything Derrida might have to say about Shakespeare's ghost and therefore he did not read this staging of a new translation. But in each of these possible cases, the visor effect would have operated all the more surely.

Specters of Marx recalls that "The one who says 'I am thy Fathers Spirit' can only be taken at his word" because the visor effect is in place. We therefore "feel ourselves seen by a look which it will always be impossible to cross" (7), meaning both a look we cannot look in the eyes or the face, and a look that is a command we cannot cross or disobey. The visor effect in this way conditions the very basis of inheritance from the law, it makes for the law of inheritance. By overlooking the visor effect, the scholar's historical criticism remains written into this scene always in the same place: the place of the legitimate son and heir. There can be only one, there should be only one. But of course there never is just one, the visor effect being also a prior pluralization of every one, everyone. If the visor effect can regulate the law as inheritance by only sons, it has this effect only to the extent that something can be made to play along the hinges or the joints of the law's power to reproduce its will through filiation. These hinges link the visor to a helmet, which bears the symbol or insignia of the king's power, a coat of arms as it is called, a coat of arms carried on a coat of armor. There is thus a visor effect, a helmet effect, and what hinges them together.

Historical criticism, and perhaps especially New Historicism, would appear to see clearly enough the helmet, that is, the chief prosthesis of power, but does not notice the visor. No doubt this is so because Horatio is taken as scholarly witness. When asked by Hamlet whether he saw the face of the Ghost, Horatio does not hesitate: yes, he saw it, because "My Lord, he wore his Beaver up." With this response, Horatio implies that because the Ghost wore his beaver (or visor) up, the spectator that he was had a clear view of whose head was protected beneath the helmet. He also implies that it would have been a different matter had the visor been worn not up but down. In this way, Horatio demonstrates that his kind of scholarship is essentially that of the spectator, one who believes, as Derrida puts it, "that looking is sufficient" and that he need not speak to the ghost or listen as it speaks to him. He is the traditional scholar, because he is the scholar who assures tradition by supposing, but only supposing, the body of the dead King beneath its prosthetic armor.

That is what the traditional scholar does, but is there any other? Any other possible scholar? A scholar of possibilities, perhaps, rather than a factual scholar or a critical scholar? For the scholar of possibilities, what should count is not whether the visor was in fact up or down, but that a hinge, a joint puts both possibilities into play in an articulation. This articulation moves or plays in its joint with a prosthetic panoply of power that seeks to make itself invulnerable. As Derrida writes, "For the helmet effect, it suffices that a visor be *possible* and that one play with it. Even when it is raised, *in fact,* its possibility continues to signify that someone, beneath the armor, can safely see without being seen or without being identified" (8). This suggests that between the traditional scholar and this other possible scholar there is not *in fact* any difference, since it is indeed this status of *fact* that is in question. Thereby in question as well is what is called history, the facts or the events of history. Between the traditional criticism of fact and this other possible scholarship, there is not a factual or actual division: rather, there would be the effect of a prosthetic membrane opening and closing, in play between them.

Between all of them, who are many.[13] I remember that I wrote somewhere closer to the beginning of this chapter that I wanted to do little more than re-read the inscription of perhaps the most idiomatic mark on *Specters of Marx*, a common enough phrase: *plus d'un/plus d'un.* I said that this phrase mutes its voice as soon as one attempts to translate it. But one could have said just as well that translation is straining there to hear a voice, so that it can decide which of all the possible plural translations is closest to the original, supposing always that the original is a single voice. In this way, translation is also a philology of voice, at least until it has to admit or take account of the visor effect under which it performs. But a visor effect refers one to vision, whereas here the effect affects voice, and therefore speech, logos, reason, the law of reason. So one would have to find another name for an apparatus that mutes all the tropes and notes of voice, thereby multiplying voice in a disseminating trait, a voice that is not one. What would one call such an apparatus? And if one calls king, for example, the one who can see without being seen behind a visor, then what would we call one who speaks without being heard, at least without being heard by those who are called scholars? We call them ghosts, perhaps, those beings whom no scholars have ever seen or heard because, as Derrida observes, "A traditional scholar does not believe in ghosts—nor in all that could be called the virtual space of spectrality. There has never been a scholar who, as such, does not believe in the sharp distinction between the real and the unreal, the actual and the inactual, the living and the non-living, being and non-being . . . in the opposition between what is present and what is not, for example in the form of objectivity" (11). As for the apparatus that can operate as the prosthetic armor of voice, perhaps one does not have to search very far for its name; perhaps it's simply what we call the "school."

That both Derrida and Greenblatt chose to end their texts with the exact same words of Marcellus has been the *fact*, the bare textual fact I've followed a certain minimal distance into each work. This fact, which anyone may quickly verify, is the very small jot of scholarship I've presumed to bring to a discussion of "Critique and Deconstruction." It's possible, however, that at the same time I have been understood to say that Greenblatt is the traditional critic and Derrida the scholar of possibilities. If so, then I cannot conclude without rectifying that misapprehension. For Greenblatt, no less than for Derrida, it is possible that the scholar he wants to hear addressed by Marcellus, the one to whom he no less than Derrida consigns his text by readdressing and repeating Marcellus's words in conclusion, be a scholar of possibilities. For Greenblatt as well the scholar must deal above all with possibility, with what he calls "the possibility of literature." Indeed, he affirms that "literary history is always the history of the possibility of literature."

This absolutely abyssal phrase is inscribed twice in the essay as if in answer to the ontological question of its title: "What is the History of Literature?" It suggests that, even though this historical critic aligns himself in the most traditional way with romantic criticism, for which ghosts are only figments of one's own imagination, even though he finds there the benefit of joining the chief school of criticism under its apotropaic armor, he may be no less ready to welcome a new scholar of possibilities. Indeed, I would say that he too is issuing an urgent call to reread *Hamlet*, and quite a few other texts, from the place or in a certain spirit of Marcellus, not the unlettered, credulous one, but the one who enjoins the scholar to speak with ghosts.

Conversely, I would argue that Derrida's gesture of inheriting not only *Hamlet* but everything that follows in European or American letters, all the visor effects or school effects conditioning the power relations called history, is a critical gesture. It is, in other words, a gesture that would respond to Marcellus by speaking to the ghosts that appear to appear behind a visor. The gesture is critical insofar as it remarks the apparatus raised and lowered at the limit between the scholar and that which he can know, that which he can teach and learn in school. But if it would also be more than that or other than that, if it would be deconstructive and not just critical-skeptical, if it would, in other words, deconstruct as well the traditional scholar's skepticism at the idea that one can speak to ghosts without first checking their ontological identity, then it will have to multiply the scenes of inheritance: of Shakespeare, of Marx, of literature, of Marxism, and thus of quite a few others. It will have to turn its critical armor into the shield of plurality, of the more than one/other than one: *le plus d'un/le plus d'un* . . .

—And *plus d'une*, as in: more than one translation/no more of one translation.
—Well said, old mole.

§ 13 The Haunts of Scholarship

The presentation and then publication of Jacques Derrida's *Specters of Marx* in 1993 was an event in more than one regard. One measure of its impact would be the number of scholarly conferences, colloquia, anthologies, and so forth that have been devoted to several of its central themes:[1] to its defense of Marxism, a certain spirit of Marxism, to be sure, but also to the condition it recognized under the name "spectrality." Doubtless whatever echoes signaled *Specters of Marx* as an event in scholarly milieux and to some degree beyond them can be attributed in part to Derrida's immense and well-deserved reputation as an agent of intellectual ferment. All of his work has provoked and continues to provoke writing, thinking, speaking, teaching, and reading, in other words, all of those activities that go on within the scholarly milieu. But *Specters of Marx* and the ideas explored there have had, if I'm not mistaken or exaggerating, an impact unlike other work of his published before or since.

Perhaps, however, I was merely in a position to sense more of this book's effects here and there, since I was responsible for or guilty of its English translation. Be that as it may, I've formed the hypothesis that this reaction can be traced to the fact that the book provoked scholars and scholarship quite explicitly. Indeed, it exhorted them to take up speaking with specters, ghosts, phantoms, spirits, and by so doing, to question the limits on what they do as scholars. The exhortation to speak with specters is repeatedly sounded throughout the work and even given a place of prominence there: the final words of the text quote once again Marcellus's plea in *Hamlet*: "Thou art a scholar; speak to it, Horatio."[2] This command to the scholar is threaded throughout the book and begins in its first pages where Derrida asserts the necessity to speak with the phantom: "It is necessary to speak *of the* ghost, indeed *to the* ghost and *with* it, from the moment that no ethics, no politics, whether revolutionary or not, seems possible and thinkable and *just* that does not recognize in its principle the respect for those others who are not . . . *there, presently* living [*pas là*, présentement *vivants*]."[3] The necessity is thus an ethical one, or rather it is of the order of justice. It is therefore a necessity of scholarship as well, at least if one believes scholarship must also serve justice, indeed before all else. The exhortation to speak of, to, and with ghosts calls upon the scholar's sense of justice, which must be made ever more acute, ever more just, and which one cannot lose sight of without losing one's way. In this sense, the exhortation to scholars, exemplarily, calls them to their greatest purpose.

To the extent that Derrida's scholarly readers recognized that they were being called upon in this way, they might have also realized quite spontaneously the apparent contradiction into which they were being led. In any case, this contradiction will not have gone unnoticed because it is laid out explicitly a few pages into the book:

> As theoreticians or witnesses, spectators, observers, and intellectuals, scholars believe that looking is sufficient. Therefore, they are not always in the most competent position to do what is necessary: speak to the specter. . . . There is no longer, there has never been a scholar capable of speaking of anything and everything while addressing himself to everyone and anyone, and especially to ghosts. A traditional scholar does not believe in ghosts—nor in all that could be called the virtual space of spectrality. There has never been a scholar who, as such, does not believe in the sharp distinction between the real and the unreal, the actual and the inactual, the living and the non-living, being and non-being . . . in the opposition between what is present and what is not, for example in the form of objectivity. (11)

So, if the scholar, as such, *en tant que tel*, is someone who, essentially, necessarily, and by definition upholds these strict oppositions, then *as scholar*, he or she can have nothing to do with phantoms. Consequently, when exhorted to speak about, to, and with specters, Derrida's scholarly readers have effectively been pushed up against the wall of these apparent limits on what a scholar does or does not do. In my working hypothesis, the result will have been to provoke at least some of these readers to consider how taking account of the general condition of spectrality has to displace the limits on scholarship and even redefine altogether the role of scholars.

By way of a small contribution to this task of redefinition, I propose to excavate somewhat a part of the history of scholarship that has determined or at least reinforced the state that Derrida ascribes to the scholar and that we can so easily confirm to be in force for scholarship everywhere today. Before getting to that, however, I'd like to attempt to make clear what it is we are talking about when we take up this condition of spectrality, at least as Derrida has proposed to understand it.

This term and those it naturally attracts—ghost, phantom, spirit, specter, spook, apparition—have a certain frightening or gothic allure and thus a power to shock. Yet, although the ghost of Hamlet's father has more than just a walk-on part in *Specters of Marx*, the terms "specter," "ghost," "phantom," etc., are not in the least reserved there for such imaginary materializations of dead loved ones—or unloved ones—come back to haunt the living. To recall the brief passage I cited earlier, specters (phantoms, ghosts, etc.) are defined in the most general terms as "those others who are not . . . *there, presently* living." Now, when you think about it, the category of "others who are not there, presently living" is quite large: it includes, as Derrida underscores, all the dead and all the still-to-be born (or hatched or cloned?). Now, if one allows the term to have this semantic range of the not-presently-living, well, then it would be easy to point out how scholarship, *in the main*, has in fact always been concerned with spectrality and with specters. There are even whole, important areas of scholarship that are concerned with nothing but specters.

Yet, one should not stop there because this category of the not-*presently* living can be shown to be still larger if one bears down on the sense of the "presently," a term that Derrida certainly does not throw around casually (moreover, it is in italics). What is the "present," what makes the present present? It is not simply a temporal distinction—present, as distinct from past and future. Presence, in both idealist and materialist traditions (for Hegel, but also for Marx), implies first of all a presence to (it)self, a self-presence and a return to self. Spectrality would thus be the condition of that which returns without presence, without present or presentable presence, without a present life, present-to-itself. Self-presence, the dream of self-presence, excludes from the circle of the *presently living* whatever does not return to its *own* life, to its *own* present. "Presently," I am suggesting, thus implies this quality of "own-ness," of *le propre*, as one would say in French. Which is to say that by "specters" one should understand not just the class of beings no longer or not yet living—the dead, the yet-to-be born—but all beings, all others, whose "own-ness" is "not mine." Spectrality would thus name a contemporary condition no less than the condition of a relation to non-contemporaries.

One can make contemporary spectrality appear or materialize by appropriating some basic tools of discourse analysis. I may very well acknowledge the presence of all sorts of other beings. These are, by all objective criteria, present with me at the same time. We are thus what is commonly called contemporaries. But do we not count many who might be specters among our contemporaries? I am really here and so are you— as for him or her, well, that's another story. The third person is used above all, if not solely in some languages, to speak of whoever is not "there," that is, in the situation of present address. According to linguists like Emile Benveniste, unlike "you" and "me," third-person pronouns should not even be called personal pronouns.[4] They refer to those who are not there when we speak of them. In effect, we speak of them as non-persons because, at that moment, the moment of speech or *énonciation*, they are not there—*pas là, présentement vivants*—and thus they cannot be addressed or address us "in person," as we say. Yet Benveniste, who is undoubtedly one of the greatest scholars of our age, would surely have balked at calling this non-person/non-thing a specter, ghost, or phantom. Moreover, he would have insisted on the simple impossibility of address to the third non-person, whose absence from the discursive space of enunciation is what is being marked by the pronominal distinction. A specter would be the impossible thing that could never appear on the horizon of the linguist's world: someone, something to which one addresses oneself and by which one is addressed even though it is *pas là*.

Linguist-scholars, however, are not the only ones to reflect on the condition of this non-presence or non-personhood of the grammatical third person. Maurice Blanchot has placed that figure at the core of his reflection on fiction, or rather on what he prefers to call simply writing, without marking any generic division but also, and more important for our concerns here, without invoking distinctions between real and non-real, being and non-being, fictional and non-fictional. Blanchot's reflection on this figure cannot be situated therefore strictly within the boundaries of scholarship just outlined. This thinking occurs rather as a *passage* across those boundaries. That is, it is concerned with the passage beyond the limits of the present first-person to the third-person who or which is *pas là*. "[T]o write," writes Blanchot, "is to pass from 'I' to 'he,' but . . . 'he' when substituted for 'I' does not simply designate another me."[5] The "he" (or "it": *il*) designates not another "me" but what Blanchot calls the neuter or the neutral, the non-person whose absence speaks in writing. This absent speech or speech of absence or of the absent is precisely what the linguist-scholar must exclude from the possibility of real speech or discourse, that is, the speech possible only between those who are present to themselves or each other as I and you, two me's, me and another me.[6]

What if, however, the scholar must also thereby exclude the very possibility of the dialogue between you and me, the "I" and the "you"? The possibility of the present possibility of speech? It is such a question that has to disturb scholarly confidence in the distinction between there and not there, *là* and *pas là*, the elemental, differential distinction of the negative marker, not or *pas*.[7] At issue would be the very possibility of naming, that is, of figuring in names and in language whatever experience you and I are trying to share or to invent with our dialogue. Such at least is a conclusion to be drawn from the written dialogue that closes a section in *The Infinite Conversation*, the book by Blanchot to which I've been referring. The exchange is inaugurated by the question about the name given or chosen for the impersonal or non-personal source to which writing returns, a return that, because it returns to no one, is what might also be called the spectral. Blanchot, however, speaks not of spectrality but of neutrality, or simply the neutral. But why this name? Thus the dialogue begins:

> —Why this name? Indeed is it a name?
> —Might it be a figure?
> —Then a figure figuring only this name.
> —And why can a single person speaking, a single speech, despite appearances, never succeed in naming it? We are obliged to be at least two to say it.
> —I know. We have to be two.
> —But why two? Why two instances of speech to say a same thing?
> —Because the one who says it is always the other.[8]

The necessity evoked here—"We are obliged to be at least two to say it," "We have to be two"—could take us back directly to the necessity, injunction, or exhortation to which Derrida gives voice in *Specters of Marx*: "It is necessary to speak *of the* ghost, indeed *to the* ghost and *with* it." The two speakers or two *paroles* represented in Blanchot's text each affirm that they speak or name only in the space opened up by the other who or which figures only in or as a name: "a figure figuring only this name." This is, I would suggest, what is also figured by the specter or the name specter, that is, by that which returns not to the same or to the self, to some me or other; rather, there is a figure of return without presence or without present being.

At the end of *Specters of Marx*, this necessity will be articulated one last time and, as in Blanchot's written dialogue, it is the very possibility of addressing and being addressed by the other, any other, that is made to turn on the spectral figure, on that which is being called specter, ghost, phantom. I cite from the last lines of Derrida's book:

> Can one, in order to question it, address oneself to a ghost? To whom? To him? To *it*, as Marcellus says once again and so prudently? "Thou art a Scholler; speake to *it* Horatio [. . .] Question *it*."
>
> The question deserves perhaps to be put the other way: Could one *address oneself in general* if already some ghost did not come back? If he loves justice at least, the "scholar" of the future, the "intellectual" of tomorrow should learn it and from the ghost. He should learn to live by learning not how to make conversation with the ghost but how to talk with him, with her, how to let them speak or how to give them back speech, even if it is in oneself, in the other, in the other in oneself: they are always *there*, specters, even if they do not exist, even if they are no longer, even if they are not yet. They give us to rethink the "there" as soon as we open our mouths . . . (176)

"They are always *there*, specters." If so, then one has every reason to be astonished that scholarship seems yet to have discovered this fact and, with it, the necessity to transform its ontological presuppositions into hauntological ones.

Under the impulse of this reawakened astonishment, I'd like to return to a key scene in the history of modern scholarship, so as to see if one can make out the outline of the specters that, while "always *there*," will have been hidden, or rather disavowed. The scene I have in mind is even an inaugural moment of sorts in the history we're talking about. If, at least, one takes scholarship not only in the sense current in modern usage of the traditional, classical, research scholar, in other words, the literary scholar, philosopher, or scientist who advances knowledge by producing, discovering, or inventing new knowledge, but also in the sense of the one who is in school, the pupil, student, or apprentice for whom scholarship is a matter of learning some part of what it has been possible for the human race to teach itself already. Well, in this latter sense at least, much of what is understood today by proper schooling or education of the young was inaugurated by Rousseau's *Emile*, as I think we could quickly agree. We could agree, that is, that Rousseau's novel treatise (which is more novel than treatise) laid down, if not for the first time, then in the most forceful fashion up to that point, many of the principles that remain touchstones of modern pedagogy, even if these are nowadays rarely traced back explicitly to the formulation Rousseau invented for them. One need not, however, be a scholar working on the original texts of pedagogical theory or its history to recognize the ways in which Rousseau's notion of natural education becomes the tutelary idea of education in the democracies that were trying to emerge in Europe or North America. One way they tried—and are still trying—to emerge, that is, to give themselves a future, was, of course, through the adoption of universal, state-sponsored, secular instruction.[9] It is well known, for example, that the educational reformers of France's Third Republic frequently invoked the name of Rousseau and the spirit of "rousseauisme," to the point that his spirit, along with Voltaire's, could be thought to have presided, at least in France, over the passage into state-mandated, universal, and compulsory primary education. So, whether or not we consider ourselves still scholars or still in school, we have all at some time been touched, shaped, formed, if not educated, by this historical invention, which has yet so largely to be invented or realized: universal literacy instruction.

For the rest of this chapter, I want to try to address questions to what I've just called the tutelary spirit of modern pedagogy. In that spirit, *Emile* must be revisited not only because it will have inaugurated a certain pedagogical scene, the scene of natural education or an education by nature, that is, by the very nature of things as they are, which is the most fitting education of a free citizen, who submits only to those constraints that result from the nature of life and never to the arbitrary constraints imposed unjustly by fellow men. Not only, then, this general scene, so powerfully evoked or invented by Rousseau, leads one back to his text, but also the very specific place given or denied in the pages of his singular educational treatise to books, reading, literacy, or simply scholarship, in the more classical sense of the term. For it was this classical model of learning from books that *Emile* famously sought to replace with its model for a nonscholarly, natural education. Our tutelary spirit will lead us, then, to reread moments from the familiar elaboration in *Emile* concerning all the pernicious effects of reading to which the traditionally schooled young have long been exposed, all that from which Rousseau plans to protect his pupil by putting off teaching him to read and to know what books are for until, *as it were*, he learns to read for himself, naturally.

Picking up the thread of this "as it were," as it were, we will try to follow, *to read* how it could happen that anyone ever learned to read naturally, as it were, for or by himself/herself. And we'll ask: will there not have to have been some spirit or specter of another, some other than the apprentice reader, present, *as it were*, at this initiation into a repetition, at this repetition of initiation, or at this initiating repetition by which Emile comes to read, finally? We are thus preparing to scrutinize how this moment of a natural reading education gets figured in the text when it is time for it to occur and we'll be on the lookout, as it were, for the specters that *Emile* is going to have to conjure up and conjure away in order to teach its pupil to read.

Or rather to let Emile teach himself to read when the time comes. For Emile learns to read, by himself, only once its usefulness to him has been made felt, "rendüe sensible." Before this can happen, the child will be spared the great misery of reading:

> In thus taking away all duties from children, I take away the instrument of their greatest misery—that is, books. Reading is the plague of childhood and almost the only occupation we know how to give it. At twelve Emile will hardly know what a book is. But, it will be said, he certainly must at least know how to read [*Mais il faut bien, au moins, dira-t-on, qu'il sache lire*]. I agree. He must know how to read when reading is useful to him; up to then it is only good for boring him.[10]

Rousseau here in effect reiterates the main tenet or pretense of this pedagogy, namely the principle of freedom from arbitrary constraint. This principle is famously represented in the earliest pages of the book by the protest against the practice of swaddling newborns. Let their limbs be free, cries Rousseau, do not bind them! In this passage from book 2, the instruments of binding are books, which are like swaddling clothes inasmuch as they bind the child's body to the sole activity of the mind, an activity moreover which is as yet useless to the child, or so it is implied here. In other words, it is assumed, rather than argued, that this utility appears only with a certain delay in childhood. In the place of any argument (and the novelty of this novel-treatise is to replace argument wherever possible by narrative), one is merely shown or told that Emile, the imaginary pupil, does not naturally learn to read before the age of twelve. The natural delay, in other words, is introduced into the narrative through the example of its principal fiction (or prosopopeia), who or which is called Emile. Naturally, Emile will not have learned to read by age twelve.

At this point, however, Rousseau's *gouverneur*/narrator is called upon to respond to an intervention from a faceless, rhetorical "on" who articulates a certain necessity. "Mais il faut bien, au moins, *dira-t-on,* qu'il sache lire," which Allan Bloom translates: "But, it will be said, he certainly must at least know how to read." The fact that the *gouverneur* recognizes this necessity without delay ("I agree" is his reply) suggests there is no need to question whether it is a necessity of reason, of natural reason, or a necessity of men, imposed by men, thus, whether it is imposed as a constraint of nature, the facts of life and death, or as an artificial constraint. This question is not explicitly posed but it is implicitly answered for Emile who will learn to read, naturally by himself, without the misery of constraint. Rousseau moves to preempt the apprenticeship of reading under the reign of necessity or constraint, that plague of childhood, when he rearticulates the law laid down by the other, the neutral, faceless, dare I say spectral "on" who or which pronounces: "he must know how to read." "I agree," responds the *gouverneur* to this ghostly intervention, adding immediately; "He must know how to read when reading is useful to him." Instead of a painful necessity, then, there would be desire to appropriate what is useful.

So, the question is: how is writing/reading useful? Rousseau will supply a general definition of the utility of this art, but he will also insist it can be made "sensible" at any age. Thus, it would seem, at any age a child can be made to feel the utility of writing, for or by himself, and therefore be able to learn the art more or less painlessly, without inflicting the kind of torment Rousseau deplores. In other words, although Emile discovers the usefulness of reading only sometime around the age of twelve, in another narrative, of another pupil, this discovery could have been made much earlier or later. But the text does not draw this inference, which makes for something of a problem in the logic of the passage we're trying to read. Specifically, the idea that writing's utility can be sensed, grasped at any age challenges the other assumption made here to which I've already pointed. It is the assumption concerning the *natural* delay affecting the appearance of this utility to Emile. But, granting the other assumption, and if one may *naturally* learn to read at any age, then it is neither more nor less natural to learn by age four or fourteen than by age twelve. None of these problems is allowed to derail what has been put in motion here once the necessity of learning to read has been made felt as desire. Emile learns to read naturally, without constraint and under the sole tutelage of his own desire, which naturally is the desire to appropriate something to himself, to interiorize it, or more simply, as we will see, to eat it.

Here is the continuation of the passage:

> If one ought to demand nothing of children through obedience, it follows that they can learn nothing of which they do not feel the real and present advantage [*l'avantage actuel et présent*] in either pleasure or utility. Otherwise, what motive would bring them to learn it? The art of speaking to and hearing from absent people [*L'art de parler aux absents et de les entendre*], the art of communicating our feelings, our wills, our desires to them at a distance [*au loin*] without a mediator is an art whose utility can be rendered palpable [*sensible*] at all ages. (Ibid.)

"L'art de parler aux absents et de les entendre" designates reading as spectral art, as the art of address to and by absent ones.[11] This spectral dimension is clearly delineated here but it is even more clearly dispatched, swallowed up, in the rush of desire to appropriate a "real and present advantage." These absent ones may be far away, *au loin*, but no distance is allowed to open up that does not arouse desire for a present advantage, meaning, present to the reader or to the one reading. There is no misery to be brooked because misery is not useful, that goes without saying. Children cannot want to learn to read if it is a misery, if it makes them miserable, if it is bad news. And by misery we must now understand whatever makes itself felt as the *absence* of a present advantage to the one reading, to the one who is learning to read because he wants to, because he wants it for himself, to himself, and all to himself. The address to and from absence produces only misery if it cannot be appropriated as and by this presence-to-itself, all to itself. Rousseau will thus extol reading as a source of pleasure and not misery, but in so doing he appears merely to apply the lesson being taught here, which is that children will learn naturally to read as soon as they see reading's usefulness.

This is where one must acknowledge the continued force of *Emile*'s example in a basic principle that still guides pedagogy today. The pleasure principle is the tutelary *gouverneur* that watches over or guides Emile's appropriation of the art of reading. And reading pedagogy has largely remained, I would argue, within the scope or under the sway of this governing principle. The pleasure principle only works, however (if it ever really works at all) on the condition of spectrality. The appropriation to the present one or to (the) one's presence is haunted from the first and in principle by a certain absence that opens up along with or simply as the possibility of communicating it and with it. The pleasure of appropriation is in principle or necessarily haunted by that inappropriability called specter, ghost, phantom. Which is why Rousseau's text cannot entirely conjure it away.

I've already remarked the shape assumed here by this specter, which is that of the third-person pronoun, the faceless, rhetorical *on*. This spectral pronoun figures prominently in the culminating act of this non-drama, this natural scene of reading's pedagogy.

A note arrives, in fact many notes or *billets*. They are to Emile, addressing Emile, who because he cannot read them must show them to another. Since the pleasure principle is presiding, the *billets* bring no misery. On the contrary, all of them arouse desire for some pleasure or gratification, ultimately for food, for what can be internalized and appropriated. Emile learns to read as a natural extension into space and time of his desire to appropriate something to himself.

Something or someone: *quelqu'un* or simply *on*. In this passage, one must pay attention to what is going on with the pronoun *on*. Its referent is shifted rapidly around in a quick succession of scenes and sentences, now this one, now that, now absent, now present, and finally at once absent and present, but just one reading, as it were, by or for himself. Because the translation has to sacrifice much of this play of the pronoun, I cite the passage first in French so as to underscore the repetitions of *on* and *quelqu'un*:

> L'intérêt présent, voila le grand mobile, le seul qui méne surement et loin. Emile reçoit quelquefois de son pére, de sa mére, de ses parens, de ses amis des billets d'invitation pour un diné, pour une promenade, pour une partie sur l'eau, pour voir quelque fête publique. Ces billets sont courts, clairs, nets, bien écrits. Il faut trouver *quelqu'un* qui les lui lise; ce *quelqu'un* ou ne se trouve pas toujours à point nommé, ou rend à l'enfant le peu de complaisance que l'enfant eut pour lui la veille. Ainsi l'occasion, le moment se passe. *On* lui lit enfin le billet, mais il n'est plus tems. Ah! si l'*on* eut su lire soi-même! *On* en reçoit d'autres; ils sont si courts! Le sujet en est si intéressant! *on* voudroit es-

sayer de les déchiffrer, *on* trouve tantôt de l'aide et tantôt des refus. *On* s'évertue; *on* déchiffre enfin la moitié d'un billet; il s'agit d'aller demain manger de la crême . . . *on* ne sait où ni avec qui . . . combien *on* fait d'efforts pour lire le reste!

Present interest—that is the great mover, the only one which leads surely and far. Sometimes Emile receives from his father, from his mother, from his relatives, from his friends, notes of invitation for a dinner, for a walk, for an outing on the water, for watching some public festival. These notes are short, clear, distinct, well written. Someone has to be found who can read them to him. This someone either is not always to be found on the spur of the moment or is paying the child back for his unwillingness to oblige him the day before. Thus the occasion, the moment, is missed. Finally the note is read to him, but it is too late. Oh, if he had known how to read himself! Other notes are received. They are so short. Their subject is so interesting! He would like to try to decipher them. Sometimes he is given help, and sometimes he is refused it. Finally he deciphers half of a note. It has to do with going tomorrow to eat custard . . . he does not know where or with whom . . . how many efforts he makes to read the rest! (117)

With one exception, the *on* here is each time poor Emile, who must find someone to read to him, someone who may not be where he or she is supposed to be, or who may be avoiding just such importunities. Someone or rather *on* reads the note to him at last, too late. The scene then consists in the one *on* learning to read in the place of the other *on*. *On* is on its own only so long as it can read from the place of the other. *On* can read to himself, or he can "lire soi-même" as Rousseau puts it, only if he reads as another and as another does, and only because one *on* can comprehend and be comprehended by another. *On* within *on*. Each one within the other. But also each without the other, each exterior to and inappropriable by the other.

The inappropriable absence of the other: this is what has to be learned and this is what reading teaches again. One has already learned it, for otherwise one could not learn it again. What we call reading in the proper sense or *à la lettre* would be but the passage through the narrow stricture of that little word "on." Like everyone, Emile must learn to read "on" for himself, or rather, "savoir lire soi-même" in Rousseau's formulation, which also makes "soi-même" into a direct object here, dividing the *même* within/without itself: to read oneself. Within itself without itself, one that comprehends another one, not the same one but the same *on* all the same. The haunted *on* of an ontology that will forever be troubled in its accounting on the basis of the one and only one. It will always be an ontology haunted by the spectral *on* within and without everyone.

Rousseau's paragraph leaves Emile struggling "to read the rest." There would never be enough space remaining to read this remains of a word, which here designates all that Emile must strive yet to read and to appropriate if he is to have the desired custard tomorrow: "It has to do with going tomorrow to eat custard . . . he does not know where or with whom . . . how many efforts he makes to read the rest!"

Before we could reach this remains, we needed to take some rather long preliminary steps in order to have a chance to be once more astonished at what is, after all, the most natural scene in the world, or so we continue to teach ourselves to believe. Now perhaps we can begin both to recognize this scene as naturally spectral and to admit that there is nothing really astonishing at all about that. For "they are always *there*, specters." And they are always teaching someone to read, which is to say, to live with specters. This is the secret of our pedagogy. One day, perhaps, we as scholars will admit to this thing we know, for having also learned it from some ghost, for example, the one we call by the name Rousseau.[12]

Nevertheless and despite the difficulty, one might try to read the *reste*. That is, to read a little more of this letter, which promises such pleasures to pupils like Emile that it has kept them learning to read naturally and painlessly for two and a half centuries at least. Or so we profess to believe as scholars. The pedagogical pleasure principle remains the creed of those who learn or teach to read and who must presume such a thing is simply possible, a possible thing, as if it were a thing rather than the specter or specterization of all things possible. And yet of course we also *know*, somewhere, consciously, unconsciously, that specters are there, always, "as soon as we open our mouths," whether or not to ingest some custard. The desire to speak with specters, to do what Rousseau calls "parler aux absents et les entendre," this is what causes to yawn open that figure of self-presence encased in the bodies of the presently living, my body or yours, always someone's, the proper and appropriated body of someone living, thus not a specter of himself or herself. But already, all the same, this living one, this reader, for instance, is specterized for being able to "parler aux absents et les entendre." Scholars know this as well but still must believe, so very absurdly, that no specters can assist them in their work, the work of a life or of living, and of learning to live.

Because I began by pointing to the event that was *Specters of Marx*, I will conclude by returning to that text or letting it return, like a specter. The opening lines of the first section, "Exordium," describe or inscribe the trace of this text's own event in or through another, through another's coming forward and speaking, *as it were*: "Someone, you or me, comes forward and says: *I would like to learn to live finally*" (xvii). This *incipit* is a spectral event, neither fictional nor nonfictional, performative, one might say, if that did not imply somewhere a self-knowing self-present first person. The phrase comes, *as it were*, from nowhere, from "someone" who says it; it opens up with a series of pronouns, beginning with the third person indefinite: *quelqu'un*, someone, "Someone, you or me . . . " Notice that the order of the pronouns is third, second, first, which reverses the ordinally numbered series but preserves, perhaps, the division between the non-personal third and personal first/second pronouns (to recall Benveniste's distinction). It depends how one interprets the play of commas, the spectral punctuation of "Someone, you or me, comes forward and says: *I would like to learn to live finally*." A specter has begun to speak, from the first word, as soon as some mouth opens and says: "Someone, you or me . . . *I*." The opening sentence opens itself to this event whereby another, another you or me but also still another other, comes forward in or as desire that calls forth something. "Someone, you or me" begins to speak, begins to write, begins to give this text to be written when he, she, or it comes forward and says "*I*," "*I would like*," "*I would like to learn to live finally*."

—Someone: a child, a student, a scholar, perhaps, an old man, a still older woman.

—Yes, perhaps, but first and finally, no one at all—*on*, I would say if we were speaking French.

—In English, someone, you or me, translates: "Someone, you or me."

—In any case, specter.

—And more than one.

§ 14   Derrida on Television, or "Applied Derrida"

A title takes place only on the border of a work; if it let itself be incorporated into the work it titles, were it only to be a part, like one of its internal elements or one of its pieces, it would no longer play the role or have the value of a title. If it were completely outside the corpus, detached and separated from it by a distance greater than that which the law, right, and code ordain, it would no longer be a title.[1]

Derrida describes thus in the most general terms the singular topology of the edge or border of works where titles take place. When the edge is that of a work of fiction—say, "The Purloined Letter" or "Counterfeit Money"—then one should remark as well, Derrida tells us, the title's propensity to fold and divide its reference undecidably, so that "it is impossible to define, determine, or specify the indivisible trait binding this title to what it is supposed to announce" (9).

Now, imagine someone, you or me, schooled in this habit of tracing the folded edges of titles; he or she, you or me, has been asked to speak at a conference under the general title of *Applied Derrida*.[2] The chances are that he or she, you but in this case me, will be tempted to linger a moment at this border, to trace one or two of its implied folds.

At first approach, the analysis of such a title appears unlikely to uncover topological or referential undecidability of the sort "Counterfeit Money" produces across any possible reading of Baudelaire's tale or, to take a different but similar example, of the sort the title of Melville's *The Confidence-Man* deploys from one end to another of that work. I mean the structural impossibility of deciding whether the title, which gives the fiction its name and a name that already designates a kind of fiction (the counterfeit coin or the confidence game), refers to some textual content—theme or story—or to the text itself in which that theme or story unfolds. The consequences of reading or receiving "Counterfeit Money" as counterfeit money or *The Confidence-Man* as a confidence game, that is, of reading or receiving these fictions as the very fictions they say they are, with a (possibly) truthful declaration of their untruth or non-truth, these consequences are considerable and, when rigorously pursued, defeat even the hardiest efforts to maintain the standard framing presuppositions with which we ordinarily preserve ourselves from the radical operations of fiction. Now, this effect has been achieved through what may be called (and indeed Derrida has called it) a certain fold or folding whereby the title, from its liminal position between the inside and outside of the fictional text—neither strictly part of that fiction nor yet strictly external to it—is folded back or we might say *applied* to the text, naming it twice, so to speak, but also thereby sending it off beyond the borders of a decidable or identifiable entity promised by a name.

It is naturally this effect of the fold or application that seems to warrant some attention to the title *Applied Derrida*. But it is the titular conjunction or juxtaposition, the application of the term "applied" to the name "Derrida" that jars with the effect of a provocation, at least if one takes that name as the signature of texts that have consistently, in some places even relentlessly, discounted or disregarded a certain notion of "application." I am not referring to any public judgments on what some have been willing to portray as misguided "applications" of his work. (Those who find it odd that Derrida has in fact never signed on to such judgments, or never lent the authority of his name to them, themselves display a stubborn reluctance to "apply" a number of the lessons of deconstruction.[3] Of course, such a judgment is itself caught up in a kind of contradiction to which I'll have to return in a moment, before leaving behind some of these folds.) No, the "application" that Derrida sets aside, with increasing insistence in recent writings, concerns what he describes as unfolding a program. A single instance can suffice to exemplify this tendency, because it concentrates a number of the motifs that have come more and more to occupy the center stage of Derrida's reflection.

In *The Other Heading*, after invoking a certain "double and contradictory injunction" for whoever is seriously concerned with European cultural identity, Derrida comments:

> Responsibility seems to consist today in renouncing neither of these two contradictory imperatives. One must therefore try to *invent* other gestures, discourses,

> politico-institutional practices that inscribe the alliance of these two imperatives, of these two promises or contracts: the capital and the a-capital, the other of the capital. That is not easy. It is even impossible to conceive of a responsibility that consists in being responsible *for* two laws, or that consists in responding to two contradictory injunctions. No doubt. But there is also no responsibility that is not the experience and the experiment of the impossible . . . [W]hen a responsibility is exercised in the order of the possible, it simply follows a direction and elaborates a program. It makes of action the *applied* consequence, the simple *application* of a knowledge or know-how. It makes of ethics or politics a technology. No longer of the order of practical reason or decision, it is beginning to be irresponsible.[4]

The application pointed to here is that of a program, which because it "makes of action the applied consequence, the simple application of a knowledge or know-how . . . [is] no longer of the order of practical reason or decision." When he adds "it is beginning to be irresponsible," Derrida activates one of the paradoxical implications of the structure of responsibility that he has been analyzing in many different contexts, most forcefully and consequently perhaps in *Politics of Friendship.*[5] It is consistently remarked of this structure that responsibility cannot be engaged programmatically, in other words, wherever it is simply a matter of unfolding in an application already decided or known consequences. This is paradoxical (in the sense of going against received opinion) because it discounts a common version of responsible action or decision as exercised first of all in function of a thorough knowledge. According to this common wisdom, to act without knowing as much as possible of the possible consequences is to act irresponsibly, blindly, and so forth. But, Derrida adds, decision is not solely a function of or on the order of knowledge; rather, if one *must* decide something it is because no degree of knowledge can reduce an undecidability. Where everything is decidable, or decided, no responsibility for a decision need be taken. That is why one can say, or must say, that applied knowledge does not decide anything and begins to be irresponsible.

I am summarizing crudely and hastily what has been very patiently worked out in a number of important texts. I do so in order to get to a point of implication in this structure when one is preparing to speak under the title *Applied Derrida*. And from there to draw some consequences for what I have announced as my own title, namely, "Derrida on Television." It would seem, *on the one hand,* that we are set up to ignore whatever responsibility can or must be taken here if, by applying "Derrida," we understand various unfoldings of a knowledge or a theory; if, that is, we *applied* the word "applied" in the sense of "to put to practical use; practical as distinguished from *abstract* or *theoretical*," which is the only currently accepted definition of the word (the sense of "folded" is given as obsolete) and it is clearly derived from the sense of the verb "apply," which is: "to bring (a law, rule, test, principle, etc.) into contact with facts, to bring to bear practically, to put into practical operation" (*OED*). At the very least, however, this application of the title, besides prescribing that we begin to be irresponsible, would leave one trying to figure out how to apply a law that is not simply a law or that is not a simple law but always the sort of double injunction or double-bind of the undecidable. And, indeed, it is under the sway of such a double-bind that one must add, *on the other hand*, this: having recalled the limits Derrida discerns on application as a mode of responsible action, having repeated in a quotation what could be called Derrida's (impossible) law of responsibility— "there is no responsibility that is not the experience of the impossible"— one is still and perhaps even more than ever seeking to apply that law, as if it were possible. As if, in other words, it were possible to apply the law according to which an application that is simply possible, of the order of the possible, does nothing responsible or for which responsibility is taken. The question begins to arise whether so far one has done anything other than double up the folds of the application mechanism and, thereby, become more than ever implicated in its irresponsibilizing movement.

If there is some countering force to call upon, and thus a chance for that invention of "other gestures, discourses, politico-institutional practices" to which Derrida refers, a chance for what, in other words, results from something other than simple application of a program, then it cannot come from a logical reduction of the contradiction. And this because responsibility, decision, invention are names for an irreducible relation to an other, which will not be accounted for by the logic of non-contradiction. As soon as by subject one understands not the subject of a discourse but first of all the subject of address, and therefore not the subject alone but irreducibly more than one, then what I am calling contradiction becomes the condition and not the negation of this subject's responsibility.

At the risk, once again, of a quotation sliced from its context, and at the more serious risk in our context of duplicating to a still higher power the folds of application, I want nevertheless to cite a passage from *Politics of Friendship*, where Derrida is working through this logic of self-contradiction as the condition of address to another who is indeed other, that is, not simply present to the one who addresses him, her, them, or that. The passage describes an imaginary scene in view of illustrating the structural condition whereby, when I call to the other or invite the other to come, my messianic phrase is capable of converting terms into their contraries:

> Imagine my having thus to command the other (and this is renunciation) to be free (for I need his or her freedom in order to address myself to the other *qua* other, in desire as well as in renunciation). I would command him or her to be capable of not answering—my call, my invitation, my expectation, my desire. And I must impose a sort of obligation on him or her to remain free, to prove thereby his or her freedom, a freedom I need, precisely in order to call, wait, invite. What I thus engage in the double constraint of a double bind is not only myself, nor my own desire, but the other, the Messiah or the god himself. As if I were calling someone—for example on the telephone—saying to him or her, in sum: I don't want you to wait for my call or ever to depend on it; go for a walk, be free not to respond. And to prove it, the next time I call you, don't answer, otherwise I'll break things off with you. If you answer me, it's all over between us.[6]

The address here submits to a terrible, even terrifying logic, whereby it must be broken off *so that it may continue*; at the same time as it calls for the other to come, it would defer that coming so as to leave "a chance to the future which one needs for the coming of the other—or for the event in general" (198). The double-bind of such an address—that of a caller but also a writer, for this imaginary phone message has been left for anyone to hear or to read—is that it calls for a response in the form of a non-response, or perhaps one should say it calls for a response that is not a reply, a replication, or a re-application of the call to itself. For that is the *hantise* here, the dreaded event of a non-event which would be the *application* of a law and yet it is the dread that, of itself, risks producing precisely what it dreads most: a *prescribed* response from the other, which is necessarily a nonresponse. This means, however, that the *proof* demanded of the other's freedom is precisely what will always be withheld by the undecidability between two versions of the response/nonresponse: the one that responds in freedom and the one that follows the prescription.[7]

What I am suggesting, then, is that between the event of invention and the application of a law or a program, there is a margin of undecidability which is precisely what calls for decisions of all sorts. It is also what can open up the field of "application" to something other than the programmatic unfolding of a law into the future without future because without event.

To give this speculation some legs to stand on besides wishful thinking, one might take the occasion of our title (which has been programmed in advance of whatever anyone may say or do here) as a chance to revive a certain *address* that has not yet been altogether forgotten, even if it may have fallen into disuse. For among its many former and current uses or applications, "to apply" has also meant "to address" or as the *OED* specifies: "To address or direct (words) to." We then find a most extraordinary illustration of this use, one which indeed can hardly be called an example since it is the verb as word of God, the Word in its beginning that was with God and that was God. If, at least, we can take Milton's word for it, and Milton's word for God's awful word uttered at the first crossroads of human history, at the point, precisely, at which the creation myth gives man and woman a history and a future together, that word is "applied."

It is the scene in Book X of *Paradise Lost* when God interrogates Eve and learns of Satan's treachery through the instrument of the serpent, which has been "polluted from the end / Of his creation." Milton then interpolates the address of God's curse upon the serpent as an application, that is, address, to Satan, to whom He is "unable to transfer / The guilt." Therefore, while the judgment on the accused serpent proceeds, as Milton notes, "without delay," the application to Satan, "first in sin," must wait— and wait:

> "Say woman, what is this which thou hast done?"
>   To whom sad Eve with shame nigh overwhelmed,
> Confessing soon, yet not before her Judge
> Bold or loquacious, thus abashed replied.
>   "The serpent me beguiled and I did eat."
>   Which when the Lord God heard, without delay
> To judgment he proceeded on th' accursed
> Serpent though brute, unable to transfer
> The guilt on him who made him instrument
> Of mischief, and polluted from the end
> Of his creation;
> . . . .
>   yet God at last
> To Satan first in sin his doom *applied*,
> Though in mysterious terms, judged as then best:
> And on the serpent thus his curse let fall. (X, 158–74)

Milton makes plain that this deferred application or address, called an oracle (X, 182), awaits its fulfillment in Christ's defeat of Satan. It is to a verse from Paul's letter to the Romans that he goes for a connection to the serpent's curse: "And the God of peace shall bruise Satan under your feet shortly" (Rom. 16:20), or as Milton rewrites the line: "The realm itself of Satan long usurped, / Whom he shall tread at last under our feet" (X, 189–90). This treading, bruising step recalls and reiterates the one that God promises to visit on the serpent "all the days of thy life" ("Upon thy belly groveling thou shalt go, / And dust shalt eat all the days of thy life" [X, 177–78]). But the oracle of the application remains thereby still promised, still to come: "shortly," writes Paul, and Milton translates "at last" just as he had written twenty lines before, "yet God at last / To Satan first in sin his doom applied."

"At last," which is to say . . . what? What of this "application" which is thus opened up in a *necessary* deflection from its proper and first addressee, or rather, applicee? The deflection or deferral was necessary because not even God, we read, was able to set it right, not even God was able to transfer guilt to him who was "first in sin," but was obliged to address it, apply it to the mediating serpent, Satan's mere instrument. Who then is going to say that the application of the law, the curse of the law, has arrived "at last" at its destination?

Which question will bring me, at last, to television and to certain other questions raised by its applications. With this medium that is above all one of programmed reception, what chance might one stand to discern an opening beyond application to the future of an address without certain arrival? And if it were possible to make a distinction between television as irresponsible application of a program (in the sense of those terms with which I began) and television as something else, no longer perhaps correctly named thereby and yet for which one may never have a better word, what would it be?

This latter question asks about the possible transformation of television, about what might be new not so much on television—a new program, as we say—but about a television without program. Raymond Williams gave this question its now classic form when he posed it thirty years ago, in *Television: Technology and Cultural Form*. In what was at once a profound act of memory, which recalled television's prehistory in other cultural forms, and a prescient assessment of the medium's immediate future, Williams posed the specificity of television in its massive, comprehensive, and yet discrete deployment of what he called "flow," which as the word says, implies a fluid movement that follows an irreversible direction, rather like a flow of lava or other substance under the pull of gravity. Williams does not himself underscore at any length this irreversibility, but it is more than just implied in his numerous indications of the limits, indeed the near-total absence, of what he appropriately terms "response" to the flow, that is, of what would be something other than mere reaction to the flow's direction.

For example, after having acknowledged and reviewed the broadened forms of public discussion and argument made possible by television, Williams comments:

> In these cases the public remains, evidently, beyond the screen; we are watching a proceeding which we can see as separate from us; we can then independently, though in effect silently, respond. But what more often happens is that a public process, at the level of response and interrogation, is *represented* for us by the television intermediaries. Not only the decisions and events, but what are intended to be the shaping responses to them, come through in a prepared and mediated form.[8]

He then goes on to remark that, like representative and centralizing processes of government, the centralizing medium of television can "exhaust and even claim to exhaust the necessarily manifold and irregular processes of true public argument" (53). What occurs, according to Williams, is that elements outside these representative structures will be governed in their efforts by the "attempt to become real—that is to say, to become present—in television terms." The protest demonstration or the march arranged to "attract the cameras" is the cited example. Once again, however, Williams points to television's capacity to recuperate response, which it does, for example, by framing a contrast

> between the apparently reasoned responses of the arranged studio discussion and the apparently unreasoned, merely demonstrative responses of the arranged and marginal visual event. This is in its turn often mediated as a contrast between serious informed responses and emotional simplifying responses. (53)[9]

This is not yet an argument about "flow," the term that Williams will introduce only in the next chapter. But in underscoring what are by now the even more familiar dynamics of the televised "response," these analyses serve to set up the concept of "flow" or "planned flow" that Williams puts forward as "perhaps the defining characteristic of broadcasting, simultaneously as a technology and as a cultural form" (86). The term is meant to correct what he sees as a misapprehension of the televisual experience, which instead of a series of discrete units or programs, must be described as a flow of images, segments, sequences, narratives, and so forth, that are run into each other without apparent relation other than sheer contiguity. It is this flow that telespectators have been conditioned to accept, to see without seeing. Even television critics like himself can overlook the significance of flow because the sort of critical response one is used to bringing to discrete cultural artifacts—books, plays, films—is a kind of tunnel vision that prevents one from seeing what is happening at the periphery. He writes: "Yet we have become so used to this that in a way we do not see it. Most of our habitual vocabulary of response and description has been shaped by the experience of discrete events. We have developed ways of responding to a particular book or a particular play . . . the specific event is ordinarily an occasion, setting up its own internal conditions and responses" (87). It is as if Williams were saying, although he does not put it this way, that flow is *meant* (for, as we shall see, the category of intention is central in this account of television as technology and as cultural form) to induce this critical blindness, this non-responsiveness so that, precisely, it may continue to flow without resistance, without obstacle, the point being above all to keep the viewer watching, whatever he or she may in fact think of what is shown. The motto of the televisual experience being described here could very well be "Go with the flow." Having written *Television* in part while visiting at Stanford University, Williams, with his sharp ear for the poetic resources of popular speech, would doubtless have picked up the expression had it been around in 1974 in California, where it would soon become something like the mantra of the so-called California lifestyle.

In a famous passage, which I will quote at length, Williams conveys more pointedly, perhaps because with more pathos, the experience of what he calls flow. At the end of this comic evocation of the English intellectual–TV critic, used to the more discreet and discrete flow of British TV, he will issue a judgment of irresponsibility that interests us. Here is the scene of judgment:

> One night in Miami, still dazed from a week on an Atlantic liner, I began
> watching a film and at first had some difficulty adjusting to a much greater

frequency of commercial "breaks." Yet this was a minor problem compared to what eventually happened. Two other films, which were due to be shown on the same channel on other nights, began to be inserted as trailers. A crime in San Francisco (the subject of the original film) began to operate in an extra-ordinary counterpoint not only with the deodorant and cereal commercials but with a romance in Paris and the eruption of a prehistoric monster who laid waste New York . . . the transitions from film to commercial and from film A to films B and C were in effect unmarked. There is in any case enough similarity between certain kinds of film and between several kinds of film and the "situation" commercials which often consciously imitate them, to make a sequence of this kind a very difficult experience to interpret. I can still not be sure what I took from that whole flow. I believe I registered some incidents as happening in the wrong film, and some characters in the commercials as in-volved in the film episodes, in what came to seem—for all the occasional bizarre disparities—a single *irresponsible* flow of images and feelings. (92; em-phasis added)

For all the self-mocking, comic effect of this scene, there is little doubt about the serious weight given to the final judgment on the "irresponsible flow of images and feelings." And yet it is not immediately apparent what prompts this specific judgment. If one analyzes the phrase, "irresponsible flow" implies that there is a responsibility to be taken, and thus a respon-sibilizable agent, actor, or subject who can be held accountable for the se-quencing of the flow, although not for its separate elements. This is an al-together ordinary rhetorical convention, whereby a qualifier is transferred from actor to act or rather to the result of some act. That result is here called "flow," which is judged "irresponsible" because, as the term itself suggests, it lays down an appearance of fluid continuity over what are— or should be—discrete elements, separate entities, distinct narratives, or different discursive genres.

In some lines omitted from the quotation above, Williams remarks that what he saw that night on Miami television struck him as a new kind of sequence for which his experience with British TV had not prepared him: "Even in commercial British television there is a visual signal—the resid-ual sign of an interval—before and after the commercial sequences, and 'programme' trailers only occur between 'programmes.' Here there was something quite different . . . " One may still ask, however, in what sense it may be judged "irresponsible" to erase these residual intervals, leaving aside any suggestion of simple bias based on nationalized televisual convention, which Williams himself, in any case, makes no attempt to disguise. The judgment, nevertheless, bears on this erasure for that is what creates the effect of flow between narrative elements that *were not intended* to be related in any way. Williams is saying, in effect, that it is irresponsible to erase the marks of discrete intentions, or to create out of these discrete intentions a single flow without assignable limits, and therefore without intention. Yet, because he cannot go so far as to suggest that there is somewhere a collective or individual intention to mean all of the "bizarre disparities" he experienced that night in Miami, because the "creation" of the flow flows not from an intention to mean but merely to continue the flow itself, he is left pointing to an apparent tautology: a flow of meanings, "images and feelings," without intention and therefore without an identifiable responsible agent, which absence is called irresponsible. This is tantamount to saying: it is irresponsible that there is no one responsible for the flow, that the flow flows on with no other purpose or end than its own flowing.

But one senses, as well, that there is a particular suffering conveyed by the passage that has little to do with anyone's intentions or lack thereof. Rather, it is the experience of a radical *dislocation*, which the night of watching Miami TV brings home, so to speak. Williams recounts the sequence of "bizarre disparities" as following upon his own displacement across the Atlantic, which had left him dazed, and it is in this daze that he watches as San Francisco becomes Paris without transition or marking of their difference, and then again as one or both of these cities become New York, which is "laid waste." The effacement of interval occurs as the collapse of distance among these localities, a reduction or even a denial of spatial difference within the unlocatable, non-localizable flow of place names that now bear only the most tenuous, fictionalized connection to the places they name. The failure to distinguish one place from another, the induced indifferentiation of cities, countries, continents, hemispheres, the disregard for discrete locality or dis-localization, that is what is irresponsible.

In the final chapter of *Television*, the dis-localization of television, understood no longer in its specificity as flow but as the technical-industrial-economic complex of production, transmission, and reception of that flow, will be repeatedly identified as the principal threat posed by and to the medium. Local, community-based television is the defense Williams calls up again and again to counteract the irresponsible forces of para-national, global, which is to say, unlocalizable—nowhere and everywhere—corporations and institutions. The dominant mood of these closing paragraphs is the imperative, the imperative to decide: "The period of social decision has then to begin now"; "In the United States the crisis of public television similarly requires immediate campaigns and decisions"; "key decisions about cable and satellites will have to be made" (147–48). At stake in all these decisions is a participatory democracy based on a "new universal accessibility," in which local control and specificity would nevertheless access and be accessed by "internationally extended television systems, making possible communication and information-sharing on a scale that not long ago would have seemed utopian" (151). As solution, Williams envisions more locally based television production, "real local bases from which some material would pass into one or other of the networks" (149).

But local autonomy cannot in itself solve the "problems of urban information flow, democratic discussion and decision-making" because it tends to "overlook the dimension that is inevitably there, beyond the community—the nation and the world with which it is inevitably involved." Williams conceives, therefore, what he calls "back-up national and international services" to fill a dangerous gap: "The back-up national and international services would protect community television from its greatest danger: that its legitimate sense of locality will leave a gap which will be exploited by wholly irresponsible institutions beyond it." This is not to say that all non-localized institutions of television are irresponsible, but it does vest the concept of televisual responsibility in what Williams calls here a "legitimate sense of locality": it is above all a responsibility *to* and *for* this sense. The responsibility to the sense of place may take the form, as it does here, of supplementing or "backing up" the community with what lies beyond it: a nation and the world beyond the nation. But this supplement only fills a gap in the legitimate sense of locality, rounding it out, so to speak, completing it and making it whole, thereby warding off the danger from those other institutions beyond the community that have no responsibility to it, that are irresponsible to that sense of wholeness and seek only to widen rather than close the gap harbored there, to dis-localize the locality. Nor is this the only or even potentially the most devastating threat of such irresponsibility: in an irony that Williams repeatedly points out, the sense of locality, which legitimates itself, which sets the measure of legitimacy and responsibility, is for that very reason available to serve as a cover or front for dis-localizing interests: "community is a word that will be exploited by commercial operators and by the political enemies of the now partly independent programming and networking authorities. . . . Again and again, unless it is specifically prevented, 'community' stations will be mere fronts for irresponsible networks which have their real centers elsewhere" (149–50).

This is to say: localization or the preservation of the sense of locality, when it is taken as the sole measure of responsibility and the single touchstone for decisions regarding television's future, cannot prevent, indeed can even aggravate, the very dis-localization and irresponsibility that Williams fears most. By itself or of itself, the sense of locality invites irresponsibility. But for Williams, necessarily, that is, by virtue of a kind of tautology, this feared outcome will fall upon the locality from beyond its borders, and therefore the paramount concern must be to enforce the distinction of the truly local, which in certain cases will mean national, from the extra-local. The case of satellite transmissions presents clearly the greatest challenge to such enforcement, but Williams is hopeful that international law will extend the concept of national sovereignty to include the "right to refuse beamed satellite signals." At present, because reception of satellite signals still depends mainly on ground stations, there are "simple practical means of control . . . which can exercise selection or censorship" and he mentions the promising solution of twelve-channel narrow-beam satellite transmission, which "in favourable geographical circumstances, would transmit only to the areas of particular nation states" (143). Aware that it "will sound strange and reactionary to defend national autonomy" in these terms, Williams is concerned above all with the potential irresistibility of satellite-beamed television which, because of the expense of the technology, would be monopolized "by a few large corporations and authoritarian governments" (144). "Corporations" and "authoritarian governments": the Cold War alternative of capitalism or communism, when relayed by satellite technology, is a recipe for the kind of dis-localisation Williams deplores.

Now, one may well wonder what to think, in the context of this generally far-sighted book, of the apparent assumption in 1974 that the Soviet Union not only could mount a global satellite service, but could be successful in defending its own borders against unwanted, non-locally originated telecommunications. In any case, the point is not that Williams failed to foresee the contrary outcomes, in which failure he was hardly alone. But perhaps there is here another indication of the limits of a logic of responsibility which is finally responsibility to a single law, the law of a single community.

That limit is traced as soon as television can no longer be located or localized in one place, as soon as it is transmitted from one locus to another, as soon as it begins what Derrida might call its "destin-errancy," which is to say, its wandering toward and from destination. As soon as there is television, in other words, there can be no such thing as truly or properly local television.[10] That is the other law, which applies to television regardless of the conditions of its so-called production, transmission, or reception. It applies, in the sense of a limiting condition, not in the sense, however, of a knowledge that can be applied, or that can unfold in a direct application. It is precisely because no one knows altogether what television is doing or will do in any one place that it can locate, in multiple locations, a responsibility, including but not limited to the responsibility to that "legitimate sense of locality" that preoccupies Williams. And because it shares with everything we call "communication" this structure of address without certain destination, this responsibility is also a response.

But TV is not an address like any other, given its power to represent—to recuperate and even exhaust—in advance the response it calls for, to respond *in (the) place of* anyone and everyone else. The development of so-called interactive TV, which Williams foresaw in 1974 and which he predicted would define its viewers as "reactive consumers" (146), can be understood as an extension rather than a reversal of this recuperative power. As if TV's programming, having run the gamut of what can be shown and said, were now reaching out through the screen to take over its own controls, the viewer having become merely a kind of device through which a closed-circuit TV watches itself and responds to itself. This would describe the ultimate dis-localization or irresponsibilization, which is the absence of any place for response, the total violence of undifferentiated space without place: TV as the modern-day Satan to whom the curse at last applies.

I return finally to my title and to the elided subject of this essay, which was supposed to be not Williams but Derrida on television. Actually, however, I have been all along reading, without citing, between the lines of the former a text of the latter that treats among other things television and that is propelled by a recognizably similar concern. That concern is the future of democracy when the formal possibility of response is increasingly confined and limited in a public space increasingly saturated by media supposed merely to reflect or represent public opinion. In fact, however, "reflection" or "representation" figure as *alibis*—literally "in another place"—for the media's place between an invisible, unlocatable "opinion" and that opinion's phenomenological appearance, in the light of day, according to the rhythm of the daily news.

To quote now from this text, titled "La Démocratie ajournée" and cleverly translated as "Call It a Day for Democracy," this "in-another-place" structure has a "disconcerting topology. How is one to identify here public opinion? Does it take *place*? Where is it given to be seen, and *as such*? The wandering of its proper body is also the ubiquity of a specter. It is not present as such in any of these spaces."[11] With the latter assertion of the unpresentability of public opinion as such, which Derrida attributes here to the ubiquity of a specter, this essay on the media parts company quite clearly with Williams, inasmuch as the latter would retain his faith that the local *as such* can be located. But such a parting of the ways only sharpens the point of the question to which each is responding, the question, precisely, of the response without which what we call democracy is not just adjourned but rather cancelled in its promise of a future and as the possibility of justice. So the question for both is how to sharpen the point of response, even and perhaps especially in those rare democratic countries, such as France, that guarantee to each of its citizens a "droit de réponse" in the public media, that is, a right to respond. The exercise of that right, however, when it is not simply made technically impossible, is, as Derrida remarks, "in general neutralized by the placement, the framing, and the delays," its sharp edges smoothed over, Williams might say, by the flow. It's all a matter, then, of sharpening the question of response, of this putative right to respond that barely exists at all. And to do so above all in the media that, far from being today just one of democracy's institutions among many others, are what give birth to the day itself, they "donnent le jour au jour même" with the daily newspaper, televised *journal,* or, switching medium yet again, web-based publications.

I have not mentioned that "Call It a Day for Democracy" is the text of an interview first published in *Le Monde.* Derrida is thus writing in response to a journalist's questions. Pointedly, however, these answers are turned back around into questions for *Le Monde,* the world of the media, and thus for everything about our democratic practices in the West that these media presume merely to *represent.*[12] To conclude, I quote the moment of sharpest thrust, three questions fired off one after the other.

Thus the right of response hardly exists. Why do people so often pretend (fiction of democracy) to be unaware of the violence of this dissymmetry, along with what can or cannot be reduced in it? Why the hypocrisy, the disavowal, or the blindness before the all-too-evident? Why is this "all-too-evident" at once as clear as the light of day and the most nocturnal face of democracies such as they are, presently? (122)

—If these are questions that call for response, that's because we already know the reply.

—Or at least how it applies today, if not into the future, at last.

§ 15 Singular Sense, Second-Hand

Le trait d'union, *là est la littérature.*
—Hélène Cixous

—It has a second hand.
—Oh, I don't care about that.

The watch had a small face ringed in a gold-colored metal that could be slid on and off a slim leather wristband. The novelty was its adaptability, the possibility of changing the color of the band. There were four of these: one of black suede, another white, a red one, and a fourth whose color I've forgotten (blue?). The whole set was presented in a long white jeweler's box that sprang smartly open and shut.

It was the first "grown-up" gift her parents had given her, its numbered face denoting a new responsibility and accountability. But from the first, this gift was confused with a verbal exchange. Years later, she would learn a very precise word for the kind of confusion that had to remain unspoken in her own idiom. In the Babel of more than one language, it was what would be called a malentendu—mishearing as misunderstanding. For lack of such a term's precision, not hearing or knowing its range across the random senselessness between idioms, the misunderstood, misheard word left traces far more durable than the object that was their concrete occasion.

"It has a second hand," said her mother after the girl had had time to give the first signs of gratified pleasure. As these did not give any indication that she had noticed the special feature, her attention was being drawn to it.

"Oh, I don't care about that," she replied.

Shocked by her daughter's bald-faced ingratitude, the older woman's face decomposed. The dismay almost choked off her voice.

"What a thing to say!"

In a flash, the whole scene came crashing down around the girl's ears, the very ears that had somehow tricked her into reading lines from the wrong script.

"It's second-hand," said her mother.

"Oh, I don't care about that," was the girl's reply.

While her own ears were ringing with the utterly plausible interference of the two declarations, the effect of which ought to have been comic but which under the circumstances stung her with the sudden and, for the moment, useless awareness of the treachery of words, her mother heard only the one version of the exchange, which cast the girl in such an inexplicably disagreeable role. Fumbling to explain what she understood too late to have happened, the girl managed only to make matters worse since it had then to come out that she saw nothing incongruous in the idea that her parents, not rich but hardly poor, might buy a used watch for their only daughter. Besides, one had only to look at it in its crisply clean box to see that the watch and its assortment of wristbands were perfectly new.

The damage was irreparable and there was no retrieving her mother's generous humor. She looked at her daughter now with mistrust, making no attempt to dispel the sense of the latter's trespass. The girl protested but only in silence. The confounding homonymy of a language had asserted itself at the very juncture of her *entente* with the being who, more than any other, was supposed to know her meaning even before she put words to it. Was this misunderstanding proof to the contrary? What had happened?

No doubt she never succeeded in convincing her mother of the innocence of the mistake, either because she rapidly gave up trying or because she herself grew to suspect that her mother's version had some truth in it. Already by then, the exchange of gifts was freighted with a certain anxiety (was she worthy of this?), but there is no telling how much this affect was a cause before becoming a result of the episode of the second(-)hand. A silence settled around the affair. Yet, there was anything but silence within where the girl kept up a running dialogue with a new, dangerous interlocutor, this mother tongue that had suddenly become the parent of monstrous offspring—the same words, plus or minus an inaudible hyphen, telling two incompatible tales. "Here, look, a second hand," in other words, an extra measure of my affection, in fact a third hand that will divide the minutes of your impatient young life so that you will see how, yes, time has not been arrested by the past but is propelling you toward whatever you wish, the gifts of the future. But also "Look, it's (only) second-hand," meaning I could do no better than an *objet trouvé* that comes with a past, tales it could tell of the times marked on some other wrist, accompanying the movements of another hand, used, a hand-me-down of unknown provenance.

An elementary lesson in the vicissitudes of speech: saying and meaning could be dissociated quite ruthlessly without, apparently, the least intention on the speaker's part. My meaning is not mine so long as it depends on hearing and therefore on others. None of these potentially interesting vistas opened up at the time. On the contrary, the lights dimmed for a while as if someone had just tripped over the Christmas tree light cord. The fault gaped too large and had to be accounted for; there was blame to be assigned.

In her internal dialogue, the girl fought off the notion that the blame should come to her: Why was Mother so unwilling to credit the reasonable explanation she had given as the disculpating truth? She awaited in vain a sign that her mother had done so—a laugh they could have shared over the bad joke, the lame pun. Instead, the dialogue pursued implacably; she must have been listening for some confirmation of the suspicion that hers was a thankless task, raising a heartless child. This might have been one of the first occasions the daughter heard her speak the words that would later become a relentless refrain, words that had the power to send her into a rage that, on the rare occasions it exploded on the outside, disturbed with disastrous effects the familial policy of silence. "You're just like your father." The words carried no perceptible tenderness for the personality of the man her mother had married after giving up plans (or so she claimed) to be a geneticist. Rather, that he had turned out to have the dominant genes, at least in the case of her daughter, was apparently a cause of considerable chagrin and no reason to cherish either that parent or his child. Decoded it meant: you are secretive, uncommunicative or, in its worst intonation, you are unfeeling, insensitive. The reproach invariably stung in its unreasonableness, as if the daughter should have chosen different genes instead of her mother a different husband. But even if it was not uttered on that occasion, like an answer to the riddle of the second(-)hand or some premature moral to the story of a barely begun life, the phrase began to resonate in an inner ear from that moment, striking a chord thereafter on the notes of her father's hearing. The resonance was dim, but that was perhaps the way her father, who had lost the hearing in his right ear at about age twelve, perceived the muted sounds of his world.

To be "just like her father" meant also therefore—but inadvertently, iron- ically—to turn a deaf ear to what others were saying. His infirmity, with its accidental etiology, had become a generation later the girl's willful disposition; his incapacity, her insensitivity. He was not to blame if he couldn't always hear. (But, to the ironic inner ear, was there not also a note of doubt even as regards that physical disability? After all, who could tell if he didn't hear or if he just pretended not to hear? The partial deafness might be a sort of reverse crutch, infirmity as prosthesis, which he relied on to blot out the world.) As for her, she had no such excuse.

This, then, was the obscure region of the fault to be avoided, if possi- ble, in her ponderings over the curious impasse into which she had been led as if by some mischievous hand turning senselessly in its own little cir- cumference. It was an impasse because the quickest exit inexorably turned out to lead right back over the gap where she was suspended again. The way out took the form of an alternative: "not my fault, therefore hers." Al- though this simple, two-step reasoning brought a certain satisfaction, it wasn't very long before the trap shut in a neat vice. The more she seized on the disculpating hypothesis, the more it grabbed her back with the proof of her ingratitude, the very charge she charged her mother with bringing against her unjustly. Round and round, the two versions always came down to and back to just one as the rotating hand swept toward to its point of departure that was never a point of arrival or rest. "If I am right—she listened to me only to hear signs of my unworthy nature— then I am wrong and in the wrong." And vice versa, or almost. The strange logic of the equation never simply reversed, an asymmetry difficult to grasp seeming to veer it towards the, for her, more discomfiting side of the balance. The hand just touched the point of her possible innocence before setting off again to pull her into the gulf of another minute of cer- tain guilt. The little measured intervals of grim satisfaction could have been enough to keep the whole thing turning indefinitely, despite the re- peated pricks to the floated balloons of her good conscience. And, indeed, perhaps it did just that for many years.

But perhaps as well, less clearly and certainly less consciously, what re- mained always just out of reach was a way to admit the fault, to assume it but as a desire that had chosen to speak at the wrong moment and in a confused manner. To have heard "it's second-hand" she had to have wished to overlook the obvious—the brand-newness of the thing that came wrapped in the absence of a past and that could change its appearance in order to efface whatever traces of wear it would inevitably accumulate. Had she wanted, then, a device that would tell a story as it told the time, a kind of book with hands and springs? A gift from the past, of the past, which is to say her mother's, her father's, some concrete link to the history of all those other hands that had left so few marks on the things she saw around her?

But that would have been unspeakable, unthinkable even, and she surely did not think it at the time.

∿

Why tell you this story of a second hand? And why tell it in the third person as if it did not happen to me, but to another? And, finally, why, if I wanted you to think it was a fiction or a story reported secondhand, do I now assume it to the order of the first-hand and first person? In other words, if the genre is autobiography, then why not mark it in the conventional fashion, by grammatical person?

Good questions. But here's the thing: the first-hand experience I related came to me only as experience of the second-hand, that is, as a repetition by another of what was not simply itself but first of all doubled, multiplied, of the order of the more-than-one. The story I wanted to tell is that of a singular articulation in this more-than-one, our so-called common language, and for that the first-person convention of autobiography seemed not only inadequate but a disavowal of the very interval or space by virtue of which the singular can be repeated. The story I've told would be about, in effect, the interval that holds apart the first-hand and the second-hand, but also the interval that alone can allow the first to be repeated in its difference from the other.

It is to this articulation of plural senses with single sense that I bring my not-autobiographical story. You will not have heard, perhaps, that the articulation happens there as what cannot be heard, as an unspoken mark of punctuation—or not.[1] You may not have heard this because between "second hand" and "second-hand" (or "secondhand") not only is the difference inaudible, but there is disagreement among the orthographic conventions governing the spacing (or not) of this word. If the OED is still a reliable guide to British usage, then "second-hand" is the preferred spelling of the adjective, as in "second-hand automobile" or "second-hand watch." However, both the Webster's Unabridged and the Random House dictionaries recommend for their primarily American users "secondhand" with no space and no hyphen, forming what is called a solid or closed compound word. British and American conventions agree, on the other hand, that the open compound "second hand" is correct when referring to the hand on a watch or clock that counts off the seconds.

According to Eric Partridge, "hyphen" is a Late Latin word that derives from the Greek *huphen* which is itself a compound word formed by the joining of *hupo*, under, and *hen*, one; literally, then, hyphen means "under one," and hence "into one" or "together."[2] From its earliest use by manuscript scribes to signal the linked syllables or letters of a word that have become separated at the end of a line, its range of later print uses has been extended considerably: the linking of commonly associated words, the affixing of occasional prefixes, the indication of a specific syntactic combination, or even a typographical convention for the representation of an abnormal speech pattern, such as stuttering or unusual emphasis on separate syllables of a word.

This variety of conventional uses (and there are still others one could mention) already points to the hyphen's double sense of articulation, which both joins what it separates and separates what it joins.[3] Unlike other conventions of punctuation, moreover, hyphenation signals articulation not at the level of propositions, clauses, or phrases but at a more elementary level of the formation of units of sense. Perhaps hyphenation does not even belong to the category of punctuation, as commonly defined, but signals a discernibly different act, which could explain in part why, in English at least, we have both this noun, "hyphenation," and a verb, "to hyphenate," whereas no equivalents circulate for the other common marks of punctuation ("periodization" and "to periodize" have ordinarily nothing to do with placing a period at the end of a sentence). Linguistic treatises one may consult on punctuation either exclude consideration of the hyphen or mention it only in passing.[4] Prescriptive manuals, such as Eric Partridge's *You Have a Point There*, classify hyphens among what it calls the "allies and accessories" of punctuation proper. The standard reference for American university presses, *The Chicago Manual of Style*, treats hyphens principally in its chapter on spelling and introduces the section with the remark that the cloudy distinctions among solid, hyphenated, and open compounds are responsible for probably "nine out of ten spelling questions that arise in writing or editing."[5] After setting out "general principles" that conform to the trend away from the use of hyphens and underscoring that this is a trend and not a rule, the same authority admits that there are "quite literally, scores of other rules for the spelling of compound words. Many of them are nearly useless because of the great numbers of exceptions" (164). This problem is itself compounded if one has to take account of differences between American and British usage, as already mentioned. According once again to the Englishman Partridge, ever since World War I, which "taught many people that superfluities should be treated as such and therefore discarded" (138), the tendency toward the formation of non-hyphenated compound words in English has accelerated, and among Americans more so than Britons. American alacrity in discarding "superfluities" alarms many Britons, says Partridge, and results in some "ugly 'continuities' (e.g., *nonresistance*)." At the same time, however, he does not seem to doubt that such ugliness is our common future as readers and writers of the English language: "so why," he asks, "resist the inevitable?" (138). Why resist, in other words, the unhypenated "nonresistance"?[6]

It is a version of that question I want to take up briefly, not, however, to explore any further what the vicissitudes of hyphenation may indicate about different national characters, even though that is doubtless a fascinating subject.[7] Rather, because it marks the space of a certain resistance to nonresistance, a minimal jot left as a reminder to hold apart the two (or more) terms that are all the same being pulled together "under one," hyphenation perhaps supplies an opening, albeit a tiny one, for remarking the insertion of singular differences within general structures of meaning. This opening can be described in one of the effects already noted, the largely non-rule-governed practice of hyphenation in different English idioms. What may be provisionally called the hypothesis of the hyphen, which for structural reasons cannot be fully raised to or posed as a thesis, is this: hyphenation makes room for or gives place to a mark that arrests the disappearance of a singular sense at the limit of common sense, common language, the rule of the under- and into-one.

At this point, one should attempt to say something general about singularity if only to demonstrate the predictable failure of any such an attempt. Fortunately, one does not have to venture into this territory unassisted. I am going to rely on two seasoned guides and two recent works elaborated around a thinking of singular articulations within the general space of sense. They will also allow us to run a few preliminary tests on the hypothesis of the hyphen.

In the introduction to his collection of essays, *Inventions of Difference:*

On Jacques Derrida, a book described by its author as "about singularity," Rodolphe Gasché sharply disputes the idea, advanced by another commentator, that "'the distinctive trait' of Derrida's writing imparts its singularity to his texts in a way that renders their generic categorization impossible."[8] This assertion, which has all the appearance of common sense, posits in effect an impermeable barrier between singular sense and, precisely, common sense. It renders singularity, as Gasché puts it, "opaque, silent, or immediate in a nondialectical sense" (14). Gasché, by contrast, wants to insist that if indeed singularity were simply inaccessible in this sense, then it would be "quite simply thoroughly unintelligible" (ibid.). That is, one could not possibly have any idea of it at all. The reasoning here might bring to mind a similar observation of Freud's concerning the unconscious drive, which "can never become an object of consciousness"; the drive has access to conscious thought only as and on condition of representation in an idea. This condition is the condition of knowing anything at all about the drive, for, as Freud puts it: "If the drive did not *attach itself* to an idea or manifest itself as an affective state, we would know nothing about it."[9] Likewise, Gasché underscores that the condition of singularity's intelligibility is its repetition "in an idealizing doubling." If one is to have any idea at all of singularity, then it "must translate itself, interpret itself as intelligible in its unintelligibility." As Freud put it, it must "*attach* itself to an idea." Or as we might now begin to be able to say with some understanding, it must hyphenate.

Gasché does not name the hyphen as such. Nevertheless, the language he selects from a passage in *Shibboleth*, Derrida's essay on the iteration of singular dates in Celan, and in particular the word "ligament" will allow us to translate, to hyphenate.

> Singularity . . . cannot be simply demarcated from the universal. As with the ciphers encountered in Celan's poetry, with the singular "chance and necessity cross and in crossing are both at once consigned. Within its strictures a ligament binds together, in a manner at once significant and insignificant, fatality and its opposite: chance and coming-due, coincidence in the event, what *falls*—well or ill-together." It is thus imperative to acknowledge this *togetherness* of the unique, the one-and-only-time, of the utter singular's refusal of all possible repetition *and* necessity, ideality, universality, in order to do justice to the singular itself. For the singular to be understood as what it is, that is, in its utter singularity, the ligament that within it holds together, each time in a singular manner, contingency and necessity, sheer punctuality and universality, must, in one way or another, be acknowledged. (15–16)

As I said, Gasché does not name the hyphen; nevertheless, the above passage, in addition to excising and then re-attaching the term "ligament," practices hyphenation at two different levels. Whether this is an accidental or necessary gesture is not a question one should rush to decide, given what the passage has to say about the coming- or falling-due together of chance and necessity and despite the fact that an accident seems indeed to have been responsible for at least one of the hyphens that shows up here.

At a first level, then, the passage repeats a translation of Derrida's sentences from *Shibboleth* that have been rendered into English with the help of two hyphenated words—or so it appears. The compound "coming-due" hyphenates the translation of "échéance," which means the coming- or falling-due of the deadline (a word that perhaps used to be hyphenated). Derrida's text, which is working to retrieve and repeat Celan's singular idiom of the date, crosses into and crosses *with* the English idiom by means of the uncommon yet intelligible open compound word: "falling-due." As for the second hyphenated word Gasché quotes, "ill-together," it turns out to have been formed by a typographical error in the quotation, both the translation and the original having used a dash here.[10] By chance, accident, or error an ill-formed word results, and it is one which says precisely, that is, badly, the ill-fitting joint of the singular's repetition in generality: "ill-together."

At a second level, Gasché's own language, as it continues after the quoted lines, picks up the hyphenating trait remarked there: he forges the four-part compound "one-and-only-time" and sets it in balance with "necessity, ideality, universality." This hyphenated general name of absolute singularity, of that which can only take up a name through universalizing repetition, has by the end of the passage, after a number of repetitions, been transformed into the common word "punctuality." "For the singular to be understood as what it is, that is, in its utter singularity, the ligament that within it holds together, each time in a singular manner, contingency and necessity, sheer punctuality and universality, *must*, in one way or another, be acknowledged." The ligament must be acknowledged. The force of Gasché's repeated imperative here carries over the force of a hyphenating punctuality or punctuation at the singular crossing of chance and necessity traced in his own text. The hyphenating imperative, in other words, dictates not just a duty to acknowledge what can and therefore must be acknowledged; it is that which is also imperatively punctuating the language of common understanding at its limits.[11]

To follow the inscriptions of this double imperative, I will turn to a second guide. Jean-Luc Nancy, no less although differently than Jacques Derrida, has set his thought within the space of articulated singularity. Nancy announces this preoccupation clearly enough in the chosen title of one collection of his essays: *Etre singulier pluriel,* that is, *Plural Singular (or Singular Plural) Being.* The reversibility of the two modifying adjectives, their co-priority and co-secondarity (with the shift in sense that is thereby allowed), supplies the syntactic and semantic matrix that is worked through most explicitly in the initial chapter of the book. I am not going to try to summarize the intricate movements of this essay. I merely want to remark the considerable extent to which the hyphenating gesture imposes itself on these pages. This can be seen, once again, at two levels.

At a first level, there is the regular and constant occurrence of hyphenated compounds, formed either through the insertion of hyphens in normally unhyphenated words (for example, pre-position, dis-position, ex-position, co-appear, co-existence, co-incidence) or through the forging of hyphenated word-phrases. The latter practice is heavily relied on as a vehicle of the exposition of "singular-plural/plural-singular-being," which is indeed, at one point at least, explicitly hyphenated in this way (58). Other formations dictated by this thinking-in-hyphenation precipitate out of the Heideggerian elaboration of *Mitsein,* which both French and English translate with the help of a hyphen: *être-avec* and Being-with. Indeed, Nancy quite clearly positions what he is doing here as what would be called in French an "explication avec" *Being and Time,* that is, an "explanation with," a coming-to-terms, and in particular a coming-to-terms with the "with" of Being-with.

After asserting that the existential analytic of *Being and Time* is "the enterprise from which all subsequent thinking derives" inasmuch as this analytic registered "the seismic jolt of a decisive rupture in the constitution or the consideration of sense," Nancy then remarks:

The analytic of *Mitsein* that appears within the existential analytic remains nothing more than a sketch; that is, even though the trait of *Mitsein* is said to be co-essential with *Dasein,* it remains subordinated to it. In this way, no doubt, the whole existential analytic hides some principle by which what it opens up is closed down. It is necessary, then, to forcibly reopen a passage through the obstruction that, without any doubt, determined the filling-in and the folding-back of Being-with by means of the "folk" and its "destiny." This does not mean that it is necessary to "finish off" an analysis that is merely sketched, or to give *Mitsein* a "principial" place that is rightly its due. Being-with no doubt escapes "in principle" both completion and the principial position. But it is necessary to go back over the trait of the sketch and bear down on it to the point where it becomes apparent that the co-essentiality of Being-with implies nothing less than a co-originarity of sense.[12]

The French word "trait" twice rendered or repeated above as "trait" means as well a line drawn, which is why it figures in the French term for hyphen: *trait d'union*, literally, line or mark of union. But it is not this semantic coincidence alone that can lead one to hear the above passage and the imperatives it issues as announcing a necessary re-hyphenation of what has been filled in, occluded, obstructed, or closed down. Nancy's language, at this point, adopts a specifically graphic description for what must be done: "go back over the trait of the sketch and bear down on it." This re-drawing of the line, however, does not figure a setting down of some boundary or limit; rather, it is always the double gesture of an articulation in difference of the singular-plural/plural-singular, of "being-many-together" (41), of "being-with-one-another" (84), of "being-each-time-with" (97).[13] These latter sort of hyphenated formations, then, which arise regularly and constantly here, carry out the graphic imperative that Nancy formulates above, the necessity of going back over the articulating trait that has been covered over or closed down.

At a second level, this graphic practice is thematized, so to speak, around the preposition "with" or "avec." Here, I will have to be even more cursory in the description of how this thematization remains a spacing practice of the sort I am calling hyphenation. What comes to be thematized in this way is a preposition, with or "avec," which is to say, a lexical unit that belongs to the class of syntactic or logical terms called syncategorems: words that do not have meaning by themselves but only when used in conjunction with another word or words. What I have called Nancy's thematization of "avec" is the movement that carries over this syncategoremic character of the pre-position into affirmations or propositions that bear out the non-categorical sense of the in-conjunction-with-another.

I will take two examples of this thematization and propose a minimal commentary on them.

A unique subject could not even designate *itself* and refer or relate to *itself* as subject. In the most classical sense of the term, a subject supposes not only its own distinction from [*d'avec*] the object of its representation or mastery; it supposes at least equally its own distinction from [*d'avec*] other subjects whose ipseity (or even, if one prefers, aseity) it can distinguish from [*d'avec*] its own center of representation or mastery. The *avec* is thus the supposition of "self" in general. But it is precisely no longer a subjacent supposition, in the mode of the infinite self-presupposition of subjective sub-stance. As its syntactic function indicates, "avec" is the pre-position of position in general, and it thus makes for its dis-position. (40; trans. modified)

In addition to the introduced hyphens in the words "sub-stance," "pre-position," and "dis-position,"[14] what one may remark here is an idiomatic effect that shows up when one translates the three occurrences of "d'avec." This French preposition in fact combines two prepositions and must normally be rendered, as here, not as "with" but "from" (i.e., the "distinction from other subjects"). Literally, "d'avec" stages a kind of tug-of-war in two directions, away from/with, and is itself an articulated formation, marked not by a hyphen but by an apostrophe. In any case, the last sentences of the passage thematize, substantialize, or categorize not the "d'avec" but the "avec," when they make of it the grammatical subject of three predicating propositions, beginning with "The *avec* is thus the supposition of 'self' in general." This movement, then, can also be described as taking the risk that such a predication or substantialization of the "avec" will once again occlude, close down, cover over, or simply drop the difference articulated in the idiomatic, untranslatable formation "d'avec."

To generalize very quickly, and without further corroboration, I would be tempted to say that Nancy's writing is quite precisely, graphically dictated by this sort of risky gesture, which then requires, as the first passage I quoted put it, a doubling back over the trait so as to bear down once again on the occluded articulation. This could explain perhaps two prevalent features of the Nancien idiom: on the one hand, the frequency of copulative propositions in the third-person present singular of the verb "to be," propositions, therefore, that take the risk of categorization, and on the other hand, the frequent imperatives, some modality of the impersonal "it is necessary," "il faut." If I am correct in reading such a text according to the hypothesis or the pre-position of the hyphen, then the "it is necessary" each time re-inscribes, bears down on the imperative Nancy relays in the wake of Heidegger's "sketch" of *Mitsein*: "it is necessary to go back over the trait of the sketch and bear down on it." In other words, the imperatives regularly issued here would be given above all or first of all to the writing itself—or to thinking, as Nancy prefers to say, for example in this sentence that combines the two features I have just isolated, the copulative proposition and the order of the imperative: "That being is being-with, absolutely, that is what we must think [*Que l'être, absolument, soit être-avec, voilà ce qu'il nous faut penser*]" (61; 83–84). This is what we might call Nancy's syncategoremical imperative, which is given to thinking, to writing, but also to reading.

I select the second example because it will bear down on the hyphen by name:

> The *with* is not "unpresentable" like a withdrawn presence or like an Other. If there is a subject only with other subjects, the "with" itself is not a subject. It is or it makes the hyphen, the mark of union/disunion, which by itself appropriates neither the union nor the disunion as substances posed under the mark: the mark is not a sign for a reality, not even for an "intersubjective dimension." It is truly—"in truth"—a line drawn on the void that it at the same time traverses and underscores, which is what makes for its tension and traction, the tension and traction—attraction/repulsion—of the "among"-us/"between"-us [*l' "entre"-nous*]. The "with" remains among or between us, and we remain among ourselves: nothing but us, but nothing but interval between us. (62; 84; trans. modified)

These sentences thematize the hyphen or rather the *trait d'union*, that is, they are general propositions on the hyphenating effects of "between," "among," or "with." And yet, just as with the previous examples, these general propositions are inflected by an idiom and thereby limited in their generality, as may be verified by attempting to translate them. Thus, for example, Nancy takes the rather considerable risk of re-inscribing the French phrase "entre nous," which is first cited and hyphenated as "l' 'entre'-nous" and then inserted twice without any further punctuation in the sentence: "L' 'avec' reste entre nous, et nous restons entre nous." What cannot be simply repeated in another idiom, English for example, are the several resonances of the phrase "entre nous," which range from the aside or the secrecy of "just between us" to the sense of a closed circle of intimacy, family, friends, or neighbors. In this latter sense, "nous restons entre nous" could therefore also mean "we are alone among ourselves, no outsider is present." It is precisely such gestures of closure or ex-clusion, whereby "we" pose and appropriate a substantial subject of community, that Nancy's re-inscriptions of the pre-positions—with, between, among—are working to expose. But this ex-position is undertaken at the risk of a re-inscription of the idiom that is "entre nous," just between us, unrepeatable or imperceptible for outsiders.

What I have just described is a marking effect of the common idiom, the possibility of a repetition of sense that exercises its tractor-like pull on the hyphenating or pre-positioned instance of the singular. Having recourse to his idiom, Nancy consigns this effect to the co-originarity and co-secondarity of a "singulier-pluriel," singular plurality/plural singularity. It is not, then, conceptual or categorical generalization as such that risks effacing without trace the singular trait here, because "entre nous" defines and performs only a *limited* generality, collectivity, or community, that which can be assembled in the *entente* of a common idiom. For this common idiom repeats singularity's effacement and, in the same trait, remarks the limit at which, *entre nous*, we will have been *overheard* by another, by a different idiom, no longer speaking therefore just among ourselves.

—What does it mean to overhear a hyphen? To overhear that which, under one, stands at the limit of a common under-standing? Is it to hear more than one should and is meant to or, on the contrary, as we can also say in our idiom by appealing to another sense, to overlook an essential something, at once under and over, before and beyond the sense of our common meanings?[15] In other words, what sense, hyphenation?

—Inaudible, odorless, tasteless, untouchable, the hyphen is finally invisible as well, even when its conventional mark has not already been effaced by the tendencies of the common idiom or editorial convention. In the sensorial array, no organ or faculty is set to read the hyphenating pulse. And yet, precisely: a pulse, the repetition of a beat, seconds ticking off beyond counting, but not to infinity, finite, rather, and always approaching the end, the one-and-only-times of our watches never quite synchronized, on the second. A sense of the singular counts with the unaccountable repetition of what has no number, not even one. The sense, perhaps, of a vigil and a vigilance, the sense of being *on watch* for the passing of the singular other.

Afterword:
On Leaving No Address

by Branka Arsić

> Blessing of the one who leaves without leaving an address.
> —Jacques Derrida

After her double "marriage," her double contract with Abelard and with God, Heloise addresses a letter to Abelard that reveals a certain confusion regarding this contract. Abelard, instead of addressing his letter to her, had sent it to a different address. Thus, Heloise warns of the letter deviating from its "true" path, which had to lead from Abelard "directly" to her. In keeping with their (marriage) contract, Heloise should have been the addressee, but that was not the case, for Abelard had addressed the letter to his friend, and this letter sent to a friend had reached Heloise "by chance," she feels: "Not long ago, my beloved, by chance someone brought me the letter of consolation you had sent to a friend."[1] Addressed by the inescapable workings of chance, it is with fervent eagerness that Heloise reads a letter not addressed to her, because the sender is someone "so dear to her heart" and because, now living at *her own* address, she hopes that she will draw strength from reading it, "at least from the writer's words, which would picture for me the reality I have lost" (ibid.). Heloise hopes that this strength will come as the effect of a certain transmutation of words into images, and that the letter's words will give her a whole panorama of the reality she no longer has. She hopes that she will get back what she has lost, that she will get back her reality. But instead of the strength she is hoping for, Heloise feels weakness; instead of consolation, she finds distress and, moreover, double distress and sorrow ("My own sorrows are renewed . . . and redoubled," 110).

Yet one might say there is something odd about Heloise's reaction. She is reading into the letter exactly what she wishes to read there: in the let-

ter addressed to his friend, Abelard describes his own history, often mentioning Heloise, and thus depicts the reality Heloise wishes to read about.
Why then, when looking at the renewed image of her own reality, instead
of taking narcissistic pleasure in the fact that Abelard is writing about her,
does Heloise feel twice the loss she did, a redoubling of sorrow? This is not
because Abelard is still faced with various predicaments and misfortunes,
but because she herself is no longer faced with his misfortunes, because he
is writing about her but not to her, because the letter also writes that
Heloise is no longer the sender's addressee. A letter arrives at Heloise's address and it says that her address is not the address of this letter; this letter
addresses her by not addressing her, it is sending her a message: you are
excluded from this message, and it writes her that it is not writing to her.
Hence the entire story of redoubled sorrow and mourning. And so the reality to which Heloise wishes to return becomes clear: she wants to be the
addressee of Abelard's letters.

Unaddressed, she herself addresses. She recalls the contract and the exchange of contracts. In keeping with the (marriage) contract, I gave you
everything, my love (of course), and my body, and my pleasure, and absolute fidelity, and I entered the monastery to show you that I am yours
forever, and I donned the veil; in short, I gave you so much, I gave you the
most there is, everything. And now that I have given you everything, you
give nothing, not a single letter, not a word, you do not write to me, you
do not address me. You give nothing because I am no longer the addressee
of your letters. Love aside, says Heloise, you owe me those letters in keeping with the contract we signed together: "Yet you must know that you
are bound to me by an obligation which is all the greater for the further
close tie of the marriage sacrament uniting us" (113). The fact that you do
not send them to me, that you no longer address them to me is a matter
not of your devotion, but of my right and your sense of fairness and your
obligation to honor the contract. "Consider then your injustice, if when I
deserve more you give me less, or rather, nothing at all, especially when it
is a small thing I ask of you and one you could so easily grant. . . . I beg
you to restore your presence to me in the way you can, by writing me
some word of comfort, so that in this at least I may find increased strength
and readiness to serve God" (117). Heloise recalls the contractual, sym-
bolic status of addressing, and asks, implores, requests, or demands to be
addressed, not by a letter that will arrive at her address "by chance" but by
a letter addressed to her; moreover, what I am asking for is so little, almost

nothing, "a small favor which you can easily grant" (116) because words come easily to you, they are no trouble to you.

However, the letter that Heloise sends to Abelard is a letter that spells out what she wants in the letter she expects from him. Heloise is asking Abelard for his signature, for his name on her address as confirmation of the contract, remarriage. In asking for Abelard's name on her address, she is asking Abelard to write out and confirm once more her name, and thus to name her. Write me in this letter "why . . . I have been so neglected and forgotten by you that I have neither a word from you when you are here . . . nor the consolation of a letter in absence?" (111). Tell me why you are depriving me of the delight of our conversations, but most important, "Tell me, I say," was it "desire, not affection which bound you to me, the flame of lust rather than love?" (116). This request (tell me . . .) should be read carefully, not because the answer to it is in any way important to Heloise's emotional life, but because it constitutes the logic of letter-writing, of sending, addressing a letter, and above all, the logic of *constituting the address*. Because when she asks for a letter, when she asks to be addressed with an answer to "tell me," Heloise is not asking Abelard to send her a picture of himself (though that is what she says: "While I am denied your presence, give me at least through your words . . . some sweet semblance of yourself" [ibid.]), she is not asking Abelard to send her himself, but rather to send her something that she does not have and cannot send him: herself. The recipient is asking the sender to send not himself, but herself in her capacity as recipient. In other words, Heloise is insisting on this correspondence not because she is asking Abelard, "Who are you?"— show me your picture. Quite the contrary, she is asking a different question, a question to which *the letter as such* is the answer. What she is really asking is: "Who am I?" She is asking the hysteric's question: tell me what kind of object I am for you and thereby confirm to me that I am for you an object. Address the letter to me, address me, *constitute me into an object*. When you write to me that I am for you an object, you will actually be writing to me that I am for myself a subject; when you write to me what kind of object I am for you, you will be writing to me what kind of subject I am for myself, you will be answering the question "Who am I?"; you will be giving me my identity, you will be making me into a subject. This is what Heloise is saying when she tells him that she is missing her own heart—in other words, herself—that she is bereft of her own being, which is with the addresser whom she is asking to address her: "My heart was not in me but with you, and now, even more, if it is not with you it is nowhere; truly, without you it cannot exist" (117). What I am telling you with this letter is that I have nothing to tell you other than this not-having, because I do not exist until you address me, your addressing me will constitute my being because my being is your addressing me and my heart lies in your letter. By thus addressing me, I am asking you to send me what I would like to send you, my very self, but cannot send because I do not have myself, I am without a name until your letter arrives. I am without an address, I am you (my heart is with you, etc.), which is why the letter that you now receive is, in this uncanny game of redoubling and mirroring, a letter *arriving from your own address;* but it is also a letter which, like any letter, seeks not its own destination but rather its starting point, its point of departure: what I am asking you for is myself. To put it in other terms: this is a letter whose destination is its own point of departure, this is a letter whose sender insists on constituting his own address: the addressee constitutes the sender, who constitutes the addressee, the address of the addressee. Literally and truly, without you it cannot exist.

Every letter is always sent from its destination insofar as the sender is the effect of having been addressed, the sender is always already the receiver: nothing could be sent had not something already been received. Just as there is no first trace, so there is no first letter, no first address that has constituted itself into an address and dispatched itself from the fullness of its own being, from itself, just as nothing has ever been sent from the fullness of being anyway, because being, fullness, is precisely that which does not send (it)self, that which "refuses to be," that which exists or is by refusing that it is (herein lies the key difference between being and not-being: not-being is not; being is, as that which resists the fact that it is, i.e., the fact that it is missing something; the difference between not-being and being is the difference between nothing and I won't). The fact that every letter is sent from (outside) its destination and so arrives at its address from its own departure point simply means that addressing constitutes the address and the name of the addressee, the name of the address, the name of the sender/recipient. *The address is the product of the work of addressing,* as is the name of the addressee. Addressing precedes naming and—to cite an old distinction—not in terms of time but in terms of logic, which means in the sense that, say, *causa sui* as the result of itself it comes timewise "after" itself as a cause, but it is logically simultaneous with itself as the cause that is its effect. The effect is simultaneous with its cause, with itself, and hence is always already divided within itself. In other words, in terms of common sense, in terms of the "vulgar notion of time," I cannot address until I write out the name of the addressee. But this vulgar circle does not affect the logic of addressing whereby addressing produces the name: the name of the addressee is established or constituted only by addressing and as the product of addressing, as Gertrude Stein attests in her favorite sentence: "I love you, Nelly. Nelly is your name, isn't it?" *I love you* is addressed before the name and arrives before the name, and the name is established as an effect of the addressing (of love), as a naming meant to allow the circle of addressing to continue ("isn't it?" seeks an answer). Thus, the logic of addressing overturns the traditional notion whereby the name has its establishing, original power of naming (creating the world), and hence it itself cannot be named: there is no name for a name, says this traditional view. And it overlooks the fact that naming, as a *process* of naming, is nothing other than sending the name, than its addressing. Addressing attests to the fact that the name is the effect of addressing, or that the name of the name is addressing. A name is not a substance or entity (not even a purely linguistic entity). A name is the outcome of the relation (addressing) that positions or establishes the address and the name (when Heloise asks for a letter, she is actually asking about her address). For this reason, the unaddressed do not have a name, however they may be called.

However, the fact that addressing precedes the name does not mean that it is addressing some sort of immanent essence, some sort of substantial identity whose fundamental attribute or expression would be a name. Quite the contrary: it means that the sender and the recipient are determined and positioned by what Blanchot designates as *"relations of strangulation where each party holds the other by the throat without seeming to do so and with cold politeness."*[2] Both the sender and the recipient are determined and positioned by the *relationship* of addressing that produces them and ties them to one another, separating each from the other, giving them their addresses. As a result of which, they strangle each other politely so as to stay alive, because they depend on each other and because, in this strangling, they are breathing life into each other; or, to put it more precisely, their mutual strangulation is the condition for them of their being able to breathe (as is always the case in the predictable, boring game of those who live from giving and receiving the work of death). This is merely another way of saying that the circle of addressing—the letter, the sender, and the recipient—is caught up in a speculative game of mirroring, of objectivation and subjectivation, in a game of splitting and redoubling. This triple redoubling has a triply redoubling effect.

Vertical redoubling, or self-subjectivation, is the effect of self-redoubling, that is, of taking oneself as the object of one's own thought. Establishing oneself as one's own object arises inasmuch as I cannot at the same time think about something and think about thinking about something. But this simple fact is very revealing, for it indicates that when it is thinking the world (things and objects in it), the subject does not have itself because it is not thinking self. And when it thinks self—that is, "its own" thought that is thinking about something (and only by thus thinking about thinking does it become "its own")—when it *addresses* self, the subject loses itself, it has itself not as a subject but as an object, as the object of its thinking, which, therefore, is fundamentally distanced from that thinking because this is not thinking. Self-distancing should be taken literally: the subject is distancing itself from its very being. But that is where the subject is lucky, because the subject is a subject only if it does not have itself, only while it is far removed from itself, only if it is lacking its being and if it does not manage to connect with its being: "What makes me me is this decision to be by being separate from being—to be *without* being."[3] To be "without" is the only happy outcome for the subject, the only way that the subject can make itself a subject. This self-reflexive twist, therefore, reveals the core strategy of appropriation and self-appropriation. Not only is every possession always already threatened, and hence so is possession of self, but also I possess myself only on condition that there is no self. "Without" is the only way to be "with." "With" means to be "with" something that is "out," and which remains there, outside. "With" is another name for distance, the distance between me and me, me and another, me and things in the world, me and the world. "With" is another name for "without," or the only way of being "without." Hence, a happy encounter between the subject and itself is possible only if that encounter keeps falling through and if the subject fails to connect with its own being. This meeting, where both the being and the subject would arrive at the appointed place at the same time, would not bring them any happiness; on the contrary, it would be a meeting between the subject and complete, utter desubjectivation, with the subject falling into a psychosis or into the immediacy of idiotism.

This is what Heloise does not know. When she says "my heart is with

you, so write to me, come, come, return my heart to me, return my being
to me, make me one with myself," what she is really saying is "will you,
please, address to me a psychosis"; she wants to move "forward" from a
hysteric to a psychotic, she wants to be without without and thus to disappear. On the other hand, Poe's Minister clearly knows the trick of meeting with being. When he addresses a stolen letter to himself, thus entering
into a "curious relation to oneself," he is actually avoiding meeting with
being.[4] To open the self-addressed letter, the letter addressed to his own
name, is to annul the difference between self as the sender and self as the
recipient, which means to annul the possibility of addressing, which requires distance (without). It is to fall into the night of absolute self-identity. Therefore, a letter to another (always another) falls under the rule of
self-splitting, self-reflection, and introspection: "The work the letter carries out on the recipient, but which is also brought to bear on the writer
by the very letter he sends, thus involves an 'introspection.'"[5] Of course,
the fact that the subject can never appropriate himself does not mean that
he ever tires of working toward (self-)appropriation, that he ever ceases to
tend to his possession or to think that he will lose something (and that always means himself). In other words, the fact that the subject is always at
a loss for his own being means that this loss is the condition of its possibility, it is what positions him firmly in relation to everything else and
everyone else.

Vertical redoubling of being, however, is also redoubled by the *objectivation of self-subjectivation* (which could be another name for the letter itself, for its materiality). To put it simply: vertical redoubling is doubled by
horizontal redoubling. In addressing and sending a letter, the sender is
sending, by virtue of this gesture alone, what he is missing (the heart, as in
Heloise's unhappy case, or the female manuscript, as in the case of Poe's
Minister) delivering and sending himself (his loss) to the gaze of the recipient, who objectifies this loss, thus subjectifying the sender. The structure
of vertical redoubling is now repeated horizontally, between the sender and
the recipient. Hence, the letter is the "objectivation of the soul" because
with the letter "one opens oneself to the gaze of others" (ibid.).

But this same objectivation of self-subjectivation, this opening oneself
to the gaze of others, presumes and says that the subject is opening himself up to his own gaze, and that by addressing his letter to another he is
also addressing this letter to himself: he sees in what he intends for the
gaze of another that which the addressee will never see, just as the gaze of

another, of course, sees in this letter that which has escaped the gaze of the sender, and which has not arrived at his address. In other words, every act of addressing always addresses two addresses, every addressing of another is at the same time a self-addressing, every addressing is necessarily split and drawn into the game of two gazes that have different vantage points in that they look at the blind spot in the gaze of the other. We shall call this *diagonal redoubling*. This redoubling of addressing explains the "nature" of every addressing and every letter: every letter is always sent from the address of the addressee and, at the same time, every letter reaches the sender from his own address. This is simply another way of saying that the act of addressing produces and repeats the strategy or logic of subjectivation. Just as the subject has itself only if his own being escapes him, *so a letter always arrives at its address provided it never arrives at that address.* It does not arrive, but not so that when it does not arrive at the named address it unerringly arrives where it should arrive, because this would merely be another way of saying that the letter always arrives at its address; and not so that there is the possibility that, taken in its materiality, it *may not* arrive; but rather so that it never arrives wherever it arrives. Both the sender and the recipient get what the other does not have, see what the other does not see. Only on the condition that the sender address part of the letter to himself does the letter arrive at the address of the recipient, who, therefore, receives the letter as something not-complete, without the truth that the sender addressed to himself in the game of self-writing: "Every letter also marks the nonoccurrence of something; every letter is always in this sense a 'dead letter.'"[6] This thesis could be bolstered by saying: *a letter by necessity never arrives at its address, a letter is what must be able not to arrive at its address.* Redoubling the addressing itself means that both sender and recipient are deprived of the very truth of the letter, which has gone to the address of the other: the truth of the letter is always addressed to the other and for the other himself—or herself. So the truth of the letter is addressed to a third party. Divided addressing always divides, it gives by taking, it positions by de-positioning.

Addressing, therefore, is demonic, if the word daimon "neither simply indicates a divine figure nor merely refers to the one who determines destiny. Considered according to its etymological root (which refers it to the very *daiomai*, 'to divide, lacerate'), daimon means 'the lacerator, he who divides and fractures'" (117–18). The demonic force of addressing means not only that what arrives at my address is always already divided and fractured, but also that it divides my address as well, it positions by the very force of de-positioning. To address means to upset, to disturb order in the house, to divide the house, to lose one's house or, more precisely, to build a divided house, into which the demon has entered while the very foundations were still being laid. Every house, every address, is a demonic house, inhabited by demons. That is why unhomelike is not the negation of homelike; rather it is one of the meanings of homelike: homelike is unhomelike. The demon of addressing watches over every address. The demonically addressed other constantly returns the demonic message that he cannot return the message. It is only thus and for this reason that the demon appears in his nature as the determiner of destiny: the addressing will keep circling, the letter will never arrive. We address simply because we do not find the answer in the way the other has addressed us. Only absolute silence in the addressing voice, only the absence of truth in the addressed letter is the cause for addressing and writing. We want to hear the truth that we will never hear, we want to read the message that will never arrive, because it always arrives at another address, it always arrives at the address where we are not, whatever the address is where we are.

Hence, addressing as an endless search for a lost object is the tireless work of mourning. This, to be sure, already points to a certain deformation in the nature of mourning, because the mourning that is addressing never stops. The search for the lost object is never done by testing a reality that would tell it to halt the search, because the actual search for the lost object *constitutes the reality* that is to be tested. One cannot test the absence of an object from a reality that is constituted as that absence and is the product of that object. For this reason, mourning is renewed, forever producing anew the reality that gives it the strength to continue its futile search: to find and appropriate what it is constitutively missing and what makes it search in the first place, the forever lost object, the elusive truth, that cannot be found even when it is "found," because what is found is never what was sought. It is not that we would never have searched had we not already found; rather we never searched for what we found; we never find anything. But the fact that we never find anything is all that we need to find. Therein lies the twist in this circle of not-having: only not-finding makes the search a success, the full success of addressing lies in what it misses. This should be taken literally: addressing always misses the addressee, but in doing so the addressing manages to address itself, to divide itself yet again, to ensure the work of addressing, positioning, self-production, the endless work of mourning. In this respect, the "work of mourning is not one kind of work among others. It is work itself, work in general, the trait by means of which one ought perhaps to reconsider the very concept of production."[7] The work of mourning is another name for work itself inasmuch as it implies constant circling between possession and dispossession. To that extent, there is nothing sorrowful about this mourning, for it is the happiness of composure, of mediation. This is not to say, of course, that the subject is not sad; it simply means that the way the subject stays alive is by mourning. The subject is always the subject of constant, never-ending grieving, and every addressing of another is compassionate.

Hence, mourning that is mourning for a lost object and an attempt to overcome the division caused by its loss, to annul the demonic division of the house so that it may finally become homelike, is nothing other than homesickness or love, insofar as love is nothing other than homesickness. This favorite joke of Freud's ("There is a joke saying that 'Love is homesickness'"), from which Freud draws anything but humorous consequences regarding the nature of what is unhomelike, should be seen in its ambivalence—in other words, in three ways.[8] First, literally: love is homesickness, "sickness of the home," the demonic division of the identity that mourns what it lacks (wholeness) and tries to find it by searching for another. Perhaps Descartes was right and maybe not all gods are demons, but the God of identity most certainly is, not only because the I is fractured, but also because it places what it lacks in someone else, mutilating him, becoming his demon. "I love you, but because inexplicably I love in you something more than you . . . I mutilate you."[9] Second, love is not only homesickness, the wounded intimacy of the whole; it is also a reflection of this illness within itself: the mourning of loss and division, grieving for the lost unity of the home, but also grieving for lost love. Love thus also appears as the apperception of mourning, provided the mourning mourns only for lost love. In other words, *love is always mourning for lost love.* Third, like any apperception, love tries to appropriate perception itself. Grieving love tries to appropriate love. That is why every act of addressing is always loving and every letter is always a love letter. Like any apperception, love too misses the perceived, love falls barren, the loving address misses the addressee. And it does so necessarily in that it is the effect of the structural paradox of love. This paradox is based not simply on the idea that identity is redoubled and therefore eludes itself, but rather on the particularity of this redoubling, on the realization that in a situation of love *redoubling is always the product of identification.* The enamored I identifies with itself (with the other) through the process of specular identification, or, colloquially speaking, it gives itself to another, it puts itself in the position of another, it becomes the gaze of another, but it is precisely this, this gaze that is the gaze of the other because it is the gaze of another, that introduces into the very center of this self-surrender the relationship of "mournfulness," distance, separation, and redoubling. The identity acquired through love is the effect of *identification, which separates.* In other words, the loving address says: I gave you everything, everything I have, which means that I gave you all that I do not have (myself), expecting in return to have (myself), but, in keeping with the just economics of this relationship, since everything I gave you is nothing, nothing is what I received. Or, to put it more precisely: "I give myself to you . . . but this gift of my person . . . Oh, mystery! is changed inexplicably into a gift of shit" (268). All the excellent opportunities the subject had to place himself in the house with closed windows and live forever in the unmitigated joy of the whole have vanished.

If this act of love is based on the sad idea that I can take possession of and appropriate my own impotence (what I cannot see, say, control, the place I cannot be, and so on) and in this way establish myself as an unfractured whole, then the actual truth about this love is jealousy. Jealousy is one mode of shit that is addressed to another, inasmuch as the "jealous operation . . . is the device of blindness" that dreams of absolute vision, of an ideal machine or disposition "designed to see in [my] place" and that "records a scene from what would be [my] point of view."[10] In other words, it dreams about appropriating the place where one is but does not see, appropriating one's every gaze and hence the other's every gaze, in every space and time that this gaze looked or will look, which means that it would appropriate the past and the future to the complete control of the gaze and thus effect the incredible appropriation of everything that eludes it, thereby finally allowing an end to the mourning. Of course, the operation of jealousy is no more successful than that of love or mourning, which is why it is always successful. For it is only because the I remains deprived of the wholeness to which it aspires (of the totality of the range of vision, time and space) that it ever manages to see anything at all, that it makes an attempt at new love, or that it prolongs mourning. This brings us closer to the following thought: if jealousy is the truth of love that addresses to another what it would appropriate and return to itself, and if this truth constantly falls through, which means that the object-love is forever being lost, as a result of which love becomes the work of mourning that preserves identity by dividing it, then jealousy is the very truth of this circular structure of redoubled addressing that redoubles. In other words, not every act of addressing is merely compassionate and hence loving. Rather, in the sense that jealousy is the truth of love, which is the truth of mourning, every addressing is jealous and every addressing to the addressee addresses jealousy.

Jealousy is actually a kind of cake made from all the ingredients that constitute addressing. This, at least, is how Freud determined the phenomenon of jealousy: "It is easy to see that essentially it [normal jealousy] is compounded of grief, the pain caused by the thought of losing the loved object, and of the narcissistic wound, in so far as this is distinguishable from the other wound."[11] So jealousy is mourning for the loss of the "deficit-surplus" that the I places in the object of love so as to appropriate itself, and the pain caused by the thought of losing the loved object is the pain caused by the thought of losing this surplus, which enables this I to see itself from an "ideal" position; it is the pain caused by the thought of losing oneself, that is, the privileged place that the I occupies in the field of vision of the Other. The jealous person mourns because he can no longer address and be addressed from this "quite satisfactory perspective: centered on the Ideal point, with a capital I." What is being mourned in jealousy is precisely this capital I, mourning for oneself. The jealous person grieves for the possible disappearance of love, which already always mourns the loss of love: it mourns the possible vanishing of the possibility of mourning-loving itself. And inasmuch as jealousy is the work of mourning directed at re-producing this position of the "capital I" (because this position makes me worthy of feeling sorry for myself), one could say that jealousy, not mourning, is another word for work, the very logic of all work and all addressing.

But is it possible to get out of this regime, is it possible to stop the specular circle of addressing? This circle can be stopped by nullifying any separation between the letter of the word and literalness, between the written letter and its meaning, the designator and the designatee, any separation between I and being. The intrusion of being into the law (letter, text, language, pact, contract) is not, however, a transgression of the law; rather it is the transgression of the very possibility of transgression, falling into the fullness of not-living, into the repose of death. The vanishing of the distance between I and being is nothing more than not-being itself. Let us imagine that Abelard took the *letter* of the text Heloise addressed to him *literally* when she asked for her heart, which is his heart; let us imagine, in other words, that he nullified any difference between the word and the thing (the heart), and that, having been thus addressed, he decided to answer this letter, to answer it literally, to the last written word, giving Heloise the thing she was asking for. In that case, Abelard would not have sent Heloise a letter, thereby prolonging the specular separation of their mutual addressing; rather he would have embarked on the long journey to Heloise's monastery, appeared in her cell, plunged a knife into his heart, attempted to remove from himself this kilogram of bloody meat, and with his dying breath, would have said: "Here, I give you what you asked for, here is your heart." The whole problem with putting an end to redoubling in this way is, of course, that it interrupts not only the circle of specular separation but also any movement, any separation, and announces the pure and simple fullness, the absolute impossibility of any kind of identity (difference), of any kind of sending, addressing, constituting. This intrusion of being into the "contract," into the letter, is therefore nothing more than the black hole of negation, an absolute, pure and simple no, the end, stop, not-being without potency. This is not only the death of the recipient (the one who plucks out the heart), but also of the sender (the one who receives the being, the heart). Quite simply, it is nullification of the loss. For not only would this imaginary Abelard fall into the fullness of being or fall out of the circle of addressing, but Heloise would truly get what she had been asking for—her loss: you want the heart, here is the heart, *eat your Dasein*, in other words, die. Abelard's heart in Heloise's mouth is exactly what will choke Heloise. Being is, so to speak, too big a mouthful, one that inevitably leads to death. This kind of outcome from the specular-speculative redoubling of addressing that begs for death is, like any simple no, trivial, which means that, as a "way out," it prevents any exit, it even nullifies the idea of an exit. The real question is: is there a possible way out of this redoubling of the circle of self-appropriation that would not be based on the idea of burial, of one's own funeral in the fullness of being, in the eternal peace of not-being?

In other words, the way out of this structure cannot be found by establishing that redoubling exists and that identity is ruled by difference, that identity is the work of differences and divisions. All traditional (modern) philosophy is based on the work of differences, on the presence of the other, on addressing negation, on addressing the outside that redoubles identity. *Cogito* is rooted in constant self-eluding. Leibnizian apperception is obsessed with the inability to establish self-identity. Transcendental apperception, though devoid of any experience, is itself the "sheer" experience of moving differences insofar as the I must be able to *follow* all of my representations, to move and to subject itself to the work of differences. The entire phenomenology of spirit is the phenomenon of this work of differences. Thus, it is not a matter of establishing that there is always redoubling, but that *there are differences between differences* and that not all redoubling is the same. Some superb misreadings of Derrida's critique of Lacan's notion of letters and addressing can be traced to the failure to distinguish between differences and redoublings. To say, for instance, that even for Lacan himself, "the letter cannot be divided because it only functions as a division,"[12] and that therefore Derrida's criticism misses the mark, is actually to fail to perceive that not all divisions are the same. To claim that division is inscribed in every letter, that every addressing is redoubling, is to nullify the difference, *the irreducible singularity of difference that distinguishes it from all other differences*, and to lapse into the Hegelian night of abstraction, where, as we know, all cows are black. It means, for instance, overlooking the essential difference that exists between the "reflexive" redoubling of addressing (something we have already analyzed), which subjects the difference to specular identification, whose effect is compassion and self-identification (the name, truth, letter, structure of question and answer, addresser and addressee), and the operation of the hymen, which undermines the actual work of double invagination. For, if double invagination can still be (or is) caught in the logic of reflexive redoubling by producing, as its effect, interiority or, to put it differently, if it is the actual effect of interiority, the operation of the hymen, on the other hand, undermines this redoubling. Not only because through its work it stops belonging "to the system of truth," and thereby "does not manifest, produce, or unveil any presence"; not only because it does not "constitute any conformity, resemblance, or adequation between a presence and a representation,"[13] but also because by thus eluding the regime of representation it is working from the other side of difference between interiority and exteriority, between being and not-being, between difference and nondifference: "It is not only the difference . . . that is abolished, but also the difference between difference and non-difference" (209). If

demonic, speculatively established identity means that identity is actually
the identity of identity and difference, that it therefore has an and-and
structure or that it is already always redoubled, then the operation of the
hymen is not merely a turnabout in this division.[14] Identity is not the difference between identity and difference, but rather the difference between
difference and nondifference, not difference and not nondifference. Identity is not not-not but rather the space between not-not, the nullification
of the very possibility of speculative redoubling: not demonizing and not
ridiculing the demon, but rather forgetting the demon. This turnabout
has capital consequences for the very possibility of addressing insofar as it
breaks demonic identity and brings about the most terrible experience,
that of *ongoing disaster,* where there is no happy division of being because
there is no being anymore, even though no one has died and no funeral
has been held.

But how is it possible to articulate and think identity? What is the difference between difference and nondifference? These questions can recall
the one posed by Aristotle: is "alteration" the same as "unqualified coming-to-be" or are "unqualified coming-to-be" and "alteration" irreducibly
different? In the event of their sameness, of their reducible differences,
"whatever 'comes-to-be' in the proper sense of the term is 'being altered'"
or is the alteration of being. This means that whatever "comes-to-be" is
the coming-to-be of the being-altered of being. Alteration is the coming-
to-be of the "change of the substratum": what is one and the same
changes, collapses, and passes, remaining one and the same, remaining
within itself different. The paradox of this position (what passes does not
pass, what collapses remains the same all the time it is collapsing) is quite
literally evident in that it concerns a certain system of seeing and a certain
way of observing. For, says Aristotle, "Alteration is a fact of observation.
While the substance of the thing remains unchanged, we *see* it altering
just as we see in it the changes."[15] We see the change but we do not see its
substratum or the continuity of its self-difference, and therefore *we do not
see* its identity. We do not see this identity, which inside itself is different
from itself, which moves in constant "confinement" and thus comes and
goes while remaining; we do not see it because we are looking from the
perspective of the regime of representation, which makes the visible constitutively elusive, not because it is hidden but because it is invisible in its
unhiddenness. Or: because we are inside the representation we do not see
the representation itself, we do not see that alteration is subordinated to

the "formal" production of this "re-" as the reproduction of the continuity of the difference of alteration. However, if we change our viewpoint, which means if instead of observing alteration we observe that alteration is a matter of observation, then we will also notice the substratum the only way it can be noticed: as the continuity of the difference of alteration. The continuity of differentiation means that differentiation is established as defined and qualified by what keeps it in continuity: by the identity of what in themselves are different substances, "for tragedy and comedy are both composed of the *same* letters" (315b). Radically different differences (tragedy and comedy) are simply aspects of the continuity of the self-differentiation of substances, as a result of which all differences between alterations must ultimately be understood not as sameness but rather as the "qualified coming-to-be and qualified passing-away" of difference, or as the production of the other from the same and, moreover, says Aristotle, as the production of the utterly other from the same.

But there are also those "who make the ultimate kinds of things more than one" and who therefore "must maintain that 'alteration' is distinct from coming-to-be for coming-to-be and passing-away result from the consilience and the dissolution of the many kinds" (314b). Insofar as identity is not the manyness of one, the difference of the same, insofar as, to quote Aristotle, there is a "radical divorce" between alteration and coming-to-be, then not only is there no continuity of difference but also, since there is no continuity of difference, differences are not "defined"—they are not qualified. In that event, coming-to-be establishes itself as *unqualified coming-to-be*. At first glance, to claim that unqualified coming-to-be exists does not confront thinking with any particular difficulty, because "if 'unqualified not-being' means the negation of 'being' in the sense of the primary term of the Category in question, we shall have, in 'unqualified coming-to-be' a coming-to-be of a substance out of not-substance" (317b). Simply put, we will return to thinking about the familiar problem of the coming-to-be of substance, the self-mobilizing of the immobile, the inscription of differences in the same, and so on. However, none of this happens, because it is in this return to the not-substance that things become radically complicated, radically in that they force thinking to the unthinkable. For, says Aristotle, "that which is not a substance or a 'this' clearly cannot possess predicates drawn from any of the other Categories either—e.g. we cannot attribute to it any quality, quantity or position. Otherwise, properties would admit of *existence in separation from sub-*

stances" (ibid.). The problem, then, lies in the following: either unqualified coming-to-be, discontinued difference is not mediated by any other property, by any other category, as a result of which it has no quantity, quality, and generally speaking, no position: it is neither here nor there, neither this nor that, neither I nor not-I, neither identity nor difference, rather it is *not-difference.* Or else properties, phenomena, positions, attributes lose their property of being attributes of something, of positioning something, belonging to something (to a substance, category) and become *independent of any substance* (or category). An attribute is no longer an attribute, which means the attribute of something or someone. A smile is no longer the smile of an I but rather a smile that smiles, a wound is no longer the wound of an I but a wound that is open and bleeding, and so on. In fact, radical separation from the substance, says Aristotle, is pure difference. Comings-to-be do not belong to something or someone; they simply come to be and become the movement of irreducible, unconnected differences, whereby—and this is the most radical consequence of this thesis—the substance itself becomes not a merely empty form, qualified not-being (insofar as the content of empty form is form itself), but rather "unqualified not-being." I becomes not-I becomes what *is not.*

If not-I is what is not, then not-I should not be taken as the "qualified-passing away" of this I, as the negation of I, as a change in the "quality" of I, its disappearance, or assumption of a different position. Not-I should be seen as neither position nor preposition. Clearly we are confronted with the difference between different types of relations. I as the product of "qualified coming-to-be" is actually the product of the relation between I and not-I: qualified coming-to-be is reducible to alteration, which means that the I is mediated by exteriority. In these "qualified comings-to-be" where every identity is multiplied and *therefore protected* in its identity, relations remain immanent to the relata, they draw them into the game of externality and interiority, all of which, however, takes place in the sphere of interiority and thus exteriority. (I is mediated by a not-I that is superceded by the coming-to-be identity of I and not-I). In unqualified comings-to-be, however, what comes-to-be is on the other side of the movement that leads from preposition to apposition to position. This unqualified coming-to-be has no quality (not-difference) and is separated from substance (difference); it *is what it is not,* neither not-difference nor difference, but rather difference between not-difference and difference, pure *relation.* Pure relation means: this relation *is not immanent to the re-*

lata in that the latter themselves (not-difference, pure difference) are not immanent to the substance; it is a relation that is outside the relata. Outside, of course, is not the same as external. External remains caught in the game of interiority and is immanent to interiority. Outside is outside the playing field of exteriority and interiority. And so when we say that identity is the difference between difference and nondifference, *the difference between the absence of position and nonexistence*, we are actually saying two things: this identity is outside, or to be more precise, it is outsideness and it is pure relation, pure relation that flickers in the night of outsideness, unconnected, without relata. But if death is not the way out into this outsideness but rather the reverse, a fall into the fullness of being, simply qualified passing-away, and if what is outside is not outside something (the game of exteriority and interiority, for instance), because that would mean that it still points to what it is outside of, insofar as it is sheer exteriority, where then is that outsideness, how does one enter it?

Blanchot described this "beyond," which is a step beyond Heloise's mirror situation, in *Death Sentence*:

For quite some time I had been talking to her in her mother tongue, which I found all the more moving since I knew very few words of it. As for her, she never actually spoke it, at least not with me, and yet if I began to falter, to string together awkward expressions, to form impossible idioms, she would listen to them with a kind of gaiety, and youth, and in turn would answer me in French, but in a different French from her own, more childish and talkative, as though her speech had become irresponsible, like mine, using an unknown language. And it is true that I too felt irresponsible in this other language, so unfamiliar to me. . . . So I made the most friendly declarations to her in this language, which was a habit quite alien to me. I offered to marry her at least twice, which proved how fictitious my words were, since I had an aversion to marriage . . . but in her language I married her, and I not only used that language lightly but, more or less inventing it, and with the ingenuity and truth of half-awareness, I expressed in it unknown feelings. . . . Even now . . . it is difficult for me to imagine what the word marriage could have awoken in her . . . marriage was not very important to her either. And yet why was it that the only time, or one of the only times, she answered me in her own language was after I had proposed marriage to her: the word was a strange one, completely unknown to me, which she never wanted to translate for me, and when I said to her: "All right, then I'm going to translate it," she was *seized by real panic at the thought that I might hit on it exactly*.[16]

Of course we will not insist on the fact that everyone in this little story, each being the product of addressing the other, is performing the work of the endless redoubling of language, that everyone is speaking his or her language as the language of the other, that everyone is speaking the language of the other as his or her own, and also that everyone is speaking the language of the other as a language different from the language of the other, as the language of a third person ("but in a different French from her own"), and so on.[17] However, what is of crucial importance here is the exiting from this game of redoubling, from the external-internal difference into outsideness. And as can clearly be seen from Blanchot's description, no one comes out of this fine game of redoubling—which in its predictability also brings the cheerful talkativeness of childishness—by decision, will, or desire; no one comes out of happiness (deficiency), out of one's own identity by will. One steps out of this game into outsideness helpless, in incredible fear, in horrifying panic, under the coercion of something that shoves us into a corner (the subway) and makes us cry, scream, but this is already a senseless scream, the scream that comes from the outsideness of every identity so as to declare that this scream no longer belongs to any I. The fact that these two people meet in a passage, in a subway passage, should be taken seriously—because the way out to outsideness leads through the passage, which is the unqualified passing away of what was qualified (I, the redoubling of language and meaning) and which leads out to outsideness, to the unqualified coming-to-be of what is or what becomes not-I.

It all starts with no indication of threat. It begins with an ordinary request: give me the word I do not know, that is what I am asking for, that is what we are constantly doing anyway. After all, these are the lines along which we establish our identities, translate ourselves to each other, speak the other languages of others, address words, so it is all quite ordinary. Give me the word, but then, suddenly, *unexpectedly,* says Blanchot, comes this terrible interruption of the everydayness of identity, suddenly comes the event: if you do not translate for me the word I do not know, I will translate it for you, although I do not know that word. What so panics this woman who is exposed to *the loving violence of another* is not simply inventing the word (that returns her to her own language, it makes her childish, opens for her the annals of her own history, lulls her into the idea of the continuity of identity), but rather the most terrible of possibilities: that the senseless word could drop from utter ignorance, from nowhere, from outsideness, into the very heart of sense and the sense of identity (the heart of sense inasmuch as we are speaking here of the triple confirmation or triple negation of the law of language-word, word-meaning, and the meaning of the marriage contract; the sense of identity insofar as identity is based on this law). It is not the law that causes panic here; it is the possibility that "I might hit on it exactly," but hit on what? Well, on the law itself. This panic is caused by the sudden realization that language in its "crude state"—language without any power (which is meaning), *illegal language, illegal law*—could "hit on it exactly," meaning hit on the language, hit on the law, hit on the I, and thereby utterly shatter it. From the outsideness of law and language comes a *completely accidental law, the event of law*, a word without any meaning, and it hits on it exactly, it hits the heart of meaning, bringing news that what constitutes the I is exposed to the unpredictable force of a shot, a shot that aims blindly but hits precisely. The sheer law, the sheer word, the word that is the absolute absence of any meaning and, as such (because meaning results from the connection of differences), is also the absolute absence of any "context," milieu, field, identity, now collapses together with meaning: words are separated from each other, "with their power, which is meaning, broken," and this broken and nullified meaning, which means the breakdown of all connections, the outsideness of connections themselves, becomes all meaning, all law. "Behind" the law lies neither the fullness of being nor the sheer absence of not-being, but rather the unbearableness of the proliferation of the law, a world in which every word is law, every movement is "law," the chaos of law, the rhythm of the happening of law, "unqualified coming-to-be," the singularity of law, the unending cluster of "accidental shots," each of which is a hit—"intervals of madness," as Blanchot puts it.

The disaster of the law is therefore also the disaster of every I. Thus this outsideness that is disaster, precisely because it is neither being nor not-being, neither the world (the world of law, identity, misaddresses) nor the absence of the world—it is the world outside the world, it is the world "if we succeed in disengaging it from the idea of order, or regularity guaranteed by law. For the 'disaster,' a rip forever ripping apart, seems to say to us: there is not, to begin with, law, prohibition, and then transgression, but rather there is transgression in the absence of any prohibition, which eventually freezes into Law, the Principle of Meaning."[18] This absence of any prohibition establishes the law of the principles of meaning as a space in which Law becomes a horror: the absolute, *unpredictable intensity of the singularity of the event of law.* Outsideness, therefore, is the Other of the Law, or the Dead Law, and he who is pushed into this outsideness is pushed into a space "bereft of light," which "refers endlessly to a dead law which in its very fall, fails yet again, the lawless law of death. The *other* of the law" (55).

The I that goes into outsideness which is the dead law is not, however, itself dead. It is the not-I and it is so because the Law has died and nothing constitutes its identity anymore. It lives in the death of the Law, which establishes a new principle of meaning: every letter, word, gesture, or decision (of the other), every sign, and each of its meanings, however contradictory these meanings may be, will be absolutely the first and the last. Not-I will live in the most dreadful ripping apart, in the simultaneousness of all laws, all meanings that do not cancel each other out. The not-I will live in constant dying, but will not die. Such is life in outsideness.

Going out into outsideness is endured as the effect of the power of the other that the I is driving into that outsideness. The way the other acts as a power that breaks the I and abolishes its identity is of crucial importance here, in that it completely changes the "logic" of reflexive addressing. In a certain sense, there is no point asking: why is the other breaking and abolishing this I; there is no point to this question because there is no "because," in other words because the work of the power of the other is not "addressed" to the I that it is abolishing, but rather is the product of the absence of any addressing: what the other is addressing to this I is not at all addressed to this I, not only in the sense that the other "did not mean" or "did not want" to attack the identity of the I, but also in the sense that the other has no knowledge of what the I receives from him as the other, because as far as he, the other, is concerned, he has not addressed anything anyway. What was addressed is the effect of an accident, an accidental overlapping, the sovereignty of accident, as Blanchot described it in *Death Sentence.* What the other addresses, by not addressing, is the effect of "inattention neither negative nor positive, but excessive, which is to say without intentionality" (ibid.). Here, however, "without intentionality" should not be taken in its commonsensical meaning of the absence of intent (I did not mean to destroy you). Here "intentionality" should be taken to mean, first and foremost, that "the stimulus exercised by the intentional object in its directedness toward the ego attracts the latter more or less forcefully, and the ego yields to it," resulting in "a tendency of the intentional object to pass from a position in the background of the ego to one confronting the ego."[19] However, if the breakdown of the I is here the effect of an absence of intentionality, that means not that the intentional object (the other) is confronted with this I, but rather the opposite, that there is no "confronting" because even the other knows nothing about it, and precisely because the other knows nothing about it—in other words, because his power as intentional object eludes him—the power of the other becomes "mortal inattention to which we are not free—or able—to consent, or even to let ourselves go (to give ourselves—up)."[20] This, then, is the absence of intentionality, whose effect overlaps with that of the presence of intentionality, in the sense that the ultimate outcome of the power of the intentional object is in fact "to submit" the I "to an effective affection." But even the I is not intentional, it is not any kind of "primitive" or savage or "original" consciousness through which the intentional object moves, thus constituting consciousness in its resistance as "not-original." Quite the opposite. The I hit by this "object" no longer has any ability or power to confront it. And so it disappears. This is intentionality without intentionality. More simply put: the word, gesture, look, which the other addresses and which will nullify the I, does not at all belong to the other, not only in the sense that belonging can always be posited as a problem (nothing ever belongs to me, etc.), but also fundamentally speaking, which means that this word or gesture is the effect of its unqualified coming-to-be, the other knows nothing about it himself, it is not connected to the other, it is the pure sovereignty of accident. Hence, the other is not my enemy. But what reaches the I does so in all its strength as the intentional object, which means that it reaches it so that the I, powerless to resist it, subordinates itself to the working of this affection, becoming utterly "eradicated" in the process. The paradox of intentionality without intentionality: nothing was ever addressed, but the I is precisely hit and so disappears. It suffers disaster.

In this respect, and in this respect alone, the other has the nature of the external cause (of that which "causes," eluding the mirror game of the spectacle), as this cause was probably most pregnantly formulated by Spinoza in the fourth proposition of the third volume of *Ethics*:

> Nothing can be destroyed except by an external cause. *Demonstration.* This proposition is self-evident, for the definition of each thing affirms, but does not deny, the essence of the thing; or, it posits but does not negate, the essence of the thing. Whilst, therefore, we attend to the thing itself alone, but not to the external causes, we shall be able to find nothing in it which can destroy it.[21]

In other words, only the I lacks the power to be powerless, is without the power to establish itself as not-I, because it is the power of self-positing and self-confirmation. The other in its nature of external cause, which breaks the I, which pushes it into a "corner," as Natalie is pushed into the corner of the subway in Blanchot's narrative, is necessary in order for the I to suffer disaster, for it to disappear as a subject and become subjectivity without any subject.[22] Subjectivity without a subject, following Spinoza's definition, means that through the working of the external cause the essence of what exists is nullified. What exists continues to exist as existence without essence. Not as existence that "precedes" and conditions essence, but literally: as existence without essence, not-I. The body. Subjectivity without a subject, because it is without a subject, is not active, *it cannot be active*, if the subject is the subject of all working, the activity of self-positing and the work of self-confirmation. Subjectivity without a subject is, therefore, passive; it is the one that suffered the other and so is passion. Passion, of course, is not desire; it does not feel a lacking, and it is not the power of impulse that leads us to actively search for the other, that propels us into a search that, as Blanchot puts it in his interpretation of Mallarmé's *Igitur*, takes place at night when one leaves the study, goes out into the city streets where one animal calls out to another, on the "first" night, in the "ordinary" night, in the night of desire, which requires darkness. Conversely, passion is a modus of the other, an affect of the other, in the place of that I: there where the I used to be is now the not-I. The essence of passion is not explained by "our essence," as Spinoza interprets it, but "it must necessarily be defined by the power of an external cause." Just as subjectivity with a subject is on the other side of the difference between being and not-being, so passion is on the other side of the difference between openness and desire. Passion is not openness, because openness is openness "to" the other, and is possible only as the openness of the interior to the external, whereas passion is outsideness. Also, passion is possible only when the I no longer has the slightest connection with itself, when it no longer has any I—in other words, when it no longer has desire. Not when desire has flagged, but when desire is completely exhausted, when the subject of subjectivity has vanished into the oblivion of nonexistence, that is, when an existence is left that exists as passion, as forever powerless powerlessness, as forever existing passion and the passivity of this passion.

To say that subjectivity without a subject is the passivity of passion indicates the nature of this passivity. For, this passivity is not contemplative insofar as contemplative passivity implies the quiet replication of cold mirrors and knows no passion. This means that passivity is not contemplative to the extent that contemplation implies a world where there is only exteriority, without the play of exteriority and interiority, as a result of which no outsideness of this world is possible.[23] Contemplative passivity is not passionate. Nor does the passivity of passion point to passivity that says: "I can be passive." To be able to be passive is the active, working passivity of a subject who has not suffered disaster and who, through its ability to be passive, appropriates and self-synthesizes. Active passivity is triggered by openness and desire. But passionate passivity is outside the difference between these two passivities; it is merely the "center" of a crazed madness, of an unthinkingness, the realization of the possibility of an impossibility. For, if it could talk, if it belonged to an I that could say I, the "formula" of this passivity would be: I cannot be passive. Not to be able to be passive is neither the weakness of contemplative passivity nor the power of active passivity, it is un-power that has exhausted absolutely every power, including the power to be powerless and weak. (Therefore, distinctions should perhaps be made between active, tired, and exhausted passivity.) The inability of this passionate or passive or exhausted passivity to be passive should be taken literally, as absolute powerlessness, meaning powerlessness to be active, but also *powerlessness to be passive*. Passive passivity is *passivity that cannot be passive*. The passion of this passivity is therefore the suffering of passivity, unendurable passion, unbearable passivity that is "borne" all the same or that simply is (there is suffering, there is passion, there is a body that suffers) because it does not "belong" to any subject that would have the power (activity or weakness) to overcome it, and because it is the sheer effect of the other in the no man's land where the I once was. "There is suffering, there would be suffering, but no longer any I suffering, and this suffering does not make itself known in the present."[24] A body that no longer belongs to anyone, that knows not of suffering, that is the sheer feeling of suffering, a feeling that vanishes the moment it appears because it is not mediated by knowledge, and that is forever renewed. Perhaps it is necessary, therefore, to drop the sentimentalist or even aesthetic image of passion as a sublime phenomenon that opens us up to the other. Conversely, this is a horror, a constant feeling of the unbearable that is not mediated and, precisely because it is not mediated, is not overcome. Passion does not mean exposing the subject to

AFTERWORD

some extreme danger; rather it emerges after this extreme danger has occurred and after the subject has disappeared: subjectivity without a subject
is existence that "lives" by dying but is never dead, because it is constantly
revived by the wound inflicted on it by the other: "The quick of life
would be the burn of a wound, a hurt so lively, a flame so avid that it is
not content to live and be present, but consumes all that is present till
presence is precisely what is exempt from the present" (51). Passionate passivity is the life of the wound, the living wound, the body that lives off of
wounds so wounding, so avid, that they exhaust all life and turn the life
of this passive existence into perpetual dying, neither life nor death, but
unlife. Unlife is the exhaustion of life, life that is lived by dying.

But if this other is the one "pressing until he crushes me" so that he
"withdraws me . . . from the privilege of the first person" (18); if, after this
collapse, "the other becomes rather the Overlord, indeed the Persecutor,
he who overwhelms, encumbers, undoes me" (19); why, then, is this
wounded body so completely, "lovingly" exposed to the other, and what
stops us from seeing this relation, or this not-relating as sadomasochistic?
The answer to this question lies in the very nature of (passive) passivity.
For (passionate) passivity is not the activity or movement of suffering that
constitutes masochistic desire; it is suffering that is inflicted, and is therefore borne; it is the nonwork of suffering, in other words, it is not under
the condition of time. One can talk about passionate passivity as subjectivity without a subject precisely because it is the subject that is always under the condition of time, because time itself is the form of the subject's
self-affecting (from St. Augustine's "in you, my soul, I measure time" to
meditative time, to time as the movement of overcoming or time as the a
priori form of the subject). Subjectivity without a subject is, therefore,
subjectivity without time, just time outside of time, time in outsideness,
where time itself stops because all of time is at its disposal. This is not to
say that outsideness is in eternity, meaning: in the outsideness of time,
where the past is conditioned by the present but always falls into the future. Analyzing Mallarmé, Blanchot describes this time outside of time as
a paradoxical condition in which the dice can be thrown only at midnight, but midnight strikes only after the dice have been thrown. In other
words, the past appears only after the present, making the present the
ever-past past, the oblivion of the present.

But let us elaborate this paradox a bit more: the fact that midnight
strikes only after the dice have been cast means that midnight never strikes

at midnight; the past in which the present vanishes appears *after* the present (always already past); the past is the future. This should not be seen as re-articulating the idea of the eternal return of the same. Here the past is not the future in the sense in which what has already happened returns, confirming itself. Quite the opposite: here the past is the future in the sense that the future is always the already unknown, it is time in which nothing has happened. The future is time without time, time without the future: "The irremediable character of what has no present, of what is not even there as having once been there, says: it never happened, never for the first time, and yet it starts over, again and again, infinitely. It is without end, without beginning. It is without future."[25] The past that vanishes into the future is hence without future, without time, outside of time. The past that makes the present disappear into the oblivion of the always already past thus itself disappears into the unknown, into the future, as if nothing had ever happened. Everything is always happening and nothing has ever happened; *everything has always already happened and everything has always yet to happen*; never for the first time, always for the first time, that is the logic of time outside time, and that is the reason why casting the dice will never abolish chance, will never abolish the "extreme law, that is: the excessiveness of uncodifiable law—that to which we are destined without being party to it."[26] Strictly speaking, this is disaster: the terrible wound inflicted on the body that suffers, but an always already forgotten wound because it is outside of time, a wound always already left to the oblivion of oblivion. The dreadful silence of a wounded body, which is forever wounded anew by the most terrible wound and which is never hurt.

To say that passionate passivity is outside of time points to the difference between innocence and inexperience; it says that subjectivity without a subject is innocent. This, of course, is not the case. The subject is not innocent, the subject is inexperienced insofar as inexperience is nothing other than experience of one's own inexperience. The subject is always the subject of disappointment (self-appropriation fails, love is unhappy, the address is misaddressed, the letter does not arrive, etc.); no matter how experienced, the subject always misses the mark, and in this sense one can say that the experienced subject is the subject who has acquired knowledge/consciousness of his own inexperience. To "acquire" experience of one's own inexperience is, of course, always under the condition of time, action, self-relation. Every activity is experience; where there is activity there is no innocence. Or, to put it differently: there is no innocent sub-ject. However, passionate passivity is outside of time and outside of work. "If spirit is always active," then subjectivity without a subject is "already nonspirit: the body in its suffering passivity—cadaverous, exposed, flat-tened, sheer surface" (40). Only the body that is sheer surface, without ac-tive, operative spirit, is passionate and passive, and it alone is innocent, because "innocence alone is nonaction." That this passionate body is ac-tually the suffering of passivity and passivity that suffers means that "suf-fering suffers from being innocent" (40–41). But this suffering that suffers does not indicate the reflexive structure of suffering and passivity that could negate innocence. That suffering suffers does not mean that suffer-ing knows it suffers, and that it therefore has a certain distance from its suffering, that it has a chance to appropriate and overcome that suffering. On the contrary, because it is the effect of absolute innocence or because it is outside of time, this suffering suffers absolutely and constantly anew. For the hurt that comes from the other is not accompanied by any "hope" that it will be overcome, or by any memory of life without hurt. Every hurt is here to stay, to stay forever, every hurt is the first and the last, ab-solute. And it is because it is inflicted on the body that is in outsideness and in the outsideness of time, that every hurt falls into the past/future, into the nonexistence of the unknown, into utter oblivion. This body is always already forgotten suffering, which always already exists forever, for-ever renewing itself. Herein lies the meaning of Benjamin's thesis that vir-ginity is renewed without moans.

Without moans means without regret. The nonreflexive structure of passive suffering also indicates that this suffering does not suffer "over" it-self, it is not suffering that pities itself or that pities the subject. This suf-fering suffers its innocence because it feels the inexorability of a "now" that disappears into oblivion, into the unknown of the future. The I has suffered disaster precisely because it has "entered" into a different time, a time without a past, without a history, without a story. Subjectivity with-out a subject is another name for "un-story,": it does not have its own story, nothing ever happened to it and therefore it has never lost anything. Every loss disappeared in the innocence of the oblivion of oblivion. This does not mean that the loss has been overcome, "repressed," or "lived through," all of which are the operations or effects of regret; it means that the loss is lost. Everything is already lost for this subjectivity because it does not know how to appropriate anything (not even loss), in other words, because it does not know how to regret, to mourn its powerlessness. Everything is always already lost, but everything is lost absolutely, in the oblivion of oblivion. Lost loss, the renewal of innocence.

Just as it does not know regret, so this passionate passivity does not know homesickness. Passive passion is not love in the sense that love presumes the work of regret, of mourning, mirroring, and self-objectification. The happening of the other that happens to this passion, and of which it is the accidental product, takes place outside the difference between subject and object; it happens as passion, in passion insofar as passion "knows no subject, no 'I' who loves 'X,' outside or before the passion,"[27] insofar, then, as passion never knows I or X, insofar as it "knows" nothing other than passion. In this sense, this passion does not happen where specular love happens, within the framework of the difference between preservation and destruction. Passion is outside of this difference, at the already ruined dividing line between preservation and destruction. Passion "takes place along the divided, ruined border of this alternative" (26). Not preservation and not destruction, but disaster and the gift of the disaster. But what is the gift of the disaster?

The gift of disaster is gentleness. Following the absolute innocence of the hymen that is renewed after every crime, this passion "knows" only gentleness. This necessarily follows from the very nature of passionate passivity. For all else (regret, love, jealousy, fury, anger, resistance, offense, hesitation, vacillation, doubt, aggression, decision, etc.) belong to the subject. The always already wounded body is therefore always the already gentle body. This gentleness, however, should never be seen as an aspect of cruelty that aims at provoking a feeling of guilt. The point is not for this living wound to say to the other: "See what you have done to me, and see how gently I answer you." This sort of cruel gentleness belongs to active passivity and its power tactics. But passionate passivity does not know any tactics; it is "pure" passion, absolute innocence that, precisely because it is absolutely innocent, can give only gentleness. For, this gentleness is not "an answer" to the other (which is why it is not cruel); it is not addressed to the other (because it has long since forgotten to say "I" and to address something like that to someone); this gentleness is a pure gift in the sense that a gift is possible only if there is no subject, only as the product of subjectivity without a subject and, hence, in the sense in which a gift is possible only as the gift of disaster, "from" disaster, from a mindless innocence that absolutely forgets it is absolutely wounded; this innocence is a gift in the sense in which a gift is possible only as giving something we do not have. For, this gentleness does not "belong" to subjectivity without a subject, insofar as nothing belongs to this subjectivity because it is without a subject. This gentleness is un-qualified coming-to-be gentleness from the space of the living wound. That is why it is a gift. Maddening, crazy gentleness, which abolishes all accounts, all reckonings, all logic, all reason, accidentally causing a madness, the madness of gentleness. From extreme hurt comes an extreme gentleness: "Madness through excess of gentleness, gentle madness."[28]

The madness of gentleness is possible only outside the world in which jealousy exists. For, if "what [jealousy] wants is proof,"[29] if jealousy is the process of reexamining the other, leveling his statements, if jealousy is inspection of the other's life, then mad gentleness is the absolute opposite of jealousy: it is the absence of questions, the nonexpectation of answers. After disaster, in disaster, there are no more questions: "The disaster does not put me into question, but annuls the question."[30] The gentleness of passionate passivity is without question and without answer, unconditional, absolute. It is clear: the killing of the answer and question, the disappearance of any addressing, is possible only as the result of the key effect of disaster: because disaster is first and foremost the destruction of specularity, the shattering of all mirrors, the abolishing of representation, but also the abolishing of appearance; it is not only a way out of the speculative structure, it is a step farther, it is the way out of phenomenology: intentionality without intentionality, the exhaustion of appearance, impossibility of representation.

Passionate passivity is precisely that: the impossibility (as powerlessness) of representation, that which cannot "constitute itself as a basis for a representation" (33). To be sure, the absence of representation is the absence of any possibility of addressing, in the sense that addressing is always already divided and is that which divides, separating every connection. Passion, however, does not address anything (the gift of absolute gentleness is not addressed precisely because it is a gift) and nothing is addressed to it because it is not any I to whom something could be addressed, and because everything that reaches this passion is the effect of the sovereignty of accident. No letters arrive from outsideness. Indeed, what would a letter from outsideness look like, who would sign it and under what name? The idea that something can be addressed from outsideness undermines the very idea of outsideness; it immediately establishes the address and the destination, the name, the route, the relays, transmission, problems of re-doubling, and so on. And the space of outsideness is outside all addresses and destinations, all routes and their junctions, all names. There are no names in outsideness, there is no one, all there is in outsideness is no one. Since addressing is disaster, outsideness is also the disaster of addresses and the disaster of one's own name.

And the absence of one's own name, as the representation of identity, takes us back to the absence of representation in the space of outsideness. However, the absence of representation is not the mere presence of pres-ence either, because presence indicates duration, and the possibility of re-presenting the present. Presence takes place in outsideness only as an in-transient moment of a forced presence, which is why it takes place absolutely, as an event of the absolute, as immediacy, "for immediacy is absolute presence—which undermines and overturns everything"; it is "no longer the desired or demanded, but violent abduction. . . . Immedi-acy not only rules out all mediation; it is the infiniteness of a presence" (24). This presence, then, is infinite because through the force of immedi-acy it "cancels out" any identity (which is necessarily finite), and absolute because it provokes disorder and disruption in the absolute (in the law and the "law" of identity). Immediacy is a happening of absoluteness, and that is why it is the absoluteness of the absolute; what is absolute can in-terrupt the absolute.

The fact that immediacy is an event of absoluteness should be taken in the double meaning of the word event (or in the double meaning of the word immediacy). Immediacy is an event in the sense of intensity, the in-tensity of immediacy. For, intensity is "the extreme of difference, in excess of the being . . . an absolute disruption" (56). Disruption, of course, is not interruption. Interruption is a break, stop, pause, hesitation, indecisive-ness, rhythm, interval, dream, and uncertainty, because after interruption what is interrupted can be renewed and "saved," and everything can turn out well, just as everything can be cancelled out, and suddenly everything can become very bad. Interruption, in this sense, is the uninterruption of constant interruptions, renewals, ruinations: "Interruption . . . having somehow the same meaning as that which does not cease" (21). But dis-ruption is the interruption of interruption and hence of continuity. Dis-ruption is the way out of interruption into what can no longer be inter-rupted: into a dreamless night, into the passivity of intervals, into uncertainty without the support of doubt. It is the effect of the intensity of immediacy, which goes beyond every being, which goes over being and goes over to the extreme, to the extreme of the extreme. In this respect, when talking about the event of the intensity of immediacy, there can be no more allusion to any interiority. For intensity can also be thought of as intensity that cuts through the interiority of a living body. But absolute intensity, which brings with it absolute disruption, does not indicate the interiority of the body; it is intensity that cuts through the body as sheer surface, existence already deprived of essence, and going to the extreme of the extreme, it carries with it this extreme of extremeness that, ultimately, something can happen to the body as well, that the body can be exposed to a certain life or a certain dying. But "for" subjectivity without a subject, living and dying are already in the domain of the gift (and not a sacrifice), they are already living and dying outside of time, in the time of the other: "To give is to give living and dying not at my time but according to the time of the other" (89). This is disaster. Or this is the smile of a wound in outsideness without a horizon. The meaning of a wound becomes comprehensible only from here, because only now does it become legible that the wound is another name for the event that does not happen to anyone anymore: "Yes, the wound is there, over there. Is there some other thing, ever, that may be legible? Some other thing than the trace of a wound? And some other thing that may ever take place? Do you know another definition of event?"[31]

Absolute presence, the immediacy of the intensity of the wound instead of representation and demonic addressing. This is what "arrives" at the "address" of subjectivity without a subject: intentionality without intentionality, addressing without addressing, the event of the wound in outsideness, where the body is exposed to the immediacy (of the law) of the other. Exposed quite literally: without refuge, without shelter, without a home (there are no addresses, backyards, gardens, or balconies in outsideness). In the no man's land of outsideness, passionate passivity is nonsituated (hence Blanchot points constantly to the anonymity of hotel rooms). This passionate passive body is where there is neither home nor dome nor arch,[32] where not even God's name has been saved, where demons do not go, precisely because they are protecting their demonic nature. Passive passion is outside the reach of demons, not appropriating but not appropriated either, the mad gentleness of a "loneliness without interiority," which forgets that it is lonely and therefore is always gentle, from the other side of the difference between happiness and unhappiness, both of which belong to the subject. The passionate passive body is simply some-body who is over there, always already there, available, given, "offered" as an "offering which has no subject," an "offering" that "offers the body which belongs to no one, in non-narcissistic suffering and joy."[33] Neither happiness nor pleasure nor desire, but joy insofar as joy itself is the pure intensity of life (the event of life, hence, the event of hurt), which is so in-tense that in passing through the I it drags the I with it, making it pass through as well, leaving behind just the flicker or echo or trace or cry of joy that no longer belongs to anyone; leaving behind joy that rejoices.

It is only from this vantage point that we can understand Derrida's sen-tence: "Blessing of the one who leaves without leaving an address."[34] To leave without an address does not mean, of course, to simply cover one's tracks, change one's name, hush up the act, just as it does not mean to die. The difference between these two possibilities is the difference between the work of self-appropriation and the fall into total sameness (death); it is the difference between life at the address of ripped-apart addressing and absolute address, the eternal destination; it is the difference between life and death, the house and the grave. But to leave no address means to leave on the other side of this difference, to live constantly traveling between the house and the grave, outside the power of the demonic but without the protection of the eternal name of God, the way passionate passivity "lives." For it lives always already unprotected and hence without any hope of being saved, but for this very reason it is completely safe, nothing can happen to it because everything has happened already, no destruction can touch it anymore; it is "indestructible because [it is] always and infi-nitely destroyed."[35] And it is indestructible because it always and infinitely forgets this destruction, in the innocence of joy from which slowly ap-pears only blessing or the gift of gentleness. A gift of which neither demon nor God is capable, but only an angel.

Provided, of course, that the angel is the one that or who suffers the event of "the possibility of the impossible, of the most impossible,"[36] and insofar as this most impossible is actually a departure into the beyond, into the *affirmation of the outside*. "Beyond," or this affirmation, should be taken not as yes or no, as the possibility of "return" or self-possession, as the possibility of death or a "contact with the other" ("It would liberate us from everything if it could just have a relation with someone,"[37] or even as a departure into nonexistence, but rather as leaving without an address, as a departure into the unconditional: "Passivity neither consents nor refuses, neither yes nor no. . . . The passive condition is no condition: it is an unconditional" (30). The unconditional is unconditionality, the absolute availability of a body, which does not ask, does not set conditions, does not answer, and at the same time, it is a body that exists in the absence of conditions, that does not have its own "condition," situation, environment, home address, or position. For this reason, here affirmation of the outside should be taken as neither yes (a readiness to change or abandon one's position) nor no (an attempt to preserve one's position), but rather as an affirmation that is in the past of every yes and every no, and which is therefore the future of every yes and every no, a future without future, a past without past, between past and future, between yes and no: the "mindlessly" innocent *patience* of passion. Waiting.

However, this waiting is not the waiting of active passivity, where waiting is a strategy developed under the condition of time. If one can even ask the question: "What is it waiting for, this passive passion of the body that belongs to no one?" then the answer would have to be: it is waiting for the intense, disastrous event of immediacy, for the body of the other that will pass through the body of this passionate passivity. But this question cannot be asked precisely because there can be no waiting for the event, and not only because waiting for the event cancels out the event in its very nature as event (the expected event is not an event), not only because there is no I here that would wait, but first and foremost because the waiting of passionate passivity is innocent, which means that every event is completely and utterly forgotten, and hence cannot be expected, for there is no experience regarding it, because no event has ever happened. This waiting is, therefore, the oblivion of waiting, or waiting that has forgotten itself, has forgotten to wait and, hence, is not addressed to anyone. This waiting is possible, of course, only outside of time, as affirmation of the outside, as affirmation of not having time. Therein lies the difference between waiting that is addressed to someone and waiting for waiting. Waiting that waits for something (for a yes or a no) is the waiting of active passivity, it is *waiting that has time*, it is the waiting of an I that has given itself time to wait. But waiting that forgets to wait, the waiting of passive passivity, is "the waiting of time itself," time that has given itself time. The waiting of passionate passivity "takes place" in the absence of time: "In waiting the absence of time reigns where waiting is the impossibility of waiting."[38] This should be taken literally: the waiting of passive passivity *has no time*. And wherever there is no time, things are urgent; wherever there is no time, it is impossible to give oneself time, there is no patience of waiting there, what reigns there is impatience. Just as this passive passivity *cannot be* passive, and yet it also cannot be active passivity, so, for the same reason, because of the utter absence of power to be and to be nonbeing, it cannot be patient either: it cannot wait. Passionate passivity, as neither the simple impatience of activity nor the patience of the waiting of active passivity, is waiting that cannot wait ("Patience is extreme urgency: I no longer have time, says patience"); it is impatient patience ("Impatience suffered and endured endlessly").[39]

The impatience of the patience of waiting outside time is the impatience of the waiting of Benjamin's New Angel. For this Angel is not merely a "personal" angel, the hidden being of an I, its secret name which is its life, a name that "gathers all the forces of life unto itself, and by which these forces can be conjured up and protected against outsiders."[40] It is not an angel that protects identity, even if this identity changes several times in the course of life, every time it reaches a "new maturity." This is not the angel of identity that conceals identity from itself (making it a secret, unknown, what is missing, lacking, an undiscovered name). Were it this sort of angel, then it would not be a New Angel. "The Kaballah relates that, at every moment, God creates a whole host of new angels, whose only task before they return to the void is to appear before His throne for a moment and sing His praises. *Mine had been interrupted in the process*; his features had nothing human about them" (712–13). The new angel is an angel who has suffered interruption, not a hymn sung in praise of God, not the void of nonexistence, not yes and not no, not words and not silence, not man and not God, not human and not inhuman, but the absolute absence of hope of return to the void or of confronting God: disrupted interruption, *stopped* in the interval, in the "in-between," in this break, the endlessness of waiting, "a meaning infinitely suspended, decried, decipherable-indecipherable."[41] The New Angel is the angel of waiting, of impatient waiting, the angel of outsideness. He who has stepped into outsideness has "learned" everything from this angel, everything, and that means the impatience of patience outside of time. For he who is outside is patient, with a patience that cannot be overcome. "Its pinions resemble those of the angel: they need but a few moments to hold it stationary in the face of the woman whom it is determined to await. But my patience has claws like the angel and razor-sharp pinions, *and makes no attempt to pounce on her*."[42] In other words, this patience has

the power of the mightiest impatience, which can eradicate everything before it, and the claws and power of slicing, but *it makes no attempt*, it does
nothing, not so as to give itself time, but rather and worst of all, because
it bears its impatience outside of time and learns from the angel, becomes
angelic; it "retreats in a series of spasms, inexorably," it retreats farther and
farther, more and more into outsideness, it is a retreat that is "that flight
into a future from which he has emerged" (713), from which appears he
who has become an angel, from which the angel appeared. The retreat
into the future is a retreat into the not-happened, into the nonexistent,
into existing in nonexistence, into oblivion and the oblivion of oblivion,
into innocence, into waiting that waits outside of time, on the other side
of speech and silence, meaning and nonmeaning; it is a retreat into "the
patience of the cry,"[43] into the joy of a voiceless cry. The retreat into the
future is a departure that leaves address behind.

—*Translated by Kristina Pribićević Zorić*

Notes

INTRODUCTION

1. Yet, of the countless works—ancient, traditional, or modern—that call themselves or are known as *The Book of* [this or that] or *The* [whatever] *Book*, irony seems rarely to have dictated the title. Just to take two recent examples: For every endlessly ironic *Telephone Book* (Lincoln: University of Nebraska Press, 1991) by Avital Ronell, there are thousands of entries, like William J. Bennett's *Book of Virtues* (New York: Simon and Schuster, 1993), that rival the Bible for titles of highest earnestness.

2. Gérard Genette, *Paratexts: Thresholds of Interpretation*, trans. Jane E. Lewin (Cambridge: Cambridge University Press, 1997).

3. Most of these essays were first delivered in public. Let this be the place to thank again all those who initially issued the invitations for these addresses: Geoff Bennington, Jean Bessière, Elizabeth Beaumont Bissell, John Brannigan, Monique Chefdor, Tom Cohen, Hafid Gafaiti, Nancy Holland, Lynne Huffer, Michel Lisse, Ian Maclachlan, Martin McQuillan, Richard Rand, Alison Rice, Ruth Robbins, Nicholas Royle, Michael Syrotinski, Christine Thuau, Julian Wolfreys.

4. Goodwin has conceded that her biography, *The Fitzgeralds and the Kennedys* (New York: St. Martin's Press, 1991), contains numerous unattributed quotations of other works. In an essay for *Time* magazine (Jan. 27, 2002), she explained that in the process of rechecking quotations, she did not verify all of her sources. "I relied instead on my notes, which combined direct quotes and paraphrased sentences. If I had had the books in front of me, rather than my notes, I would have caught mistakes in the first place and placed any borrowed phrases in direct quotes."

5. As cited by Derrida (in "Force of Law: The 'Mystical Foundation of Authority,'" trans. Mary Quaintance, *Cardozo Law Review* 11, nos. 5–6 [July/Aug.

1990], p. 959), this quotation is somewhat faulty although doubtless it does not miss Levinas's meaning in the sentence from which it is lifted: "Mais nous voulons aussi montrer comment en partant du savoir identifié avec la thématisation, la vérité de ce savoir ramène à la relation avec autrui—c'est-à-dire à la justice," Emmanuel Levinas, *Totalité et infini: Essai sur l'extériorité* (The Hague: Martinus Nijhoff, 1961), p. 62.

6. Jacques Derrida, *The Post Card: From Socrates to Freud and Beyond*, trans. Alan Bass (Chicago: University of Chicago Press, 1987), p. 7.

7. Plato, *Phaedrus* 275E, cited here in translation by Harold North Fowler, Loeb Classical Library (Cambridge, Mass.: Harvard University Press and London: William Heindemann, 1982), p. 565.

8. For a thoughtful and careful guide to such a new thinking of responsibility, see Thomas Keenan, *Fables of Responsibility: Aberrations and Predicaments in Ethics and Politics* (Stanford: Stanford University Press, 1997).

9. One should not read here a defense of "relativism," in any of the uses of the term bandied about today and even though it has become commonplace to assign deconstruction or Derrida's thought to the relativist side of an opposition with absolutism. So long as one is restricted to such binary possibilities, then crude approximations like this will have to do. But deconstruction, need one say it, has never been resigned to binary thinking; it could even be said to proceed from the deconstruction of any relativist/absolutist polarity.

10. See pretty much anything Derrida has written in the last ten or fifteen years.

11. Sigmund Freud, "Negation," trans. Joan Riviere, in James Strachey, ed., *Standard Edition of the Complete Psychological Works of Sigmund Freud* (London: Hogarth, 1961), vol. 19, p. 236. In *Vocabulary of Psychoanalysis*, Jean Laplanche and Jean-Baptiste Pontalis clarify that Freud reserved the term *Verleugnen*, rather than *Verneinung*, to name the refusal to perceive a fact in the exterior world. It is this former term that the editors of the *Standard Edition* translate by "disavowal." See also Alan Bass, *Difference and Disavowal: The Trauma of Eros* (Stanford: Stanford University Press, 2000).

12. For example, "the responsible decision must be this impossible possibility of a 'passive' decision, a decision of the other-in-me who will not acquit me of any freedom or any responsibility." Derrida, "As If It Were Possible, 'Within Such Limits,'" in *Negotiations: Interventions and Interviews, 1971–2000*, ed. and trans. Elizabeth Rottenberg (Stanford: Stanford University Press, 2002), p. 357.

13. "For, just as popular superstition divorces the lightning from its brilliance, viewing the latter as an activity whose subject is the lightning, so does popular morality divorce strength from its manifestations, as though there were behind the strong a neutral agent, free to manifest its strength or contain it. But no such agent exists; there is no 'being' behind the doing, acting, becoming; the 'doer'

has simply been added to the deed by the imagination—the doing is everything. The common man actually doubles the doing by making the lightning flash; he states the same event once as cause and then again as effect. The natural scientists are no better when they say that 'energy *moves*,' 'energy *causes*.' For all its detachment and freedom from emotion, our science is still the dupe of linguistic habits; it has never yet got rid of those changelings called 'subjects'" (Friedrich Nietzsche, *The Genealogy of Morals*, trans. Francis Golffing [New York: Doubleday, 1956]), pp. 178–79.

14. See below "'Fiction' and the Experience of the Other," and "The Experience of Deconstruction."

15. As is clearer in French, Derrida actually distinguishes between psychoanalytic "refoulement" and this other, specifically historical "répression." The translator, Alan Bass, adquately renders these as, respectively, "repression" and "suppression" but then qualifies them both as "historical" ("the analysis of a historical repression and suppression of writing") through a misreading of the phrase "analyse d'un refoulement et d'une répression historique [singular] de l'écriture."

16. "Freud and the Scene of Writing," p. 198. The translator has again overlooked the precise syntax of "rapport d'appartenance *pensée*," in which *pensée* modifies "appartenance" and not "rapport." Alan Bass translates: "a *conceived* relationship of belonging."

17. The name of fiction, however, is certainly problematic, as was already indicated above with the reference to "legal fiction." For more discussion of this problematic name, see "'Fiction' and the Experience of the Other."

18. See especially "'Fiction' and the Experience of the Other," "To Give Place," and "Democracy's Fiction." The reading of *The Aspern Papers* is found in the opening chapter, "Deconstruction and Love."

19. See J. Hillis Miller, *Speech Acts in Literature* (Stanford: Stanford University Press, 2001), pp. 9–11. It was Miller's highlighted reading that first pointed in the direction of James's preface. See as well chapter 6 of Miller's *The Ethics of Reading: Kant, de Man, Eliot, Trollope, James, and Benjamin* (New York: Columbia University Press, 1987) for a longer reading of James's preface that has great pertinence for our discussion here. For other recent critical work on the New York edition prefaces, see David McWhirter, ed., *Henry James's New York Edition: The Construction of Authorship* (Stanford: Stanford University Press, 1995); and John H. Pearson, *The Prefaces of Henry James: Framing the Modern Reader* (University Park, Pa.: Pennsylvania State University Press, 1997).

20. Henry James, *The Art of the Novel* (New York: Charles Scribner's Sons, 1934), p. 327. Later in the same passage, James will mention "the intelligent but quite unindividualised witness of the destruction of 'The Aspern Papers'" (329).

21. Toward the end of the preface, James will cite approvingly the model of Flaubert (347). For Maurice Blanchot, Flaubert's fiction is likewise the model of

a narrative space in which "the ideal is still the form of representation of classical theater" and the impersonal narration remains that of the disinterested subject of aesthetic distance and enjoyment. See below chapter 8, "'Fiction' and the Experience of the Other."

22. On the collaboration between James and Coburn, see Ira B. Nadel, "Visual Culture: The Photo Frontispieces to the New York Edition," in McWhirter, ed., *Henry James's New York Edition*.

23. The phrase is Emerson's, which puts what James says here, remarks Hillis Miller, "under the aegis of Emersonian high-minded New England solemnity" (*Speech Acts in Literature*, p. 9).

24. This language of testimony returns once more in the succeeding lines: "All of which means for [the artist] conduct with a vengeance, since it is conduct minutely and publicly attested."

CHAPTER I

1. *The Ear of the Other: Otobiography, Transference, Translation*, trans. Peggy Kamuf and Avital Ronell (New York: Schocken Books, 1985), p. 85.

2. Although the term is here being used in the limited sense of a written text, one should endeavor to keep in mind a general notion of "text" as whatever is constituted by repeatable marks or traces.

3. For instance, the ethical philosopher Martha C. Nussbaum has evinced how much she clings to this notion. Quoting Zarathustra's model, "of all that is written, I love only what a man has written with his blood," she characterizes her reaction to, in her terms, "Derrida's perceptive and witty analysis of Nietzsche's style" in *Eperons*: "After reading Derrida and not Derrida alone, I feel a certain hunger for blood; for, that is, writing about literature that talks of human lives and choices as if they matter to us all" (*Love's Knowledge: Essays on Philosophy and Literature* [New York and Oxford: Oxford University Press, 1990], p. 171). In other words: too much attention to textuality leads to bloodlessness. But is that a good or bad thing? Says who? As for the relation Derrida himself discerns between literature and bleeding, see "Syringe (at the point)" in this volume.

4. "How to love anything other than the possibility of ruin. Than an impossible totality?" Nicholas Royle quotes these lines from Derrida's *Memoirs of the Blind* before advancing his own affirmation of a phrase he once heard Derrida pronounce, at another improvised discussion: "Deconstruction is love." Royle comments: "Deconstruction is love. That would be the final aphorism here, but only on condition that it could never be mine—or Jacques Derrida's either" (Nicholas Royle, *After Derrida* [Manchester: Manchester University Press, 1995], pp. 139–40).

5. The discussion from which these remarks are taken followed a lecture by Derrida on Nietzsche's signature: "Otobiographies: The Teaching of Nietzsche

and the Politics of the Proper Name," trans. Avital Ronell, in *The Ear of the Other*.

6. For Bill Martin, the limits of a "fully predictive science" appear with the example of love. He writes: "For example, if all of the physical, and even chemical determinants of a loving relationship could be specified, and if such a relationship could be fully contextualized in terms of economic, political, and other material factors, would we have really described even one instance of love?" (Bill Martin, *Humanism and Its Aftermath: The Shared Fate of Deconstruction and Politics* [Atlantic Highlands, NJ: Humanities Press, 1995] p. 17). Martin appears to suggest, however, that his "example" is just one among many he might have chosen.

7. In both the original French and the English translation, the phrasing can be construed as also meaning it is he himself who accompanies this gesture, he accompanies it by and as affirmation; deconstruction, therefore, is not just something he *does* but something he accompanies affirmatively. And therefore something that accompanies him. If this were an essay, necessarily interminable, on "love" in the writings of Jacques Derrida, then among all the other texts one would have to invoke and attempt to read is *Politics of Friendship* and in particular a chapter titled, with echoes of Blanchot, "The One Who Accompanies Me": see *Politics of Friendship*, trans. George Collins (London: Verso, 1997).

8. Does the distinction between the partiality of love and impartial justice hold up or is it also deconstructible? That question may be addressed in Derrida's essay on "the possibility of justice," which evokes the idea of undeconstructible justice, the justice deconstruction is mad about, perhaps even madly in love with. "This 'idea of justice' seems to me to be irreducible in its affirmative character, in its demand of gift without exchange, without circulation, without recognition or gratitude, without economic circularity, without calculation and without rules, without reason and without rationality. And so we can recognize in it, indeed accuse, identify a madness. . . . And deconstruction is mad about this kind of justice. Mad about this desire for justice" (Jacques Derrida, "Force of Law: The 'Mystical Foundation of Authority,'" trans. Mary Quaintance, *Cardozo Law Review*, vol. 11, nos 5–6 [July/Aug. 1992]).

9. Jean-Luc Nancy, "L'amour en éclats," in *Une pensée finie* (Paris: Galilée, 1990), pp. 247–48.

10. We should note, however, that as an affirmation of love, in all its infinite manners, the marking force of the idiom bears little resemblance to what in common psychological parlance is called "self-affirmation." Indeed, if that popular pedagogical or pop-psychological slogan means, as it appears to most often, the self's triumphal movement out from under the sway of others, then the affirmation of love's idiom admits, and affirms, a contrary movement. For the idiom of love can only affirm in itself that which has already carried it off toward another's address, bearing it away, always in its own manner.

11. *Politics of Friendship*, p. 228.

12. The order of acceptation in the OED records first this "proper" sense, the most widely understood sense: "That disposition or state of feeling *with regard to a person* which (arising from recognition of attractive qualities, from instincts of natural relationship, or from sympathy) manifests itself in solicitude for the welfare of the object, and usually also in delight in his or her presence and desire for his or her approval; warm affection, attachment." Emphases have been added to the key or determining phrase here: "with regard to a person." Consider, however, the first sense in the French *Robert*, which prefers "humanized entity" to "person": "Disposition à vouloir le bien d'une entité humanisée (Dieu, le prochain, l'humanité, la patrie) et à se dévouer à elle." The distinction between person and humanized entity (or personification) will be pursued below, not directly but allegorically, as it were.

13. But also—why ever not?—soap operas, fanzines, rave music, whatever.

14. For an unflinching, even a *cruel* (i.e., "bloody") analysis of *Romeo and Juliet*, see Derrida, "Aphorism Countertime," trans. Nicholas Royle, in *Acts of Literature*, ed. Derek Attridge (New York and London: Routledge, 1992); also see, in this volume, "Syringe (at the point)."

15. In particular, in *Speech and Phenomena*, trans. David B. Allison (Evanston: Northwestern University Press, 1973); for more clarification of this notion of iterability, see below "Deconstruction and Feminism."

16. Doubtless a principal reason deconstructive thought has been excoriated as "negative" is that it does not deny this condition of iterability. On the contrary, it affirms iterability as the possibility of addressing/being addressed by love.

17. This is also, therefore, the "site" of mourning. See Derrida, *The Work of Mourning*, ed. Pascale-Anne Brault and Michael Naas (Chicago: University of Chicago Press, 2001), for example: "When I say Roland Barthes, it is certainly him whom I name, him beyond his name. But since he himself is now inaccessible to this appellation, since this nomination cannot become a vocation, address, or apostrophe . . . it is him in me that I name, toward him in me, in you, in us that I pass through his name. What happens around him and is said about him remains between us. Mourning began at this point. But when? For even before the unqualifiable event called death, interiority (of the other in me, in you, in us) had already begun its work. With the first nomination." (46). See as well the editors' introduction, "To Reckon with the Dead: Jacques Derrida's Politics of Mourning," p. 10.

18. In "The One Who Accompanies Me," in *Politics of Friendship*, Derrida characterizes what is "most beautiful and most inevitable about the most impossible declaration of love," one which would declare love by *prescribing* that the other be free not to respond, "for," he writes, "I need his or her freedom in order to address myself to the other as other, in desire as well as in renunciation" (*Pol-*

itics of Friendship, p. 174). But since the prescription in advance cancels the free-dom it prescribes, this declaration of love remains the most impossible. For a brief discussion of this passage, see below "Derrida on Television," and for Cixous's similar reflection on a declaration of the love that would not destroy the other's freedom, see below "To Give Place."

19. "I can arrive at the papers only by putting her off her guard, and I can put her off her guard only by diplomatic practices. Hypocrisy, duplicity are my only chance. I am sorry for it, but for Jeffrey Aspern's sake, I tackle the main job" (Henry James, *The Aspern Papers*, in *Great Short Works of Henry James* [New York: Harper and Row, 1996], p. 222. All further references to the novel, in parentheses, will be to this edition of the 1888 original text.

20. Such figures, in other words, work to provoke "that impulse of identifica-tion which is indispensable for reading" that Derrida mentions in the passage cited at the beginning of this chapter.

21. A recent critic sees an allusion to the "green Shade" in Marvell's poem "The Garden": "The Mind, that Ocean where each kind / Does streight its own resemblance find;/ . . . /Annihilating all that's made / To a green Thought in a green Shade"; see Jeanne Campbell Reesman, "'The Deepest Depths of the Ar-tificial': Attacking Women and Reality in 'The Aspern Papers,'" in *"The Finer Thread, the Tighter Weave": Essays on the Short Fiction of Henry James*, ed. Joseph Dewey and Brooke Horvath (West Lafayette: Purdue University Press, 2001), pp. 49–50.

22. The detail of the "button" is alone enough to justify comparing this text's secret or not-so-secret economy to that of Poe's "Purloined Letter," in which a "trumpery filigree card-rack of pasteboard . . . hung dangling by a dirty blue rib-bon, from a little brass knob just beneath the middle of the mantle-piece." Rather than holding a "trumpery filigree card-rack," rather, that is, than this dangling apparatus in which Lacan, at least, identifies the phallus of the woman, James's text places the button on a secretary, a piece of furniture but also some-one, most often a woman, who, like Miss Tita with her aunt, accompanies an-other, writes another's letters, and keeps another's secrets. Whereas Poe's narra-tive needs someone like Dupin to put his hands on the hidden letter, James's has the force, "the force of soul," to depict the inviolable secret of the secretary.

23. Because, as was suggested in the previous note, James's novel shares many features with Poe's "The Purloined Letter," central elements of Derrida's famous analysis of the latter can be carried over to the former. In particular, there would be much more to say in a longer reading with regard to this structure of the non-arrival of a letter even when it has apparently arrived at its destination. See Der-rida, "Le facteur de la vérité," in *The Post Card: From Socrates to Freud and Be-yond*, trans. Alan Bass (Chicago: University of Chicago Press, 1986).

24. Regarding the indeterminacy of Tita's age and relation to Juliana, critics

have not failed to wonder whether she could not be the illegitimate daughter of Juliana and Aspern, although this possibility is never entertained by the narrator; see James Gargano, "'The Aspern Papers': The Untold Story," *Studies in Short Fiction* 10 (1973); and John Carlos Rowe, *The Theoretical Dimensions of Henry James* (Madison: University of Wisconsin Press, 1984), pp. 105–6.

25. At least in the original, 1888 version. For the New York edition of 1908, James, among other numerous emendations, changed this character's name to Tina.

26. A less rapid discussion of this text could bring out that such a state of non-declaration, specifically the withheld or suspended declaration of love, informs all the interactions among the three characters. The only love declared is that of the narrator for Jeffrey Aspern, unless it is for himself. As for James, his preface to the New York edition of the novel becomes the occasion to profess love only for the cities of Venice and Florence, and to "lay it on thick" in this reminiscence of how he came to write the novel: "So it is at any rate, fairly in too thick and rich a retrospect, that I see my old Venice of 'The Aspern Papers,' that I see the still earlier one of Jeffrey Aspern himself, and that I see even the comparatively recent Florence that was to drop into my ear the solicitation of these things. I would fain 'lay it on' thick for the very love of them—that at least I may profess; and, with the ground of this desire frankly admitted. . . ." Henry James, *The Art of the Novel* (New York: Charles Scribner's Sons, 1950), p. 161.

27. This fading of the erotic hallucination could call to mind the sort of deconstruction of sense certainty that Paul de Man has elaborated through an attention to textual figurality. He writes, for example, in his essay on Rousseau's *Nouvelle Héloïse*: "Like 'man,' 'love' is a figure that disfigures, a metaphor that confers the illusion of proper meaning to a suspended, open semantic structure. In the naïvely referential language of the affections, this makes love into the forever-repeated chimera, the monster of its own aberration, always oriented toward the future of its repetition, since the undoing of the illusion only sharpens the uncertainty that created the illusion in the first place" (Paul de Man, *Allegories of Reading: Figural Language in Rousseau, Nietzsche, Rilke, and Proust* [New Haven, Conn.: Yale University Press, 1979], p. 198); and elsewhere, in a footnote, "Rather than being a heightened version of sense experience, the erotic is a figure that makes such experience possible. We do not see what we love but we love in the hope of confirming the illusion that we are indeed seeing anything at all" (de Man, "Hypogram and Inscription," in *The Resistance to Theory* [Minneapolis: University of Minnesota Press, 1986], p. 53; my thanks to Nicholas Royle for reminding me of this note).

CHAPTER 2

1. For an overview of the debate, see Juliet Mitchell's introduction to *Feminine Sexuality: Jacques Lacan and the École Freudienne,* ed. Mitchell and Jacqueline Rose (New York: Norton, 1982), pp. 13–24.

2. *The Standard Edition of the Complete Psychological Works of Sigmund Freud,* ed. James Strachey (London: Hogarth Press, 1953–74), vol. 18, p. 169; quoted in Kofman, *The Enigma of Woman: Woman in Freud's Writings,* trans. Catherine Porter (Ithaca, N.Y.: Cornell Univ. Press, 1985), p. 177, n. 19.

3. *Standard Edition,* vol. 11, p. 205.

4. *Standard Edition,* vol. 22, p. 125.

5. I have discussed at greater length the (theological) implications of this position "without-jealousy" in another essay on Derrida, "Reading Between the Blinds," which is the introduction to *A Derrida Reader* (New York: Columbia University Press, 1991); see esp. pp. xxxi–xxxv.

6. *Oeuvres et lettres* (Paris: Pléiade, 1953), pp. 776, 781–82; my translation.

7. Melanie Klein takes over the classical distinction in her differentiation of envy from jealousy when she adapts these terms to her developmental model. As one of her commentators explains: "Melanie Klein, in *Envy and Gratitude,* makes a proper distinction between the emotions of envy and jealousy. She considers envy to be the earlier of the two, and shows that envy is one of the most primitive and fundamental emotions. Early envy has to be differentiated from jealousy and greed. Jealousy is based on love and aims at the possession of the loved object and the removal of the rival. It pertains to a triangular relationship and therefore to a time of life when objects are clearly recognized and differentiated from one another. Envy, on the other hand, is a two-part relation in which the subject envies the object for some possession or quality; no other live object need enter into it" (Hanna Segal, *Introduction to the Work of Melanie Klein* [London: Hogarth, 1973], p. 40).

8. *La jalousie amoureuse,* 3rd ed. (Paris: PUF, 1985), p. 371; my translation.

9. For a helpful survey of the distinction envy-jealousy, see Rosemary Lloyd, *Closer and Closer Apart: Jealousy in Literature* (Ithaca, N.Y.: Cornell University Press, 1995), pp. 2–5

10. Both jealous and zealous are derived from late Latin *zelosus, zelus.*

11. "Certain Neurotic Mechanisms in Jealousy, Paranoia and Homosexuality," *Standard Edition,* vol. 18, p. 223; my emphasis.

12. See Kofman, *Enigma of Woman,* pp. 50–65.

13. In a review article of *The Enigma of Woman,* "The Third Woman" (*Diacritics,* [Summer 1982]), Elizabeth Berg has argued that just such a displacement is effected by the third woman in Kofman's reading, the woman who is neither a

hysteric nor a narcissist. "In her refusal to recognize sexual difference—in refusing castration—she has moved beyond the economy of truth to affirm, simultaneously or in turn, both her masculinity and her femininity. . . . Like the
fetishist, who posits the possibility of the phallic mother, the affirmative woman
affirms her femininity while refusing to be castrated" (19). The question might
still be asked whether an affirmation of the "phallic woman" (Berg writes, "The
phallic mother—or the phallic woman—is not a fantasm to be dismissed, or
simply the product of the child's imagination; she is the reality of woman who is
beyond the 'truth' of castration," ibid.) must not also be displaced—actively,
strategically—by, for example, the "generalized fetishism" Derrida works out in
Glas and Kofman takes up again in "Ça cloche" (*Lectures de Derrida* [Paris:
Galilée, 1984]).

   14. The tendency to collapse historically and conceptually different notions of the "subject" has contributed to a certain confusion about what we
are even talking about. In an attempt to sort out this confusion, Jean-Luc
Nancy has described debates about the "subject" as "most often false debates
of opinion rather than serious debates of concepts around the subject: debates
of the type 'death of the subject—return of the subject,' in which the subject
becomes a kind of strange little clown that can leave and come back; or else
debates of the 'ontology versus subjectivity' kind; and of course debates in
which, without any precautions, people jumble up together what is meant by
the subject in philosophy, what is meant by the subject in psychology, and
what is meant by the subject in psychoanalysis. These are debates that, in
large measure, owe their existence, and often their foolishness, to the confusion among meanings or to the absence of clear and distinct meanings"
(Nancy, "Un sujet?" in *Homme et sujet* [Paris: Harmattan, 1992], pp. 49–50;
my translation).

   15. See Judith Butler, *Gender Trouble*, on this exasperated "etc." that so often
concludes the list of predicates elaborated by what she calls "theories of feminist
identities" ([New York: Routledge, 1989], p. 143). See as well Butler's fine analysis of the "subject" of feminism. Given the overall direction of this analysis, one
might wonder about her retaining the category of identity for a politics even as
she forcefully critiques what is called identity politics in general. The reconcep-
tualizing of identity as an "effect," rather than a constitutive ground, cannot
rule out that embracing such an effect will entail the very consequences one
wishes to avoid. What she describes as the "critical task," which is "to locate
strategies of subversive repetition enabled by [the constructions of identity],"
coming as it does at the end of the book, may sound an upbeat note in part because it has forgotten the warning issued at the beginning of the same book:
"strategies always have meanings that exceed the purposes for which they are intended" (p. 4).

16. In Derrida's idiom, this figure of non-return also clearly says non-appropriation. That which "ne revient pas" to someone—does not come back or return to—is out of his or her purview; it does not belong to him or her. The expression also has the sense, as it does in English, of not recurring to memory, as in "it isn't coming back to me," that is, I can't remember it. With this latter sense, there is an opening onto the unconscious as the uncanny site of expropriation within the ego. One of Derrida's most important texts on this figure of non-return is "Le facteur de la vérité" (in *The Post Card: From Socrates to Freud and Beyond*, trans. Alan Bass [Chicago: University of Chicago Press, 1987]), in which Lacan's notion of the phallus as transcendental signifier is deconstructed as that to which all signification would return as to its final destination.

17. Samuel Weber has argued persuasively that one should take account of a shift in Derrida's writing after the early texts of the 1960s and 1970s. He characterizes this shift as one that moves deconstructive thinking from a putative and always finally "fictional" position external to the discourses it examines, to a quasi-narrative position within the limits of the deconstructible. For Weber, the latter position or strategy, which is exemplified by texts like "Envois" and "To Speculate—on 'Freud'" in *The Post Card*, is the more effective or powerful one; see Weber, "Reading and Writing *chez* Derrida," in *Institution and Interpretation* (Minneapolis: University of Minnesota Press, 1987). Without contesting that evaluation, I have chosen to "go back" to an early text so as to isolate a particular theorem that will remain in force in everything Derrida will later write; see note 19 below.

18. Jacques Derrida, *La voix et le phénomène* (Paris: Presses Universitaires de France, 1967); trans. David B. Allison as *Speech and Phenomena* (Evanston, Il.: Northwestern University Press, 1973). Page references will be given in the text to both the French and English editions; the translation will on occasion be modified.

19. In a later text, Derrida has reiterated what he there calls this "aporia" of "my death": "Is my death possible? Can we understand this question? Can I, myself, pose it? Am I allowed to talk about my death? What does the syntagm 'my death' mean? . . . 'My death' in quotation marks is not necessarily mine; it is an expression that anyone can appropriate; it can circulate from one example to another. . . . If death . . . names the very irreplaceability of absolute singularity (no one can die in my place or in the place of the other), then all the *examples* in the world can precisely illustrate this singularity. Everyone's death, the death of all those who can say 'my death' is irreplaceable. . . . Whence comes a first exemplary complication of exemplarity: nothing is more substitutable and yet nothing is less so than the syntagm 'my death'" (*Aporias: Dying—Waiting (for One Another) at the "Limits of Truth,"* trans. Thomas Dutoit [Stanford: Stanford University Press, 1993], 22–23).

20. "Unsealing ('the old new language')," trans. Peggy Kamuf, in Derrida,

Points . . . Interviews, 1974–1994, ed. Elisabeth Weber (Stanford: Stanford University Press, 1995), 118.

21. Nor should we confuse this finite, excessive singularity with the concept of the "individual," which, as Jean-Luc Nancy writes, misses singularity through a certain process of formalization: "However the *singular being,* which is not the individual, is the finite being. What the thematic of individuation lacked, as it passed from a certain Romanticism to Schopenhauer and to Nietzsche, was a consideration of singularity, to which it nonetheless came quite close. Individuation detaches closed off entities from a formless ground. . . . But singularity does not proceed from such a detaching of clear forms or figures (nor from what is linked to this operation: the scene of form and ground, appearing [*l'apparaître*] linked to appearance [*l'apparence*] and the slippage of appearance into the aestheticizing nihilism in which individualism always culminates). Singularity perhaps does not *proceed* from anything. It is not a work resulting from an operation. There is no process of 'singularization,' and singularity is neither extracted, nor produced, nor derived" (Nancy, *The Inoperative Community,* trans. Peter Connor et al. [Minneapolis: University of Minnesota Press, 1991], 27). See as well, below, "Singular Sense, Second Hand."

22. On this notion of "the invention of the possible," see "Psyche: Invention of the Other," trans. Catherine Porter and Philip Lewis, in *Reading de Man Reading,* ed. Wlad Godzich and Lindsay Waters (Minneapolis: University of Minnesota Press, 1989) and "The Other Fiction" in this volume.

23. Thus it would not be altogether anachronistic or simply facetious to say that Marie-Antoinette, for example, was tried and executed on the strength of the argument: the personal is the political; see Chantal Thomas, *La Reine scélérate: Marie-Antoinette dans les pamphlets* (Paris: Editions du Seuil, 1989).

24. See Nancy Fraser, *Justice Interruptus: Critical Reflections on the "Postsocialist" Condition* (New York: Routledge, 1997), esp. chap. 3 ("Rethinking the Public Sphere: A Contribution to the Critique of Actually Existing Democracy"), for a useful critique of how Habermas's notion of the "public sphere" has been taken up by contemporary feminisms.

25. Such a politics would always risk resembling liberal anti-regulationist policies that favor the free market and individual enterprise. It would, in other words, maintain an ambiguous alliance with the individualism and liberalism of traditional American ideology that produces the dissimulation of the "political" as the "personal" in the first place.

26. See Drucilla Cornell, *Beyond Accommodation: Ethical Feminism, Deconstruction, and the Law* (New York: Routledge, 1991), 21–78, for a critical analysis of three different versions (in Robin West, Julia Kristeva, and Hélène Cixous) of the maternal feminine.

27. On this structure of the "yes" as an original repetition, see especially Derrida, "A Number of Yes," trans. Brian Holmes, in *Qui Parle* 2, no. 2 (Fall 1988)

and "Ulysses Gramophone: Hear say yes in Joyce," trans. Tina Kendall and Shari Benstock, in *James Joyce: The Augmented Ninth*, ed. Bernard Benstock (Syracuse: Syracuse University Press, 1988).

28. The affirmation would concern the *subject* of feminism in another sense, as in what feminism is *about*. We are saying, then, nothing more, nothing less than this: feminism is not *about* the appropriation of power; it is *about* justice.

CHAPTER 3

1. This chapter was initially written for a conference on "Unofficial Knowledge" organized in 1994 at King's College, Cambridge University by Jonathan Burt, Simon Goldhill, Maud Ellmann, John Forrester, and Peter de Bolla.

2. "Combien de personnes, de villes, de chemins, la jalousie nous rend ainsi avides de connaître! Elle est une soif de savoir grâce à laquelle, sur des points isolés les uns des autres, nous finissons par avoir successivement toutes les notions possibles sauf celle que nous voudrions. . . . Et je comprenais l'impossibilité où se heurte l'amour. Nous nous imaginons qu'il a pour objet un être qui peut être couché devant nous, enfermé dans un corps. Hélas! Il est l'extension de cet être à tous les points de l'espace et du temps que cet être a occupés et occupera. Si nous ne possédons pas son contact avec tel lieu, avec telle heure, nous ne le possédons pas. Or nous ne pouvons toucher tous ces points. . . . De là la défiance, la jalousie, les persécutions" (*La Prisonnière*, vol. 3 [Paris: Gallimard, Bibliothèque de la Pléiade, 1988], pp. 593; 607–8; English translation from *In Search of Lost Time*, vol. V, trans. by C.K. Scott Moncrieff and Terence Kilmartin, revised by D.J. Enright [New York: Modern Library, 1993], pp. 106; 125).

3. "Ne pas voir ce qu'on voit, voir ce qu'on ne peut pas voir et qui ne peut pas se présenter, telle est l'opération jalouse. Elle a toujours affaire à de la trace, jamais à de la perception" (*Glas* [Paris: Galilée, 1974], p. 240; trans. John P. Leavey, Jr. and Richard Rand [Lincoln: University of Nebraska Press, 1986], p. 215). I have also commented on this passage in "Reading Between the Blinds," introduction to *A Derrida Reader: Between the Blinds* (New York: Columbia University Press, 1990), pp. xxxv ff. That essay was prompted by, and is a reflection on, the phrase "In everything I talk about, jealousy is at stake" [Dans tout ce dont je parle, il y va de la jalousie], which one may read at the end of Derrida's essay on Levinas "At This Very Moment In This Work Here I Am" (*A Derrida Reader*, p. 437).

4. For a detailed reading of the handkerchief's theme throughout the play, see Harry Berger, Jr., "Impertinent Trifling: Desdemona's Handkerchief," in *Shakespeare Quarterly*, vol. 47, no. 3 (Fall 1996).

5. In her very suggestive study of the relations between jealousy and narrative fiction, *Closer and Closer Apart: Jealousy in Literature*, Rosemary Lloyd quotes lines from Proust that resonate in an interesting way with Derrida's assertion: "As there is no knowledge, so one can almost say there is no jealousy, save of oneself" (Ithaca, N.Y.: Cornell University Press, 1995), p. 14.

6. "La jalousie n'est souvent qu'un inquiet besoin de tyrannie appliqué aux choses de l'amour" (598).

7. See above, "Deconstruction and Feminism: A Repetition"

8. Martin's character throughout the film is developed as having a heightened and acute awareness of language, in contrast with Andy, who must learn from Martin how to describe what he sees in less imprecise language. In particular, he makes Andy aware of visual metaphors when the latter says to him, as they are taking leave of each other, "See you around." Martin replies: "So to speak."

9. A less cursory reading of the film would have to add to these several determinations of this scene's significance that of another, similar scene between Martin and Celia: the latter has brought Martin to a concert hall to experience his first live concert. When the opening measures of Beethoven's Fifth are sounded, Martin says "My God," and reaches for his heart. Celia is moved to tears by his reaction. But instead of sealing some bond between them, this experience is followed in the next sequence by Martin's most vigorous rejection of Celia's most aggressive attempts to arouse his desire.

10. For a stunning working through of prosthetic operations, in film, in fiction, in "life," see David Wills, "De la lettre au pied," in *Le passage des frontières: Autour du travail de Jacques Derrida*, ed. Marie-Louise Mallet (Paris: Galilée, 1994), and especially *Prosthesis* (Stanford: Stanford University Press, 1996).

11. "La jalousie qui a un bandeau sur les yeux n'est pas seulement impuissante à rien découvrir dans les ténèbres qui l'enveloppent, elle est encore un de ces supplices où la tâche est à recommencer sans cesse" (III, 657).

12. " . . . j'aurais voulu non pas arracher sa robe pour voir son corps, mais à travers son corps voir tout ce bloc-notes de ses souvenirs et de ses prochains et ardents rendez-vous" (III, 601).

13. "Ce qu'elle disait, ce qu'elle avouait avait tellement les mêmes caractères que les formes de l'évidence—ce que nous voyons, ce que nous apprenons d'une manière irréfutable—qu'elle semait ainsi dans les intervalles de la vie les épisodes d'une autre vie dont je ne soupçonnais pas alors la fausseté. Il y aurait du reste beaucoup à discuter ce mot de fausseté. L'univers est vrai pour nous tous et dissemblable pour chacun. Le témoignage de mes sens, si j'avais été dehors à ce moment, m'aurait peut-être appris que la dame n'avait pas fait quelques pas avec Albertine. Mais si j'avais su le contraire, c'était par une de ces chaînes de raisonnement (où les paroles de ceux en qui nous avons confiance insèrent de fortes mailles) et non par le témoignage des sens. Pour invoquer ce témoignage des sens il eût fallu que j'eusse été précisément dehors, ce qui n'avait pas eu lieu. On peut imaginer pourtant qu'une telle hypothèse n'est pas invraisemblable. Et j'aurais su alors qu'Albertine avait menti. Est-ce bien sûr encore? Le témoignage des sens est lui aussi une opération de l'esprit où la conviction crée l'évidence. . . . Mais enfin j'aurais pu être sorti et passer dans la rue à l'heure où Albertine m'au-

rait dit, ce soir (ne m'ayant pas vu), qu'elle avait fait quelques pas avec la dame. Une obscurité sacrée se fût emparée de mon esprit, j'aurais mis en doute que je l'avais vue seule, à peine aurais-je cherché à comprendre par quelle illusion d'optique je n'avais pas aperçu la dame, et je n'aurais pas été autrement étonné de m'être trompé, car le monde des astres est moins difficile à connaître que les actions réelles des êtres, surtout des êtres que nous aimons . . . " (III, 694).

14. On Descartes' automaton, hypothesized in the Second Meditation, see Andrzej Warminski, "Spectre Shapes: 'The Body of Descartes,'" *Qui Parle?*, vol. 6, no. 1 (Fall/Winter 1992), pp. 93–112.

15. The examples: "We have often seen her sense of hearing convey to Françoise not the word that was uttered but what she thought to be its correct form, which was enough to prevent her from hearing the implicit correction in a superior pronunciation" (248–49). The other example is the word "pistière" which the butler hears instead of "pissotière" (ibid.). Proust seems to want to contain this kind of error within the servant class, with its "inferior" language skills.

16. In his study of Proust, *La jalousie: Étude sur l'imaginaire proustien* (Arles: Actes Sud, 1993), Nicolas Grimaldi attempts to analyze the paradoxes of possession without ever putting in question the status of his own assumption that, in the sexual act, the woman is somehow literally "possessed" by the man. Because he uses this "metaphor" throughout as if it denoted a self-evident event, he is reduced to repeating as analysis what are in fact the most discouraging commonplaces that buttress the phallocentric vision of desirable femininity, for example: "thus every woman when finally known and possessed reduces the vastness of the world, which she had led us to imagine, to the reality of her own person" (p. 33). The "us" of that final sentence, an exclusive, unreflected, masculine "us" which is constant throughout the book, says it all.

17. "L'image que je cherchais, où je me reposais, contre laquelle j'aurais voulu mourir, ce n'était plus l'Albertine ayant une vie inconnue, c'était une Albertine aussi connue de moi qu'il était possible . . . c'était une Albertine ne réflétant pas un monde lointain, mais ne désirant rien d'autre . . . qu'être avec moi, toute pareille à moi, une Albertine image de ce qui précisément était mien et non de l'inconnu" (III, 583).

18. On lying in Proust, see J. Hillis Miller, "Fractal Proust," in *Black Holes* (Stanford: Stanford University Press, 1999), pp. 431–39, odd-numbered pages.

19. "Il me semblait à ces moments-là que je venais de la posséder plus complètement, comme une chose inconsciente et sans résistance de la muette nature" (III, 581).

20. " . . . jeunes filles, o rayon successif dans le tourbillon où nous palpitons de vous voir reparaître en ne vous reconnaissant qu'à peine, dans la vitesse vertigineuse de la lumière"; "Pour comprendre les émotions qu'ils donnent . . . il faut calculer qu'ils sont non pas immobiles, mais en mouvement, et ajouter à

leur personne un signe correspondant à ce qu'en physique est le signe qui signifie vitesse" (III, 573, 599).

21. In another text on Proust (see above, n. 18), J. Hillis Miller discusses at
length aspects of telephoning in the *Recherche*, although not in direct relation to
jealousy; see his *Speech Acts in Literature* (Stanford: Stanford University Press,
1999), pp. 185–98.

22. "Mais déjà une des Divinités irascibles, aux servantes vertigineusement ag-
iles, s'irritait non plus que je parlasse, mais que je ne dise rien. 'Mais voyons, c'est
libre! Depuis le temps que vous êtes en communication, je vais vous couper.'
Mais elle n'en fit rien, et tout en suscitant la présence d'Andrée, l'enveloppa, en
grand poète qu'est toujours une demoiselle du téléphone, de l'atmosphère parti-
culière à la demeure, au quartier, à la vie même de l'amie d'Albertine. 'C'est
vous?' me dit Andrée dont la voix était projetée jusqu'à moi avec une vitesse in-
stantanée par la déesse qui a le privilège de rendre les sons plus rapides que l'é-
clair" (III, 608).

23. The infinity of the other, the absolute alterity of the time of the other or
diachrony: this would be the place to invoke the thinking of Emmanuel Levinas,
for example on the other's freedom, which "could never begin in my freedom,
that is, abide in the same present, be contemporary, be representable to me"
(*Otherwise than Being, or Beyond Essence*, trans. Alphonso Lingis [The Hague:
Martinus Nijhoff Publishers, 1981], p. 10).

24. "Alors sous ce visage rosissant je sentais se réserver comme un gouffre
l'inexhaustible espace des soirs où je n'avais pas connu Albertine . . . je sentais que
je touchais seulement l'enveloppe close d'un être qui par l'intérieur accédait à l'infini . . . m'invitant sous une forme pressante, cruelle et sans issue, à la recherche
du passé, elle était plutôt comme une grande déesse du Temps" (III, 888).

CHAPTER 4

1. The essay was commissioned to discuss gender for a volume on the work of
Jacques Derrida. Hence, its original title was "Derrida and Gender: The Other
Sexual Difference" (in Tom Cohen, ed., *Jacques Derrida and the Humanities: A
Critical Reader* [Cambridge: Cambridge University Press, 2001]).

2. Although this incommensurability is well known to translators between
the two languages, it has not to my knowledge been the object of much if any
reflection by those who regularly write about the relation between "sex" and
language. The title of a collective work directed by Luce Irigaray, for example,
Sexes et genres à travers les langues (Paris: Grasset, 1990), seems to promise just
such an engagement with this difference between English and at least the other
languages represented in the collection (French and Italian). But any reader
with this expectation who reads through the collection, beginning with Irigaray's own long introduction, is very soon disappointed. It is partly this over-

sight, which is certainly not limited to Irigaray and her epigones, that this chapter seeks to interrogate.

3. Judith Butler, *Gender Trouble: Feminism and the Subversion of Identity* (New York: Routledge, 1990), p. 6.

4. In a subsequent book, *Bodies that Matter: On the Discursive Limits of "Sex"* (New York: Routledge, 1993), Butler's analyses more frequently refer to language theory, for example, in readings of Lacan. But all questions of language difference or translatability are no less left aside than in the earlier work, as if one could safely consider them to be without real pertinence for determining the "discursive limits of 'sex.'" A discussion of the "materiality of the signifier" (pp. 67–72), for example, remains altogether within a conceptual generalization of that materiality, so that the relations examined between subject and signifier are at every point subsumed to a general law of signification, which is described as if it were never "embodied" in a particular language or idiom.

5. In this Butler would seem to be taking most of her cues from Foucault. The point is not that she, any more than Foucault, would maintain that the "apparatus of production" constitutes an origin or originary structure. Rather, because Foucauldian critique dismisses altogether the question of origin, it does not open onto what Derrida has called arche-writing, "writing" before any distinction of writing from its others and as the possibility of all such distinctions. See on this question Derrida's essay on Foucault's *Madness and Civilization*, "Cogito and the History of Madness," trans. Alan Bass, in *Writing and Difference* (Chicago: University of Chicago Press, 1978); and, for an excellent guide to the debate between Foucault and Derrida, Niall Lucy, *Debating Derrida* (Carlton: Melbourne University Press, 1995).

6. *Gender Trouble* refers very little to any work of Derrida. One should perhaps understand this relative absence as a more or less active effacement, rather than just a neutral non-appearance, since Butler does make use of recognizably Derridean terminology. The term *différance*, for example, is deployed at one point but is implicitly attributed to Irigaray and given an oddly restrictive sense (40).

7. Butler often effects this reinscription more or less explicitly through a kind of translation. The need to translate another language, however, rarely if ever prompts any remark as to the referential constraints of the target language, English. For instance, an essay on Simone de Beauvoir begins by citing the famous line from *The Second Sex*: "One is not born, but rather becomes, a woman." Butler then proceeds to offer a paraphrase that ignores whatever implications follow from the fact of de Beauvoir's own language: "Simone de Beauvoir's formulation distinguishes sex from gender and suggests that gender is an aspect of identity gradually acquired" ("Sex and Gender in Simone de Beauvoir's *Second Sex*," *Yale French Studies* 72, p. 35). De Beauvoir, of course, any more than anyone else writ-

ing in French, says literally nothing about gender, and consequently about its possible distinction from sex. For a similar commentary on the same Beauvoirian formulation, see *Gender Trouble*, pp. III–12.

8. This condition has certainly not been missed by Derrida's readers and has prompted enormous commentary, both favorable and unfavorable. To take only a recent index, several book titles in the last few years mark the conjunction of either Derrida's name or deconstruction with an interest in sexual difference: for example, Diane Elam, *Feminism and Deconstruction* (New York: Routledge, 1994); Nancy J. Holland, ed., *Feminist Interpretations of Jacques Derrida* (University Park: Pennsylvania State University Press, 1997); Penelope Deutscher, *Yielding Gender: Feminism, Deconstruction, and the History of Philosophy* (London and New York: Routledge, 1997). Ellen K. Feder, Mary C. Rawlinson, and Emily Zakin, eds. *Derrida and Feminism* (New York: Routledge, 1997); Drucilla Cornell, *Beyond Accommodation: Ethical Feminism, Deconstruction, and the Law* (New York: Routledge, 1991).

9. Human cloning, would not be, of course, the reproduction of some self itself and still less by itself. Nevertheless, it still seems to be this impossible scenario of self-reproduction that is behind both a general fascination with cloning and the counter-measures put in place to contain it. The fact that a president of the United States (Clinton) could call for a voluntary prohibition on human cloning research, until the bioethical implications of the practice can be fully understood (!), suggests that such an extraordinary measure has to be taken to maintain or reinforce a taboo. Taboos do not just prohibit; they also surround the prohibited object or practice with a sacred aura fed by desire. Science, which believes it has nothing to do with taboos, has found a spokesman prepared to defy the ethical reservations of the political establishment. His name is Dr. Richard Seed. When in 1998 Seed announced his plan to pursue human cloning research as an alternative therapy for infertility, he caused a media flurry, in the course of which this renegade physicist described cloning as but the technical, scientific realization of the doctrine that man is made in God's image. "God made man in his own image," he is quoted as saying. "Therefore He intended that man should become one with God. Man should have an indefinite life and have indefinite knowledge. And we're going to do it, and this is one step" (http://www.brentmorrison.com/9801Clones_Richard_Seed.htm). It is not just with his name, then, but also by virtue of this discourse that Seed seems particularly well placed to make more apparent the ancient desires that foment the issues around cloning.

10. Of these, "hymen" and "invagination" commonly carry a reference to the female body. Derrida was led to comment on the choice of these terms in an interview that deals largely with sexual difference: see Jacques Derrida and Christie V. McDonald, "Choreographies," in Peggy Kamuf, ed., *A Derrida Reader: Between the Blinds* (New York: Columbia University Press, 1991), p. 453.

11. Butler, like Foucault but with a very different resonance, hardly ever refers to Heidegger. Whereas Foucault would have, to some considerable extent, presupposed a reading of Heidegger within the context in which he wrote, Butler in her context cannot and does not presuppose any such reading. This difference of address no doubt affects a considerable number of American adaptations of Foucault's thought and not just Butler's.

12. Jacques Derrida, "*Geschlecht,* différence sexuelle, différence ontologique," in *Psyché, Inventions de l'autre* (Paris: Galilée, 1987), p. 396; trans. Ruben Berezdivin, "'Geschlecht': Sexual Difference, Ontological Differenece," in Kamuf, ed., *A Derrida Reader,* p. 381. Further references to both the original and the translation will be given in that order in the text.

13. As given in French in Derrida's essay, these possible translations of *Geschlecht* are listed as "sexe, genre, famille, souche, race, lignée, génération." Although "genre" is in turn translated (or not) as "genre" in the English version, one could argue that this is an instance where Derrida is using the term to mean something very close to gender.

14. In fact, the principal part of the reading of the dispersion, and even decomposition, of the term *Geschlecht* through Heidegger's text will be consigned to another essay, which is a companion to this one: "Heidegger's Hand (*Geschlecht* II)" (trans. John P. Leavey, Jr., in John Sallis, ed., *Deconstruction and Philosophy: The Texts of Jacques Derrida* [Chicago: University of Chicago Press, 1987]). There will also be a third *Geschlecht* essay: "L'oreille de Heidegger: Philopolémologie (*Geschlecht* IV)" (in Jacques Derrida, *Politiques de l'amitié* [Paris: Galilée, 1994]). On the missing number in this sequence—*Geschlecht* III—see "Heidegger's Hand," p. 183.

15. David Krell, *Intimations of Mortality: Time, Truth, and Finitude in Heidegger's Thinking of Mortality,* as cited in Jacques Derrida, "Heidegger's Hand (*Geschlecht* II)," pp. 191–92. As for the standard meanings of *Geschlecht,* Krell writes: "First, it translates the Latin word *genus,* being equivalent to *Gattung: das Geschlecht* is a group of people who share a common ancestry. . . . Of course, if the ancestry is traced back far enough we may speak of *das menschliche Geschlecht,* 'human kind.' Second, *das Geschlecht* may mean one generation of men and women. . . . Third, there are male and female *Geschlechter*" (ibid.).

16. Such, at least, is Derrida's contention. In a note, included only in the subsequent publication of "*Geschlecht*" in the collection *Psyché,* Derrida insists on this trace of inscription in the word. The first two "Geschlecht" essays sketch, he writes, "in a barely preliminary fashion, an interpretation to come in which I would like to situate *Geschlecht* in the path of Heidegger's thought. In the path also of writing and printing, to which we are led by the marked inscription of the word *Geschlecht.* I am leaving this word here in its language for reasons that

should become clear in the course of this very reading. And it is indeed a question of 'Geschlecht' (of the *word* for sex, race, family, generation, lineage, species, genre/gender) and not of *the Geschlecht*: we will not be able to traverse so easily toward the thing itself (the *Geschlecht*) across the mark of the word ('Geschlecht') in which, much later, Heidegger will remark the imprint of the blow or the strike (*Schlag*)" (*Psyche*, p. 395; my trans.).

17. Concerning this term, Joan Stambaugh writes, in the preface to her new translation of *Being and Time*: "Heidegger frequently employs quite common vocabulary in uncommon ways. Here the most visible example is his use of the word Dasein which, besides having a long history as a philosophic term . . . is a word that belongs to everyday conversation. One of Heidegger's intentions in *Being and Time* is to re-appropriate that word and give it new meaning without completely repudiating its sense" ([Albany: State University of New York Press, 1996], p. xiii). She also explains her adoption of the hyphenated form, *Da-sein*. "It was Heidegger's express wish that in future translations the word *Da-sein* should be hyphenated throughout *Being and Time*. . . . Thus the reader will be less prone to assume he or she understands it to refer to 'existence' (which is the orthodox translation of Dasein) and with that translation surreptitiously bring along all sorts of psychological connotations. It was Heidegger's insight that human being is *uncanny*: we do not know who, or what, that is, although, or perhaps precisely because, we *are* it" (xiv). It should be remarked that Heidegger is here giving instructions to his future *translators*. And he tells them in effect not to translate Dasein but only to hyphenate it. It is thus something like a spaced-out proper name, a quasi proper name. Such a quasi proper name might be thought of as the respondent or correspondent of the quasi transcendental. On this latter notion, see Geoffrey Bennington, "Derridabase," in Bennington and Jacques Derrida, *Jacques Derrida* (Chicago: University of Chicago Press, 1993), pp. 267–75.

18. Martin Heidegger, *Being and Time*, trans. John Macquarrie and Edward Robinson (New York: Harper and Row, 1962), p 67; *Sein und Zeit* (Tübingen: Max Niemeyer Verlag, 1993), pp. 41–42.

19. Derrida and McDonald, "Choreographies," in Kamuf, ed., *A Derrida Reader*, 453.

20. Such attention to gesture could be said to characterize Derrida's approach to philosophical texts in general, which he reads first of all as doing or attempting to do something. As such, it is not thematized more here than elsewhere. Yet it is doubtless significant that the essay in which Derrida continues this reading of *Geschlecht* in Heidegger is titled: "Heidegger's Hand (Geschlecht II)."

21. Derrida has often interrogated idiomatic French expressions formed with "raison." In *Given Time*, the expressions "donner raison à l'autre" (to concede that the other is right) and "avoir raison de l'autre" (to prevail over the other) receive

thorough attention as key to what is at stake in the opening of a gift "*destined* not to have reason, to be wrong, as if one had to choose between reason and gift (or forgiveness). The gift would be that which does not obey the principle of reason: It is, it ought to be, it owes itself to be without reason, without wherefore, and without foundation" (*Given Time: I. Counterfeit Money*, trans. Peggy Kamuf [Chicago: University of Chicago Press, 1992], p. 156). For another deployment of the idioms of "raison," in an essay on Heidegger, see "How to Concede, with Reasons," trans. John P. Leavey, Jr., in Derrida, *Points . . . Interviews (1974–1994)*, ed. Elisabeth Weber (Stanford: Stanford University Press, 1995).

22. The necessity of this syntax of "without" has been shown by Derrida at several junctures, notably in his readings of Blanchot. See in particular "The Law of *Genre*," an essay on the notion of *genre*, the false friend of "gender," where the necessity is retraced in its most generic terms: "I would speak of a sort of participation without belonging—a taking part in without being part of, without having membership in a set. The trait that marks membership inevitably divides, the boundary of the set comes to form, by invagination, an internal pocket larger than the whole; and the outcome of this division and of this unbounding remains as singular as it is limitless" (Derrida, "The Law of Genre," trans. Avital Ronell, *Glyph* 7, p. 206). The invagination described here would be another term with which to name the strange movement of displacement that reinscribes all oppositions within an itself that is itself without closure. On the choice of this term, see above, note 10.

23. This topos of natural discretion or modesty that must cover sexual coupling was most forcefully put in place perhaps by Rousseau, who argued as well, of course, that the responsibility for this modesty has always been assigned to the female of the species. Whenever "sexual difference" is being thought solely on the basis of this discreetly hidden genital act, then it remains also to some extent a Rousseauvian difference.

24. Heidegger's initial use and subsequent abandonment of quotation marks on the word "Geist" is one of the principal indices Derrida follows in another text so as to reconstruct the liminal movement of a certain "spirit" through Heidegger's thought. At the point at which the distinction of use from mention is invoked, Derrida makes clear that he is interested above all in demonstrating its problematic limits: "In order to describe this situation, let us momentarily, for convenience, provisionally resort to the distinction put forward by speech-act theory between *use* and *mention*. It would not be to Heidegger's taste, but perhaps what is at stake is also to put the limits of such a distinction to the test" (*Of Spirit: Heidegger and the Question*, trans. Geoffrey Bennington and Rachel Bowlby [Chicago: University of Chicago Press, 1987], p. 29). Derrida has persistently questioned this conceptual distinction in speech-act theory, most notably in his response to John Searle, one of the theory's foremost spokesmen; see *Lim-*

ited Inc, trans. Samuel Weber (Evanston, Ill.: Northwestern University Press, 1988), especially pp. 81–85.

25. In *Given Time,* Derrida situates this figure of "giving life" along a "fold of undecidability": "To give time, the day, or life is to give nothing, nothing determinate, even if it is to give the giving of any possible giving, even if it gives the condition of giving. What distinguishes in principle this division from the transcendental division it resembles? One perceives there no longer the sharp line that separates the transcendental from the conditioned, the conditioning from the conditioned, but rather the fold of undecidability that allows all the values to be inverted: the gift of life amounts to the gift of death, the gift of day to the gift of night, and so on" (*Given Time,* p. 54). If one extrapolates from this to what is being advanced here about a sexual difference that "gives life" before or beyond the sense of engenderment, then it would occupy that "fold of undecidability" Derrida has elsewhere called "quasi transcendentality" (see above, note 17).

26. This includes all texts Derrida has signed or will sign. See, however, especially the discussion of Hegel's signature on the conceptual machinery of the dialectic, in *Glas,* trans. John. P. Leavey, Jr. and Richard Rand (Lincoln: University of Nebraska Press, 1986).

CHAPTER 5

1. *Antigone,* trans. Paul Roche (New York: New American Library, 1958), p. 180; for a remarkable new reading of Antigone's exceptionalism, see Judith Butler, *Antigone's Claim* (New York: Columbia University Press, 2002).

2. Nicole Loraux, *Tragic Ways of Killing a Woman,* trans. Anthony Forster (Cambridge, Mass.: Harvard University Press, 1987).

3. Martin Heidegger, *Being and Time,* trans. John Macquarrie and Edward Robinson (New York: Harper & Row, 1962), §47, p. 284.

4. On the sexual neutrality of Dasein and Derrida's deconstructive reading of its place in Heidegger's thought, see, above, "The Other Sexual Difference."

5. Although essentially correct, there is in fact a passing reference to a woman in Melville's narrative: the woman who comes to clean the lawyer's offices at night.

6. *The Gift of Death,* trans. David Wills (Chicago: University of Chicago Press, 1995), pp. 75–76; *Donner la mort* (Paris: Galilée, 1999), p. 107.

7. In this regard, Derrida can be read as finding the same pattern of "giving oneself one's own death" that he finds in Freud's *Beyond the Pleasure Principle* in "To Speculate—on 'Freud'" in *The Post Card,* trans. Alan Bass (Chicago: University of Chicago Press, 1987).

8. Sarah Kofman, *Rue Ordener, rue Labat,* trans. Ann Smock (Lincoln: University of Nebraska Press, 1996), p. 23.

9. This text of Kofman's has and doubtless will continue to solicit readers' responses. Several are collected in the fine volume of essays edited by Kelly Oliver and Penelope Deutscher: *Enigmas: Essays on Sarah Kofman* (Ithaca, N.Y.: Cornell University Press, 1999). See in particular, Kelly Oliver, "Sarah Kofman's Queasy Stomach and the Riddle of Paternal Law"; Tina Chanter, "Eating Words: Antigone as Kofman's Proper Name"; and Diane Morgan, "'Made in Germany': Judging National Identity Negatively." See also Verena Andermatt Conley, "For Sarah Kofman, on *Rue Ordener, rue Labat*," in *SubStance* 81 (1996), pp. 153–59; and Frances Bartkowski's introduction to her translation of other autobiographical fragments by Sarah Kofman ("Eating Her Words: Autobiographical Writings of Sarah Kofman," in *SubStance*, 49 [1986], pp. 6–8). In 1997, *Cahiers du Grif (nouvelle série)* published a special issue on Sarah Kofman (no. 3).

CHAPTER 6

1. "—Parce que le rêve secret de l'écriture, c'est d'être aussi délicate que le silence.—Mais est-ce qu'il y a une écriture d'une telle délicatesse?—Il y en a une, mais je ne l'ai pas. Parce que pour écrire délicatement de la délicatesse, il faudrait pouvoir non-écrire.—Il faudrait pouvoir écrire l'effacement. Mais est-ce qu'on peut 'écrire' l'effacement?" (Hélène Cixous, *Limonade tout était si infini* [Paris: Editions des femmes, 1982], pp. 252–53; my translation).

2. "Comment faire pour que soit libre? Souci: Peur que l'aimer lui fasse loi."

3. "La légèreté aussi pèse. Ce qui j'ai à dire est plus léger que la légèreté ou n'est pas. Le mot 'légèreté' est déjà un poids. Il n'y a pas de mot assez léger pour ne pas alourdir la légèreté de la légèreté. Et ce que j'ai à dire est du domaine de la légèreté propre."

4. Mireille Calle-Gruber makes a similar remark in an interview with Cixous: "By 'theory' you are referring in particular here to a north-American situation . . . which, under the name of 'feminist theory,' has excluded your books of fiction, limiting itself to a few essays or articles. . . . One must wonder how this happens. What happens—or does not happen—when one does so little justice to a body of work?" (Hélène Cixous and Mireille Calle-Gruber, *Hélène Cixous, Rootprints: Memory and Life Writing*, trans. Eric Prenowitz [London and New York: Routledge, 1997], p. 4).

5. "The Laugh of the Medusa," trans. Keith Cohen and Paula Cohen, *Signs* 1/4 (Summer 1976); and "Castration or Decapitation," trans. A. Kuhn, *Signs* 7/1 (Fall 1981). In 1991, Morag Shiach, in the bibliography of her *Hélène Cixous: A Politics of Writing* (London and New York: Routledge, 1991), listed fifteen essays or extracts from essays by Cixous translated in various journals or collections, as well as several works for the theater. At that time, which is when this essay was

first written, only two complete translations (*Angst* and *Dedans*) of Cixous's twenty-four or more (depending on how you count) "fictional" texts had appeared. Since then, at least six other fictional texts have been translated and doubtless more are forthcoming.

6. In her introduction to *Revaluing French Feminism: Critical Essays on Difference, Agency, and Culture* (Bloomington and Indianapolis: Indiana University Press, 1992), Nancy Fraser writes that "for many English-speaking readers today 'French feminism' simply *is* Irigaray, Kristeva, and Cixous" (1). This repetition by rote feeds Fraser's complaint, which seems to be primarily that there has been a misapprehension of "a much larger, more variegated field" (ibid.). This is, of course, quite true. And yet, although her introduction makes a point of mentioning other feminist thinkers in France, the anthology she is introducing (and which she edited with Sandra Lee Bartky) conforms pretty much to what she calls the "curious synecdochic reduction" (ibid.) by concentrating its essays on Irigaray and Kristeva, adding only an essay by Sarah Kofman to the mix. It would thus seem that the principal "revaluation" this anthology proposes is to eliminate altogether Cixous, whose name indeed is never again mentioned by any of the contributors.

7. Hélène Cixous and Catherine Clément, *The Newly Born Woman*, trans. Betsy Wing (Minneapolis: University of Minnesota Press, 1986). Originally published as *La jeune née* (Paris: Union Générale d'Edition, 1975).

8. *Sexual/Textual Politics: Feminist Literary Theory* (New York: Methuen, 1986), p. 102.

9. Moi's general disregard for what she calls here "style" should be surprising if one recalls that the subtitle of *Sexual/Textual Politics* is "Feminist Literary Theory." After a first section on "Anglo-American Feminist Criticism," however, the second part of the book is titled "French Feminist Theory"; hence the announced "literary" component seems to have slipped into the crack between Anglo-American "criticism" and French "theory."

10. Moi, however, manifests no awareness at all of Cixous's constant and various political activities. Like Gilbert or Fraser, she is content to "read off" Cixous's "politics" from a very few texts, which are moreover being read in the most reductive fashion.

11. At the beginning of his now famous essay "Resistance to Theory," Paul de Man observes that an inherent difficulty for literary theory is that it must "start out from empirical considerations" if it is not to ground itself in "an *a priori* conception of what is 'literary' by starting out from the premises of the system rather than from the literary thing itself—if such a 'thing' exists" (In de Man, *The Resistance to Theory* [Minneapolis: University of Minnesota Press, 1986], 4–5). This opening statement, and its reprise in the essay's conclusion regarding theory's impossibility ("Nothing can overcome the resistance to theory since theory *is* itself this resistance" [19]) may stand here synecdochically for what we are calling "theory"'s limits.

12. See Jacques Derrida, "La double séance," in *Dissémination* (Paris: Editions du Seuil, 1972), p. 234.

13. "Je dirai: aujourd'hui l'écriture est aux femmes. Ce n'est pas une provocation, cela signifie que: la femme admet qu'il y ait de l'autre. Elle n'a pas effacé, dans son devenir-femme, la bisexualité latente chez la fille comme chez le garçon. Féminité et bisexualité vont ensemble. . . . A l'homme, il est bien plus difficile de se laisser traverser par de l'autre. L'écriture, c'est en moi le passage, entrée, sortie, séjour, de l'autre que je suis et ne suis pas, que je ne sais pas être, mais que je sens passer, qui me fait vivre,—qui me déchire, m'inquiète, m'altère, qui?—une, un, des?—plusieurs, de l'inconnu qui me donne justement l'envie de connaître à partir de laquelle s'élance toute vie. Ce peuplement ne laisse ni repos ni sécurité, trouble toujours le rapport au 'réel,' produit des effets d'incertitude qui font obstacle à la socialisation du sujet. C'est angoissant, ça use; et pour les hommes, cette perméabilité, cette non-exclusion, c'est la menace, l'intolérable. . . . Que soit 'féminine' une certaine réceptivité, c'est vrai. On peut bien sûr exploiter, comme l'Histoire l'a toujours fait, l'accueil féminin en aliénation. . . . Mais je parle ici de la féminité comme conservant en vie l'autre qui se fie à elle, la visite, qu'elle peut aimer en tant qu'autre. . . . Par la même ouverture, qui est son risque, elle sort d'elle-même pour aller à l'autre, voyageuse de l'inexploré, elle ne dénie pas, elle approche, non pour annuler l'écart, mais pour le voir, pour faire l'expérience de ce qu'elle n'est pas, qu'elle est, qu'elle peut être" (158–59).

14. "This Essentialism Which Is Not One: Coming To Grips With Irigaray," *Differences* 1 (Summer 1989): 40.

15. For more on hyphenization as mark of heterogeneity, see below, "Singular Sense, Second Hand."

16. "Ce fut comme si la foudre m'avait frappé. J'ai éprouvé au contact de ces cheveux une douleur inavouable à mes amis, mais c'était *une joie* qui m'a causé cette douleur: je n'ai pu retenir mes larmes. Elles semblaient jaillir directement de mon coeur. Alors, comme si par la violence du ruissellement, une toile de nuit était arrachée de mes pupilles, j'ai cru voir—je mens—: j'ai vu—avec certitude,—de mes yeux comme si je voyais soudain la lumière."

17. Here is how the writer, Oskar Baum, who is the O. in Cixous's recounting, himself describes the episode: "Kafka's first gesture as he came into my room left a deep impression on me. He knew he was in the presence of a blind man. And yet, as Brod was introducing him, he bowed silently to me. It was, you might think, a senseless formality in my case, since I couldn't see it. His hair, which was smoothed down, touched my forehead for a moment as he bowed, probably because the bow that I made at the same time was a little too violent. I was moved in a way that for the moment I could see no clear reason for. Here was one of the first people in the world who had made it clear that my deficiency was something that concerned nobody but myself—not by making allowances

or being considerate, not by the faintest change in his bearing. That was what he was like. He stood so far from the accepted utility formulas, that he affected one in this way. His severe, cool reserve was so superior in depth of humanity to the ordinary run of kindness—which I otherwise recognize when I am first introduced to people in a pointless increase in warmth of words, or tone of voice, or shake of the hand" (cited in Max Brod, *Franz Kafka: A Biography*, trans. G. Humphreys Roberts and Richard Winston [New York: Schocken Books, 1960], pp. 107–8).

18. "Ce qui rend cette scène si fragile, un mot pourrait la briser, c'est qu'elle n'a pour ainsi dire presque pas de lieu, parce qu'elle s'est passée dans l'invisible. L'indicible délicatesse du geste: c'est de faire signe à voir devant un homme aveugle: et ainsi de ne pas le priver du plus diaphane respect."

19. In a like manner, Kant defines duty [*Pflicht*] as the respect owed not to anyone or to one's fellow men, but to the moral law; cf. *The Critique of Practical Reason*, part 1, book 1, chap. 3.

20. In the first published version of this text, in 1995, I had insisted here that O. *alone and no other* perceived and thus received this address. But this singularization is in fact not a necessary condition here; it is an accidental or contingent one. Kafka himself or anyone else at the scene might have perceived in some fashion the glancing touch, even if only for O. could it be phenomenalized as the feeling of hair grazing his own forehead. Jacques Derrida has pointed out that I make a similar error in another text of mine; see his "Provocation: Forewords," in *Without Alibi*, ed. and trans. Peggy Kamuf (Stanford: Stanford University Press, 2002), pp. 282–83, n. 5.

21. "Dans le mouvement du désir, de l'échange, [l'homme] est partie *prenante*: la perte, la dépense, est prise dans l'opération commerciale qui fait toujours du don un don-qui-prend. Le don rapporte. La perte se transforme au bout d'une ligne courbe en son contraire et lui revient sous forme de gain.

Mais est-ce qu'à cette loi du retour la femme échappe? Est-ce qu'on peut parler d'une autre dépense? En vérité, il n'y a pas de don 'gratuit.' On ne donne jamais pour rien. Mais toute la différence est dans le pourquoi et le comment du don, dans les valeurs que le geste de donner affirme, fait circuler; dans le type de bénéfice que tire le donateur du don, et l'usage qu'il en fait. . . .

Elle aussi donne pour. Elle aussi donnant se donne—plaisir, bonheur, valeur augmentée, image rehaussée d'elle-même. Mais ne cherche pas 'à rentrer dans ses frais.' Elle peut ne pas revenir à elle, ne se posant jamais, se répandant, allant partout à l'autre" (160–61).

22. Jacques Derrida, *Given Time, I: Counterfeit Money*, trans. Peggy Kamuf (Chicago: Chicago University Press, 1992), pp. 13–14; emphases in the original.

23. "L'ineffaçable de l'histoire, c'est l'effacement de F.: pour faire un geste aussi délicat, il faut être devenu aussi transparent qu'une libellule, aussi léger qu'une sauterelle . . . "

24. There are other creatures on the list, *hirondelle, gazelle,* and *tourterelle,* but it also includes *aile, ocelle, femelle, jumelle, échelle, demoiselle, sorcellerie, patelle, étincelle, appel, dentelle, élégance* ("élégance de sauterelle," 262), *lamelle, cellule* ("C'est la cellule mélodique de tout un livre," p. 275), *frêle,* and the proper names Kohelet and Dominicella. One could also follow the other syllable "-li" toward the "Livre Ultime" and, of course, the first syllable of the ultimate sentence "limonade tout était si infini." And the syllables come together in one of the key words of the text: *délicatesse.* As disseminated, disseminating points, the syllables also pinpoint the resistance of the text to translation.

25. "Comment faire pour lui dire 'je veux que tu te saches libre' sans que la phrase l'attrape entre ses pattes de mots, même pour la caresser et, dans son désir de lui confier sa bonne intention, l'oblige à freiner? . . . Et la question est: peut-on donner sans faire part? Comment faire part sans parole? Le silence aussi est de parole. . . . Car penser les mystères du donner, qui sont aussi délicats que les ailes de papillon, demandait une délicatesse de même nature exactement. Rien que d'y penser lui faisait sentir son propre pesant."

CHAPTER 7

1. "The grammatical model of the question becomes rhetorical not when we have, on the one hand, a literal meaning and on the other hand a figural meaning, but when it is impossible to decide by grammatical or other linguistic devices which of the two meanings (that can be entirely incompatible) prevails." Paul de Man, "Semiology and Rhetoric," in *Allegories of Reading: Figural Language in Rousseau, Nietzsche, Rilke, and Proust* (New Haven, Conn.: Yale University Press, 1979), p. 10.

2. On the relation of literary studies to the modern scientific university, see my *Division of Literature, or the University in Deconstruction* (Chicago: University of Chicago Press, 1997); and Bill Readings, *The University in Ruins* (Cambridge, Mass.: Harvard University Press, 1996), esp. the chapter "Literary Culture."

3. On this ambivalence as an irreducible feature in the "humanities," see Samuel Weber, "Ambivalence: The Humanities and the Study of Literature," in Weber, *Institution and Interpretation* (Minneapolis: University of Minnesota Press, 1987).

4. J.L. Austin, *How to Do Things with Words,* 2d ed., ed. J.O Urmson and Marina Sbisà (Cambridge, Mass.: Harvard University Press, 1975), p. 22; italics in the original. Subsequent page references will be given in the text in parentheses. For an admirably probing analysis of Austin's text, see J. Hillis Miller, *Speech Acts in Literature* (Stanford: Stanford University Press, 1999), chap. 1. Miller draws out, in particular and with great clarity, the extent to which Austin's lectures do *not* exclude the "literary" in that, for example, they include many citations and allusions to literary works.

5. Jacques Derrida, "Signature Event Context," in *Glyph* I (1977), pp. 190–91.

6. Hillis Miller argues very persuasively that Austin should indeed be read as seeking to shore up clear moral distinctions and that these are, moreover, always tilted in the direction of historically determined privileges (e.g., of class or gender); see Miller, *Speech Acts in Literature*, esp. pp. 55–59.

7. For a discussion of experience and poetry, see Walter Benjamin, "On Some Motifs in Baudelaire," in Benjamin, *Illuminations*, trans. Harry Zohn (New York: Schocken Books, 1969). Benjamin's interpretation of Baudelaire's experience pays particular attention to the distinction between *Erlebnis* and *Erfahrung*, that is, between a lived moment and experience that enters memory. For a clarification of this distinction in Benjamin's thought, see Benjamin, "Central Park," trans. Lloyd Spencer, *New German Critique* 34 (Winter 1985), p. 57, n. 32a.2.

8. See, for example, Nancy, *L'Expérience de la liberté* (Paris: Galilée, 1988), p. 25; and Lacoue-Labarthe, *La poésie comme expérience* (Paris: Christian Bourgois, 1986), p. 30; see as well, below, "The Experience of Deconstruction."

9. "This Strange Institution Called Literature: An Interview with Jacques Derrida," in Derek Attridge, ed., *Acts of Literature* (New York: Routledge, 1992), p. 46. Subsequent references will be included in the text in parentheses.

10. Both translations have been given of Blanchot's term "le neutre." There are in fact three extant English translations of this essay: "The Narrative Voice (the 'he,' the neuter)," trans. Lydia Davis, in *The Gaze of Orpheus and Literary Essays* (Barrytown, N.Y.: Station Hill Press, 1981); "The Narrative Voice or the Impersonal 'He,'" trans. Sacha Rabinovitch, in *The Sirens' Song: Selected Essays by Maurice Blanchot* (Bloomington: Indiana University Press, 1982); and most recently, "The Narrative Voice (the 'he,' the neutral)," trans. Susan Hanson, in *The Infinite Conversation* (Minneapolis: University of Minnesota Press, 1993). I follow Susan Hanson's translation and will therefore refer more consistently to "the neutral."

11. Maurice Blanchot, *The Infinite Conversation*, trans. Susan Hanson, pp. 383–84; subsequent page references will be included in the text.

12. On this phrase as marking the anteriority of response in relation to any knowledge, see Samuel Weber, "La surenchère (Upping the Ante)," in *Le passage des frontières: Autour du travail de Jacques Derrida*, ed. Marie-Louise Mallet (Paris: Galilée, 1994), p. 147.

13. Jill Robbins, *Altered Reading: Levinas and Literature* (Chicago: University of Chicago Press, 1999), pp. 152–53.

14. The term "récit" means narrative, story, recounting. But it also carries the mark of repetition, of citation. It thus conjoins the remarking of the mark with the citation of some other speech. On the question of the *récit* in Blanchot, a question that is more precisely a demand, see Jacques Derrida, "Survivre," in *Parages* (Paris: Galilée, 1986), esp. pp. 130–52.

15. These last words of the text are followed by the signal for a final footnote, which begins: "It is this voice—the narrative voice—that I hear, perhaps rashly, perhaps rightly, in the narrative by Marguerite Duras that I mentioned [*Le ravissement de Lol V. Stein*]." The note then proceeds to justify in a few lines this reference to Duras's *récit*. But it also might be taken to suggest that one read the final lines of the text precisely in the sense of such an admonition to avoid confusing narrative voice with the voice of some character, Lol V. Stein, for example, whose "oblique voice" would be that of "misfortune, or of madness." Read in this sense, the final sentence of the text wards off the sort of psychological criticism that has been the mainstay for so long of writing about narrative fiction, including Duras's.

CHAPTER 8

1. Jean-Luc Nancy recalls the origins of the word experience (*peirā, ex-periri*) and revives its links to perilousness, *periculum* (trial, attempt, proof, danger, risk), as well as to pirates (*peirātēs*), those who operate beyond the limit (*peirā*) of a certain law. It is this expropriating piracy within fundamental experience that Nancy emphasizes in his reflection on the experience of freedom: "In a sense, which here might be the first and last sense, freedom, to the extent that it is the thing itself of thinking, cannot be appropriated, but only 'pirated': its 'seizure' will always be illegitimate" (*The Experience of Freedom*, trans. Bridget McDonald [Stanford: Stanford University Press, 1988], 20). A more extensive, less provisional approach to the questions raised here would have to trace out not only Nancy's continued reliance on the term "experience" (once it has been wrenched out of its positivist sense) but also Derrida's. A possible place to begin the latter task might be in the essay "Signature Event Context," where Derrida proposes to extend the law of the grapheme, that is, of the "differential mark cut off from its putative 'production' or origin" to all "experience." He writes: "And I shall even extend this law to all 'experience' in general if it is conceded that there is no experience consisting of *pure* presence but only of chains of differential marks" ("Signature Event Context," trans. Samuel Weber and Jeffrey Mehlman, in Derrida, *Limited Inc* [Evanston, Il.: Northwestern University Press, 1988], p. 10). Derrida will later refer to deconstruction as the experience of the impossible.

2. Narrative theory is a theory of repetition inasmuch as it depends on what Didier Coste calls "the narrative paradox," namely: "In order to understand 'X has changed,' I have to accept that X remains X whether p or -p is true about it." For Coste, as for most narratologists, X represents a subject, "a character." See his *Narrative as Communication* (Minneapolis: University of Minnesota Press, 1989), p. 9; see also below, "The Other Fiction."

3. "The Uncanny" in Freud, *Writings on Art and Literature*, ed. Neil Hertz (Stanford: Stanford University Press, 1997), p. 217; the German text is found in

Freud, *Gesammelte Werke*, Band 12 (Frankfurt am Main: S. Fischer Verlag, 1966), pp. 229–68.

4. Of all recent work, none is more exhaustive, inventive, and far-reaching in its implications for thinking about literature than Nicholas Royle's *The Uncanny* (New York: Routledge, 2003). Royle makes every turning in Freud's essay answer to his probing interrogations and establishes connections throughout Freud's corpus. He also surveys widely the critical literature on the essay and uncanniness in general. Samuel Weber is another prominent thinker who has returned more than once to Freud's essay: see "Uncanny Thinking" and "The Sideshow, or: Remarks on a Canny Moment," both in *The Legend of Freud*, expanded edition (Stanford: Stanford University Press, 2000); other benchmark readings can be found in Sarah Kofman, "The Double is/and the Devil: The Uncanniness of *The Sandman*," in *Freud and Fiction*, trans. Sarah Wykes (Boston: Northeastern University Press, 1991); Hélène Cixous, "Fiction and Its Phantoms: A Reading of Freud's *Das Unheimliche*," *New Literary History* (Spring 1976); and Neil Hertz, "Freud and 'The Sandman,'" in *The End of the Line* (New York: Columbia University Press, 1985). Derrida has likewise repeatedly signaled his attentive reading of Freud's essay. He even suggests in a note that "The Double Session" is "in sum" a rereading of "Das Unheimliche" (Derrida, *Dissemination* [Chicago: University of Chicago Press, 1981], p. 220 n. 23). There are two further notes in "The Double Session" that invoke Freud's essay, one of which gestures toward the problematic taken up here: "It should not be forgotten," Derrida remarks, "that in *Das Unheimliche*, after having borrowed all his material from literature, Freud strangely sets aside the case of literary fictions that include supplementary resources of *Unheimlichkeit*" (268 n. 67).

5. See Freud, "The Claims of Psycho-Analysis to Scientific Interest," in *Standard Edition*, vol. 13. Samuel Weber notes that if "the uncanny remains a marginal notion even within psychoanalysis itself," this may be attributed to the fact that "psychoanalysis, today as in Freud's lifetime, seeks to establish itself in stable institutions, to ground itself in a practice and a theory that rarely question the established conceptions of truth and the criteria of value that prevail in the societies in which it is situated" (*The Legend of Freud*, 20).

6. "Ja, der Autor dieser neuen Unternehmung muss sich einer besonderen Stumpfheit in dieser Sache anklagen, wo grosse Feinfühligkeit eher am Platze wäre. Er hat schon lange nichts erlebt oder kennen gelernt, was ihm den Eindruck des Unheimlichen gemacht hätte, muss sich erst in das Gefühl hineinversetzen, die Möglichkeit desselben in sich wachrufen" (*Gesammelte Werke*, vol. 12, p. 230).

7. See Freud, *Writings on Art and Literature*, which includes in the appendix a "List of Writings by Freud Dealing Mainly or Largely with Art, Literature or the Theory of Aesthetics," p. 263. There are 22 items on the list.

8. In her incomparably fine reading of Freud's essay, which she likens to a

"strange theoretical novel" ("Fiction and Its Phantoms," p. 525), Hélène Cixous touches on this episode and its degrees of repetition not yet recognized as such by its author, or rather by its victim. She writes: " . . . and Freud wanders—in obsessive turns. One other winding, and instead of the distress which Freud claims to have experienced, we should be confronted with the irresistible comedy of Mark Twain. Question: how many repetitions are necessary before distress turns into comedy? The 'degree' of repetition supposes the type of reflection that Freud scrupulously refrains from undertaking: he wants to remain sexually on this side of ridicule. . . . " (540).

9. The irreducible necessity of this fiction is remarked but also covered over by the hypothesis of unconscious functioning. It is finally perhaps this hypothesis that would be at stake for Freud in the distinction of real from fictional experience, since one must not be left to conclude that the unconscious is a kind of fiction.

10. The story Freud read appears to have been a tale by L. G. Moberly titled "Inexplicable" and published in *The Strand* in 1917. It has been collected in *Strange Tales from The Strand*, ed. Jack Adrian (Oxford: Oxford University Press, 1991). (My thanks to Kathleen Chapman and Michael Du Plessis for putting me on the right track.) Since the initial publication of this chapter, I've been able to read the pages in Nicolas Royle's *The Uncanny* that treat this anecdote and set Freud's faulty or disavowed memory over against a reading of the story. Royle too asks the question of where the story begins and brings out in numerous ways Freud's resistance to literature as a space in which the uncanny can be thought; see Royle, *The Uncanny*, pp. 134–40.

11. Such reading experience may be termed primitive in a strict sense: a primary experience, a first and then sole experience. The crocodile story, Freud understands, would not sustain a similar effect upon a second reading. A primitive reading experience is one that cannot be repeated to the same effect, because this effect depended above all on one remaining ignorant of the story's end. Those fictions we call literary, on the other hand, bear up under repeated readings. Literature, in the modern sense, is quite simply the institution of (its own) repetition, its self-disseminating, self-(dis)possession in multiple copies, editions, and critical readings.

12. For more sustained engagements with this reading, see the essays by Kofman, Cixous, Weber, and Hertz cited above.

13. Referring to the final scene on the parapet, Sam Weber writes: "Freud, it seems, has eyes only for the Sandman: fascinated, he stares at him and simply refuses to see Clara. Not so poor Nathanael" ("The Sideshow, or: Remarks on a Canny Moment," 223).

14. In *The Birth of Tragedy* §15.

15. Sarah Kofman was perhaps the first to signal this possible renaming when

in 1974 she titled a long essay on Derrida "Un philosophe 'unheimlich'" (reprinted in Kofman, *Lectures de Derrida* [Paris: Galilée, 1984]).

CHAPTER 9

1. This chapter was first written for the conference titled "Deconstruction Reading Politics" organized by Martin McQuillan at Staffordshire University in July 1999.

2. Maurice Blanchot, *Thomas l'obscur*, rev. ed. (Paris: Gallimard, 1950), p. 27; my trans.

3. Philippe Lacoue-Labarthe and Jean-Luc Nancy, *The Literary Absolute: The Theory of Literary in German Romanticism*, trans. Philip Barnard and Cheryl Lester (Albany: SUNY Press, 1988). See also the introduction to my *Division of Literature, or the University in Deconstruction* (Chicago: Chicago Univerity Press, 1997).

4. René Wellek and Austin Warren, *Theory of Literature*, 3rd ed. (New York: Harcourt Brace, 1956), chap. 5. The first edition was published in 1949.

5. "The work of art, then, appears as an object of knowledge *sui generis* which has a special ontological status. It is neither real (physical, like a statue) nor mental (psychological, like the experience of light or pain) nor ideal (like a triangle). It is a system of norms of ideal concepts which are intersubjective" (p. 156). Thus, the obligation to "see" the totality of the work commands that one grasp this system of intersubjective ideal concepts.

6. *Poésies, Une saison en enfer, Illuminations*, ed. Louis Forestier (Paris: Gallimard, 1965), p. 200; my trans.

7. Jacques Derrida, *On the Name*, trans. David Wood (Stanford: Stanford University Press, 1995), p. 28.

8. Here a discussion of the Fifth Amendment to the U.S. Constitution would be in order. Since the protection it offers against compelling anyone "to be a witness against himself" is specifically limited to criminal procedures, it would seem not to institute in any sense an originary right of nonresponse.

9. Monica Lewinsky and Andrew Morton, *Monica's Story* (New York: St. Martin's Press, 1999), pp. 175–211.

10. A better nominee for this title might be Philip Roth's *The Human Stain* (New York: Vintage, 2001), which transposes this event of impeachment into a fictional allegory of considerable interest and subtlety.

CHAPTER 10

1. The pretext was given by Jean Bessière and Monique Chefdor as a colloquium held at the Université de Picardie Jules Verne in June 1990 and titled "Déconstruction et esthétiques romanesques." An earlier version of the present essay was originally published in French in *Etudes romanesques 2: Modernité, fiction, déconstruction*, ed. Jean Bessière (Paris: Lettres Modernes, 1994).

2. See John Searle, "The Logical Status of Fictional Discourse," *New Literary History* 6, no. 2 (1975).

3. Didier Coste, *Narrative as Communication* (Minneapolis: University of Minnesota Press, 1989), p. 36.

4. Jacques Derrida, "Psyche: Inventions of the Other," trans. Catherine Porter, in Wlad Godzich, ed., *Reading de Man Reading* (Minneapolis: University of Minnesota Press, 1989), p. 42.

CHAPTER 11

1. The first version of this chapter was written for the colloquium "Passions de la littérature. Avec Jacques Derrida," organized by Michel Lisse at the Catholic University of Louvain (Belgium) in 1995, and initially published, in French, in *Passions de la littérature. Avec Jacques Derrida*, ed. Michel Lisse (Paris: Galilée, 1996). As Michel Lisse writes in his preface to that volume, the subtitle indicates "the desire to accompany [Jacques Derrida] in his passions for literature, as he has taught us to do" (9). It is a desire that accounts as well for the packed itinerary traced here through numerous writings of Derrida's on literature, poetry, painting.

2. On the "tout-dire" of literature, see above, "Deconstruction Reading Politics."

3. Jacques Derrida, "Aphorism Countertime," trans. Nicholas Royle, in *Acts of Literature*, ed. Derek Attridge (New York: Routledge, 1992), p. 416.

4. Charles Baudelaire, *The Parisian Prowler*, 2d ed., trans. Edward K. Kaplan (Athens: University of Georgia Press, 1997), 4; the translation will occasionally be modified.

5. In *Voyous* (Paris: Galilée, 2003), Derrida once again invokes a *pointe acérée*, this time pointing to the sharp tip of the extreme difficulty of a "*reasonable* transaction between two antinomic rationalities" (217).

6. In his celebrated reading of Baudelaire's poem "Le soleil," Benjamin describes the figure there of the poet as fencer or dueler ("Je vais m'exercer seul à ma fantasque escrime") as the privileged image of the poet at work. Although he cites in passing from the last sentence of "Le *Confiteor* de l'artiste" ("où l'artiste crie de frayeur avant d'être vaincu"), he does not turn his attention to the dueling scene it stages, perhaps because the poet here is not shown fending off the shocks of a modern urban landscape; see Walter Benjamin, *Baudelaire, un poète lyrique à l'apogée du capitalisme*, trans. Jean Lacoste (Paris: Payot, 1982), pp. 100–101.

7. "Se faire mal" is an ordinary locution, meaning to hurt or injure either oneself (reflexive) or one another (reciprocal). But it can also be forced grammatically to say something like a botched or poor self-production.

8. Elsewhere, I have analyzed various "feminine" dynamics in Baudelaire; see "Baudelaire au féminin," in Kamuf, *Signature Pieces: On the Institution of Au-*

thorship (Ithaca, N.Y.: Cornell University Press, 1988), and "Baudelaire's Modern Woman," *Qui Parle?* 4, no. 2 (Spring 1991), pp. 1–7; see also Elissa Marder, *Dead Time: Temporal Disorders in the Wake of Modernity (Baudelaire and Flaubert)* (Stanford: Stanford University Press, 2002). Marder calls attention in particular to the fact that Benjamin never fully examines "the multiple ways in which . . . feminine figures mediate the experience of shock" in Baudelaire (33).

9. See, above, "The Other Sexual Difference," n. 24.

10. Jacques Derrida, "Que cos'è la poesia?" trans. Peggy Kamuf, in Kamuf, ed., *A Derrida Reader: Between the Blinds* (New York: Columbia University Press, 1991).

11. Ibid., p. 229

12. Jacques Derrida, *Circumfession*, trans. Geoffrey Bennington, in Geoffrey Bennington and Jacques Derrida, *Jacques Derrida* (Chicago: University of Chicago Press, 1993), pp. 3–8. Because what follows alludes to many intricacies of this text, a brief description is in order. *Circumfession* was written to accompany Geoffrey Bennington's presentation of Derrida's thought for a French publisher's series on contemporary thinkers or writers. Bennington's text, *Derridabase*, runs along the top two-thirds of each of the book's pages, while *Circumfession* is printed like a running footnote on the bottom third. Derrida's text was written after Bennington's and on a kind of dare to exceed in some way the "data base" that the latter had compiled of the key operative notions of his own thinking. The result, *Circumfession*, is at once a conjoined reflection on confession and circumcision, an ongoing commentary on Augustine's *Confessions*, and the record of his mother's dying. The text is composed of fifty-nine "periods," sections of almost exactly equal length (as measured by the number of lines that fit on a computer screen), each of which is confined within one long sentence.

13. This recalls the phrase from Derrida's *Glas* that is placed in epigraph to the volume in which *Circumfession* appears: "Dès qu'il est saisi par l'écriture, le concept est cuit," which can be rendered more or less as: "As soon as it is seized by writing, the concept is cooked, crocked, finished."

14. In "trouver la veine," "veine" has also two figurative senses: inspiration and luck.

15. For a very lucid discussion of confessional power in its dependence on fiction, see Derek Attridge, "Deconstruction and Fiction," in Nicolas Royle, ed., *Deconstructions: A User's Guide* (New York: Palgrave, 2000).

16. That is, St. Augustine.

17. Cutting oneself off from/with: this awkward wording attempts to render the double preposition "d'avec" that Derrida exploits on pp. 226–27; for more uses of this idiom, see below, "Singular Sense, Second-Hand."

18. Jacques Derrida, "+R (Into the Bargain)," in *The Truth in Painting*, trans.

Geoff Bennington and Ian McLeod (Chicago: University of Chicago Press, 1987), pp. 163–62.

19. I allude to Derrida's book of essays on Blanchot, *Parages* (Paris: Galilée, 1986).

20. Fifty-nine was Derrida's age in 1989, when he wrote *Circumfession*. As for the figure thirty-nine in "Aphorism Countertime," written in 1986, its significance, if it has one, is not obvious.

CHAPTER 12

1. "Critique and Deconstruction" was the title of the conference, organized by Geoff Bennington at the University of Sussex in 1998, where a first version of this chapter was presented.

2. See Geoffrey Bennington's essays on Kant and frontiers: "La frontière infranchissable," in *Le passage des frontières: Autour du travail de Jacques Derrida*, ed. Marie-Louise Mallet (Paris: Galilée, 1994); "The Frontier: Between Kant and Hegel," in *Legislations: The Politics of Deconstruction* (London: Verso, 1994) and *Frontières kantiennes* (Paris: Galilée, 2000).

3. For a Bourdieusian study of scholarly criticism in the recent American university, see John Guillory, *Cultural Capital: The Problem of Literary Canon Formation* (Chicago: University of Chicago Press, 1993).

4. See Derrida's characterization of Marx's own distinction between *Geist* and *Gespenst* as regards Hegelian idealism: "For there is no ghost, there is never any becoming-specter of the spirit without at least an appearance of flesh, in a space of invisible visibility, like the dis-appearing of an apparition. For there to be ghost, there must be a return to the body, but to a body that is more abstract than ever. The spectrogenic process corresponds to a paradoxical *incorporation*" (*Specters of Marx: The State of the Debt, the Work of Mourning, and the New International*, trans. Peggy Kamuf [New York: Routledge, 1994], p. 126).

5. See my "Violence, Identity, Self-Determination, and the Question of Justice: On *Specters of Marx*," in Hent De Vries and Samuel Weber, eds., *Violence, Identity, Self-Determination* (Stanford: Stanford University Press, 1997).

6. Since the original publication of his essay, Greenblatt has rectified the omission somewhat, at least nominally. In his *Hamlet in Purgatory* (Princeton, N.J.: Princeton University Press, 2002)—which so admirably extends the scope of "What Is the History of Literature?" that almost no trace of the original essay remains except the preoccupation with the Ghost of *Hamlet*—a note acknowledges that *Specters of Marx* "has many acute observations about the functioning of the ghost in Shakespeare's play" (297 n. 17). The same note also glosses "hauntology" as "a queasy awareness of a suppressed politics," which, as a take

on Derrida's neologism, is curious enough to lead one to ask: whose queasiness over which suppression?

7. Since Greenblatt's own *Renaissance Self-Fashioning: From More to Shakespeare* (Chicago: University of Chicago Press, 1980), there have appeared countless studies of Shakespeare or the English Renaissance that explicitly invoke New Historicism. A representative selection of this work is found in Richard Wilson and Richard Dutton, eds., *New Historicism and Renaissance Drama* (London and New York: Longman, 1992). For some reflections on how New Historicism inflects the legacy of Marxist literary criticism, see Carolyn Porter, "Are We Being Historical Yet?" in David Carroll, ed., *The States of "Theory": History, Art, and Critical Discourse* (New York: Columbia University Press, 1990). Interestingly, Porter's essay begins by quoting Edward Pechter, writing in *PMLA* in 1987: "A specter is haunting criticism—the specter of a new historicism."

8. For some reasons why such a model of competing "schools" is always inadequate as a description of the field on which "theory" is deployed, see Derrida, "Some Statements and Truisms about Neologisms, Newisms, Postisms, Parasitisms, and Other Small Seismisms," trans. Anne Tomiche, in Carroll, *The States of "Theory,"* op. cit.

9. I have done so in an unpublished lecture, "Undying Literature," delivered at the University of Wales, Cardiff, May 1998.

10. Stephen Greenblatt, "What is the History of Literature?" in *Critical Inquiry* 23, no. 3 (Spring 1997): p. 478.

11. Greenblatt has earlier situated his essay as a response to just such a call for renewal: "the time has come," he writes, "to renew on our own terms . . . the reason, if we have one, to study literature" (462).

12. It was originally written to be delivered as the keynote lecture at a conference titled "Whither Marxism?" organized by Bernd Magnus and Stephen Cullenberg at the University of California, Riverside in 1993. For more on the scene of this lecture, see "Translating *Specters*: An Interview with Peggy Kamuf" in *Parallax* 20 (July–Sept. 2001).

13. For a very different and forceful mobilization of hauntological possibilities for literary scholarship, see Christopher Peterson, "The Haunted House of Kinship: Miscegenation, Homosexuality and William Faulkner's *Absalom, Absalom!*" *The New Centennial Review* 4, no. 1 (Spring 2004), and "Possessed by Poe: Reading Poe in an Age of Intellectual Guilt," in *Cultural Values* 5, no. 2 (April 2001).

CHAPTER 13

1. In addition to the occasion for an earlier version of this chapter (the conference "La joie de revivre" organized by the graduate students in French at UCLA in April 2000, under the direction of Alison Rice and Christine Thuau), see in

particular Michael Sprinker, ed., *Ghostly Demarcations: A Symposium on Jacques Derrida's "Specters of Marx"* (New York: Verso, 1999); and *Parallax* 20 (July–Sept. 2001), a special issue on the New International, ed. Martin McQuillan.

2. See, above, "The Ghosts of Critique and Deconstruction."

3. Jacques Derrida, *Specters of Marx: The State of the Debt, the Work of Mourning, and the New International,* trans. Peggy Kamuf (New York: Routledge, 1994), p. xix; *Spectres de Marx: L'état de la dette, le travail du deuil et la nouvelle Internationale* (Paris: Galilée, 1993), p. 15.

4. See in particular Emile Benveniste, "Relationships of Person in the Verb," in *Problems in General Linguistics,* trans. Mary Elizabeth Meek (Coral Gables: University of Miami Press, 1971), pp. 199–201.

5. Maurice Blanchot, "The Narrative Voice (*the "he," the neutral*)," in *The Infinite Conversation,* trans. Susan Hanson (Minneapolis: University of Minnesota Press, 1993), p. 380; for more discussion of Blanchot's thinking of the third person, see above, "'Fiction' and the Experience of the Other."

6. Cf. Benveniste, "Relationships of Person in the Verb," p. 199: "'I' and 'you' are reversible: the one whom 'I' defines by 'you' thinks of himself [*sic*] as 'I' and can be inverted into 'I,' and 'I' becomes a 'you.'"

7. See Blanchot, *Le pas au-delà* (Paris: Gallimard, 1973); and Derrida, "Pas," in *Parages* (Paris: Galilée, 1986).

8. Blanchot, "The Wooden Bridge (*repetition, the neutral*)," in *The Infinite Conversation,* p. 396. Once initiated in these final lines of the section, the dialogic or polylogic form continues through the next section, "Literature One More Time."

9. I have written elsewhere about this development from different angles; see my *Division of Literature, or the University in Deconstruction* (Chicago: University of Chicago Press, 1997), especially chapters 1, 2, and 5.

10. Jean-Jacques Rousseau, *Emile, or On Education,* trans. Allan Bloom (New York: Basic Books, 1979), p. 116; the original to which I am referring is *Emile, ou de l'éducation,* in *Oeuvres complètes,* vol. 4, eds.Bernard Gagnebin and Marcel Raymond (Paris: Gallimard, Bibliothèque de la Pléiade, 1969), pp. 357–58.

11. Allan Bloom's translation of this phrase attenuates significantly this spectral dimension: "hearing from absent people." To hear *from* absent ones is not the same as hearing them ("les entendre"), which is what Rousseau effectively wrote.

12. In this sense, Derrida's *Of Grammatology* undertook, *avant la lettre,* a hauntological or spectrological analysis of Rousseau's text (or specter). It thus inaugurated a new spectral scholarship, and not only for Rousseau scholars, of course.

CHAPTER 14

1. Jacques Derrida, "Title (to be specified)," trans. Tom Conley, *SubStance* 31 (1981): 8 (trans. modified).

2. The conference took place at the University of Luton in 1995, and was organized by John Brannigan, Ruth Robbins, and Julian Wolfreys; see Brannigan et al., eds., *Applying to Derrida* (Basingstoke: Macmillan, 1996).

3. For example, in *Double Reading: Postmodernism after Deconstruction* (Ithaca, N.Y.: Cornell University Press, 1993), Jeffrey Nealon professes bafflement that Derrida has not publicly disassociated his own practice of deconstruction from those of Jonathan Culler or Paul de Man, to which it is frequently assimilated and which, on Nealon's reading, are egregious misappropriations. Yet, Nealon himself gives the key to this enigma in the conclusion of his own exposé, where he endorses what "Derrida has shown quite clearly," namely that "the subject's inscription of an authorizing signature cannot and does not stop the play of substitutions and appropriations" (48). The only baffling thing, then, is why Nealon believed he had to step in and stop the play.

4. Jacques Derrida, *The Other Heading*, trans. Pascale-Anne Brault and Michael B. Naas (Bloomington: Indiana University Press, 1992), p. 44; I have modified the translation slightly and emphasized "applied" and "application."

5. Jacques Derrida, *Politics of Friendship*, trans. George Collins (London: Verso, 1997).

6. *Politics of Friendship*, 174; trans. modified.

7. For another version of this aporia of address to the other's freedom, see, above, "To Give Place: Semi-Approaches to Hélène Cixous," for example, the narrator's question in *Limonade*, "How can I say to her 'I want you to know you are free' without the sentence catching her between its paw-like words . . . "

8. Raymond Williams, *Television: Technology and Cultural Form* (New York: Schocken Books, 1974), p. 52.

9. Interestingly, Williams confines his critique here to this effect and does not note the potential such filming of "alternative" responses presented for more direct suppression, rather than merely marginalization. Police around the world, however, have seen and exploited this potential, beginning perhaps with the FBI in the 1960s, but also the Chinese authorities, who played back Western TV news footage of the events of May–June 1989 captured off the satellite relays, and the Los Angeles Police Department in 1992 after the civil disturbances in that city. These uses of television or video for surveillance, as witnessing technology (cf. the Rodney King arrest), and in military weapons are wholly absent from Williams's analyses, which is not to be explained simply by the date of his study (1974). Much subsequent writing on television, at least in the United States and Britain, has tended to operate the same exclusions: see, for example, Richard Di-

enst, *Still Life in Real Time: Theory after Television* (Durham, N.C.: Duke University Press, 1994) or the essays in the anthology edited by E. Ann Kaplan, *Regarding Television: Critical Approaches* (Frederick, Md.: University Publications of America, 1983). A notable exception is Samuel Weber's *Mass Mediauras: Form, Technics, Media* (Stanford: Stanford University Press, 1996), in particular the essay "Television: Set and Screen." I have discussed some aspects of video surveillance and the "replay" effect in my "The Replay's the Thing," *Opera Through Other Eyes*, ed. David Levin (Stanford: Stanford University Press, 1993). For a remarkable reflection on surveillance technology, see *CTRL [SPACE]: Rhetorics of Surveillance from Bentham to Big Brother*, ed. Thomas Y. Levin, Ursual Frohne, and Peter Weibel (Cambridge: MIT Press, 2002).

10. Or, as Samuel Weber puts it: "The *vision* [television] shows is . . . intrinsically split, both *right here* in front of us, and at the same time *elsewhere, out there* in *another place*. The duplicity of the vision it both represents, presents and elicits appears to move in two very divergent directions at least. . . . *Either* it can encourage the more or less unconscious effort to *overlook the split* and the separation and to see the splitting image as though it were the spitting image. *Or*, when the institutions that promote and channel that overlooking have relinquished much of their authority, it can make room for that 'demonical ambiguity' of the lines of demarcation, which then reemerge with startling clarity" ("The Parallax View," in *Assemblage* 20 [April 1993] 89).

11. *The Other Heading*, p. 87.

12. This is by no means an isolated instance in which Derrida turns the occasion of a press interview into a practical demonstration of the limits imposed by the media on the receivability of an interviewee's responses. I have analyzed elsewhere at greater length Derrida's contestatory practice in interviews; see my "Tape-Recorded Surprise: Derrida Interviewed," in *Nottingham French Studies* no. 1, 42 (Spring 2003).

CHAPTER 15

1. What does remain "audible" here, however, are the traces of the first, oral presentation of this address, at a conference titled "Sensual Reading," organized by Ian Maclachlan and Michael Syrotinski, University of Aberdeen, July 1996.

2. See Eric Partridge, *You Have a Point There: A Guide to Punctuation and Its Allies* (London: Hamish Hamilton, 1953), p. 134.

3. For a more complete inventory and a very witty analysis of hyphenation, see John McDermott, *Punctuation for Now* (London: MacMillan, 1990), pp. 113–28. McDermott cites the "conventional wisdom" that "dashes divide and hyphens join," but is then careful to observe that "the hyphen performs two apparently contradictory tasks. It holds together two (or more) word-elements that would not normally occur in combination (such as, well, *word-elements*, or *fish-*

hooks), and keeps apart word-elements which, though linked, must be shown as separate (such as *word-elements* or *fish-hooks*)" (113–14). On the "conventional wisdom" regarding hyphens, see Harold Herd, *Everybody's Guide to Punctuation* (London: Allen and Unwin, 1925), who reduces the hyphen to a single function: "The hyphen is used to join two words together" (38). (My thanks to Peter Krapp for these references.)

4. See, for example, Charles F. Meyer, *A Descriptive Study of American Punctuation* (Ann Arbor, Mich.: University Microfilms International, 1983); and Geoffrey Nunberg, *The Linguistics of Punctuation* (Stanford: Center for the Study of Language and Information, 1990).

5. *Chicago Manual of Style*, 13th ed. (Chicago: University of Chicago Press, 1982), p. 162.

6. To illustrate: in the first published version of this essay (in *Sensual Reading: New Approaches to Reading in Its Relations to the Senses*, Michael Syrotinski and Ian Maclachlan, ed. [Lewisburg, Pa.: Bucknell University Press, 2001]), the American copyeditor regularly deleted any superfluous hyphens, for example, in "nonhyphenated" in the preceding sentence.

7. Studies of punctuation in English frequently accept to speculate rather freely, or all too predictably, on the socio-psychological determinants of the general differences between American and British usage in this domain. In the appendix to Partridge's book, "A Chapter on American Practice," John W. Clark comments on Partridge's repeated assertion that "American punctuation tends to be more rigid than British, and more uniform, more systematic," for which reason it is also, in Clark's estimation, "easier to teach and, once learnt, easier to use." Two "facts" are then adduced to explain this difference: the greater tolerance for "individualism and independence" in Britain than in the U.S., and the greater reliance among "cultivated" Americans on written rather than oral/aural tradition. These facts are in turn attributed to various ambient conditions: greater "fluidity" of American social classes, greater frequency of successful social climbing among Americans, which also produces greater anxiety among Americans about "correctness" or idiosyncrasies. "In short," he concludes, "an American is likely to punctuate unconventionally only because he [*sic*] doesn't know any better; a Briton, at least the typical British writer, because he [*sic*] is jolly well sure he does" (211–12).

8. Rodolphe Gasché, *Inventions of Difference: On Jacques Derrida* (Cambridge, Mass.: Harvard University Press, 1994), p. 13; Gasché is quoting from Mark C. Taylor, "Failing Reflection," in *Tears* (Albany: SUNY Press, 1990), p. 101.

9. "The Unconscious," in *Standard Edition of the Complete Psychological Works*, ed. and trans. James Strachey (London: Hogarth Press), vol. 14, p. 177; my emphasis.

10. Gasché is quoting from the selections of Joshua Wilner's translation of

Shibboleth included in *Acts of Literature*, ed. Derek Attridge (New York: Routledge, 1992), p. 398; for the original language, see *Schibboleth, pour Paul Celan*
(Paris: Galilée, 1986), p. 43.

11. This punctuality, if not punctuation, could also be seen as a point of articulation with Roland Barthes's distinction between the *punctum* and the *studium*
as he elaborates it throughout his *Camera Lucida: Reflections on Photography*,
trans. Richard Howard (New York: Hill and Wang, 1981).

12. Jean-Luc Nancy, *Being Singular Plural*, trans. Robert D. Richardson and
Anne E. O'Byrne (Stanford: Stanford University Press, 2000), pp. 93–94, trans.
modified; *Etre singulier pluriel* (Paris: Galilée, 1996), pp. 117–18.

13. In French: "l'être-à-plusieurs-ensemble," "être-les-uns-avec-les-autres,"
"l'être-à-chaque-fois-avec."

14. In fact, the last word falls at the end of a line and therefore the hyphenation may be dictated by typographic convention. However, Nancy elsewhere
hyphenates the word "dis-position" in this way.

15. A children's primer, originally published in 1824, makes this point about
overheard punctuation in riddling rhyme. Here are the first two stanzas:

> Young Robert, could read, but he gabbled so fast;
> And ran on with such speed, that all meaning he lost.
> Till one Morning he met Mr. Stops, by the way,
> Who advis'd him to listen to what he should say.
> Then, ent'ring the house, he a riddle repeated,
> To shew, without stops, how the ear may be cheated.
> "Ev'ry lady in this land
> "Has twenty nails upon each hand
> "Five & twenty on hands & feet
> "And this is true without deceit."
> But when the stops were plac'd aright,
> The real sense was brought to light.

This primer, *Punctuation Personified: or Pointing Made Easy, by Mr. Stops*, was
reprinted in 2002 by Optical Toys, Putney Vermont.

AFTERWORD

1. Abelard and Heloise, *The Letters of Abelard and Heloise*, trans. Betty Radice
(New York: Penguin Books, 1974), p. 109. Only one aspect of Heloise's addressing Abelard is of interest to us here. For a highly developed analysis of the strategy of this correspondence, see Peggy Kamuf, *Fictions of Feminine Desire: Dis-
closures of Heloise* (Lincoln: University of Nebraska Press, 1982).

2. Maurice Blanchot, "Idle Speech," in *Friendship*, trans. Elizabeth Rottenberg (Stanford, Ca.: Stanford University Press, 1997), p. 123.

3. Maurice Blanchot, *The Space of Literature*, trans. Ann Smock (Lincoln: University of Nebraska Press, 1989), p. 251.

4. Jacques Lacan, *The Seminar of Jacques Lacan, Book 2: The Ego in Freud's Theory and in the Technique of Psychoanalysis, 1954-1955*, ed. J. A. Miller, trans. Sylvana Tomaselli (Cambridge: Cambridge University Press, 1988), p. 199.

5. Michel Foucault, "Self-Writing," in *Ethics: Essential Works of Foucault, 1954–1984*, vol. 1, ed. Paul Rabinow (New York: Penguin Books, 1997), p. 217.

6. Giorgio Agamben, *Potentialities: Collected Essays in Philosophy*, trans. Daniel Heller-Roazen (Stanford, Ca.: Stanford University Press, 1999), p. 269.

7. Jacques Derrida, *Specters of Marx: The State of the Debt, the Work of Mourning, and the New International*, trans. Peggy Kamuf (New York: Routledge, 1994), p. 97.

8. Sigmund Freud, "The 'Uncanny,'" in *Writings on Art and Literature*, ed. Neil Hertz (Stanford, Ca.: Stanford University Press, 1997), p. 221.

9. Jacques Lacan, *The Four Fundamental Concepts of Psychoanalysis*, ed. J. A. Miller, trans. Alan Sheridan (New York: W.W. Norton, 1998), p. 268.

10. Kamuf, above, p. 70.

11. Sigmund Freud, "Certain Neurotic Mechanisms in Jealousy, Paranoia and Homosexuality," in *Sexuality and the Psychology of Love*, ed. Philip Rieff (New York: Touchstone Books, 1997), p. 150.

12. Barbara Johnson, *The Critical Difference* (Baltimore, Md.: Johns Hopkins University Press, 1988), p. 139.

13. Jacques Derrida, *Dissemination*, trans. Barbara Johnson (Chicago: University of Chicago Press, 1981), p. 208.

14. "Double invagination . . . makes no sign beyond itself, toward what is utterly other, without becoming double or dual, without making itself be 'represented,' refolded, superposed, re-marked, within the enclosure, at least in what the structure produces as an *effect of interiority*" (Jacques Derrida, "Living on. Border Lines," trans. James Hulbert, in Harold Bloom et al., *Deconstruction and Criticism* [New York: Seabury Press, 1979], pp. 100–101).

15. Aristotle, "On Generation and Corruption," in *The Basic Works of Aristotle*, ed. Richard McKeon (New York: Random House, 1941), 314b.

16. Maurice Blanchot, *Death Sentence*, in *The Station Hill Blanchot Reader*, trans. Lydia Davis (Barrytown, N.Y.: Station Hill Press, 1999), pp. 173–74; emphases added.

17. For an analysis of "the language of other" spoken here by the narrator and Natalie, see Derrida, "Living on. Border Lines," pp. 147–51.

18. Maurice Blanchot, *The Writing of the Disaster*, trans. Ann Smock (Lincoln: University of Nebraska Press, 1995), p. 75.

19. Edmund Husserl, *Experience and Judgment*, trans. James S. Churchill and Karl Ameriks (Evanston, Ill.: Northwestern University Press, 1973), p. 77.

20. Blanchot, *The Writing of the Disaster*, p. 55.

21. Baruch de Spinoza, *Ethics*, ed. and trans. G. H. R. Parkinson (Oxford: Oxford University Press, 2000), p. 170.

22. Blanchot, *The Writing of the Disaster*, p. 30.

23. Studies of the passivity of contemplation (connected with the study of intentional types) presumed (as developed in Bruno's philosophy) that the world is an endless multitude of mirrors, images, and surfaces that are reflected in each other by simple contradiction, by sheer presentation that prevents duplication of the image: he who contemplates becomes that which contemplates (always something else) and he becomes that absolutely, without redoubling the image in itself and in its representation. The observer's spirit, therefore, is not a reflecting spirit that redoubles the image; on the contrary, it is merely the eye by means of which images are presented—the surface of the quiet, cold mirror that becomes the image it reflects. Consequently, every spirit is the eye, every eye the image and every image—the eye. But the eye is nothing more than a passive plane that becomes a different plane. The synthesis of the two surface-images is not, however, done by the eye, by the movement of the image that is moved by infinite stupidity. Such a conceived contemplative world is one of small, local, passive beings of images that are themselves mere nodes of passive contemplative syntheses (the overlapping of two images, etc.). But, precisely because there is nothing in this world of spirit other than the eye-image, the passive being here *does not suffer* any change; it is simply a change that changes. This means that the passivity of contemplation does not point to passion and suffering. The being that does not know the difference between notion and observation, as Schelling explained in his treatise on Bruno, is nothing more than the passive, impersonal, nonpassionate, quiet reflection of the surface. The world of passive contemplation is not, however, the "world" of outsideness, for two reasons. First, because there is no outsideness in the world of passive contemplative syntheses, since there is no difference between outside and inside; rather everything is always outside. Second, stemming from the first, because everything is outside, since only node-images exist, neither human nor inhuman, neither personal nor impersonal, neither vegetable nor mineral; in this world there is no I that could *suffer* going out into outsideness.

24. Blanchot, *The Writing of the Disaster*, p. 15.

25. Maurice Blanchot, *The Space of Literature*, trans. Ann Smock (Lincoln: University of Nebraska Press, 1989), p. 30.

26. Blanchot, *The Writing of the Disaster*, p. 2.

27. Kamuf, "Deconstruction and Love," above, p. 30.

28. Blanchot, *The Writing of the Disaster*, p. 7.

29. Kamuf, "Jealousy Wants Proof," above, p. 66.

30. Blanchot, *The Writing of the Disaster*, p. 28.

31. Jacques Derrida, "Sauf le nom (Post-Scriptum)," trans. John P. Leavey, Jr., in *On the Name* (Stanford, Ca.: Stanford University Press, 1995), p. 60.

32. For an analysis of the dome, arch, home, and body as houses, see David Wills, *Prosthesis* (Stanford, Ca.: Stanford University Press, 1995), pp. 176–214.

33. Blanchot, *The Writing of the Disaster*, p. 29.

34. Hélène Cixous and Jacques Derrida, *Veils*, trans. Geoffrey Bennington (Stanford, Ca.: Stanford University Press, 2001), p. 42.

35. Blanchot, *The Writing of the Disaster*, p. 30.

36. Derrida, "Sauf le nom (Post-Scriptum)," p. 43.

37. Blanchot, *The Writing of the Disaster*, p. 5.

38. Maurice Blanchot, *Awaiting Oblivion*, trans. John Gregg (Lincoln: University of Nebraska Press, 1999), p. 52.

39. Blanchot, *The Writing of the Disaster*, p. 31; *The Space of Literature*, p. 173.

40. Walter Benjamin, "Agesilaus Santander (First Version)," trans. Rodney Livingstone, in *Selected Writings: Vol. 2, 1927–1934*, ed. M. W. Jennings et al. (Cambridge, Mass.: Harvard University Press, 1999), p. 712.

41. Blanchot, *The Writing of the Disaster*, p. 51.

42. Benjamin, "Agesilaus Santander (First Version)," p. 713.

43. Blanchot, *The Writing of the Disaster*, p. 51.

Index

M E R I D I A N

Crossing Aesthetics

Giorgio Agamben, *The End of the Poem: Studies in Poetics*

Theodor W. Adorno, *Sound Figures*

Louis Marin, *Sublime Poussin*

Philippe Lacoue-Labarthe, *Poetry as Experience*

Ernst Bloch, *Literary Essays*

Jacques Derrida, *Resistances of Psychoanalysis*

Marc Froment-Meurice, *That Is to Say: Heidegger's Poetics*

Francis Ponge, *Soap*

Philippe Lacoue-Labarthe, *Typography: Mimesis, Philosophy, Politics*

Giorgio Agamben, *Homo Sacer: Sovereign Power and Bare Life*

Emmanuel Levinas, *Of God Who Comes to Mind*

Bernard Stiegler, *Technics and Time, 1: The Fault of Epimetheus*

Werner Hamacher, *pleroma—Reading in Hegel*

Serge Leclaire, *Psychoanalyzing: On the Order of the Unconscious and the Practice of the Letter*

Serge Leclaire, *A Child Is Being Killed: On Primary Narcissism and the Death Drive*

Sigmund Freud, *Writings on Art and Literature*

Cornelius Castoriadis, *World in Fragments: Writings on Politics, Society, Psychoanalysis, and the Imagination*

Thomas Keenan, *Fables of Responsibility: Aberrations and Predicaments in Ethics and Politics*

Emmanuel Levinas, *Proper Names*

Alexander García Düttmann, *At Odds with AIDS: Thinking and Talking About a Virus*

Maurice Blanchot, *Friendship*